D1169470

THE BLUEGRASS READER

MUSIC IN AMERICAN LIFE

A list of books in the series appears at the end of this book.

THE
Bluegrass
Reader

EDITED BY

Thomas Goldsmith

UNIVERSITY OF ILLINOIS PRESS

Urbana and Chicago

First Illinois paperback, 2006
© 2004 by the Board of Trustees
of the University of Illinois
All rights reserved
Manufactured in the United States of America
2 3 4 5 6 C P 5 4 3 2 1
∞ This book is printed on acid-free paper.

The Library of Congress cataloged the cloth edition as follows:
The bluegrass reader / edited by Thomas Goldsmith.
p.   cm. — (Music in American life)
Includes bibliographical references and index.
ISBN 0-252-02914-3 (cloth : alk. paper)
1. Bluegrass music—History and criticism.
I. Goldsmith, Thomas, 1952– . II. Series.
ML3520.B54   2004
781.642—dc22   2003019686
PAPERBACK ISBN 0-252-07365-7 / 978-0-252-07365-6

Sounds, and sweet aires, that give delight and hurt not:
Sometimes a thousand twangling instruments
Will hum about mine ears; and sometimes voices.

———————————————

WILLIAM SHAKESPEARE

The Tempest, ACT III, SCENE 2

Contents

PART 2: The Reseeding of Bluegrass, 1960–79

PART 3: Another Roots Revival, 1980–2000

Preface

In putting this book together, I spent a few years looking for the best writing about bluegrass that I could find. In doing so I drew upon more than thirty-five years as a fan and sometime-player of this music and a sometime-writer about it.

I grew up and now live again in the bluegrass haven of Raleigh, North Carolina, where Bill Monroe and Flatt and Scruggs once held forth at radio station WPTF. My deep involvement began in my early teens with exposure to Lester and Earl on local television, to Bill Monroe in recordings, and to exciting explorations of a local scene that featured the New Deal String Band.

Luckily, my father, Richard Goldsmith, had a friend in Cherrill Heaton, a fellow North Carolina State professor and banjo player who introduced me to *Bluegrass Unlimited* in its earliest editions. I have played bluegrass on guitar and mandolin, along with other styles, for many years. I've appeared on recordings by Hazel Dickens, the Whitstein Brothers, and others, although I certainly claim no exalted level of expertise. I have also written bluegrass songs, with a personal high point coming with the Nashville Bluegrass Band's wonderful recording of my tune "Old Devil's Dream."

I began to write about bluegrass when I became a staff music reporter for the *Nashville Tennessean* in 1985 and a frequent contributor to *Bluegrass Unlimited* a few years later.

This volume is intended to present particularly strong, influential, and representative writing about bluegrass. The selections come mostly from magazines and other periodicals and also from books, album liner notes, and other sources.

Together, they form a sort of linear history of bluegrass, although not a comprehensive one. I have learned as a daily journalist and editor that almost anyone's idea of what should run on the front page of a newspaper will to some degree conflict with other people's opinions. Similarly, I am sure that anyone with a knowledge of bluegrass would be likely to come up with a different list of key articles about this music.

My editor, Judith McCulloh, asked, "What articles about bluegrass would you want to have with you on a desert island?" That question, along with its intriguing images of a leisurely idyll focused on bluegrass journalism, gave rise to many choices. Thus, I began with articles that seemed indisputably to hold key places in the history of writing about bluegrass: Alan Lomax's *Esquire* article, Mayne Smith's groundbreaking thesis, Ralph Rinzler's *Sing Out!* piece on Bill Monroe, Mike Seeger's Folkways liner notes, Jim Rooney's book on Monroe and Muddy Waters, and so on. More recently, Tom Piazza's book on Jimmy Martin and David Gates's article on Ralph Stanley in *The New Yorker* seemed significant. These tended to be pieces with circulation outside the small circles in which bluegrass fans traveled during the music's first decades.

That articles display a high level of expertise and good writing was another consideration. In addition, some provide what seem to me an important, specific context. For example, the pieces on Rudy Lyle, Jim Shumate, and Kenny Baker vividly illustrate the importance of side musicians. Murphy Henry's IBMA speech about women in bluegrass, along with Pete Wernick's response, casts light on another long-standing facet of the style.

Other stories, such as the articles on Hot Rize and Peter Rowan, seemed central to my thesis that innovation and return to tradition come in discernible waves in bluegrass. Articles from daily newspapers and *Creative Loafing,* a free publication, show that good writing about bluegrass is increasingly available to people who may not specifically follow the style.

In matters of style, I have followed Tom Ewing's sensible suggestion and used "silent" corrections for matters of punctuation and the many misspellings of names that I encountered. For example, Bill Monroe's bluegrass band was called the Blue Grass Boys, a name that's widely misspelled.

Original notes follow the italicized word *note* and are bracketed; my notes are numbered. Articles have been reprinted as they first appeared, with exceptions that are noted.

Again, it's likely that someone's favorite article may not be reproduced here. In a few cases, copyright or other issues prevented publication of some that would have worked well. In the end, it's my hope that this book presents an enjoyable and well-lit path through the fascinating, heartfelt music called bluegrass.

Acknowledgments

A book such as this one is by its nature a work of collaboration. It would not exist without the permission of dozens of writers and publishers to allow use of their copyrighted works. That means I owe a heartfelt debt of gratitude to all contributors for their gifts of a particular piece of bluegrass history.

Before I even started reaching early contributors, including Jim Rooney and Jack Bernhardt, however, I owed a debt of gratitude to Neil Rosenberg, whose writing about bluegrass is in my view unparalleled. He put thought and effort into the idea of a bluegrass reader some years ago. I heard that he had put the book aside to pursue other interests and got in touch with Judith McCulloh, eventually my editor at the University of Illinois Press, who queried Neil about the possibility of my doing the book. He not only agreed but also made available the original list of articles he had put together when thinking about the collection.

That list formed the early foundation of this volume; indeed, a number of the stories Neil had in mind are present in its finished form. In addition, he allowed use of several key articles and served as a reader at various stages. It's safe to say that Neil Rosenberg's support was absolutely vital to my work on this book.

More key help came from Sharon Watts and Pete Kuykendall at *Bluegrass Unlimited.* Because *BU* has been the journalistic touchstone of this music for nearly forty years, this book leans heavily on articles published there. Sharon helped make that possible by personally locating and sending permission forms to dozens of contributors past and present.

Whatever understanding I have of bluegrass has been vastly enriched by my good fortune in being able to interview and be around some of the great founders of the music. Bill Monroe, Earl Scruggs, Mac Wiseman, Jim and Jesse McReynolds, the Osbornes, and others have given freely of their time and insights.

Judy McCulloh showed endless patience, understanding, and encouragement through what turned out to be a much longer process than either she or I had expected. Many thanks to her and to others on the University of Illinois Press's staff.

Ronnie Pugh and Lauren Bufferd at the Country Music Foundation provided help as I plowed through hundreds of articles from all sorts of sources, and indefatigable typists Jean Lewis and Kristi Bryan risked their wrists to save mine.

A special thanks goes to Tom Ewing, a distinguished Blue Grass Boys alumnus and journalist who pointed out myriad potential errors of fact and judgment. Jon Weisberger and Lance LeRoy also deserve credit for catching points well worth consideration. Neil Rosenberg and another reader who shall be nameless made numerous suggestions that resulted in a stronger work.

My parents, Richard and the late Mary MacMillan Goldsmith, encouraged my dual loves of music and writing, even interrupting the previously sacrosanct dinner hour during the 1960s so we could watch Lester and Earl on television each Saturday night.

My former partners, the late Walter Hyatt, Champ Hood, and Steve Runkle, joined in and nurtured my love of bluegrass.

Finally, my eternal thanks to my wife, Renee, and children, Kelsey, Hudson, and Nate, who uncomplainingly gave up whatever familial duties I might have fulfilled during the many hours I spent on this volume.

THE BLUEGRASS READER

From the Big Bang to the Big Time

1939–59: The Big Bang

People often think about bluegrass music as an ancient style, something that men and women played on Appalachian porches long years ago before electricity came.[1] Indeed, its authentic connection to folk roots form a large part of the tenacious appeal of bluegrass music. That sense of the ancient reach of bluegrass has endured, from its origins in the hillbilly music of the 1930s and 1940s to its post-millennial sales of millions of records by Alison Krauss and the multi-million-selling *O Brother, Where Art Thou?* soundtrack.

Some key dates, however, make it clear that bluegrass as it is known today is fewer than eight years older than rock 'n' roll. It was September 1946 when founding father Bill Monroe's "classic" bluegrass band hit its legendary stride in the studio. July 1954 brought Elvis Presley's Sun Records breakthrough, including a jiving version of Monroe's "Blue Moon of Kentucky."

Like rock 'n' roll, bluegrass exploded out of a post–World War II atmosphere as more Americans opened their ears to more different kinds of music than ever before. All around the country, musicians were stretching, grasping for new sounds and approaches. Country blues went fully electric in Chicago, bebop boiled over as jazz hit the hippest notes yet, and country music followed Hank Williams into newer, sexier, and more hard-hitting territory. What was happening in bluegrass was every bit as galvanic.

What is bluegrass, exactly? For now, try this definition, remembering that bluegrass wasn't widely known by that name until the mid-1950s or later. It is an expansive, twentieth-century, acoustic string-band music based in traditional styles, including fiddle tunes, blues, and southern church music, and it features high-pitched lead and harmony singing and emphasizes instrumental virtuosity on fiddle, banjo, mandolin, guitar, and acoustic bass.

---

1. David McCormick, "Kentucky Site Blooms as Site of Bluegrass Birth," *Nashville Banner,* June 4, 1984, C2.

Unlike early rock 'n' roll, which tended quickly to lose its grounding in traditional music, bluegrass has clung to its roots in old-time country music, blues, gospel, and balladry. Indeed, no other style has so continually checked its advances against what many consider to be its unparalleled early years.

In an age when musical trends flit by like models on a Paris runway, bluegrass has endured—and changed—certainly long enough for its history to have a shape. To examine the contours of the growth of bluegrass, this book will separate the history into three roughly twenty-year periods: from 1939 to 1959, from 1959 to 1979, and from 1979 to the millennium.

Again, in general, the first period encompasses the first "big bang" of bluegrass and the disciples who helped create a golden era. Artists led by Monroe set a bluegrass standard that still commands a wide following.

A "reseeding" of the style, fueled by interest in areas outside the South, in cities, and on college campuses, had its roots in the late 1950s and saw continued growth for the next two decades. The urbanites, hippies, and others who flocked to bluegrass brought it the widest following yet.

A return to the acoustic, rootsy beginnings of bluegrass reoccurred in the late 1970s and early 1980s, again with long-lasting fallout.

Finally, perhaps the biggest surge yet for bluegrass occurred during the years surrounding 2000. Evidence includes the popularity of Krauss; the successful bluegrass recordings of major stars, notably including Dolly Parton; and the overwhelming sales and reach of the *O Brother* soundtrack.

///

Inevitably, the epic starts with Monroe, the great Kentucky-bred singer, mandolinist, and songwriter who was born in 1911 and possessed strong will and musical genius in equal measure. As Monroe told it in interviews he started giving in the 1960s, his childhood in rural Rosine, Kentucky, was straight out of the nineteenth century.

Backbreaking farm work, the beauty of nature, moonlight rides on horseback, trips to church in a wagon, and just the occasional community ballgame to break the lonely monotony of country life—all formed the "true life" foundations upon which Monroe built his music. In conversation, he often seemed as eager to get across what could be called the cultural roots of bluegrass as he was its musical basis.[2]

As for his stylistic touchstones, the timing of Monroe's birth meant that he experienced nourishment from the store of traditional music—his mother's fiddling and songs, his fiddling Uncle Pen's canon of old-time tunes, his black mentor Arnold Shultz's bluesy fingerpicking, and his church's stark harmonies—before he heard country music on commercial radio and records. Once those two institutions started preserving and broadcasting country music in the 1920s, Monroe immersed

---

2. Thomas Goldsmith, "At Seventy-five, Bill Monroe Continues to Sow New Bluegrass Pastures," *The Tennessean* (Nashville), Sept. 7, 1986, SC7.

himself, eventually citing commercial pioneers such as the energetic fiddler Clayton McMichen and the folk-oriented Bradley Kincaid as early favorites.

By his late teens Monroe had left Kentucky and become a working man in the Chicago area while also developing his mandolin playing and singing in a band with older brothers Birch and Charlie. It was during the 1930s, however, with the band stripped down to a duet with Charlie, that Monroe's musical energy and innovation began to explode.

By the time the Monroe Brothers, seasoned by years of touring and broadcasting, first recorded in 1936, their sound charged off the grooves of Bluebird seventy-eights. And Bill Monroe's stark tenor and quicksilver mandolin—not yet fully improvised but full of energy and excitement—formed the driving force of the brothers' hit sound.

The notoriously contentious brothers split in 1938 and started separate bands. By October 1939, Monroe had landed at the Grand Ole Opry, debuting his Blue Grass Boys with a fuel-injected version of the old Jimmie Rodgers blue yodel tune "Mule Skinner Blues." The music was faster, higher, more inventive, and more aggressive than almost anything that had come before. In years to come, Monroe would make the case that bluegrass was born when he started his own band. It is a point that has occupied untold hours of bluegrass debate.

Now Monroe was not alone in pepping-up old-time country music. As far back as the 1920s, acts such as Charlie Poole and the North Carolina Ramblers and Gid Tanner's Skillet Lickers brought new energy and commercialism to venerable fiddle tunes, heart songs, and minstrel show numbers.

In the 1930s, bands such as the Morris Brothers and Mainer's Mountaineers were also adapting for the new electric era the mountain-born picking and sentimental nineteenth-century songs at the heart of the country repertoire. In the hill country of the Carolinas, banjo pioneers, including Smith Hammett, Fisher Hendley, and Snuffy Jenkins, revved up the five-string banjo with a three-finger style that was to metamorphose into one of bluegrass's defining sounds. Roy Acuff had come on strong out of East Tennessee, combining an old-time fiddle sound with modern-era showmanship and a throbbing vocal delivery that brought him Opry stardom in the late 1930s. Elsewhere in the country universe, western swing king Bob Wills had transformed Texas fiddling and uptown jazz into a new style that inevitably influenced the open-eared pickers of the day.

Whatever the true founding date of bluegrass, it's clear that Monroe headed a band of musical revolutionaries that forever changed the way people sang, played, and wrote songs in a country string band. His fierce intensity about music galvanized the particles of change floating about in the country music of the day. Part of this drive arose from pure sibling rivalry. Monroe wanted to do more than simply churn out more of the music that had brought him stardom with Charlie. He wanted music that had "everything of its own."[3]

---

3. James Rooney, *Bossmen: Bill Monroe and Muddy Waters* (New York: Dial Press, 1971), 32.

Through the early days of the Blue Grass Boys, Monroe tried a variety of instruments as he groped for a sound—a jug, a swing-inflected accordion as played by the accomplished Wilene (Sally Ann) Forrester, and David (Stringbean) Akeman's two-finger banjo style. Most fans and historians would agree that all the elements fell into place in the mid-1940s when first guitarist Lester Flatt and then banjo player Earl Scruggs joined the Blue Grass Boys on the far-reaching Grand Ole Opry radio show in Nashville. Flatt's mellow lead vocals at once nourished and challenged Monroe's peak-scaling tenor. In the same way, Scruggs's pyrotechnic three-finger banjo gave useful battle to the leader's racing mandolin.

Maybe, as Monroe said later, his vision for what was to be called bluegrass had been clear from the beginning. Certainly, performances such as a 1941 version of the instrumental "Back Up and Push," recorded years before Flatt and Scruggs joined the band, captured a band with great drive, inventiveness, and authority.

In September 1946, Monroe, Flatt, Scruggs, and the great fiddler Chubby Wise recorded for the first time, producing such enduring tracks as "Blue Moon of Kentucky" and "Will You Be Loving Another Man?" By the recording sessions of October 1947, the crew was melding their talents in perfectly balanced and nuanced tunes such as "It's Mighty Dark to Travel," "I Hear a Sweet Voice Calling," "Little Cabin Home on the Hill," "My Rose of Old Kentucky," "Blue Grass Breakdown," and "Sweetheart, You Done Me Wrong." Monroe had met the men who would be remembered as his most perfect complement. And it was this sound that quickly reverberated through the South, inspiring a group of talented young musicians who heard in the new approach a way to channel their own energies.

Monroe, Flatt, Scruggs, and Wise, along with their fellow pioneers Mac Wiseman and the Stanley Brothers, were the collective brain trust that started bluegrass. Their work expanded and modernized the common means of singing country music and playing some down-home instruments: the mandolin, banjo, fiddle, guitar, and upright bass. Their approaches to their vocals and to those instruments grew out of equal parts new influence and new inspiration, a formula that meant picking would keep getting hotter for half a century and more. Just as the Beatles kicked up the general level of pop songwriting and performance in the 1960s, so Monroe and other pioneers raised the level of expectation in the hillbilly universe.

The sound of southern string music had mostly emerged in performers' homes and communities until country radio and records arrived in the 1920s. Even then, although their repertoires were touched by parlor songs and minstrel shows, most country performers of the 1920s and 1930s would have fit right in at a family reunion or schoolhouse gathering. In the hands of Monroe and company, however, the music raced higher and faster, built for speed and not necessarily for comfort.

Bluegrass from its earliest days was a commercial proposition designed for radio, records, and performances in front of admission-paying crowds. Bluegrass has also, from its founding years, demanded high levels of expertise and dedication. Compared to the (mostly) more easygoing pickers of mainstream country music, bluegrass players must master blistering speed and have the ability to produce high levels of volume and inventiveness to match that of the style's leaders.

Even the specific instruments played by the founding pickers had immense influence. Monroe's Gibson F-5 mandolin, the big Martin D-28 guitar played by Flatt, and the Gibson Mastertone banjo wielded by Scruggs became the instruments of choice. Throughout the history of bluegrass, especially beginning in the 1960s and early 1970s, collecting and preserving desirable vintage instruments became part and parcel of the bluegrass experience. Mandolins like Monroe's and big-bellied, pre-World War II Martin "dreadnought" guitars came to bring fabulous prices. The network of instrument collectors and fans also served as another means for information about bluegrass to spread beyond its relatively limited early audiences.

From Monroe, bluegrass learned not only its musical parameters but also a lonely, obsessed sense of destiny. It is true that Monroe started his Blue Grass Boys as a commercial enterprise, heading for the Grand Ole Opry and considerable popular success, beginning in 1939. He was also, however, on a mission. Monroe wanted to give back to farm and country people his imagistic reworking of the sounds he heard while growing up in Rosine. Moreover, he was recreating a fabled childhood that included moonlight rides with his Uncle Pen, bereft days after both parents had died and his brothers went away, and fiddle tunes that literally echoed (as he wrote in his hit "Uncle Pen") "high on a hill and above the town."

When Monroe's sales and attendance wilted in the heat of rock 'n' roll, he approached music with at least as much fire and creativity as he had during his years of chart popularity in the 1940s and early 1950s. Whatever temporary studio concessions he may have made to electric instruments, commercial repertoire, or session players, he clung to steadfast ideas of the essential nature of bluegrass. Of course, that essential nature kept changing for Monroe as years passed.

Arguments have flamed for decades over what defines that essence. A related debate concerns the identity of its founding spirit. Did bluegrass spring full-blown from the forehead of William Smith Monroe, or did the style really blossom when Earl Scruggs first brought his heroic five-string to the band in 1945? This book will not claim to resolve either dispute for all time (as if it could) but will try to shed some light on the controversies that make the style so involving to hear and study.

Mike Seeger, Alan Lomax, and Ralph Rinzler, working ten to fifteen years after bluegrass had assumed its "classic" shape, collectively provided an intellectual framework for the large body of journalism that was to come. Seeger, in his liner notes to the groundbreaking album *Mountain Music Bluegrass Style* (1959), nailed a pretty good definition at a point when the music had only been called "bluegrass" for a few years. "Bluegrass," the notes begin, "the term, came into use in the early 1950s, originally referring to the music of Bill Monroe, from the Bluegrass State and his Bluegrass [*sic*] Boys, a group that for twenty years has appeared on the Grand Ole Opry in Nashville and made records for Bluebird, Columbia and Decca. Bluegrass describes a specific vocal and instrumental treatment of a certain type of traditional or folk-composed song." The description continues, detailing a "high-pitched, emotional singing style" and an acoustic instrumental approach highlighted by Scruggs-style banjo, Monroe's driving mandolin, open-string guitar à la Flatt, and an acoustic bass underpinning. Also in 1959, in a widely cited article in *Esquire*, Lomax, a folk scholar and collector, coined the phrase "folk music in overdrive" to describe bluegrass. It was Rinzler, however, an East Coast musician and traditional music figure, who brought Monroe to the forefront of folk fans' consciousness with "Bill Monroe—'The Daddy of Bluegrass Music,'" which appeared in *Sing Out!* in 1963 in response to an earlier *Sing Out!* piece that emphasized Scruggs.[4]

Another cornerstone was "An Introduction to Bluegrass," an in-depth look at the style by Mayne Smith in a 1965 issue of the *Journal of American Folklore*.[5] In addition, *Bluegrass Unlimited* has provided more than three decades of writing about the style and offering a forum for never-ending controversies, among them, What is bluegrass? Who started it? Is it ever all right to use amplified instruments? and, When bluegrass artists start selling lots of records outside the field, should purists hate them?

Arguments about who did what notwithstanding, it's clear that the powerhouse sound of the 1940s' Blue Grass Boys erupted like an undersea earthquake, sending tidal waves throughout mountain-style string band music.

In an aftershock that for years overshadowed the original event, Flatt and Scruggs severally left Monroe in 1948, to wind up as duet band leaders with their own sound. Just as Monroe had tried to develop a style distinguishable from the Monroe Brothers, the team soon came up with a strong collective identity built on Flatt's heartfelt vocals and Scruggs's banjo mastery.

Both leaders kept turning out compositions, eventually building their own "classic" repertoire that did not rely heavily on material they'd made famous with Bill Monroe. Their Foggy Mountain Boys attracted some of the best musicians in the business. In several cases these were players who had already worked with Monroe or were to join him later. The act deemphasized the mandolin and tended to perform in a more relaxed style than the Blue Grass Boys.

In time—Flatt and Scruggs were a duo for twenty-one years—the mandolin disappeared, the swoop of the Dobro became key to their sound, and their approach to vocal harmony departed almost completely from Blue Grass Boys formulations. In place of the terse duets, occasional trios, and gospel quartets that Monroe used, Flatt and Scruggs "stacked" harmonies four and five parts high on many secular and gospel numbers.

4. Mike Seeger, "Mountain Music Bluegrass Style," liner notes for *Mountain Music Bluegrass Style*, Folkways FA2318 (1959); Alan Lomax, "Bluegrass Background: Folk Music with Overdrive," *Esquire* 52 (Oct. 1959): 108; Ralph Rinzler, "Bill Monroe—The Daddy of Blue Grass Music," *Sing Out!* 13 (Feb.–Mar. 1963): 5–8.
5. Mayne Smith, "An Introduction to Bluegrass," *Journal of American Folklore* 78 (1965): 245–56.

The group had tremendous strengths all its own. Scruggs was the top man on the banjo; there was no denying that. In addition to largely developing the rippling, syncopated, three-finger style, he also kept inventing new approaches and techniques. Flatt was not only a toweringly influential singer and songwriter but also an effortless stage personality who felt as much at home at Carnegie Hall as in a country schoolhouse.

The band's more accessible sound and unflagging work ethic, as well as the managerial acumen of Scruggs's wife, Louise, meant that Flatt and Scruggs kept prospering throughout the 1950s when many country and bluegrass acts hit hard times. During the 1960s they crossed over into mainstream recognition through shows in cities and on college campuses, television appearances, and the use of their music on movie soundtracks. Whether hard-core bluegrassers liked it or not, many Americans first heard bluegrass via Flatt and Scruggs's appearances on *The Beverly Hillbillies* television show or through the recording of "Foggy Mountain Breakdown" on the soundtrack to the popular and influential movie *Bonnie and Clyde* (1967).

Flatt and Scruggs had their own television show as early as 1955.[6] The syndicated half hour sponsored by Martha White Flour brought their images and music into dozens of television markets across the Southeast and Midwest. It was just one example of the reach of television in spreading bluegrass. Acts including the Stonemans, Don Reno and Red Smiley, and Jim and Jesse McReynolds also had local or syndicated television shows. The breakup of Flatt and Scruggs in 1969 over musical and personal issues symbolized a split between the tradition-based approach favored by Flatt and the more adventurous and trendy direction advanced by Scruggs.

Because bluegrass was slow to create a collective identity, especially under that name, the story of the music's early years is largely contained in the history of its pioneering acts. In the late 1940s, festivals, record companies, magazines, and night clubs specifically designated as "bluegrass" remained years in the future. Mostly confined to the South, the sounds of Monroe and Flatt and Scruggs spread, as it were, underground. A sense of bluegrass as the centerpiece of a movement, of a style that was somehow "cool" to embrace, lingers to the present.

The mesmerizing early music of Bill Monroe and his Blue Grass Boys affected two brother teams; Ralph and Carter Stanley and Jim and Jesse McReynolds had grown up just a few miles apart in Virginia's Clinch Mountain region. Both sets of brothers heard the new sounds and transmuted them through musical structures they had already set up. The Stanleys, who began their joint career as leaders of the Clinch Mountain Boys in 1946, tuned in to the mountain-grown, archaic side of Monroe's formulation. They incurred his anger early on by a too slavishly imitative recorded version of "Molly and Tenbrooks," a racehorse tune he had performed and recorded but had not released.[7] There's no doubt that the Stanleys listened close-

6. Author interview with Earl Scruggs, summer 1998.

7. Neil Rosenberg, "From Sound to Style: The Emergence of Bluegrass," *Journal of American Folklore* 80 (1967): 143–50.

ly to the Blue Grass Boys and modeled part of their sound on those musicians. Ralph Stanley had been playing old-time banjo and then learned the hot, three-finger style he heard from Snuffy Jenkins and then Scruggs.

They had already worked toward their own firm musical direction, which was built on the Appalachian tunes and picking of family members but had innovations such as the high third vocal part added by Monroe-style mandolinist Darryl (Pee Wee) Lambert. Carter Stanley's soulful, unstrident lead vocal was married to Ralph's heart-stopping tenor, creating a bluegrass blend that has moved and inspired generations of fans. Carter, who briefly worked with Monroe in the early 1950s, was also an excellent songwriter and front man. His death came just as bluegrass festivals were beginning to lure large new audiences to bluegrass in the later 1960s.

Ralph moved his right-on-time banjo and mountain tenor to the forefront of the Clinch Mountain Boys. In later years, when many men would have taken comfortable retirement, Ralph Stanley has become an icon of hard-core traditional music. His mountain-grown tenor and austere persona appeal both to the bustling alternative-country scene and to the mass audience that appreciated *O Brother, Where Art Thou?*

The Stanleys can be thought of as the third major act of bluegrass, following Monroe and Flatt and Scruggs. These acts mostly sprang from what purists like to call the "true vine." That is, they grew up in the South, surrounded by family and community members who played old-time country music in styles handed down from person to person, or, in some cases, they took part in "singing schools" in which they learned the vocal techniques of old-time church music. The true-vine description particularly holds true for Monroe.

Lester Flatt, born in 1914, was also picking and singing before electric media became a major force. Scruggs and the Stanleys, born in the mid-1920s, drew as young men both from country tradition and from radio and recordings. In the later 1990s, Scruggs clearly recalled coming in from working in the fields for a midday meal and tuning in to banjo player Fisher Hendley and the Aristocratic Pigs, a favorite radio act of the 1920s and 1930s.[8]

As the Monroe influence spread, "his" sound started to change in interesting ways, fueled by a slightly younger group of musicians who liked all kinds of different styles, as creative musicians tend to do. Throughout bluegrass history, an energizing—although sometimes exhausting—tension has reigned between the forces of Monroe-style traditionalism and musicians who brought in new influences. Monroe complicated that debate through the years with his own ongoing innovations and by embracing some of the acts that headed in new directions.

Another eclectic and an indispensable player in early bluegrass—indeed, in its entire history—was the great singer Mac Wiseman. Virginia-born in 1925, Wiseman

---

8. Tom McCourt and Nabeel Zuberi, "Music on Television," Museum of Broadcast Communications Web-site, posted 1998.

was already playing and singing by the age of twelve. In liner notes to a 1990 album, he recalled tuning in to country music on the radio while still a schoolboy, enjoying especially the music of Charlie Poole, guitarist-vocalist Riley Puckett, and the Carter Family.[9] Wiseman was also one of the few pioneering bluegrass artists who had formal musical training. By 1946 he had earned a spot playing bass and singing with Molly O'Day, the Kentucky-born traditional country singer who wielded significant influence on bluegrass. Then Wiseman moved in quick succession through the top acts in the field, becoming an early member of both Flatt and Scruggs's Foggy Mountain Boys and the Blue Grass Boys.

Singing tenor with Lester Flatt and lead with Bill Monroe, Wiseman was key to some of the most memorable vocal blends in the music's history. On the Monroe classic "Can't You Hear Me Calling," the lead vocal part, later described by Wiseman as "higher than a hawk's nest," gave solid underpinning to Monroe's blues-driven harmonizing. Through a long career as a recording artist that followed his star sideman years, Wiseman showed familiarity with folk, country, and pop music as well as with the mountain-style renderings that got him his start.

Banjo and guitar master Don Reno figures in two periods of Blue Grass Boys history. Hailing from an area of South Carolina not far from Scruggs's early stomping grounds, Reno was also listening to Snuffy Jenkins and developing his own revved-up version of the three-finger style. In 1943, by Reno's account, he came within a doctor's opinion of joining Monroe's lineup but was declared fit for military service. He returned after Earl Scruggs left and played banjo for Monroe for a year, unfortunately during a period when Monroe did not go in the studio.

Reno went on to form one of the great acts of the style with guitarist and vocalist Arthur Lee Smiley, much better known as "Red." Reno and Smiley developed an ear-catching duet style after meeting in 1950 in fiddler Tommy Magness's band. Recording and performing, with breaks, throughout the 1950s and early 1960s, the duo relied on Smiley's smooth lead and Reno's tenor singing, hot picking, and strong songwriting for a series of hits on the King label. With material ranging from "I'm Using My Bible for a Road Map" to "I Know You're Married but I Love You Still," they carved out an undying spot in the hearts of bluegrass fans. Reno's banjo work in particular continues long after his death to influence new generations with its inventive single-note runs and jazzy influences.

After the "classic" Blue Grass Boys disbanded, Monroe attracted a long series of musicians, including many who would become giants as band leaders or sidemen. Following Wiseman as lead singer in the Blue Grass Boys was Jimmy Martin, an East Tennessee native who recorded and performed with Monroe beginning in 1949. Just twenty-two when he joined the band, Martin possessed a striking country voice and a bluesy yelp. He performed with the band off and on until 1954, also

---

9. Mac Wiseman, with Paul F. Wells, "From Grass Roots to Bluegrass: Some Personal Reminiscences," liner notes to CMH Records CD-9041 (1990).

doing time with the Lonesome Pine Fiddlers and the Osborne Brothers during that period.

As a Blue Grass Boy, he played alongside other notable Monroe sidemen, including banjo player Rudy Lyle and fiddler Charlie Cline. Like Wiseman, Martin learned to match Monroe's sometimes bewildering notions of harmony. Listen to the 1950 cut of the Monroe-Martin duet "I'm Blue, I'm Lonesome" for an example of Monroe's startlingly unconventional take on country singing. Martin also brought a strong rhythm guitar style punctuated with staccato runs on the bass strings; a notable example is the Flatt-inspired "G-run" that punctuates "Uncle Pen."

After a partnership with the Osbornes, Martin started his own band and attracted a stellar cast of sidemen to the Sunny Mountain Boys.[10] He developed a style he called "Good 'n' Country," which married high-level picking and tight harmonies to the hard country style then prominent on the charts. A notable Sunny Mountain Boy was banjo player J. D. Crowe, who—using Sonny Osborne as one model and Martin as an exacting teacher—added strikingly bluesy licks and quirky figures to the Scruggs technique he'd mastered.

Another team with a broad musical base was formed by Jim and Jesse McReynolds, who started out learning from family members but also tuned in to the many brother teams that preceded them. The smooth singing and strong songwriting of Opry-star brothers Alton and Rabon Delmore were particularly influential. Slightly younger than Scruggs and the Stanleys, the McReynoldses took a few more years to emerge with a highly polished style that leaned on those brother-smooth harmonies, a mainstream country approach, and Jesse's articulate mandolin reworking of five-string banjo style.

Like many early acts later known as bluegrass, the McReynoldses had no particular intention of veering from the mainstream of country music or of limiting themselves to the precepts of Bill Monroe. In an interview during the 1980s, Jesse made clear the influence that record companies could have on artistic direction. The brothers, he noted, had thought of themselves as country artists until they were signed to a major label. "We really got into the bluegrass sound when we started recording for Capitol Records" in 1952, McReynolds said. "We were hesitating over whether we'd even feature the five-string banjo, but it turned out that [producer] Ken Nelson was expecting us to record as a bluegrass band, so that's what we did."[11]

Jim and Jesse even spent time in Kansas during the early 1950s, working as a western harmony act in the vein of Foy Willing. They were one of the most far-ranging early bluegrass acts, recording Chuck Berry tunes and truck-driving music as well as folk, straight country, and more conventional bluegrass fare.

Up in Ohio, a young Bobby Osborne had started his musical career playing

---

10. Neil V. Rosenberg, "Jimmy Martin: *You Don't Know My Mind*," liner notes to Rounder Records CDSS21 (1990).

11. Thomas Goldsmith, liner notes to *Jim and Jesse and The Virginia Boys: In the Tradition*, Rounder Records 0234 (1987).

guitar and singing like Ernest Tubb. Sparked by what he heard from Monroe and Flatt and Scruggs, Osborne wended his way through several bands—including the Lonesome Pine Fiddlers and the Stanley Brothers—and military service before starting yet another influential brother team. Bobby and Sonny Osborne created a powerful, border-crossing bluegrass style by combining hard-core Monroeisms with inventive picking, a distinctive, sky-high vocal blend, and a sense of what the wider country scene was about.

The story of the early years of bluegrass is in the annals of these pioneering acts. It is also, vitally, the stories of some figures whose names are even further from being household commodities, the Lonesome Pine Fiddlers and Connie and Babe; radio stations, including WCYB in Bristol and WSM in Nashville; venues such as Sunset Park and Boston's Hillbilly Ranch; record men such as Jim Stanton of Rich-R-Tone Records and Sydney Nathan of King; and talented sidemen, including the fiddler Jim Shumate and the hard-driving banjo man Rudy Lyle. Also in the first two decades came the stirring of interest in bluegrass from city-bred folk fans, including Mike Seeger, Alan Lomax, and Ralph Rinzler. From that outside interest came the seeds of a revival that would take bluegrass from southern towns, schoolhouses, and backroads to the cities of the world.

1960–79: The Reseeding of Bluegrass

From the late-1950s' vantage point of Bill Monroe and other veterans, bluegrass must have seemed a mature style that they had mined thoroughly. As it evolved, however, bluegrass encompassed several instrumental and vocal approaches rolled into one genre. Among styles thought of as bluegrass were the hell-for-leather, complicated instrumentals composed by Monroe and others; the fiddle-led waltzes tied closely to 1940s' country music; bluesy, three-chord tunes not too different from the honky-tonk hits of the day; and the complex, banjoless vocal quartets of bluegrass gospel.

The leading acts of the field were thoroughly exploring the bluegrass cosmos that came out of the big bang, but learning about bluegrass, for a slowly expanding universe of fans, was like opening a novel from an unknown writer of brilliance. As the elusive East Coast beat scene and the nascent West Coast counterculture offered glimpses of the 1960s that were to be, another group of young men and women found meaning in bluegrass.

"I was an instinctive loner and straight arrow with no conventional adolescent rebellion or crisis coming of age," wrote Norm Carlson in his revelatory history of the Stanley Brothers Fan Club. "My change from adolescence to adulthood was my emergence as a participant in the world of bluegrass and old-time music through the Campus Folksong Club at Purdue University and through the Stanley Brothers Fan Club in the world at large."[12]

---

12. Norman Carlson, "The Stanley Brothers Fan Club and a Twenty Year Bluegrass Odyssey," *Bluegrass Unlimited* 21 (Jan. 1987): 7.

The influence of the folk boom on bluegrass has been well documented, as befits its importance in the style's history. During the same period, however, other young musicians were devoting themselves to bluegrass in California, Ohio, Pennsylvania, and other parts of the country, including New England, where bluegrass took root during the 1950s.[13] Such fiery new musicians as Del McCoury, Larry Sparks, and Vic Jordan emerged to take important roles in advancing bluegrass. Just as the mainstream country scene was finding new energy from the non-Nashville likes of Merle Haggard and Buck Owens, players who had grown up in the bluegrass tradition were bringing new sounds to the table.

Of course, musicians and fans are an ornery lot and not easily pinned down. Enthusiast Carlson came to bluegrass through his love of hillbilly music. Others arrived through the folk-music boom that had deep roots in the political activism of the 1940s. Whatever their entry point, the new generation of fans, many of whom were also budding musicians, burned with the energy and excitement of bluegrass at its best. One valuable contribution was their tendency to look on bluegrass as a whole, think deeply about it, and use the drive and means at their disposal to purvey it to a much wider audience.

To some new partisans, bluegrass summed up the authenticity they craved, the hard connection to the real world many found lacking in Eisenhower's America or academia. To others it was a more enticing sister to country music. With this handful of enthusiasts began the first reseeding of bluegrass, an era that saw Monroe receive credit as founding father, another generation of talented musicians take the music in some surprising new directions, and the rise of bluegrass festivals and bluegrass-centered record labels.

As rock 'n' roll flourished, bluegrass wilted. There are, of course, degrees to which that common perception rings more or less true. Flatt and Scruggs, for instance, enjoyed consistent success through the 1950s, earning country hits and, increasingly, audiences from towns, campuses, and cities across the nation. Monroe's commercial fortunes faltered, although he kept making great music.[14] Like country music in general, bluegrass tended to be washed from the mainstream of American pop culture by rock 'n' roll, although there is no doubt that notable performers still made memorable music during this period. Monroe, Flatt and Scruggs, Reno and Smiley, the Stanleys, Jimmy Martin, and the Osbornes, among others, created some of the most compelling, hard-core bluegrass ever during the 1950s. It is worthwhile to ask whether bluegrass even needed "reviving" in the later part of that decade.

The bellwether of the style, Monroe, recorded fourteen sides in 1958. They were mostly gospel tunes but also included the folky "Gotta Travel On," his only country chart record of the period, and the brilliant instrumental "Scotland," with its tonal allusions to Monroe's beloved bagpipes. His output dropped to eight sides in

---

13. Tom Teepen, untitled article from the program book for the Dayton Bluegrass Reunion, April 4, 1989.

14. John W. Rumble, liner notes to the boxed set *The Music of Bill Monroe: From 1936–1994,* MCA 11048 (1994), 66–67.

1959, the most notable of which was the bluesy vocal "Dark as the Night, Blue as the Day."

Monroe's creativity had not ebbed, but he was scarcely burning up the charts. Flatt and Scruggs, however, had their biggest popular success until the television stardom that lay ahead, with their 1959 recording of "Cabin on the Hill." The Osbornes made their high lead harmonies immortal with the 1958 career song "Once More." Reno and Smiley, Jimmy Martin, and the Stanley Brothers all made appearances on the *Billboard* country charts.

The adventurous music of Reno and Smiley in particular offered hints of the genre-crossing direction that bluegrass was to take during the 1960s and 1970s. Reno in particular liked to employ his banjo wiles on Tin Pan Alley songs, straight-ahead country, and even rock 'n' roll.[15]

Bluegrass music still had its chief public profile as a corner of the commercial country industry, albeit in an era when country itself was at a low ebb in popularity. Although the name *bluegrass* for the music was relatively well established by the late 1950s, many acts still considered themselves country music performers. Many would resist a strict labeling as "bluegrass" for decades. As late as 1998, Ralph Stanley evasively labeled his style "what they call the old-time mountain style of what they call bluegrass music."[16]

The significant revival that bluegrass came to enjoy stemmed at least in part from the music's presentation in a different context. Instead of a corner of a slumbering country scene, bluegrass came to be seen as "folk music in overdrive." The folk boom and its fallout brought an infusion of interest, energy, and, inevitably, money from a new direction.

A date to remember: October 10, 1958. "Tom Dooley," a slicked-up version of a mountain murder ballad, hit the top of the charts for the Kingston Trio. The West Coast pop-folk group's continued use of a banjo, including a version of Scruggs picking by Dave Guard, helped ignite further interest in the five-string already popularized by folk guru Pete Seeger.

In New York City, Eric Nagler wrote in his entertaining history of bluegrass in Greenwich Village, several banjo-pickers were already working hard to emulate Scruggs by 1957 and 1958. A piece on bluegrass in the folk music magazine *Caravan* by picker Roger Lass returned repeatedly to the importance of the banjo, including much more information on Scruggs's banjo-tuners than on Bill Monroe's music.[17]

By 1959, the same year Mike Seeger wrote his perceptive liner notes to the *Mountain Music Bluegrass Style* LP, other significant currents were moving. Seeger himself had been playing mountain music with true-vine friends, including Hazel Dickens, since 1954. Seeger's piece on the banjo-picking contest at Sunset Park, Pennsylvania,

---

15. Fred Bartenstein, "The Carlton Haney Story," *Muleskinner News* 2 (Sept. 1971): 8–10, 18–21.

16. Ben Ratliff, "Grand Elder of Bluegrass Keeps It Modest," *New York Times,* May 20, 1998, B1.

17. Eric Nagler, "An Unnecessarily Wordy and Frankly Inaccurate History of the Development of Bluegrass in Washington Square Park and the Surrounding Village from 1958 to 1967," *Bluegrass Bulletin* 1 (March 1968): 56; Roger Lass, "Bluegrass," *Caravan* 12 (Aug.–Sept. 1958): 20–23.

published in the pioneering folk publication *Gardyloo,* had shown a vibrant cross-cultural scene already in the works.[18]

Dickens, the West Virginia–born singer and songwriter, was to start a pioneering female bluegrass act with California-bred Alice Foster. Rinzler, from New Jersey, had come out of the Swarthmore College folk scene to start the Greenbriar Boys, one of the earliest urban bluegrass acts, and the influential Friends of Old Time Music in New York City. Rinzler also gave bluegrass-style picking an immeasurable boost with his 1961 discovery of Doc Watson, the North Carolina guitar wizard who influenced generations of players with his complex flatpicking and finger-style guitar.

This period of "outside" interest in bluegrass included what could be called its cultural disconnects. Young Hunter S. Thompson offered up a withering, proto-gonzo look at a 1961 Greenbriar Boys performance in Greenwich Village. Musician Michael Melford, writing in *Autoharp,* and blues chronicler Sam Charters in *Sing Out!* turned in two different takes on Boston's famous Hillbilly Ranch. Melford's was raucous and unflinching, and Charters offered a more romanticized view.[19]

Amherst-educated banjo innovator Bill Keith, an early Blue Grass Boy from beyond the true vine, left Monroe for reasons that included Monroe's decision to perform on the *Hootennanny* television show that had blackballed Pete Seeger.

Ralph Gleason, a renowned jazz critic, seemed amazed in a newspaper article that Monroe was reaching up-scale credibility in San Francisco. Another jazz guru, Nat Hentoff, offered an appreciative review of Flatt and Scruggs in *Cosmopolitan.*[20]

Starday Records' attempt to sell more bluegrass records by piggybacking on the folk boom backfired. "The people that bought Bluegrass by mail order from Jimmie Skinner, Wayne Rainey, Starday and other sources seemed to identify Bluegrass with so called 'Beatniks,' 'Draft Dodgers,' 'Civil rights demonstrators,' and the like including subversives, homosexuals, pill and dope takers, and, as a result, Bluegrass sales to the country music market took one hell of a beating," Starday president Don Pierce wrote to *Bluegrass Unlimited.*[21] Starday, a country label formed in 1952 and for a while affiliated with Mercury, became heavily bluegrass-identified in 1958 when Pierce took it independent. Such central figures as the Stanley Brothers, Jim and Jesse, and the Country Gentlemen recorded for Starday.[22] The label also recycled Flatt and Scruggs' Mercury sides.

18. "Hazel Dickens: The Working-Class Conscience of Harlan County, USA," *Unicorn Times* (Aug. 1977): n.p.; Mike Seeger, "Late News Report from Sunset Park, West Grove, Penn. Five-String Banjo Picking Contest," *Gardyloo* (Jan. 1959): 23–24.

19. Hunter S. Thompson, "New York Bluegrass," in *The Fear and Loathing Letters,* vol. 1: *The Proud Highway: Saga of a Desperate Southern Gentleman, 1955–1967* (New York: Villard, 1997), 303–5; Michael J. Melford, "Working the Hillbilly Ranch," *Autoharp,* no. 27, Dec. 18, 1965; Sam Charters, "The Lilly Brothers of Hillbilly Ranch," *Sing Out!* 15 (July 1965): 19–22.

20. Ralph J. Gleason, "On the Town: Blue Grass Boys' Mountain Music," *San Francisco Chronicle,* May 9, 1963, 43; Nat Hentoff, "*Cosmo* Listens to Records," *Cosmopolitan* 160 (April 1966): 28.

21. William Henry Koon, "Grass Roots Commercialism," *Journal of American Folklore* 7 (1971): 5–11.

22. "Formation and Growth of a Record Company: Starday Records," *Disc Collector,* no. 14 (1960): 34–35.

The reach of record companies that concentrated on bluegrass, or gave it significant attention, also increased during this period. In 1959, Charles R. Freeland and friends in the Washington, D.C., area founded Rebel Records, to become one of the first labels to concentrate its resources on bluegrass. By the early 1960s, collector Dave Freeman had started County Records to preserve and record old-time and bluegrass music. His catalog offered information and reviews of not only his own releases but also of related records of interest to fans. Freeman purchased Rebel in 1980.

In a development that was to have far-reaching implications for bluegrass and other traditional styles, Massachusetts-based Rounder Records got its start as a counterculture-style "collective" beginning in 1970. Principals Ken Irwin, Bill Nowlin, and Marian Leighton presided as the label prospered, eventually recording dozens of bluegrass acts as part of Rounder's eclectic stylistic base.

Inevitably, all the activity surrounding bluegrass was to create a new nucleus of acts, many of which took Monroe-style bluegrass as a departure point rather than the Holy Grail. The musicians in groups such as the Country Gentlemen, the Charles River Valley Boys, and, later, the New Grass Revival had deep grounding and great expertise as bluegrass pickers. But they also listened to, and loved, jazz, blues, other folk-based styles, and, eventually, rock 'n' roll. "As John F. Kennedy had evoked a new era upon taking office in 1961, so countless younger Americans were living it out in their own terms in the milieu of the folk revival, where the nation's oldest sounds were telling new stories," critic Greil Marcus wrote in reference to Bob Dylan in 1999.[23]

Formed in 1957, the D.C.-area Country Gentleman became a key act to the late 1950s and early 1960s' broadening of the bluegrass audience. Lead singer Charlie Waller's baritone formed the basis of a vocal blend not too distant in sound from the folk-boom acts of the day. Picking by such adventuresome players as mandolinist John Duffey and banjo player Eddie Adcock presaged the wild-and-woolly musical approaches of the "progressive bluegrass" movement that was a decade or so down the road. Similarly, the Gents' use of material from outside the standard bluegrass canon paved the way for free spirits, including the New Grass Revival, J. D. Crowe and the New South, and North Carolina's New Deal String Band.

On the West Coast, a group first known as the Country Boys released its first recording in 1959. Led by mandolinist Roland White and containing a future guitar superstar in his brother Clarence, the group later took the name "Kentucky Colonels" and became a significant new source of creativity in the field. The Whites didn't emerge from the folk revival, but their music came to be affected by it. Clarence adopted Doc Watson's guitar techniques to mainstream bluegrass after hearing Watson at a famous folk club, the Ash Grove, in Los Angeles. The group was embraced by folk festivals on both coasts.[24]

---

23. Greil Marcus, "Young Man Blues," *San Francisco Examiner Magazine*, Oct. 16, 1999.
24. Peter Kuykendall, "The Kentucky Colonels," *Bluegrass Unlimited* 3 (April 1969): 3–4.

In Boston, a guitar-playing New Englander named Jim Rooney interrupted his
studies at Harvard to team with Bill Keith, who was attending Amherst. Their recordings featured Rooney's easy-going vocals and Keith's well-thought-out reworking of five-string banjo technique. Keith used open strings and left-hand patterns
to reproduce each note of fiddle tunes instead of the approximation usually produced in Scruggs style.[25] An enduring bluegrass debate centers on whether this complex, much-imitated style originated with Keith or with southerner Bobby Thompson. Another great banjo player, Vic Jordan, takes the position that the two men
developed the approach independently and at about the same time. Years after his
recordings with Monroe, Keith said, "It had come time for that."[26]

In any case, Keith's expertise caught Monroe's musicianly ear; it didn't seem to
matter that the younger man didn't always play Scruggs style. Between 1963 and 1966,
such non-southern pickers as Keith, Richard Greene, Lamar Grier, and Peter Rowan joined Monroe's band for some memorable shows and recordings. The interaction with skilled young musicians benefited Monroe, then in his early fifties, just as
it did the players. "The man's playing a third more mandolin than he was four years
ago," long-time Monroe fiddler Kenny Baker said in 1968.[27] The presence in the band
of high-level players, including a young Del McCoury, who did come "from the
tradition," meant that players of all backgrounds were uniting under the bluegrass
banner.

With Rinzler taking on managerial duties, Monroe's recordings and tour dates
received additional attention and creative input. Landmark albums such as *Bluegrass Instrumentals* and *The High Lonesome Sound* collected significant Monroe
recordings and presented them with full liner notes and tributes to his central role
in bluegrass. Tour dates began to draw such nontraditional fans as Jeanne Morgan,
who wrote about a 1967 date at the Ash Grove for the *Los Angeles Free Press:* "Scin-
tillating particles of sound weaving out—leaping and spraying from Bill Monroe's
boys standing up there on the Ashgrove stage last Sunday night in their straight suits
and ties and farmer's hats—yeah, farmer's hats made of some fine straw substitutes
with a black and gold shimmer."[28]

Based on their ages, levels of income and education, geographic location, and
initial exposure to it, bluegrass music interested a surprisingly wide range of fans,
according to a survey in *Muleskinner News* in 1973.[29] People of varying backgrounds
had also begun to be exposed to one another as part of the continuing phenomenon known as the bluegrass festival. More than just a place to hear music, as one
might at an isolated concert, festivals became a means for fans from all over the map

25. R. J. Kelly, "Bill Keith: Sharing a Banjo Tightrope," *Bluegrass Unlimited* 19 (Jan. 1985): 13–17.
26. Author interview with Vic Jordan, summer 1999; Kelly, "Bill Keith."
27. Alice Foster, "Kenny Baker," *Bluegrass Unlimited* 3 (Dec. 1968): 8–11.
28. Jeanne Morgan, "Down Home with Bill Monroe at the Ash Grove," *Los Angeles Free Press,*
May 19, 1967, n.p.
29. Fred. O Bartenstein, "The Audience for Bluegrass: *Muleskinner News* Reader Survey," *The
Journal of Country Music* 4 (Fally 1973): 74–105.

to hear bands, buy merchandise, take part in informal jam sessions, and, vitally, feel part of the interconnected web of bluegrass.

An actual date for the first bluegrass festival has remained a matter of dispute among fans and scholars. Multi-artist shows with bluegrass headliners occurred as early as 1960, but a 1965 show in Virginia provided the model for the modern festival: an event that consciously promotes bluegrass as a style with a discrete identity and a fascinating history. Carlton Haney, the entrepreneur who promoted the "first festival" in Fincastle, Virginia, said that the idea occurred to him after a backstage jam session in a Grand Ole Opry dressing room in 1957. Haney thought, correctly, that fans would buy into a recreation of the event, in which current and past Blue Grass Boys summoned up Monroe's music of several decades.[30]

In addition to their many music revelations, festivals spawned an often-uncomfortable life-style. As Connie Walker, wife of New Grass Revival member Ebo Walker, wrote, "For the bluegrass widow, summer means extensive grocery shopping, pulling out bedrolls and camping equipment, dusting off coolers and canteens, and relocating the first aid kit, calamine lotion, and all those maps which never seem to include places such as Bean Blossom, Knob Noster and Camp Springs."[31] The large numbers of women who have become bluegrass performers instead of "widows" make Walker's otherwise vivid reminder of life in the campgrounds seem dated. "Have a bluegrass festival in your own home this summer!" an RCA Records advertisement cheerfully suggested in July 1974, evidence that festivals had become a major component of bluegrass marketing.

Both fans and musicians were willing to endure significant hardships to devote themselves to bluegrass. With Monroe as an overriding although often inscrutable mentor, bluegrass offered a hypnotic lure—music that was deeply rewarding and a sense that performers and followers were part of an exclusive cult, holders of knowledge and lore unavailable to the less discriminating. In Don Reno's wonderful formulation, musicians sometimes felt they were "on the side of the unknown" but kept on working anyway.[32]

Such dedication kept many brilliant musicians hanging on to bluegrass for years after conventional wisdom, difficult conditions, and low pay might have told them to move on. Some, such as the great fiddler Kenny Baker, roamed back and forth from music to "real jobs"—in Baker's case, the coal mines.[33]

Dating back to the early Blue Grass Boys, grinding travel conditions wore on performers. "We both just got tired of being on the road," Lester Flatt, talking about his and Earl Scruggs's separate departures from Monroe in 1948, told journalist Don Rhodes in 1978. "Sometimes we would go three days without taking our shoes off.

---

30. Bartenstein, "The Carlton Haney Story."

31. Connie Walker, "The Plight of the Bluegrass Widow," *Muleskinner News* 3 (May 1972): 60–61.

32. Peter Wernick, "Interview with Don Reno—September 1965," *Bluegrass Unlimited* 1 (Feb. 1967): 2–4.

33. Foster, "Kenny Baker."

Earl and I had done most of the driving for Monroe's group and we were just tired of traveling." Journalist Tom Teepen presented an updated version of road life in a 1972 *Muleskinner News* piece focused on rising star Larry Sparks. "It has been a twenty-eight-hour day," wrote Teepen, who accompanied Sparks on a road trip. "You get those on the road sometimes."[34]

Bluegrass journalism—hitherto scattered among daily newspapers, a few academic journals, music trade papers, and some general interest magazines—found a focus beginning with the founding in 1966 of *Bluegrass Unlimited*. The magazine was formed by a brain trust of banjo player–disc jockey–producer Pete Kuykendall, record collector–label owner Richard Spottswood, DJ Gary Henderson, Rebel Records owner Richard Freeland, and Dianne Sims, the original editor.[35] The magazine has simultaneously boosted bluegrass and made room for the many controversies that have hovered over it from the beginning.

"Nine ideas, that's all we got, and so by 1948, they were all gone," Sonny Osborne said about bluegrass songwriting in a no-holds-barred *BU* interview taped in 1969. "Let's take a look at the instrument that is always the number 1 subject of controversy—the five-string banjo," Country Gentleman mandolinist John Duffey wrote in *Bluegrass Unlimited* in 1967. "To some of you there is only one way to play and that is 'Scruggs Style.' BOSH. If you think a fast roll would sound good in the middle of 'Bringing Mary Home' then your musical taste is in the part of your anatomy on which you sit!"[36] Duffey was among the many musicians who took pen in hand, some to vent and others to produce more traditional journalism.

Meanwhile, Fred Bartenstein, a Harvard student and bluegrass enthusiast, took a summer job working for Carlton Haney in 1969. Bartenstein put together *Muleskinner News,* which was, as far as he knew, the program for Haney's Camp Springs festival that Labor Day. When Bartenstein noticed that Haney was selling subscriptions, he learned the magazine would become his responsibility. Bartenstein went on to edit *Muleskinner News* until 1975 and remembers it proudly as filling a niche that no other magazine occupied. "My magazine focused more on the professional industry, although there was some overlap with *Bluegrass Unlimited,*" he told me in 2002. "Our editorial vision was that bluegrass was a professional art form and not a hobby."

Bluegrass talents, including Jim and Jesse and the Osbornes, successfully competed for popular success on two fronts: the bluegrass-centric festival circuit and the reviving country scene. Both acts earned Grand Ole Opry membership in 1964, joining Monroe and Flatt and Scruggs as purveyors of bluegrass on the still-influential country radio show.

---

34. Don Rhodes, "Lester Flatt: Talking with a Bluegrass Giant," *Pickin'* 6 (1979): 27; Tom Teepen, "Larry Sparks . . . on the Road," *Muleskinner News* 3 (Nov. 1972): 8–12.

35. Neil Rosenberg, *Bluegrass: A History* (Urbana: University of Illinois Press, 1985), 224–26.

36. John Duffey, "So You Don't Like the Way We Do It (or Damn Your Tape Recorder)," *Bluegrass Unlimited* 1 (April 1967): 3–4.

Ralph Stanley refocused the Clinch Mountain Boys on the lonesome side of bluegrass, building a wide and loyal following. He also nurtured the careers of Larry Sparks, Keith Whitley, and Ricky Skaggs, all of whom started with either the Stanleys or with Ralph Stanley as teenagers.

The Osbornes were at the center of one of the many bluegrass controversies of the 1960s. Purists erupted when the brothers turned to electrified instruments so they could compete with other acts on country package shows. To Sonny, the reason for doing so was clear. If the Osbornes wanted to sell more than their usual eleven thousand records, they had to make themselves heard. Like other acts that plugged in during the 1960s and 1970s, the Osbornes have followed changing tastes and better sound reinforcement back to an acoustic sound in recent years. In 1967 the brothers recorded one of the most universally recognized bluegrass numbers, "Rocky Top." The Felice and Boudleaux Bryant rouser leached into the southeastern consciousness as the University of Tennessee victory song but earned cordial hatred from the many bands and audience members who grew weary of it.

The same cross-currents of traditionalism and innovation that were bringing excitement to the bluegrass scene contributed to the demise of one of its hallmark acts, Flatt and Scruggs. After years of success in all sorts of media, Lester Flatt and Earl Scruggs came to a parting of the ways in early 1969. For bluegrass, the split had all the significance of the Beatles' breakup, to come a year later, for the pop world. The duo had arisen from the wellspring of bluegrass, the classic Bill Monroe band that defined the style between 1945 and 1948.

Flatt, almost ten years older than Scruggs, had become increasingly dissatisfied with the hip new musical direction favored by his banjo-playing partner and Scruggs's talented sons. The two men started new musical enterprises, with Flatt inheriting most of the former Foggy Mountain Boys and Scruggs starting a group with sons Randy and Gary and, later, Steve. The breakup was fueled by personal as well as musical differences, and Flatt and Scruggs remained estranged for years.

New talents who were to broaden the sound and acceptance of bluegrass for years continued to appear. Long-time performers, including Alice Foster (known today as Alice Gerrard), welcomed a scene-shaking newcomer in the person of Sam Bush, whom she profiled for *Bluegrass Unlimited* in 1969. "It is Sam and other young musicians like him who will be maintaining the traditions of bluegrass and keeping the music alive for future generations to enjoy," John Kaparakis wrote in an October 1969 *Bluegrass Unlimited* article on the Bluegrass Alliance.[37]

Sam Bush and other musical expeditionists, including J. D. Crowe, John Hartford, and David Grisman, were taking bluegrass into unexpected realms in the late 1960s and early 1970s, mixing the music with the crackle of r&b, the roar of rock, the improvisatory genius of jazz, and the sentimentality of the singer-songwriter

---

37. Alice Foster, "Sam Bush," *Bluegrass Unlimited* 4 (Nov. 1969): 11–12; John Kaparakis, "The Bluegrass Alliance," *Bluegrass Unlimited* 4 (Oct. 1969): 12–14.

movement. The elements came together in the New Grass Revival, a band that Bush headed beginning in 1972. As Monroe's Blue Grass Boys had done, the Revival bestowed a name on a genre; "newgrass" became a commonly accepted title for the style that Bush and others played.

Bush played exciting, energetic music on the fiddle, mandolin, and guitar and created memorable sounds that respected few boundaries. By 1979 the band hit the road, working as the backup band for the legendary pop/r&b session pianist and songwriter Leon Russell, an indication that the expertise demanded by bluegrass would translate into many other genres.

Inventive acts featuring varying mixes of traditional bluegrass and new sounds were being heard courtesy of J. D. Crowe and the New South, the Seldom Scene, Country Gazette, the Dillards, and musical amalgams such as Old and In the Way, a marriage of eclectic performers that included Grisman, rocker Jerry Garcia, and veteran fiddler Vassar Clements. The pop-folk act called the Nitty Gritty Dirt Band brought legions of new fans into bluegrass when it teamed with Earl Scruggs, Jimmy Martin, Doc Watson, and others on the three-album set *Will the Circle Be Unbroken* (1972).

Just as musicians of different backgrounds joined forces, festivals took on a cross-cultural aspect as newly interested rockers and hard-core bluegrass fans showed up at events from coast to coast.

Instrumental styles continued to evolve, Jack Tottle wrote in a 1972 piece focused on the mandolin, as players worked outward from the hard-bluegrass foundation purveyed by Monroe and others. Steve Arkin's *Pickin'* article on banjo styles tells a similar tale.[38]

In 1979 bluegrass lost, in the death of Lester Flatt, one of its links with the still-revered founding days. Flatt's words to Georgia journalist Don Rhodes offered the great singer's rationale for his career and life: "I'd like to be remembered as someone who tried to play it straight right to the end with the sound he started with."[39] After years of estrangement from his old partner Earl Scruggs, Flatt enjoyed a brief reunion, in a Nashville hospital room, of the friendship that had done so much to make bluegrass an enduring and vital style.

1980–2000: Another Roots Revival, a New Crop

Even as bluegrass was being taken to its outer limits through fusion to other forms, signs and portents of another stylistic wave arose. There was a growing sense that perhaps bluegrass had wandered too far and that it was time to return once again to the thrilling sounds of the late 1940s and early 1950s, to the synoptic gospels of

---

38. Jack Tottle, "Bluegrass Mandolin $\frac{1}{3}$rd Century Later," *Bluegrass Unlimited* 6 (March 1972): 5–9; Steve Arkin, "Banjo Playing: Reno, Thompson, Scruggs, Keith Style and Beyond," *Pickin'* 1 (Oct. 1974): 12–17.

39. Don Rhodes, "Talking with a Bluegrass Giant," *Pickin'* 6 (Feb. 1979): 27.

bluegrass. Even some prime exponents of newgrass started saying the wellspring of the music had been too much diluted.

Exploratory takes on traditional forms had tended to become the rule, not the exception, in the field. During the late 1970s and early 1980s—when the United States as a nation was embracing Ronald Reagan–style conservatism—a series of developments in bluegrass meant that the music was digging down to its roots for inspiration. As always, such movements are not easily pinned down. In most of the music cited here, the old-style bluegrass being revived was a key element in new formations and not the be-all and end-all of specific acts. Outside inspiration for a "new traditionalism" came as early as 1975 in the person of Emmylou Harris, whose hit "If I Could Only Win Your Love" featured trilled mandolin and bluegrassy harmonies on an old Louvin Brothers tune. By 1980 Harris brought together several acoustic music luminaries, including Ricky Skaggs, for her *Roses in the Snow* LP, once again focusing a larger audience on a tradition-heavy bluegrass sound. The duet album that Skaggs, who had been experimenting with more progressive sounds, recorded with Tony Rice (*Skaggs and Rice,* SH-3711) in 1980 marked a return to mandolin-and-guitar basics.

Banjo player Pete Wernick, interviewed in 1979, drew a distinction between learning bluegrass from the masters, as he had done in the 1960s, and absorbing the music at one remove: "At this point I consider myself lucky to have heard early Monroe, Flatt and Scruggs, the Stanley Brothers, etc., at that stage, because I got into bluegrass earlier on in my listening, whereas now people will listen to an awful lot of, well, Alan Munde, who is great, but it's not the roots. It takes folks a long time to develop a concern for the roots. I think it's important to get as deep an understanding as you can of the basis of bluegrass as well as the later development of the music." Wernick's interview came in a *Bluegrass Unlimited* piece on his new band, Hot Rize, formed after he had spent several years exploring a variety of musical directions with the Ithaca, New York, act Country Cooking and as a solo artist. The article deals at some length with Wernick's earlier career, in particular his use of the electronic effect called the "phase shifter," before mentioning that Hot Rize as a group features bluegrass music as played before 1955.[40]

Hot Rize, whose other musical emphasis was original tunes as composed by group members, including future star Tim O'Brien, was one of several groups of the day that focussed on the pioneering sounds of bluegrass. (Of course, Ralph Stanley had continued to work in a traditional vein all along, and other acts, notably the David Grisman–inspired West Coast players, kept merging bluegrass with other styles.)

The turn of the 1980s brought a measurable return to hard-bluegrass values. In several instances, the musicians involved had, like Wernick, been prominent in acts

---

40. Dick Kimmel, "Hot Rize: Pete Wernick's Secret Ingredient," *Bluegrass Unlimited* 13 (March 1979): 13–18.

that took bluegrass far beyond the original Monroe model. "I love Bill Monroe, Ralph Stanley and Don Reno. I think the world of them and I love their music, but I can't make a living doing what they do, and I shouldn't be condemned for it," said a defensive J. D. Crowe in 1974, discussing his band's use of electrified instruments and drums.[41] It's indicative of how much bluegrass had changed that it was even considered necessary to remind musicians and fans of its roots.

By 1980 Crowe and guitarist Tony Rice, also a New South member in 1974, had come together for a different reason: to revive the Monroe–Flatt and Scruggs repertoire for fun and profit. Crowe and Rice were joined by sometime Monroe fiddler Bobby Hicks, veteran mandolinist Doyle Lawson, and West Coast bass player Todd Phillips in the vastly influential Bluegrass Album Band. Rolling out standards such as "Your Love Is Like a Flower" and "Take Me in the Lifeboat" on its eponymous first Rounder LP, the all-star group brought high standards of picking, singing, and recorded sound to the traditional repertoire. With a series of Rounder albums and, later, CDs, the attention these leaders paid to the older sounds was key to refocusing a generation of new pickers.

Known as the most uncompromising of the new traditionalist bluegrass acts, the Johnson Mountain Boys had roots in the Washington, D.C., scene of the mid-1970s. They gained national attention, beginning in 1980, with their first recording for Rounder. The back-to-basics stance and coats-hats-ties look of members Dudley Connell, Eddie Stubbs, Eddie D'Zmura, Richard Underwood, and Larry Robbins became news. Robert Kyle, writing about the Johnson Mountain Boys' signing in the Washington newsletter *Blueprint,* made much of their youthfulness and old repertoire and of their daring in not playing newer, hipper styles. "Would Dudley Connell," Kyle concluded, "ever considering adding some new grass to his repertoire? (Connell replied:) 'If I had to compromise my style, I'd quit.'"[42] Bill Vernon, in liner notes for the live album commemorating the group's 1988 farewell concert, made it clear that the Johnson Mountain Boys remained true to the end to their hard-core image.

In a 1970 profile, Alan Steiner called Peter Rowan a "wandering boy" who was returning to "his roots."[43] Veteran fans remembered Rowan as one of the city-bred pickers who enlivened Bill Monroe's band in the 1960s and then left to chase other musical visions. But after playing with the experimental band Earth Opera, the country-tinged rock act Seatrain, and the all-star units Muleskinner and Old and In the Way, Rowan returned to an acoustic sound and bluegrass emphasis, beginning in the late 1970s. He also cited an increasingly commercialized pop/rock scene as a reason to return to bluegrass.

---

41. Mary Jane Bolle, "Happy Medium—J. D. Crowe and the New South," *Bluegrass Unlimited* 8 (Feb. 1974): 7–9.

42. Robert Kyle, "Untitled," *Blueprint,* Dec. 2–7, 1980, 1–2.

43. Alan Steiner, "Peter Rowan: Wandering Boy Returns to His Roots," *Bluegrass Unlimited* 13 (Feb. 1979): 12–13.

For many musicians the urge to play hard-core bluegrass had never gone away. It emerged in late-night picking sessions, under shade trees at festivals, and, increasingly, in informal side bands or occasional collaborations. One of the most influential of these was the just-for-fun collection of players called the "Dreadful Snakes," whose name simultaneously honored a Monroe song title ("The Little Girl and the Dreadful Snake") and poked fun at the entire bluegrass canon. Members Bela Fleck, Blaine Sprouse, Pat Enright, Mark Hembree, Jerry Douglas, and Roland White all had ties to more serious, big-name bluegrass enterprises, including New Grass Revival, the Whites, Bill Monroe, and the Osborne Brothers. When they started gathering as an informal band in 1982, however, they produced down-the-line, 1940s' style bluegrass mixed with the off-the-wall musician's humor that's more often saved for backstage or the tour bus.

The Dreadful Snakes gave fans an unusual look at the inside wit of the bluegrass world, where the stone faces musicians wear onstage often mask mordant humor and total lack of reverence toward bluegrass icons. "Well, we'll twist a bluegrass tune a little bit," Fleck said of the Snakes' repertoire. "We'll slither around a few bluegrass tunes. We do a version of 'Little Girl and the Dreadful Snake' that is pretty X-rated."[44] A few years earlier, one of the preeminent authorities in bluegrass and old-time music, Middle Tennessee State University professor Charles Wolfe, had offered *BU* readers a hilarious "retrospective" of early bluegrass acts, including Medwick's Incredible Sheep and Lepingwell Freeze and his Briscoe Bird Pushers.[45]

The Snakes provided a spawning ground for the Nashville Bluegrass Band, whose creative approach to tradition helped define the style for a new era. Bluesy tenor singer Pat Enright, Monroe-style mandolinist Mike Compton, and bassist Mark Hembree, formerly of the Blue Grass Boys, were called by banjo player/vocalist Alan O'Bryant for a put-together date in 1984. Although rootsy bluegrass underpinned their sound from the beginning, the band also employed other discrete elements in building a recognizable sound. Its hard-won command of the galvanizing sounds of black gospel quartets in particular helped the Nashville Bluegrass Band stand out. In addition, members worked hard to find suitable tunes by a new generation of songwriters, and their acquaintance with old-time and Celtic styles made for an instrumental sound that relied on a balanced ensemble sound as much as on mind-boggling dexterity.

A road accident of the kind that lives in the nightmares of musicians disrupted the band significantly in 1988 but resulted in an all-star concert to aid the band.[46] By the late 1980s, a lineup of Enright, O'Bryant, fiddler Stuart Duncan, mandolinist Roland White, and bassist Gene Libbea was consistently keeping the band in the forefront of bluegrass acts. More recently, White returned to a solo career,

---

44. Alynn Thomas, "The Dreadful Snakes," *Bluegrass Unlimited* 19 (June 1985): 27–28.
45. Charles Wolfe, "*The Early Days of Bluegrass, Vol. 117*," *Bluegrass Unlimited* 13 (Dec. 1978): 20–21.
46. Lance Cowan, untitled press release from publicity firm Network Ink, Aug. 15, 1988.

Compton came back to the band's mandolin slot, and Dennis Crouch replaced Libbea.

Mandolinist-singer Doyle Lawson, a veteran of Crowe's band, Jimmy Martin's band, and the Country Gentlemen, started his own act, Quicksilver, in 1979. Like the Nashville Bluegrass Band, Lawson broadened the bluegrass repertoire with high-intensity renderings of gospel music, both from his family background in white "southern gospel" and from tunes learned from black gospel recordings. Lawson's bands, through several changes of personnel, have maintained high standards of picking and singing, presenting a carefully rehearsed, tradition-mindful sound that nonetheless breathes with energy and excitement. Quicksilver's many gospel recordings have ensured them a place in Christian-music venues as well as on the bluegrass circuit.[47]

Also emerging on record during the 1980s was Stanley Brothers–style singer James King, who recorded for the traditionally oriented WEBCO label of Virginia. Founded in 1980 by Wayne Busbice, brother of the pioneering mandolinist Buzz Busby, WEBCO presented historical recordings of acts that included Busby, Jim Eanes, and Bill Harrell.[48] Combining 1950s' tunes by the Stanleys, Jimmy Martin, and others with his true-vine compositions, King enjoyed some early success but left the business for a while only to emerge in 1994 on Rounder. By the later 1990s his emotional, hard-edged recordings were regularly topping bluegrass charts.

A major event for bluegrass music came in 1978 with the founding of North Carolina–based Sugar Hill Records by Dave Freeman and Barry Poss of County Records. Doyle Lawson, the Seldom Scene, Carl Jackson, Marty Stuart, Doc Watson, and the Nashville Bluegrass Band all recorded for Sugar Hill, which Poss owned as of 1980 until a sale to the Welk Music Group in 1998. Significantly for widespread recognition of bluegrass, Sugar Hill released Ricky Skaggs's 1979 solo debut, *Sweet Temptation*. With contributions by Emmylou Harris, the Whites, Jerry Douglas, and Tony Rice, the record created a stir for Skaggs.

By the late 1970s, Skaggs, born in 1954, had been a professional entertainer for nearly a decade. With his early singing partner Keith Whitley, he had joined a memorable version of Ralph Stanley's band in 1971. The two teenagers helped Ralph Stanley recreate the classic Stanley Brothers sound and made names for themselves in the process. Playing fiddle, mandolin, and guitar adeptly and singing lonesome, country-tinged tenor, Skaggs shone as a member of J. D. Crowe's New South and the Country Gentlemen before starting his own band, Boone Creek, with Jerry Douglas, banjo player Terry Baucom, bassist Steve Bryant, and guitarist Wes Golding. Beginning in 1979, Skaggs played in Emmylou Harris's high-profile Hot Band,

---

47. Frank Godbey and Marty Godbey, "Doyle Lawson and Quicksilver," in *The Encyclopedia of Country Music: The Ultimate Guide to the Music,* comp. by the staff of the Country Music Hall of Fame and Museum, ed. Paul Kingsbury (New York: Oxford University Press, 1998), 292.

48. John S. Emerson, liner notes to *WEBCO Classics Volume Two: James King,* WEBCO CD 6002 (1994).

which at various times included Rodney Crowell, guitar great Albert Lee, and future Music Row power Tony Brown.

The *Sweet Temptation* album produced a minor country hit, a version of the Stanleys' "I'll Take the Blame," in 1980, enough to get Skaggs signed to Epic Records in Nashville. A series of remarkable recordings ensued, with Skaggs as producer and artist overseeing music that combined bluegrass, 1950s' country, country rock, and a pinch of singer-songwriter lyricism.

One key to his success was a remarkable band that included electric guitar hotshot Ray Flacke, veteran bluegrass fiddler Bobby Hicks, steel guitarist Bruce Bouton, and former Poco drummer George Grantham. The harmonies were a little slick by some bluegrass standards, and the solos were as apt to be electric guitar as bluegrass mandolin. Hits such as "Highway 40 Blues," "Crying My Heart Out over You," and the Monroe tribute of "Uncle Pen," however, represented a real step forward for mainstream country and a hugely increased presence for bluegrass songs and sounds in the mainstream.

By 1985 Skaggs had earned the Country Music Association's Entertainer of the Year Award, a high point of commercial acceptance for him. After he helped open the door to a more traditional sound, a new generation of country music stars emerged during the second half of the 1980s, including Randy Travis, Clint Black, Alan Jackson, Garth Brooks, and many others. Skaggs's mainstream career was to fade in time, but that turn of events would later benefit bluegrass as a whole.

As Skaggs's recordings featured some of his long-time bluegrass associates as instrumentalists and singers, talents including Jerry Douglas and Bela Fleck started turning up on a number of mainstream country and pop records. It was part of a growing recognition that bluegrass picking had reached an even greater level of proficiency, and that uses for that artistry existed outside the strictly bluegrass world. Douglas in particular became ubiquitous as a session musician, employing sense-defying speed and virtuosity when necessary and tastefully plying his wide, electric-guitar-inspired vibrato and harmonic sense. In a 1986 interview, Skaggs marveled at Douglas's technique: "I think in a way Jerry has done as much to stop the progression of the Dobro as he has to promote it. . . . Because when you hear Jerry play you say there's no way on God's green earth that I could ever play that lick. But if you're really into the instrument, you're not going to quit; it's just going to be an inspiration to you."[49]

From the beginning of the style, the instrumental mastery of bluegrassers had been key to attracting fans. When "new acoustic" arose during the 1980s, bluegrass and bluegrass-trained musicians had the chops to work at the heart of that demanding style. Led by pickers David Grisman, Tony Rice, Mike Marshall, Mark O'Connor, and Tony Trischka, new acoustic music combined mainstream jazz, bluegrass, blues, and world musics among other styles.

49. Author interview with Ricky Skaggs, Sept. 1986.

Significant recognition of bluegrass from the mainstream music industry came with the establishment of a bluegrass category of the Grammy Awards by National Academy of Recording Arts and Sciences. The first recipient, appropriately, was Bill Monroe for his LP *Southern Flavor* (1988).

Channeling the excitement surrounding both bluegrass veterans and newly emerging stars became the role of the style's trade association, the International Bluegrass Music Association. With long-time booking agent and manager Lance LeRoy as a driving force, talks about starting the organization began in the mid-1980s. Bill and James Monroe, *BU* editor Pete Kuykendall, LeRoy, and eventual IBMA director Art Menius met in Nashville in the summer of 1985 with a board of directors elected by August of that year.[50] The first trade show took place in Owensboro, Kentucky, in 1986.

One of the sensations of the IBMA convention in 1987 was the emergence of the teenaged Alison Krauss. At sixteen, Krauss had been winning fiddle contests for four years and presented a startlingly high level of musicianship and singing with her band, Union Station, as well as a confident stage presence that was an easy indicator of incipient stardom. Her 1987 debut album, *Too Late to Cry,* received a major push from Rounder Records, which has been a key player in her overwhelming success.

More than any other new performer of the late twentieth century, Krauss has brought bluegrass—and bluegrass-inflected styles—to a much wider audience. By 1996 she had sold more than two million copies of the album *Now That I've Found You: A Collection,* also winning multiple Grammys and awards from the Country Music Association. The disc's title track, a remake of a 1960s' hit by the Foundations, sat side by side with tunes by the Beatles and Bad Company as well as complementing the songwriter fare that Krauss increasingly favored. Union Station has included many strong performers, among them John Pennell, Tim Stafford, Adam Steffey, Dan Tyminski, and Ron Block. They benefited from Krauss's insistence that her band receive equal attention onstage and in interviews.

Echoing the long debate over innovation and traditionalism in bluegrass, fans and critics took sides over Krauss. With her expert fiddling and bluegrass-inflected singing, she brought new levels of performance and public attention to the style. But the old question was trotted out again: Is it bluegrass? For hard-liners it probably made it worse that Krauss, who does indeed love hard-core bluegrass, seemed congenitally unable to talk the talk about the importance of traditionalism. "I think whatever we have slipped by somebody is great," she said when *Rolling Stone* asked whether she had changed the general perception about bluegrass.[51]

Undeterred by perceptions of what she should be or how she should sound, Krauss forged ahead, diverging almost completely from a straight bluegrass sound

---

50. Jack Bernhardt, "Art Menius: Working to Make Bluegrass Grow," *Bluegrass Unlimited* 5 (Nov. 1987): 54–58.

51. Jim Macnie, "Country Artist of the Year: Alison Krauss," *Rolling Stone,* Jan. 25, 1996, 48.

on the *Forget about It* disc (1999). The band continued to feature a mix of material in concert, with the venerable "Wild Bill Jones" appearing side by side with tunes by pop tunesmiths Todd Rundgren and Michael McDonald.[52]

Not only was Krauss the highest-profile act of the bluegrass resurgence of the 1990s, but she also provided the prime example of how high the stock of women had risen in the field. Her emergence came in the context of high levels of critical and fan attention to acts, including the Front Porch String Band's Claire Lynch, Laurie Lewis, Dale Ann Bradley, and even an acousticized Emmylou Harris, who spotlighted bluegrass with her Nash Ramblers Band.

Picker and journalist Murphy Henry championed the cause and history of women with her *Women in Bluegrass* newsletter, which began in 1994. Going back to Wilene (Sally Ann) Forrester's early membership in Monroe's band and Bessie Lee Mauldin's stint as a Blue Grass "girl" in the 1950s and 1960s, female pickers and singers have had a role in bluegrass. A few performers—notably singer-guitarist Delia Bell, vocalist-instrumentalist Gloria Belle Flickinger, and vocalist-guitarist Betty Fisher—recorded and toured during the later 1950s and 1960s.[53] It was during the 1970s, however, that an explosion of female performers hit the scene, powered by societal changes and the examples of others, including Harris.

It wasn't easy for women to enter the field, dominated as it was by the patriarchal figure of Bill Monroe. Singers in particular ran into the musical conservatism of bluegrass, which dictated that certain songs had always been performed in certain keys and should not be changed just to suit the vocal range of a woman.[54] Murphy Henry remained a dependable chronicler and champion of female players and singers. In an address to the IBMA convention in 1998 she brought more attention to the issues and earned a response in the pages of *Women in Bluegrass* from IBMA stalwart Peter Wernick.[55]

The Texas-bred Dixie Chicks brought bluegrass instrumentation, at least, into the forefront of the mainstream country music scene in the later 1990s with their use of banjo and fiddle on recordings and—maybe as important—on music videos. Their irreverence and hip fashion sense helped link bluegrass to the MTV glitz that had permeated country music. Acousticized picking highlighted some of the Chicks' earlier hits, and their blockbuster 2002 release *Home* placed new emphasis on the bluegrass side of their sound.

52. Ben Ratliff, "Focusing on the Music, Not on Those Playing It," *New York Times*, Nov. 19, 1999, B30.

53. Mary A. Bufwack and Robert K. Oermann, "Little Darlin's Not My Name," in Mary A. Bufwack and Robert K. Oermann, *Finding Her Voice: The Saga of Women in Country Music* (New York: Crown, 1993), 454–59.

54. Thomas A. Adler, "Is There a Link between Bluegrass Music and Sexuality?" *Women in Bluegrass* 19 (Spring 1999): 1–6.

55. Murphy Henry, "'Women in Bluegrass': Keynote Address at the IBMA Trade Show," *Women in Bluegrass*, no. 18 (Nov. 1998): 2–5; Pete Wernick, "Keynote: Bones to Pick," *Women in Bluegrass*, no. 18 (Fall 1998): 8–9.

Innovation continued within the bluegrass framework as well. As Stacy Phillips pointed out in a comprehensive story in *Strings,* everyone from Bobby Hicks to highly accomplished newcomers, including Aubrey Haynie, was coming up with exhilarating new music on the fiddle.[56] Guitarist Bryan Sutton, who came to widespread attention in Skaggs's band, attracted a lot of attention with his startling technique, command of several styles, and deep grounding in bluegrass and tradition.

By the early 1990s a shifting lineup of top-shelf musicians, many of whom had already worked in established acts, started forming new groups, including IIIrd Tyme Out and Blue Highway. Members of Doyle Lawson's Quicksilver Band, the New Quicksilver, and the Bluegrass Cardinals united in IIIrd Tyme Out, which quickly built a following and earned stacks of IBMA awards and spots on the bluegrass charts. Blue Highway, which included former members of Union Station, started its career on Rebel but moved to Skaggs's Ceili Music label and then to Rounder. Dobro player Rob Ickes, who supplanted Douglas as Dobro player of the year in IBMA voting in 1998, became a particular standout. The Lonesome River Band and lead singer Ronnie Bowman combined hard bluegrass with striking new material to win legions of new fans. Artists including singer-songwriter Larry Cordle brought a taste of hard country to bluegrass. Cordle's tradition-lauding tune "Murder on Music Row" created a sensation in 1999 and won several top country-music industry awards following its recording by Alan Jackson and George Strait.

On the sometimes wearying topic of where bluegrass stands on the tradition-innovation continuum, there's evidence at both ends. Krauss had the biggest sales ever in bluegrass with an approach that stepped freely through tradition to being not too different from the female balladeers of pop's Lilith Fair. Skaggs, however, enjoyed an overwhelming career revival by sticking closer to bluegrass dogma than he had since his days as a star sideman. Krauss—and the others coming up with new approaches—nonetheless used techniques that originated with the founding masters.

Strikingly, the 1990s saw a return to the decades-old practice of gathering around a single microphone to sing and play in concert. Old-time and early bluegrass styles took a place of prominence in the Coen Brothers film *O Brother, Where Art Thou?* That film's popularity and its soundtrack's notably high level of sales sparked plenty of conversation about how big this music could be if only a wide audience was exposed to it. Other cinematic fare included *Down from the Mountain,* a documentary of a concert featuring performers from *O Brother,* and music in the Appalachian-themed *Songcatcher.*

The pioneering stalwarts of bluegrass, who had never stopped touring, welcomed the new popularity of bluegrass with the same stoicism with which they had greeted the grim, slow years of the 1950s. Increasingly imbued with a kind of bluegrass sainthood, Monroe continued to perform at festivals, concert halls, and the

---

56. Stacy Phillips, "From Bluegrass to Newgrass," *Strings* 13 (Dec. 1998): 100–107.

Opry and kept recording, appearing in the studio as late as 1996, the last year of his life. A "funeral service" for Monroe at the Ryman Auditorium in 1996 included much sober piety and an all-out version of Monroe's instrumental "Raw Hide" led by Marty Stuart.

Ralph Stanley also enjoyed the fruits of decades of making great music, assembling a long list of bluegrass and country stars—even the folk legend Bob Dylan—to appear on the well-received *Clinch Mountain Country* two-CD set. The Osbornes, freed of their electrified instruments, upheld high standards of musicianship on the Opry and elsewhere.

Others' fortunes were not as starry. Bluegrass old-timers gave nods of recognition when writer Tom Piazza, a great admirer of Jimmy Martin's music, portrayed Martin as embittered, paranoid, and disconnected in a magazine article that became a much-discussed book in 1999.[57] Musicians and fans mourned the passing of figures such as bassist Roy Huskey Jr., fiddler Randy Howard, pioneering performer Wilene (Sally Ann) Forrester, the great musician-songwriter-historian John Hartford, and bluegrass-country pioneer Jim McReynolds.

Yet signs continue to pile up that the peak of interest in bluegrass had depth and staying power. Skaggs had come back from a faltering mainline country career to produce one of the key recordings of the 1990s in *Bluegrass Rules,* a blistering, hard-core assemblage that, unexpectedly, far outsold any of his more recent, commercially aimed efforts. In response, he launched his own label, Ceili Records, and quickly signed Del McCoury and other leading exponents.

A piece on Skaggs by Jon Weisberger, a reliable bluegrass journalist, in the alternative country publication *No Depression* was evidence of the credibility bluegrass had earned with followers of the authenticity-hungry alternative country movement. Moreover, "alt country" and rock star Steve Earle picked McCoury and band to back him on *The Mountain,* a high-profile, all-bluegrass album. The resulting tour and publicity brought much new attention to bluegrass but alienated some bluegrassers, including, ultimately, McCoury himself.[58]

Also in 1999, Dolly Parton devoted the first of two albums to bluegrass, using pickers that included Sam Bush and Jerry Douglas to record songs by Lester Flatt, Johnny Cash, and others. It was, Parton said, a musical trip back to her East Tennessee childhood and her early days on the Opry, where she performed alongside Monroe, Flatt and Scruggs, Jim and Jesse, and others. During the same period, Bob Dylan increased his occasional in-concert performances of bluegrass tunes to the point where renditions of "Hallelujah I'm Ready" or "I Am the Man, Thomas" became nightly occurrences. "My songs come out of folk music," Dylan told *New York Times* reporter Jon Pareles in 1997. "I love that whole pantheon. To me there's no

---

57. Tom Piazza, *True Adventures with the King of Bluegrass* (Nashville: Country Music Foundation Press and Vanderbilt University Press, 1999).

58. Jon Weisberger, "Going Back to Old Kentucky: Ricky Skaggs Rediscovers the Rules of Bluegrass," *No Depression,* no. 12 (Nov.–Dec. 1997): 56–63; Baker Maultsby, "Progress Rooted in Tradition: Del McCoury Talks about Work with Bill Monroe, Steve Earle," *Creative Loafing,* July 10, 1999.

difference between Muddy Waters and Bill Monroe."[59] Dylan was often quoted as describing his participation in the Ralph Stanley tribute CDs as the highlight of his career.

The profile of bluegrass continued to rise in several media. The august Grand Ole Opry, faced with declining attendance and infrequent performances by a new generation of stars, began to lean heavily on its bluegrass cast members and a healthy number of guest appearances by bluegrass acts. The trend was noticeable by the late 1990s, when guest artists included Del McCoury, the Nashville Bluegrass Band, Lynn Morris, J. D. Crowe, Larry Stephenson, Blue Highway, and Doyle Lawson. Ralph Stanley received a long-overdue Opry induction in 2000.

Public radio became a vital outlet, both on several bluegrass-specific shows on stations across the country and on Garrison Keillor's *Prairie Home Companion*. Acts including Parton and the Earle/McCoury collaboration brought the music to broadcast and cable television. Krauss appeared on a new disc by the classical crossover trio of Edgar Meyer, Yo-Yo Ma, and Mark O'Connor. The young and expansive acoustic act Nickel Creek, starring mandolin's maturing wunderkind Chris Thile, reached a much-needed younger demographic of fans via sparkling performances and broad media exposure.

Public radio also nurtured the magazine *Bluegrass Now*, which started in the early 1980s as *Bluegrass Picking Times*, a free newsletter from public radio station KUMR-FM in Rolla, Missouri, according to founder Wayne Bledsoe. The newsletter's popularity led to the independent launch of *Bluegrass Now* in December 1990. "The objective of *Bluegrass Now*," Bledsoe wrote to me in 2002, "was to combine a fan publication with a trade magazine and I think we have been very successful in giving the reader the highest level of both features."

Several books came out that offered in-depth looks at key figures and at the style itself. Among them were John Wright's *Traveling the High Way Home: Ralph Stanley and the World of Traditional Bluegrass Music*, Richard D. Smith's *Can't You Hear Me Callin': The Life of Bill Monroe, Father of Bluegrass*, Carl Fleischhauer and Neil V. Rosenberg's, *Bluegrass Odyssey: A Documentary in Pictures and Words*, and Tom Ewing's *The Bill Monroe Reader*.[60]

As renewed tides of traditionalism swelled through bluegrass in the late 1990s and early 2000s, Earl Scruggs stuck to his individualistic course. Since the breakup with Lester Flatt in 1969, Scruggs had taken his banjo into new territory time and time again. Whether working with his sons in the Earl Scruggs Revue, with Bob Dylan on a television documentary, or with the Nitty Gritty Dirt Band on their

---

59. Jon Pareles, "A Wiser Voice Blowin' in the Autumn Wind," *New York Times*, Sept. 28, 1997, 2:1.

60. John Wright, *Traveling the High Way Home: Ralph Stanley and the World of Traditional Bluegrass Music* (Urbana: University of Illinois Press, 1993); Richard D. Smith, *Can't You Hear Me Callin': The Life of Bill Monroe, Father of Bluegrass* (New York: Little, Brown, 2000); Carl Fleischhauer and Neil V. Rosenberg, *Bluegrass Odyssey: A Documentary in Pictures and Words, 1966–86* (Urbana: University of Illinois Press, 2001); Tom Ewing, ed., *The Bill Monroe Reader* (Urbana: University of Illinois Press, 2000).

excursions into bluegrass, Scruggs was determined to build on his bluegrass roots and not just revisit them.

Visitors to his rare shows or to the star-studded picking parties he and wife, Louise, held at their Nashville home could attest to his continuing vitality as a musician. *Earl Scruggs and Friends,* which he released in 2001 (a project for which I helped prepare promotional material), presented a mega-version of those down-home parties—Scruggs in sympathetic interaction with his talented guests. The disc's electrified, all-star version of the venerable "Foggy Mountain Breakdown" won a Best Country Instrumental Performance Grammy for Scruggs in 2001.

The Internet's ability to reach fans easily helped retailers and publications, including *iBluegrass* and the venerable *Bluegrass Unlimited,* both of which have devoted considerable resources to Web presences.

Word of stars' involvement, new acts, and festivals competed for space with historical disputes, personal mud-slinging, and a mind-boggling array of other topics on BGRASS-L, the on-line discussion forum that created a bluegrass e-community during the 1990s. Moderated by veteran bluegrasser Frank Godbey, the "L" served as the community bulletin board and radio talk show equivalent for far-flung fans from several continents. Tidbits such as "Jammandments" (rules for taking part in bluegrass picking sessions) turned up, along with age-old disputes over who started what style when, or whether a specific act was really (you guessed it) bluegrass at all.

The death of Bill Monroe in 1996 was an incalculable blow to bluegrass. Whatever the arguments may have been about the exact nature of the big bang, there was no disputing Monroe's central role to the music throughout its history. Somehow the music rebounded, as it always has. Through years in which, as Monroe once remarked, "no one knew what this music was or why it was being brought out," and through dilutions and changes that threatened to kill it as a discrete style, bluegrass not only endured but also prevailed.[61] As of this writing, it's possible to make a case that bluegrass is more popular now than ever. Fueled by technological change, listeners' hunger for true-vine authenticity, and a vastly talented crop of new musicians, bluegrass seems certain to carry Monroe's lonely vision deep into a new century.

---

61. Author interview with Bill Monroe, 1987.

1

The Big Bang

1939–59

Jim Rooney represents several exemplars in bluegrass. He was first known as a musician, one of the original urban folkies and the duet partner of banjo innovator Bill Keith. As is the case with talented folks like Mac Wiseman, Mike Seeger, and John Hartford, he also has led a number of professional lives. Rooney has had careers as manager of Boston's renowned Club 47, manager of Bearsville Studios, studio engineer for the legendary Jack Clement, music publisher, and producer. During the 1980s and 1990s he enjoyed significant success as publisher of a number of Garth Brooks hits and producer of Hal Ketchum, Nanci Griffith, John Prine, and many others. All that aside, he created a landmark work for bluegrass with the publication in 1971 of *Bossmen: Bill Monroe and Muddy Waters.* The first Monroe profile approaching book length, Rooney's work showed his keen and insightful appreciation of Monroe and bluegrass.

1

"Bossman Bill Monroe"

JAMES ROONEY

Bill Monroe was the youngest in his family. His people were farmers, working hard to get a living out of the hills around Rosine, Kentucky. It's pretty country there. You pass by today on the "Bluegrass Turnpike" and the hills are deceptively inviting, green, undulating waves.[1] Pretty to look at but hard to work. Bill's mother died in 1921 when he was a boy, barely ten years old. When Bill was in his teens his older brothers went North to look for work. Bill's father died, leaving him alone at the age of seventeen.[2]

With no family to keep him there in Rosine, Bill set out to join his brothers Charlie and Birch, who were now living outside of Chicago in Whiting, Indiana.

> If you was raised on a farm you would know of hard times and you didn't get things as a kid that you do now. On Saturday I would get a nickel to buy some candy with and that's all I got all week. And one pair of shoes a year and two pairs of overalls. Have shoes to wear in the wintertime and go barefooted in the summertime. If you plowed for your father it felt good to your feet to follow

---

1. It's officially called the Bluegrass, or Western Kentucky, Parkway.
2. Bill was sixteen when his father died on January 14, 1928 (*The Bill Monroe Reader,* ed. Tom Ewing [Urbana: University of Illinois Press, 2000], 215n6]).

that plow and stay in that furrow with the fresh ground turning over there. You didn't mind. There wasn't no radios, nothing; you didn't hear no music—just what you played—and farm work. And you wondered what life would have been like in a town or in a city, but I was afraid to tackle it. But I reckon my people figured I would never make anything there and that they should try to get me out of there to where I could make a decent living. Course my father and mother died and a little later on Uncle Pen passed away and Uncle Birch Monroe died, so there wasn't very many of the Monroes left there—just some cousins.

But Bill's imagination and his mind were still in those hills back in Kentucky. As the youngest in the family he had been a little quieter and more observant than the others. His eyes were crossed and weak, but his ears were sharp and they took in all of the sounds around him. Those sounds haven't left Bill to this day, and they formed the basis for his musical development.

I have always been proud of the people I came from in Kentucky and growing up the way that I did in the country and to learn what old-time music was really all about and to study it ever since I was a young boy and then to make it do something later on in years and to originate a music.

The first music I heard was Uncle Pen and Uncle Birch and a man by the name of Clarence Wilson, and they played numbers like "Soldier's Joy." Each town maybe had a little band, you know. I knew a little band eight or ten miles from us by the name of Foster String Band—that was back in the twenties, and I remember a band that had a fiddle, a Hawaiian guitar, mandolin—they might have had a banjo. They played breakdowns, dance music and a few waltzes and a little Hawaiian music. Maybe there would be one man who would know a solo, and there was one fellow singing "Greenback Dollar."

There's a long ridge back home called Jerusalem Ridge, and I remember we had to cross that and go on down about a mile to where we come to this real old house called the Lizer place, and this man, Clea Baze that played the fiddle, he lived there. We'd walk back there with a coal oil lantern, and we got there that night and there was a good many in the room listening to them play and they sat in the middle of the room and I thought that was awful pretty music . . . numbers like "Turkey in the Straw" and that kind of stuff. They'd play "Cacklin' Hen" and he could really play that. It was something to go knowing you was going to hear some music that night.

At these gatherings the music was largely oriented toward instrumental music for dancing. On Sundays there was a different form of music—hymn singing in the old Sacred Harp way at the community singing schools. Based on a five-note scale, this music was very open, unlike the closer sound of more modern music. In secular music this open sound would be called "lonesome," and to the people around Rosine, that "lonesome sound" seemed to fit right with life in the mountains.

Another sound that seemed to fit in was the sound of the blues.

I remember in Rosine this colored man would haul freight from the train station to six or seven stores bringing each man what he wanted. And he would be riding his mule on those muddy roads just whistling the blues. And you could tell by the way he whistled that he was the bluest man in the world. Many days through people's lives the blues will touch them. Might not have started out on a Monday—might have been a blue Monday—but sometime through that week they'd have felt the blues. If you can sing. If you made up words as you went along you'd make them up to suit yourself, to suit the mood you was in. You would gradually touch the blues someplace.

Every boy growing up meets men that he looks up to and admires. There were two men who impressed Bill as a boy and whose music found an important place in his music as it developed. One was a black blues player who used to live near Rosine called Arnold Schultz.

The first time I think I ever seen Arnold Shultz . . . this square dance was at Rosine, Kentucky, and Arnold and two more colored fellows come up there and played for the dance. They had a guitar, banjo, and fiddle. Arnold played the guitar but he could play the fiddle—numbers like "Sally Goodin." People loved Arnold so well all through Kentucky there; if he was playing a guitar they'd go gang up around him till he would get tired and then maybe he'd go catch a train. He lived down at a little mining town—I believe it was called McHenry—or on down further. I used to listen at him talk and he would tell about contests that he had been in and how tough they was and how they'd play these two blues numbers and tie it up. And they had to do another number and I remember him saying that he played a waltz number and he won this contest. And just things like that I have never forgot. He thought it was wonderful that he could win out like that and I admired him that much that I never forgot a lot of the things that he would say. There's things in my music, you know, that come from Arnold Shultz—runs that I use in a lot of my music. I don't say that I make them the same way that he could make them 'cause he was powerful with it. In following a fiddle piece or a breakdown, he used a pick and he could just run from one chord to another the prettiest you've ever heard. There's no guitar picker today that could do that. I tried to keep in mind a little of it—what I could salvage to use in my music. Then he could play blues and I wanted some blues in my music too, you see.

Me and him played for a dance there one night and he played the fiddle and we started at sundown and the next morning at daylight we was still playing music—all night long.

And of course, that automatically made you be dancing on Sunday, but that is really the truth—I could say that I have played for a dance all night long. I played the guitar with him. I just could second fair—probably any guitar man in the country could've beaten me but anyhow I played guitar for him. I believe it was the next day about ten o'clock there was a passing train come down through and stopped at Rosine and I believe he caught that train and went back home and that was about the last time I ever saw him.

I believe if there's ever an old gentleman that passed away and is resting in peace, it was Arnold Shultz—I really believe that.

From this time on Bill felt that the blues was a natural part of him and his music. It didn't seem any different from being "lonesome." It was all there together in those hills.

The other man who had a major influence on Bill at this age was his Uncle Pen Vandiver.[3]

> He fiddled all of his life. To start out with, he was a farmer for a long time. There was four in his family. His wife and two children. The boy's name was Cecil and I believe he passed away first and then the daughter and the mother. And then Uncle Pen came to live with us. He would leave out on Monday morning and go through some part of the country and he would go to visit some people—he might know them, I guess. And he would have something to trade on and he would trade. He was the kind of man, you know, who needed the boots. He needed that extra change of money. Then he would go on—maybe spend a night with somebody else up the road. But he would always make his circle. And sometimes he would start out with nothing much and come back maybe leading a cow—he always rode a horse back or a mule—and maybe he'd sell the cow to somebody and start all over again. Might have been a bad life for a lot of people, I guess. But there's not too many people who can trade and come out winners. But he was one who didn't have to come out too much, but that was his way of making a living. Later on, he got throwed by a horse and broke his hip and he was a cripple. He was on crutches the rest of his life. His last days in Kentucky, me and him would play for square dances wherever they would want a fiddle and a guitar. You know, I rode behind him and we'd take out and go back through the country maybe three or four or five miles and play for a square dance at somebody's home, you know. They'd clear a room out and me and him would play for the dance. And we'd make three or four dollars apiece, something like that. And he'd always give me just as much as he made. If it was six dollars he'd give me three of it.
>
> It learns a boy to have someone like that to show him. It gives him experience. And at the same time my uncle was getting some enjoyment out of it.
>
> And he had the best bow movement with a fiddle bow that you have ever seen in your life. He could really shuffle.
>
> A lot of Uncle Pen's fiddling is in bluegrass music. It learned me how it had to be played to be good back when I was really young. You could hear him and you could tell that he could really fiddle. But if you had never heard him, the people in the community could tell you how he could fiddle. And you had to go along with them because there was that many that would tell you how he could really fiddle. So you knew when you was young that he was a wonderful old-time fiddler. It's got its part in bluegrass music.

So, for his seventeen years Bill Monroe had absorbed and retained a lot of music. He instinctively valued the culture he grew up in and learned from it. He wasn't thinking about it especially. It was just in him. At the moment he was concerned

---

3. Monroe's uncle was Pendleton Vandiver.

with finding Birch and Charlie and getting a job and making some money. He left his home never to return. All he needed he brought out with him.

By the late twenties, the mid-Northern cities were becoming heavily industrialized. The automobile industry was the cause of much of the expansion. Oil refineries, steel mills, and automobile plants needed large numbers of unskilled laborers and found their supply in the young men fleeing the hard-pressed rural areas of the South. They came from the Carolinas, Tennessee, Alabama, Mississippi, and Kentucky—strong young men, used to hard work. They came to the factories and refineries hoping to get money for a better life than they had left behind at home. Sometimes the supply of labor was greater than the demand, and a young boy like Bill, fresh from the country, took a while to get started.

> It was hard getting work when I went up there. It was ten weeks before I got a job. Birch didn't get a job for a long time, Charlie had trouble with his foreman and after a little while lost his job. So I was the only one working. There was places like Standard Oil Refinery and Sinclair. I worked there, you know. I worked in the Barrel House for close to five years.
>
> Many's a day I stacked a thousand barrels—two thousand barrels. We could unload a freight car in forty-five minutes. There would be two inside the car and two or three of us outside and they would spin those barrels down on you and you would have to catch them—just like playing ball. And then we would clean barrels with gasoline. Some of them weighed one hundred and fifty pounds and that was some hard work, I'll tell you.
>
> I made forty cents an hour, then forty-five cents an hour. Every two weeks Charlie or Birch would come with me to get my pay. Fifty or sixty dollars was all I could seem to make. And we would pay the rent and buy groceries and I would set aside three dollars for streetcar back and forth. And I never could put any money away it seems. They hung right on. If I rode a streetcar going to a dance why they knew that I would pay the way for them to go. Every place I went they went.
>
> I worked every day for five years and all I got out of it was I spent forty dollars for a mandolin and I got a couple of suits of clothes.
>
> I've often wondered if I was doing the right thing. I guess I was. It wouldn't be right not to support your people.
>
> We lived in Whiting for a short time. And then we moved over to East Chicago, Indiana—about four or five miles from there and we lived there for the rest of the time until we left the country.

While Bill was working at Sinclair there was very little opportunity to play much music. What music he did play was with Charlie and Birch for little house parties and dances in the area where they would make about five dollars apiece, but there wasn't enough money in it to make it worth doing full time. Music was fast becoming the major broadcast item on radio, however, and WLS in Chicago had started a program featuring old-time and country music every Saturday night. By 1932 the WLS Barndance audience had grown to such an extent that the station sent out a traveling show to cover this listening territory.[4] Charlie, Birch, and Bill sensed an opportunity to make their music pay off better than it had.

> At that time you couldn't hardly get a job playing music that paid any money. WLS in Chicago was about the only place up there that really paid any good money, and you got very little on smaller stations without you didn't have a sponsor, you know; they would take you in and give you so much a week. If you went out and played for a square dance you might make three or four or five dollars a night. We'd get maybe twenty-five dollars for the three of us or the four of us if somebody was playing bass fiddle or something. While I worked there at Sinclair, WLS, they wanted a road show, and they put their people out on it that they thought would draw good, like Arkansas Woodchopper and people like that.[5] And they had a set of square dancers at the theater and they wanted a set on the road, so Charlie and Birch and me and another feller had us a set of square dancers, you know, and we danced for WLS on the road. I don't know how long. And they paid twenty-two dollars and a half a week. Per man. Of course that far back you could get a room for seventy-five cents—a good room. You could get a steak for thirty-five cents. So it was pretty good money.
>
> I'd take off two weeks and then I'd go back. But then I got to taking off so much that I had to finally quit the job.
>
> We played a lot of times seven days a week. We had a Packard we would travel in. We played mostly through Indiana and Illinois and maybe a few days in Wisconsin and Michigan. It give us some experience and give us a chance to travel. That's something.
>
> I never had done before then, you know, was to travel any, you might say. And all the time we was dancing, we was practicing on the side with music and playing whenever somebody wanted us to play.

This was Bill's first taste of being a full-time musician, and he liked it a lot better than working in the barrelhouse at Sinclair. The money wasn't bad, and his music was improving with all of the work. Originally he had taken up the mandolin as a third choice. Charlie had the guitar and Birch the fiddle, and, being the smallest, Bill had been left with the mandolin to play.

> The thing I really wanted to play was the fiddle. Of course, there wasn't a chance—Birch, he was going to play the fiddle.
>
> I really wanted to play guitar too—the way Arnold Shultz played it with a straight pick. If I'd have fooled with the guitar I would have been a blues singer and I never would have fooled with a mandolin and me and Charlie would never have worked together. It might have been a different setup all the way around. I'd probably have been a blues singer playing the guitar.

4. WLS Barn Dance, later the National Barn Dance.

5. Arkie the Arkansas Woodchopper (Luther W. Ossenbrink) was a staple of the National Barn Dance from 1929, when it began as the WLS Barn Dance, until it went off the air in 1960. Wayne W. Daniel, "Arkie the Arkansas Woodchopper," in *The Encyclopedia of Country Music: The Ultimate Guide to the Music,* comp. by the staff of the Country Music Hall of Fame and Museum, ed. Paul Kingsbury (New York: Oxford University Press, 1998), 15.

He was growing to like the mandolin though and was beginning to explore its possibilities. His rhythm playing was getting good and solid, and he was starting to play a little lead, picking out the melodic line the way he had heard it on the fiddle.

> When I started to play the mandolin I wanted to be sure that I didn't play like nobody else, and I was going to have a style of my own with the mandolin. And I worked it out until it did become a style. Years ago people played a little on the mandolin just to fill in or to be playing. But to have heard really good fiddle players back in the early days—Clayton McMichen and people like that— and to really get on a mandolin and play the old-time notes that's in a fiddle number has really helped to create an original style of music on the mandolin.

When the Barndance tour finally ended, they went to work on another local radio station in Gary, Indiana—eleven dollars for six programs a week. Shortly, however, they were to find that their touring had paid off. They got a call to come out to Iowa and work there. Birch decided that traveling wasn't the life for him and he went home. But Charlie and Bill—now known as the Monroe Brothers—decided to make a go of it. The depression had started to hit hard, and they seemed to be doing better playing music than they would have trying to find regular work.

> This company out of Shenandoah, Iowa, they wanted us to come out there and go to work—I believe it was called Texas Crystal Company. And we worked there for three or four or five months and then they sent us to Omaha. While we was there at Shenandoah, they had a little barn dance they had on Saturday night. It was for Henry Fields—he had a big store there and a radio station too— a thousand watts, I guess.[6] So that give us some more experience. And then we moved to Omaha for the same company and stayed there, I guess, maybe a year, year and a half. And moved from there to Columbia, South Carolina.

It was a full three years, and Charlie and Bill found that they had gained quite a following as a result of their radio broadcasts.[7] They weren't alone in the field by any means. There were the Callahan Brothers, the Morris Brothers, the Delmore Brothers, and many others, each with their own sound. Charlie and Bill, however, seemed to stand out from the others by virtue of their high, clear voices. Bill's tenor was way up there, and it had that "lonesome" quality along with some blues feeling that made it immediately identifiable.

They had speed, too, and Bill's mandolin playing was more dynamic and melodic than anyone else's playing at the time. He was creating a style on the instrument that also distinguished the Monroe Brothers from their competitors.

Soon Victor Records (the Bluebird Label) got word that the Monroe Brothers were in the Carolinas and had a following and signed them up.

---

6. Henry Field owned Field's store.

7. Tom Ewing notes that best current estimates are that the Monroe Brothers were at KFNF in Shenandoah for three months in 1934 and then at WAAW in Omaha, Nebraska, for six months. They arrived in Columbia, South Carolina, sometime in 1935.

Our first record was in 1936. We was in Greenville, South Carolina, then. They'd heard about us. We hadn't been down in the Carolinas very long then. And I think they sent a man down from Charlotte to Greenville, South Carolina, to see if we would come and record, you know—for Victor records. We was playing shows then and we was drawing good crowds. But you know you didn't charge much—fifteen for children and twenty-five for grown-ups. Playing schoolhouses and courthouses—I believe we was playing two programs a day when we was in Greenville. We played one in Charlotte of a morning, say at seven o'clock, then we'd drive to Greenville for a twelve. We had a hundred miles to drive. Played two shows a day.

So we decided we would record, and I remember when we got to the recording studios. It was kindly of a warehouse place where they had it. Just where they kept their records and everything—their supply of records that they sent out to different places. The Delmore Brothers was recording, and Arthur Smith, and they stopped their session and let us take over and start recording 'cause we just had a short time, you know, in order to get back and play a show that night.

Their recordings enabled them to reach a greater audience, and the Monroe Brothers soon became the phenomenon of the Carolinas.

"What Would You Give in Exchange for Your Soul?" was the first record that was ever released. It was backed up by "This World Is Not My Home." And it really sold good. It was a powerful hit in the Carolinas. We didn't make much money out of it—maybe a cent-and-a-half a record—but it was in depression days and us playing shows and having good crowds the depression didn't hurt us after we got down in that part of the country, 'cause it was a lot more money than we had ever made, you see. We really did have big crowds. For a schoolhouse, we'd pack it twice or three times, or a courthouse, we'd pack it, say, three times. And it didn't take much advertising. People listened strictly to your program and you didn't have to put up much paper for your advertising. We worked on a percentage with the schools. I believe they got 30 or 35 percent. And then after that was over with, why, we busted it down the middle.

We would generally stay in a place a year-and-a-half, and then we would move on to another town, you know; I think we moved from Greenville to Raleigh, North Carolina, and stayed there a year-and-a-half or two years.

The move to Raleigh was the last move that Charlie and Bill made together. They had been together steadily for six years, working hard and traveling a lot, and somehow it seemed that there was always a little friction between them. Bill was several years younger than Charlie and had always been treated as the young brother. He now felt that he had proved himself an equal. He was vigorous, competitive, and proud of the way he had come up. He heard music differently than Charlie. He kept hearing a bigger sound closer to the groups he had heard as a boy, with a fiddle in there along with the mandolin, guitar, and bass. He heard a stronger beat, too, with more syncopation going against the beat, the way it happened in blues. Somehow what he and Charlie were doing, good as it was, and successful as it was, didn't satisfy Bill personally or musically. He had to get on his own.

If we'd have had a manager, you know, no telling how far we could have gone. But so many times brothers can't get along good, you know. One wants to be the boss and the other one's mad because he does and so it was just better that we split up. Monroe Brothers was great, but Bill Monroe and his Blue Grass Boys are greater. It's a different style from what the Monroe Brothers had. Monroe Brothers didn't have no beat, and the Bluegrass Boys have a beat to their music.

Took me about a month to get a new band together. I think I rehearsed every day for a month. To start with I was getting a singer and a guitar man. That's what I wanted to carry, you know—have some good singing. So that was the first thing that I done. I hired Cleo Davis. And then I got a fiddle player. Art Wooten was his name. And after I got that, the next man I hired, he played a jug, you know, it sounded like a bass. His name was John Miller, from Asheville. And he could play spoons and bones, you know, and could play good comedy—played blackface comedian. We was there in Asheville, North Carolina, three months after I got the Blue Grass Boys together. I had tried to work over in Little Rock, Arkansas, but it played out there so I came to Asheville. Then I moved to Greenville and the jug player stayed with us a short time, and then I got a bass man, Amos Garen.[8] And we worked there, I guess, and went to Nashville and tried for the Grand Ole Opry and made it there.

The Grand Ole Opry had been going for about ten years when Bill joined it.[9] The emphasis during its early years was on old-time music and comedy. It was a blend of medicine show, minstrel show, and revival meeting. Uncle Dave Macon, "The Dixie Dewdrop," set the style with his freewheeling, nonstop delivery of jokes, old-time banjo tunes, and comic songs. His voice was tough and leathery and needed no amplification. Uncle Dave's home was on a stage in a tent with a thousand weather-beaten faces in front of him creased with smiles. Along with Uncle Dave went Sam and Kirk McGee "from sunny Tennessee," the Fruit Jar Drinkers, and the Crook Brothers. The music was old-time string-band music, flavored with some blues and novelty tunes. At the time much comedy was done in blackface, and two of the most popular minstrel comics were Jamup and Honey. Another early star on the Opry was an exceptional harmonica player named DeFord Bailey. He was the only Negro ever to be a regular member of the Opry.

A year before Bill joined the Opry another new face appeared—a young fiddle player and singer from Tennessee named Roy Acuff. He wasn't a great fiddler, but his voice was unlike anyone else's—mournful, choked with emotion—the first of the "heart" singers. When Bill arrived Roy Acuff was already on his way to becoming a big star, but Bill's music was different from Acuff's and he didn't worry. He also knew it was different from the old-timers on the show, although it had its roots in old-time music. He knew that his "Blue Grass Boys" were ready and that his music would make its mark.

8. "John Miller" was Tommy (Snowball) Millard, and "Amos Garen" was, correctly, Walter (Amos) Garren (personal communication from Tom Ewing, 2003).

9. Born on November 28, 1925, but not called "the Opry" until 1927, the show was near its fourteenth birthday when Monroe joined in October 1939.

When I started on the Grand Ole Opry, I had rehearsed and we was ready. Our music was in good shape. We had a good fiddler with us—for bluegrass in them days—Fiddlin' Art Wooten. And my singing was high and clear, you know, and I was in good shape, and we was ready to go on the Grand Ole Opry. Really the only competition we had there was Roy Acuff, and they was two different styles altogether.

Charlie and I had a country beat I suppose, but the beat in my music—bluegrass music—started when I ran across "Mule Skinner Blues" and started playing that. We don't do it the way Jimmie Rodgers sung it. It's speeded up, and we moved it up to fit the fiddle and we have that straight time with it, driving time. And then we went on and that same kind of time would work with "John Henry" and we put it on that. And when we started here on the Grand Ole Opry, "Mule Skinner Blues" and "John Henry" were the numbers we tried out with. And it was something different for them, and they really wanted it. It's wonderful time, and the reason a lot of people like bluegrass is because of the timing of it.

And then we pitched the music up where it would do a number some good. If you play in B-natural and sing there and your fiddle is right up there playing where you're at and the banjo, well it just makes it a different music from where it would be played if it was just drug along in G, C, or D.

The old-time sound, if they was playing in A they played in Open A. They wouldn't note when they should have been noting, and that's where bluegrass has been a school to a lot of entertainers—or been a help to 'em. It's not only in bluegrass but in the country field too. It's been kindly like a teacher for so many country-music singers and the musicians to follow the ideas of bluegrass players if the bluegrass people could play right and was doing it right. And that's where bluegrass has helped country music. To me bluegrass is really the country music. It was meant for country people.

The country people certainly lost no time in letting Bill know their reaction to the new sound. When he finished playing his new version of the "Mule Skinner Blues" for the first time on the Opry, the house came down.

I know when we started there that "Mule Skinner" was the first number to ever get an encore there. Started getting so many that other numbers would get 'em too. They had to put a stop to it.

The other musicians on the Opry knew that here was a man to be reckoned with. Bill broke precedents right and left.

We was the first to ever wear a white shirt on the Opry or wear a tie. We was the first outfit to ever play in B-flat or B-natural and E. Before that it was all C, D, and G. Fiddle men had a fit and they wouldn't hardly tackle it and they'd swear that they wanted to play straight stuff and they figured that that's where I should sing. And that's where bluegrass really advanced music.

The first quartet I sang on the Grand Ole Opry—back in them days I sang a high lead with a tenor under it and Tommy Magness sang baritone and Cleo Davis sang bass. And we sung "Farther Along" and it was really good. There wasn't a quartet on the Grand Ole Opry before us.

Bill stopped the show every week with his high singing and jumping band. Every week thousands of people listening to their radios out in the country through Tennessee, Kentucky, Alabama, Mississippi, the Carolinas, and everywhere the Grand Ole Opry reached were struck by this new voice, this new style. Bill Monroe and his Blue Grass Boys were talked about over many a Sunday dinner in that fall of 1939. By the start of the new year the people running the Opry decided it was time to start booking Bill out to play shows.

> We worked on the Grand Ole Opry about ten weeks before they would even try to book me. Our first date was out of Nashville about twenty-five or thirty miles. I remember we taken in forty-five or sixty-five dollars—somewhere in that neighborhood. But you was still getting a small admission fee. And then we started out playing in Alabama. Seemed like that was the first state seemed like we could draw good in. And then it went to spreading, you know, into West Virginia and Kentucky, and, of course, I held a good standard in the Carolinas. They remembered me there.

Excerpted from *Bossmen: Bill Monroe and Muddy Waters* (New York: Dial Press, 1971), 21–35. Reprinted by permission of the author.

Marty Stuart, born in 1958 in Philadelphia, Mississippi, has made a difference as a brilliant musician beginning in the 1970s, a rockabilly-tinged country star beginning in the 1980s, and a strong chronicler and spokesman for traditional country music throughout his career. His first high-profile gig came as a teenaged sideman for Lester Flatt, whose band he joined in 1972. He has been active as a writer, journalist, and collector of country memorabilia since the 1970s. In this piece for *The Journal of the American Academy for the Preservation of Old-Time Country Music*, Stuart combines a fan's enthusiasm and a musician's perspicacity. His account of the Flatt and Scruggs story somewhat overlaps, and offers a different perspective on, Jim Rooney's section on Bill Monroe's development of his "classic" band.

2

"Flatt and Scruggs"

MARTY STUART

Lester Flatt's singing and Earl Scruggs' unique banjo-picking were the cornerstones of an act that took bluegrass around the world.

In 1972, when he was thirteen years old, Marty Stuart's parents gave him permission to go on the road with Lester Flatt. Flatt and Scruggs had parted three years before. When Lester died in 1979, Marty went on to play with Vassar Clements, Doc Watson and Johnny Cash. Today Marty is a close friend of Louise and Earl Scruggs and a solo artist in his own right. Herewith his look back at a classic act. If you go to any bluegrass gathering today, many of the songs and licks you hear come from Flatt and Scruggs.

Transcription from Interview with Lester Flatt in 1978

December 1945: The Grand Ole Opry, Nashville. Lester Flatt was a member of Bill Monroe's Blue Grass Boys. Lester recalls a certain audition:

"Bill came and found me and said, 'I want you to come and hear this young banjo player from North Carolina and see what you think.' I told him as far as I was concerned he could leave it in the case. You see, the kind of banjo style that we'd had in the band up until now was what Stringbean was playing. It would remind you of the old-time lick like Uncle Dave played. It was a fine style and I loved String, but it would really drag the tempo down. Stringbean had left the group, and the thought of another banjo didn't thrill me. But when I got backstage, there was a crowd gathered around to watch this boy. I worked my way through to where I could hear him and see him, and I was just dumbfounded. I had never heard anybody pick a banjo the way he did. He'd go all over the neck and do things you couldn't hardly believe. Bill said, 'What do you think?' I said, 'If you can, hire him—whatever the cost.'"

Obviously, the banjo player was Earl Scruggs. He went on to join the Blue Grass Boys along with Lester Flatt, Chubby Wise, Howard Watts and Monroe. From 1945 to 1948, they became the master architects of the music that we know today as bluegrass. This band was hard-driven, full of fire and rhythm, yet founded on the lonesome sound that has always been the cornerstone of Monroe's music. They went on to record such standards as "Will You Be Loving Another Man?," "Mighty Dark to Travel," "Wicked Path of Sin," and "Little Cabin Home on the Hill" for Columbia.

Monroe was in extreme demand, and as Scruggs later stated, "The road seemed endless. We would travel sometimes for days without pulling our shoes off in that old stretch limousine." The salary was $60 a week. So, during Christmas break in 1948, Flatt and Scruggs talked about the possibility of striking out on their own. The two men took stock of their assets. Lester had been gaining experience as an emcee with Monroe and was also writing songs. In addition, he had a unique guitar style: the now-famous Lester Flatt G-run that he had stumbled onto and made his own. And there was nothing in the country like Scruggs. His three-fingered style had already brought him wide acclaim; it would go on to revolutionize the banjo.

With those unique features to sustain them, along with some money Flatt had saved, the two decided to strike out on their own. They gave their two-week notices to Monroe and moved their camp to Danville, Virginia, to organize. [*Note:* The split infuriated Monroe. He would keep them barred from the Opry for years to come.

Lester and Bill did not speak to each other for twenty years. Finally Monroe invited him to play his Bluegrass Festival in Bean Blossom, Indiana. That reunion, in 1970, became a historic musical occasion.][1]

During the late 1940's and 50's, acts did business by moving into a region, getting a radio show, finding a sponsor and promoting a product. They built their following by doing personal appearances at night in the towns within listening distance of the station. Since you were only as good as the power of your station, it's easy to understand why a spot on WSM, with its fifty thousand watts of power and a prestigious show like the Grand Ole Opry, was coveted by all entertainers.

Lester was a great emcee—he could convincingly sell any product. He also knew how to build and promote the individual members of the band. The group translated to country audiences in a big way. By now they had adopted the name Lester Flatt, Earl Scruggs and the Foggy Mountain Boys, a name they took from the old A. P. Carter song, "Foggy Mountain Top." Some of the songs they recorded for Mercury during this period were "Foggy Mountain Breakdown," "Down the Road," "God Loves His Children," "Pike County Breakdown," "Doin' My Time" and "Old Salty Dog Blues."

Flatt and Scruggs worked at stations in Bristol and Knoxville, Tennessee; Lexington, Kentucky; Roanoke and Richmond, Virginia; Mount Airy and Raleigh, North Carolina; Crew, Virginia; Tampa, Florida, and others during the next four years. In these "B" markets, "Off Broadway" if you will, they established an act that would later go on to dazzle the world.

Monroe continued creating his own sound at WSM. The Stanley Brothers were scoring with their lonesome brand of music out of the hills of Virginia. But it was Flatt and Scruggs who first put entertainment and their music together to make the act commercially viable. Lester and Earl were good businessmen who believed in giving the people what they wanted. Their drawing card was Earl's banjo. In addition, Flatt had great secular songs and gospel quartet songs, plus fiddling and, usually, a vaudeville-style comedian. All in all, they had the ability to make you want to go to work if you had heard them early in the morning, or they could make you forget every trouble you ever had by the time you left the schoolhouse after an evening concert, with that new songbook under your arm. They were truly like neighbors.

Flatt was a master at recitations, the most popular one in later years being "Father's Table Grace," a story about an old man's prayer at the family dinner table asking the Lord to watch over and care for his son who was about to go out into the world. This song and Lester's powerful delivery brought tears to the eyes of many hard-hearted country men.

In May of 1953, Mr. Efford Burke, a traveling flour salesman, caught one of their shows. When he left, he took along a glowing report and a poster of Flatt and Scruggs

---

1. Monroe actually had relatively cordial relations with Flatt and Scruggs until they came to WSM, visiting with them often in east Tennessee (editor interview with Mac Wiseman, 2000). The reunion took place in 1971.

to Mr. Cohen Williams, the president of the Barry-Carter Mill and Company (manufacturer of Martha White Foods in Nashville). Burke sold Cohen Williams on the fact that these were the boys who could cause biscuits to boom and flour to flow throughout the South.

The act Martha White was sponsoring at this point was Milton Estes and his Musical Millers. However, Estes' brand of music wasn't translating that well to people in the South. Flour sales were marginal. Cohen Williams informed the station officials that he was bringing in Flatt and Scruggs. Management was not enthused—they were trying to remain loyal to Monroe. But Martha White sponsored a 5:45 A.M. radio show as well as a portion of the Opry, so the company had some clout. In June of 1953, Flatt and Scruggs broadcast their first early morning radio show over WSM. Their contract with Martha White was a handshake, and the association lasted well over twenty years.

In 1955, Williams purchased television time on WSM, giving Flatt and Scruggs their own show. It turned out to be a classic, stirring the demand for biscuits and the band. During that period, Elvis Presley was putting a major dent in record sales and attendance at country music shows around the country. Flatt remembered entertainers complaining about how rock 'n' roll was killing their business, but the Foggy Mountain Boys had as much work as they wanted, traveling over 2,500 miles a week, doing television in six different cities. They performed on television during the day and played shows at night within the region, as they had on radio.

As the era of TV came into its own, they became the first bluegrass act to have their own syndicated show. In 1955 they added the dobro guitar to the band, considered a controversial move by bluegrass purists. The fraternity of players in the Foggy Mountain Boys were innovators and stylists as well. Some of the alumni included dobroist Josh Graves, mandolinist Curly Seckler, fiddler Benny Martin, bassist Jake Tullock, fiddler Paul Warren and vocalist Mac Wiseman.

A fact often overlooked in the Flatt and Scruggs story is the role played by Louise Scruggs, who began managing the band in the 50's. She gained a reputation fast as a no-nonsense businesswoman and was responsible for taking them to heights as yet unmatched by any bluegrass band. She was a true pioneer and a credit to the country music industry.

As with any musical campaign, it's the politics that finally matter. Cohen Williams resisted going over Opry manager Jim Denny's head, but when Denny left and Dee Kilpatrick took over in 1956, Cohen secured Lester and Earl a spot on the Opry.[2] Here they were—after years of slugging it out on the back roads—finally on "Broadway." Throughout the South and Southeast, everywhere within reach of WSM's signal, they were a household word, and all of this without a bona fide radio hit or widespread national exposure.

To some, being different is a curse, to some a blessing. It worked in Flatt and

2. Flatt and Scruggs joined the Opry in 1955 (author interview with Louise Scruggs, 2003). Jim Denny left in 1956.

Scruggs' favor. As the folk music boom was peaking, Lester and Earl were well established on Columbia Records. Since Columbia had Bob Dylan—the prince of this new movement—I'm sure the company looked at their roster to see who else worked. In Nashville, it was Johnny Cash and Flatt and Scruggs. They were the real thing. The band became an attraction at college campuses across the country. Landmark performances such as their concert with Merle Travis at Carnegie Hall on December 8, 1962, and later at the Newport Folk Festival, fueled their legend. When they came to New York for the Carnegie Hall show, columnist Dorothy Kilgallen wrote in *The New York Times:* "The hicks from the sticks are coming to town. I want to warn you in time to get out."[3] But when the band walked out on stage to a capacity crowd that evening, Flatt replied, "I see a lot of you folks didn't read your papers today."

When Flatt and Scruggs were in Hollywood working a series of live shows, TV producer Paul Henning took some of their music into the boardroom of CBS-TV along with his idea for a show. The idea clicked, *The Beverly Hillbillies* were born and the boys wrote the theme song—"The Ballad of Jed Clampett," a Number One hit in 1963. When Henning wrote them into the script of one episode of the popular show, he had the wisdom to let them just be themselves. They were great characters.

The Beverly Hillbillies wasn't their only brush with Hollywood. Their original version of "Foggy Mountain Breakdown," recorded in December of 1949, wound up on the soundtrack of the 1967 film *Bonnie and Clyde.* The film's success raised Flatt and Scruggs and the banjo to new heights. Their producer during this period was Columbia veteran Don Law. A. P. Carter's catalog came back to life as Flatt and Scruggs re-recorded a number of Carter Family songs as well as songs they themselves had written or collected. The critics said Flatt and Scruggs played "folk music with an overdrive."[4]

Successful as it was for Lester and Earl, their folk period remained for them the first step away from the hardcore sound of their old Mercury and early Columbia recordings and toward a more Nashville-oriented sound, embellished and enhanced by studio musicians such as Charlie Daniels and Charlie McCoy. After Don Law retired, Columbia assigned ex-bluegrasser Bob Johnston to produce the band. Johnston's big hits were the Bob Dylan albums he was producing in Nashville. More and more Dylan songs showed up on Lester and Earl's records, along with drums. Paul Warren's fiddle was downplayed. The best thing that can be said about the band's last two or three albums is that they were innovative.

///

Flatt and Scruggs' last performance together was February 22, 1969, on the 8:00 portion of the Opry. The reason they split after all those years still seems evident in

---

3. Kilgallen wrote for the now-defunct *New York Journal-American.*

4. Alan Lomax's influential "Bluegrass Background: Folk Music with Overdrive," *Esquire* 52 (Oct. 1959): 108, includes what is apparently the first appearance of this phrase. The article's October 1959 publication date puts it out of the context of Stuart's chronology here.

the fact that when Lester regrouped with the Nashville Grass, he went back to playing "Salty Dog Blues" while Earl and his sons established the Earl Scruggs Revue and headed into the future. There were court battles, allegations and bitter feelings that lasted into the next decade.

Lester passed away on May 11, 1979, after an extended illness. Earl is now semi-retired, only rarely performing although still very much in demand.[5] He and Louise live in Madison, Tennessee, behind a friendly veil of mystique. [*Note:* In 1985, six years after Lester's death, Flatt and Scruggs were inducted into the Country Music Hall of Fame. Earl's acceptance speech is one of the most eloquent speeches I've ever heard. He simply said, "Thank you."]

Postscript: The Happy Ending—Spring 1979: Nashville

Bob Dylan was playing Nashville. When I was introduced to him, he asked, "Aren't you that kid that plays the mandolin with Lester Flatt?" I said yes. Dylan asked, "How is Lester anyway?" I said, "He's dying. I don't think he's going to live long." He wondered if Lester and Earl talked anymore. I told him I didn't think so. He said that was sad because Abbott and Costello were always going to speak, but they never quite got around to it before one of them died. Dylan kind of left it at that, but he said what I had been thinking for a long time. I was scared to death, but I went up to a pay phone and called Earl and asked him if I could come and talk with him. As always, he said yes. When I got there, I told him that I thought the end was real soon for Lester and I wished that he would consider going to see him one last time. Scruggs did, and that's just one more reason why I love him, because that took a whole lot of courage.

Originally published in the *Journal of the American Academy for the Preservation of Old-Time Country Music* 152 (Dec. 1991): 9–11. Reprinted by permission of *Country Music* magazine.

"It has been said that books like these are usually written by frustrated musicians. In my case, nothing could be closer to the truth," Rich Kienzle wryly observed in the introduction to his *Great Guitarists* (1985). Throughout an extended career in music journalism, Kienzle has written perceptively and with a player's insight on musicians in blues, country, jazz, and rock as well as bluegrass. In this Stanley Brothers profile, he recounts the career of an act that offered multiple moods and directions—humor, devotion, modified pop, and aching-heart songs among them—within the relatively narrow confines of mountain-based bluegrass. Of the first wave of bluegrass musicians, Ralph Stanley remains the most musically active,

5. As of 2003, Scruggs was far from retired. He was performing and recording regularly, putting out *The Three Pickers* CD on Rounder along with Doc Watson and Ricky Skaggs.

attracting new fans, including the many millions of folks who bought the *O Brother, Where Art Thou?* soundtrack. Stanley's blood-chilling version of "Oh Death" opened countless ears to the archaic, unaccompanied gospel style, although some justly criticized the directors' decision to have the song emerge from the hood of a robed Klansman.

3

"The Stanley Brothers"

RICH KIENZLE

Together with Bill Monroe and Flatt and Scruggs, Ralph and Carter Stanley, the Stanley Brothers, made up the ruling triumvirate of early bluegrass music. Forty-three years ago, the Stanleys formed their Clinch Mountain Boys group in Virginia; though they began by following the lead of Monroe, within a few years they were helping set standards with their own unique style, a style built around finely honed instrumental work and some of the greatest, most moving vocal harmonies ever recorded.

Today their influence remains immense—and not just among bluegrass purists. Emmylou Harris has recorded Stanley songs; their music was a major source of inspiration for her classic *Roses in the Snow* album. ("The Darkest Hour Is Just before Dawn" was one of several Stanley tunes she covered on that one). Ricky Skaggs and Keith Whitley got some of their earliest professional experience working as a duo with Ralph Stanley and the Clinch Mountain Boys when both were still teenagers.

Carter Glen Stanley, born in 1925, and Ralph Edmond Stanley, born in 1927, grew up in Dickenson County, Virginia, in the western region of the state, a hotbed of traditional mountain music that produced the Carter Family, the Stonemans and many others. Their father worked in the lumber business and Lucy Stanley, their mother, taught Carter to play banjo. He moved to guitar after Lucy taught Ralph (who sang tenor) to play five-string banjo at a time when the prevailing playing style was much like that of Grandpa Jones.

The brothers attended Irvington High School in Nora, Virginia, where Carter was class president. In 1943, with World War II raging, he joined the Army Air Corps; Ralph served with the Army in Europe. Both were discharged in 1946 and at that point went into music professionally. Before joining the service, Carter had worked in the band of a local musician named Roy Sykes along with singer-mandolinist Darrell (Pee Wee) Lambert, who played and sang much like Bill Monroe.

In 1946 the Stanleys and Lambert formed the Stanley Brothers and the Clinch Mountain Boys. They joined newly opened WCYB radio in Bristol, Virginia, a town that had been a focal point for mountain music for decades, and started performing around the area.

Though they began by playing pre-bluegrass mountain music, that quickly changed. Ralph shifted his technique on the banjo from the frailing style to a finger-picked style much like that of Earl Scruggs. With Lambert's Monroe-like singing and mandolin work, they were able to move whole-hog into bluegrass, doing their first recordings for the tiny, regional Rich-R-Tone label in the fall of 1947.

By 1948 the Stanleys were not only popular around the area, they even competed with Flatt and Scruggs, who'd left Monroe and were also working in Bristol. Their Rich-R-Tone recording of "Little Glass of Wine," released in the spring of 1948, enjoyed regional success. Both Ralph and Carter were Monroe fans. Later in 1948, they recorded Monroe's "Molly and Tenbrooks." They even featured expertly done performances of Monroe favorites on stage, learned from listening to his spots on the Grand Ole Opry. This made them formidable bluegrass performers at a time when the music was still new.

One thing their expert copying *didn't* do was help their stock with Monroe, who disliked other artists performing his songs. He was upset with the Stanleys (though they later became good friends), and when his own label, Columbia, signed Ralph and Carter in 1949, that tore it. Monroe refused to renew his contract with Columbia when it expired that year and moved to Decca (now MCA), where he remains some forty years later.

The Stanleys' Columbia career lasted until 1952 and yielded stunning bluegrass music that firmly established them as one of the top acts in the field. In time they created a style of their own that differed from Monroe's, which eased the problems between them considerably.

Nevertheless, amazingly enough, in 1951, the brothers disbanded briefly. Ralph left music, while—irony of ironies—Carter joined Monroe as lead singer and guitarist. Though Carter was with the Blue Grass Boys only a brief time, a mutual respect developed between Monroe and both brothers that eventually blossomed into close friendship.

Late in 1951 the Stanleys reunited. A youthful Bobby Osborne replaced Lambert, and the brothers continued working and developing their own sound. In addition to Ralph's and Carter's eerie vocal harmonies, some of the greatest ever achieved, their sound included Ralph's banjo work and the brilliant crosspicked guitar of George Shuffler, who used a flatpick to create an effect similar to fingerpicking. Shuffler joined the band in 1952 before its final session for Columbia and worked on and off with the Stanleys for years.[1]

By the time they signed with Mercury in 1953, Ralph and Carter had gained considerable ground in the field. Keep in mind that this was the period when the popularity of bluegrass was on the rise nationwide. In 1954, after Elvis recorded his speeded-up version of Monroe's "Blue Moon of Kentucky," the Stanleys recorded their own version with Monroe's blessing.

---

1. Shuffler played bass with the Stanleys in the 1950s and did not record as their lead guitarist until 1960, Tom Ewing points out.

They changed band members numerous times and spent the years between 1958 and 1960 alternating sessions for Starday and King Records. Their studio stamina was nothing less than awesome. During one King session on September 14, 1959, they taped a phenomenal twenty-five songs! By 1959 they were based in Florida, but made the same jump back and forth between Starday and King in 1960 before signing a longer contract with King.

All in all they produced over twenty albums' worth of material for King, a great deal of gospel, along with traditional folk tunes ("Darling Nellie Gray") and country hits of the day ("Window Up Above"). They tried at various times to cross over to the mainstream country charts, but only one single, "How Far to Little Rock," reached Number 17 on the *Billboard* country charts, in 1960. As was the case with other King Record country artists, they recorded occasional oddities in other styles, such as Hank Ballard's rhythm-and-blues hit, "Finger Poppin' Time."

The brothers continued working steadily throughout the early 1960s, Carter handling most of the lead vocals and emcee chores while Ralph concentrated on banjo and tenor vocals. They performed in England in 1966 before returning to work various shows in the U.S. On October 20, 1966, they performed at Bill Monroe's music park in Bean Blossom, Indiana—their final appearance as a team. Carter's hard living was affecting his health; he fell ill with liver disease and died on December 1, 1966.

Suddenly Ralph was leader and frontman of the Clinch Mountain Boys. He replaced Carter with Larry Sparks, who went on to greater fame in bluegrass and later played with Roy Lee Centers.[2] Stanley continued to record for King, now as a solo artist, and he remained there until 1969. In 1971 he founded his own bluegrass festival, giving a memorial award in Carter's name to individuals active in promoting bluegrass.

In the early 1970s he hired the duo of Ricky Skaggs and Keith Whitley. Both were only teenagers, and initially worked only summers with Stanley, but their youth and love for the Stanley Brothers' music revitalized Ralph. Skaggs once recalled Ralph being so impressed with his and Whitley's ability to sing harmony that he resurrected a number of Stanley songs he hadn't performed on stage since Carter's death. Skaggs and Whitley recorded with Ralph as well as on their own—some of those records were reissued after Skaggs and Whitley became stars in the 1980s.

Today Ralph Stanley, one of the elder statesmen of bluegrass, continues performing and recording. The Stanley Brothers act exists only in memory—and on records—but Ralph Stanley plays on, upholding a proud and honorable musical tradition.

Originally published in the *Journal of the American Academy for the Preservation of Old-Time Country Music*, undated clipping in the files of the Country Music Foundation. Reprinted by permission of *Country Music* magazine.

---

2. This sentence could be misread to indicate that Sparks and Centers performed together. Both played with Ralph Stanley separately.

I f there was one godfather for the progressive bluegrass movement of the 1960s
and 1970s it was Don Reno. The South Carolinian's early musical experiences with
the Morris Brothers, an old-time country act, and proto-rockabilly Arthur Smith
(the guitarist, not the fiddler) show his familiarity with country roots and his willingness to go beyond them. Although not in the household-word category of Monroe or Flatt and Scruggs, Reno's duet act with guitarist-vocalist Red Smiley has remained vastly influential through the years. Reno's often-jazzy, single-string banjo
eruptions were widely imitated by younger pickers until the melodic style championed by Bill Keith came to hold sway for a time. He was also a notable guitarist. The
writer of this piece, Peter Wernick, is yet another in the musician-journalist camp.
He's been known as a stellar banjoist and collaborator for nearly forty years, serving as a linchpin in groups including Country Cooking and Hot Rize. As seen here,
Wernick's dedication to bluegrass goes back long before his "Dr. Banjo" title. He
interviewed Reno when the bluegrass festival itself was new.

4

"Interview with Don Reno"

PETER WERNICK

The following interview was taped by Peter Wernick of WKCR, New York, N.Y., at
the first annual Roanoke Bluegrass Festival in September 1965. We are grateful to
Mr. Wernick for allowing us to reprint it here.

(Pete = Peter Wernick) (Don = Don Reno)

Pete: We're talking with one of the real kings of the five-string banjo here, Don
Reno, and it's a real pleasure speaking with you, Don. You put on a real fine show
last night.

Don: Thank you very much. I'm really enjoying myself here at this big bluegrass
festival that Carlton Haney's presenting and especially meeting all you fine dj's and
folks that are associated with bluegrass music.

Pete: Who are the people that you have in your band with you now, Don?

Don: I have Sid Campbell on flat top guitar, Ronnie Reno, my son, plays mandolin . . .

Pete: How do you think he is coming along, by the way?

Don: Well, I may be a little prejudiced because I'm his dad, but I think the boy
is doing real well. Then we have Duck Austin playing bass and we'll be pulling a real
surprise on you about a fiddle player a little bit later on.

Pete: Now questions about you yourself. How did you get started playing music?

Don: Well, as far back as I can remember, about the age of five years old, I found myself with a banjo in my hand, playing one of the old tunes that I probably heard somebody playing and I knew that I loved instruments and the sound that came from them. So I became solely dedicated to music at a very early age. At the age of twelve years I went into the business professionally at WSPA radio in Spartanburg, S.C., with a group known as the Morris Brothers, Wiley and Zeke. They were very popular entertainers back at that time. Then a little later on in my career I went to work with Arthur Smith. "Guitar Boogie" was one of the records that we recorded in Washington, D.C., right after the war I believe. We just thought we would do a flip side; it turned out to be a 2½ million-seller. Do you remember that?

Pete: Sure.

Don: And then from Arthur I went into the service, into the horse cavalry, was stationed at Fort Riley, Kansas. From there I went overseas, came back and did a little bit of playing around Spartanburg again until the latter part of 1947, then I went to work with Bill Monroe and the Blue Grass Boys at the Grand Ole Opry.

Pete: There are some interesting stories about how you joined up with Bill Monroe. Would you like to recount this?

Don: Well, it's kinda funny in a way. In [1943] while I was working with Arthur Smith, before I went into the service, Bill Monroe and the Blue Grass Boys came through with a tent show.[1] Sam and Kirk McGee and Clyde Moody were working with Bill at that time along with Cousin Wilbur. Chubby Wise was playing fiddle with Bill.

I got into a jam session in a hotel room with them across from the radio station and Bill tried to hire me then to go with him. I told him that I was under the gun to go in the service and if I didn't go in the service or if something happened that I was physically defected I would be glad to come to work with him. I turned out to be A number 1, they took me. So, when I returned from overseas I kind of had the thought in mind I might go out there and work with Bill if he was still in operation. When we got back I learned that a good friend of mine, Earl Scruggs, was working with Bill. Then one Saturday night I tuned in the Grand Ole Opry and didn't hear the golden tones of Earl's banjo and I says, "Well now, let's see here, what's going on?" Then I heard Bill announce that he was looking for a five-string banjo-picker and I was determined to have the job. I felt like I could hold up my end of the horn if I did some real intense rehearsing out behind the barn. I left for Nashville, Tennessee, and got there and found Bill was in Taylorsville, North Carolina, so I headed back to Taylorsville. When I got into Taylorsville, I think they'd been on the stage about maybe five or ten minutes, so I figured the proper thing to do was uncase my banjo and start work, which I did, and I got the job. It was a real pleasure working with Bill. You learn something from him that I don't think you

---

1. This date ran as 1945 in the original story. In a May 2000 letter to me, Wernick confirmed that Reno used the date 1943 on the original tape. The incorrect date was the result of a faulty transcription.

could learn from anybody else. A certain type of feeling that you pick up. That excitement. Something that he puts into you.

Pete: A lot of bluegrass musicians say the same thing about Bill Monroe. They don't know exactly what it is, but they learned a lot from singing with him. How long did you actually stay with him?

Don: A little over two years.[2]

Pete: Did you record anything with him by the way?

Don: Yes, I recorded some of the early stuff with Bill.[3] I've recorded so many numbers in the past ten years I can't remember half the stuff that I recorded with my good buddy Red Smiley. From Bill, I came back to Greenville, S.C. I had a nephew at that time that was like a son to me who was a guitar picker and he wanted me to come home and organize our own group, so I did. I went to Greenville, S.C., and organized the Tennessee Cutups. From there we went to Roanoke, Va., and became associated with Tommy Magness, an old-time fiddler, one of the best, used to [be] on breakdown stuff . . .

Pete: Didn't you record some gospel things with . . .

Don: With Tommy, yes we did. I became associated with Red Smiley through Tommy in 1950. 1951 we left Roanoke and went to Wheeling, W.Va., and worked up there with Toby Stroud, then back to South Carolina and Red and I became partners. I took him in as a partner with the Tennessee Cutups and I think we worked almost a year down there and business was real bad. We were on the side of the unknown, so to speak, at that time, and that's very poor country to go to and try to organize a band anyway. The people are just not there and the money's not there either. So we disorganized in the spring of '52 after recording sixteen sides for King and the first release came out I think about six weeks after we disbanded. If we'd stuck it out about six more weeks we'd a been all right. "I'm Using My Bible for a Road Map" you know was one of our biggest records. I went back to work with Arthur Smith in Charlotte, N.C., and worked till '55 and then Red and I organized again. Went to Richmond, Va., and from there to Roanoke, spent ten years in Roanoke. Red's health became bad. He is still in Roanoke, doing the early morning TV show we started in '56 and I'm out on the road touring because I like to meet people. Red's health just won't permit him to take the strain of the road.

Pete: Is that the reason that you finally broke up your partnership after all those years?

Don: Yes, that's the reason. Red Smiley is certainly a wonderful guy. I enjoyed working with him and I'll always treasure about three hundred records that we made together.

Pete: More specifically, about the way you play. You are of course considered one of the finest banjo players today, by just about everybody. Your style is somewhat

---

2. Reno worked with Monroe from March 1948 to July 1949.

3. Reno didn't record with Monroe during the time he worked for him, Tom Ewing notes (personal communication, 2003), but they did record together in 1962, backing Rose Maddox on her Capitol album *Rose Maddox Sings Bluegrass* (T1799).

different. How did you actually start the ideas of your style? You didn't follow Scruggs exactly, and you picked your own things.

Don: Well, in the beginning, Earl and I followed the same guy, Snuffy Jenkins, Columbia, S.C. We played the same style. Actually, I was the first man with the style, but I went overseas and Earl didn't go in the service and he got to the front with it first so it was his baby, so I said the only thing I can do is start another style so I did. Taking stuff from the guitar and transplant it onto the neck of the five-string banjo.

Pete: On the background that you use for slow songs, you have an approach that is sometimes called jazzy. How did that come about?

Don: Well, I have a certain amount of blues in me it seems like, and when I feel something I try to give it to people through the sound of the banjo. I just play what I feel. That's where my style actually comes from now.

Pete: What kind of advice can you give to banjo players that are starting off that maybe would try to learn from some of the things you do?

Don: Well, they could probably learn some of the things from listening to records that we've put out in the past, or try and catch us on a personal appearance. I'm always glad to show any banjo-picker anything that I can. It's actually not as hard as it sounds once you actually see it done, I guess. Learn the neck of the banjo as much as you can so you'll know where you are on the neck and when you hear something from somebody else's instrument then you'll know where he is and you can put it on your instrument.

Pete: How do you think bluegrass music should sound? What are your aims in getting the sound of bluegrass music? What do you try to do with it?

Don: I've tried to push it as hard as I could and as far as I could. I think, honestly speaking, and I'm a close watcher of the business, bluegrass is fast coming to the top. It's not reached its peak by a long shot, but I think it will reach its peak in the next five years. Musicians, let's give this for instance, in New York City today who are playing five string banjo, mandolin and fiddle bluegrass style that five or ten years ago probably had never heard of it, and they like it. It's the music that gives you a feel. It'll make you laugh, it'll make you cry, it'll make you want to dance. There's about seven moods in bluegrass music and when you get your mood changed about seven times in thirty minutes you've got a tiger by the tail, I'll tell you. That's my viewpoint on bluegrass music.

Pete: You are one of the best I've heard on the flat top guitar, lead flatpicking things. How did you pick up this style of guitar?

Don: When I started in the business, I tried to learn as many phases as I could, widening my scope to the extent that I could make a living by staying in the music business.

I always loved the guitar and I learned the guitar along about the time I did the banjo. It was give or take, I liked the guitar better than I did the banjo and at one time I went to guitar completely and forgot the banjo for about two or three years. There was a gentleman I took under my wing at the age of fourteen and taught him guitar, then worked some twin stuff with him for a while. You may have heard of him, Hank (Sugar Foot) Garland.

Pete: Sure. Certainly.

Don: Of course, Hank passed me so far and so fast, I forgot about guitar pick-ing. He's great. But we did have some fine arrangements worked out on hoedown stuff, twin style, even back in 1946. And then when I gave guitar up to go back to the banjo it seemed like there was more demand for a five-string banjo than there was for a guitar.

Pete: So you stayed with it then?

Don: I decided that if I was going to have to play banjo I might as well learn how. I've spent a lot of time and effort and research on the five-string banjo. I'm proud of it and I think every American should be, because it's the only American instrument that we own that was invented and made in America.

Originally published in *Bluegrass Unlimited* 1 (Feb. 1967): 2–4. Reprinted by permission of the author and *Bluegrass Unlimited*.

Jimmy Martin has been one of the most colorful and creative figures in bluegrass since his arrival on the scene as the successor to Mac Wiseman in Bill Monroe's band. A distinctive lead singer and guitarist, he's earned a place on anyone's list of the music's masters, although his outspokenness and sometimes abrasive person-ality have colored his legend, too. Chronicling him here is Neil Rosenberg, author of the definitive volume *Bluegrass: A History* and countless articles on the music since the 1960s. A banjoist who worked for Monroe, managing band contests at his Bean Blossom festivals in the 1960s, Rosenberg has also worked as a semiprofessional mu-sician; author of books, including a forthcoming collaboration with Charles Wolfe on Monroe's music; and professor of folklore at Memorial University of Newfound-land at St. John's. He is an open-eared listener and graceful writer who's done more than perhaps any other scholar to forge a detailed, objective history of the music he loves.

5

"Jimmy Martin: *You Don't Know My Mind*"

NEIL V. ROSENBERG

One Saturday in the winter of 1949–50, Jimmy Martin rode the bus from his home in the mountains of East Tennessee to Nashville. He'd been playing and singing music most of his life, and the previous year he'd even been on a radio program in Morristown. Now, at twenty-two, he was making his living as a house painter. When he reached Nashville, Jimmy walked to the Ryman Auditorium where he saw one

Grand Ole Opry show. Afterwards he went to the backstage door, and talked himself into an audition with Bill Monroe, whom he'd often heard but never before seen. Monroe's guitarist and lead singer, Mac Wiseman, was leaving and Bill was looking for a replacement. Martin sang "The Old Cross Road" with Monroe. Fiddlin' Chubby Wise listened to Monroe and Martin singing together for the first time, played "Orange Blossom Special" to Jimmy's guitar backup, and told Monroe "He's flat got it!" Jimmy Martin had been in the right place at the right time with the right stuff.

In the next four years he would work off and on with Monroe and participate in some forty-six of Monroe's most memorable recordings. Among the dozen duets he sang with Bill were classics like "Memories of You," "Letter from My Darlin'" and "The Little Girl and the Dreadful Snake." As a guitarist he laid down the rhythm for "Raw Hide" and "New Mule Skinner Blues," and put in that essential "G run" on "Uncle Pen." He sang lead in trios like "On and On" and quartets like "Walking in Jerusalem."

If Jimmy Martin's musical career had ended after those four years with Monroe, he would still be a bluegrass legend. But he did much more—so much that when in 1971 the Nitty Gritty Dirt Band came to Nashville to record their tribute to the country music greats who'd inspired them, they invited Martin to contribute five of his songs (including "You Don't Know My Mind," the original of which is on this album) to their award-winning set—and he's included again on the band's new sequel set. Again Martin was in the right place at the right time with the right stuff.

While Martin's reputation began with the Monroe days, and was reaffirmed by the "Will the Circle Be Unbroken" recordings, it is the recordings on this album which established Jimmy Martin as one of bluegrass music's great originals. Made in the decade between 1956 and 1966, they feature what Martin has called his "Good 'n' Country" sound. Although he sometimes recorded with a fiddle in the band, his instrumental sound highlights the guitar, banjo and mandolin. Martin has worked hard with his Sunny Mountain Boys to create unique instrumental and vocal arrangements. When musicians talk about Martin's sound you hear these arrangements described with words like "tight" and "driving." For those who followed bluegrass in its formative years, this was the right stuff at the right time.

At the center is Martin's forceful rhythm guitar, punctuated with bass runs, and his distinctive singing style. Master of a variety of vocal approaches depending upon the type of song, Martin lends personal conviction to sad story songs, comic novelty numbers, gospel pieces, and up-tempo bluegrass love lyrics. An essential part of his vocal style is the subtle breaking of the voice into falsetto for just a phrase or a syllable to convey a feeling of emotion. Listen, for example, to the first verse of "Ocean of Diamonds," where such breaks can be heard on "champagne," "over," "need," and "love." And while Martin's great vocal blend with his harmony singers—particularly Paul Williams—has been acclaimed by bluegrass fans, many of his most popular numbers have been vocal solos like "Don't Give Your Heart to a Rambler" and "Sunny Side of the Mountain."

Two musicians in particular helped to shape Martin's sound—mandolinist Paul Williams (who is heard on ten of the cuts on this album) and banjoist J. D. Crowe (heard on nine cuts). The Martin-Williams duets like "Hold Whatcha Got" and "What Would You Give in Exchange?" reveal a blend unexcelled in the music. And the trios, where Crowe joined in with the baritone part, have been among the most copied of all of Martin's songs: "Ocean of Diamonds," "Sophronie," "Rock Hearts," and "Homesick" are fine examples of this.

East Tennessee native Paul Humphries took the name Williams when he began his musical career in the early fifties. He was guitarist and featured singer with the Lonesome Pine Fiddlers, and when this West Virginia band moved to Detroit in 1954 he met Jimmy Martin, who at that time was working with the Osborne Brothers. In 1955, Martin formed his own band; his first mandolinist-tenor singer was the late Earl Taylor, who is heard on this album, along with banjoist Sam (Porky) Hutchins, on "Hit Parade of Love," from Martin's first Decca session. By 1958 both Hutchins and Taylor had left Martin; Jimmy replaced Taylor with Williams. His tenor voice had a fuller and less sharp-edged sound than that of the other tenor singers with whom Martin had worked and recorded. Likewise, Williams' mandolin, a round-hole Gibson F-4, had a more mellow tone than that of the F-5s played by most bluegrass mandolinists. On Martin's shows, he was regularly featured as a lead singer—a role he is heard in on "Stepping Stones" in this album.

Lexington, Kentucky, native J. D. Crowe was a teenager picking on the radio with Esco Hankins when Jimmy Martin first heard him and just out of high school when Jimmy hired him to replace Hutchins. Martin worked with the lanky youth to create the banjo sound still associated with the Sunny Mountain Boys. Crowe, who has always stressed mastery of timing and tone on the banjo, came to Martin with an intimate knowledge of Scruggs' technique and a taste for blues and rhythm-and-blues music. To this Martin added, through coaching, licks and rhythmic ideas he'd picked up from Rudy Lyle and Sonny Osborne, the two great banjoists he'd worked with previously. From this emerged one of the most admired banjo styles in bluegrass today. Built on an impeccable sense of rhythm, Crowe's banjo work features straight-ahead solid solo breaks and carefully worked out backup riffs which complement the vocals. On top of this, with "Hold Whatcha Got," Crowe created a unique style of playing single-note leads. Martin foregrounded Crowe's talent as an instrumentalist in solos such as "Red River Valley" and "Crowe on the Banjo," both included on this set. Crowe has gone on to become a great band leader in his own right, another reflection of his experience with Martin.

Crowe and Williams left the Sunny Mountain Boys in 1961 and 1962 and were followed by a succession of fine musicians who met Martin's exacting standards, including Paul Craft, Bill Yates, Vernon Derrick, and Bill Emerson—all heard in cuts on this album.

During the years covered by this reissue collection, Martin moved from the bars of Detroit to a two-year stint on the Louisiana Hayride at KWKH in Shreveport (1958–60), and another two years at the World's Original Jamboree on WWVA in

Wheeling, West Virginia. In 1962 he moved to his present home, near Nashville. He recorded for Decca/MCA until 1974, when he moved to Gusto, his present label. Over the years he has received many awards from the bluegrass and country music industry and is today recognized as one of the bluegrass greats.

Liner notes for *You Don't Know My Mind* (Rounder Records CDSS21, 1990). Reprinted by permission of the author and Rounder Records.

Mac Wiseman, a true founding father of this music, had been making records for fifty-four years by the time the CD *From Grassroots to Bluegrass* came out on CMH Records. And he's remained active well into the new century, apparently never losing his enthusiasm for the music that wasn't even called "bluegrass" until he had been involved for a decade or so. This piece offers invaluable insight into the music that just preceded the "golden era" of the 1940s, forming not only the backdrop but also the real fabric of bluegrass. Wiseman is a key figure of the country industry, serving as a hit recording artist, sideman, record executive, unofficial historian, and reliable spokesman for bluegrass and country music. Wells is the director of the influential Center for Popular Music at Middle Tennessee State University.

6

"From Grass Roots to Bluegrass: Some Personal Reminiscences"

MAC WISEMAN, WITH PAUL F. WELLS

For over ten years I've wanted to do an album that would pay tribute to some of the artists who were the pioneers of what is now known as bluegrass music. With all due respect to Bill Monroe, artists such as Mainer's Mountaineers, Molly O'Day, Roy Acuff, Karl and Harty, the Carter Family, and others whose songs are heard here, also did a lot to establish bluegrass.

I have very fond memories of the songs in this collection. I've sung most of them many times over the years, particularly back in the days of live radio, but as near as I can recall (with the exception of "Salty Dog Blues," which I recorded with Lester Flatt in the late '60s) I haven't recorded any of them before.

My dad had one of the first radios and one of the first Victrolas in our community. This was in the early '30s, and I can pinpoint that period of time because I can remember where we were living. When the depression hit, and I was about six years old, we moved to my mother's old home place up in Augusta County in the Shenandoah Valley of Virginia. This was about a hundred miles north of Roanoke—we were seven or eight miles out in the country, but Staunton and Waynesboro were the larger towns near there, and Charlottesville was just due east across the mountain.

On Saturday nights a lot of the neighbors would gather and listen to the live country music programs—not only the Opry, but at that time there were good country music programs coming from Chicago—and they'd run on into the wee hours of the morning. The folks would stay and just listen to the old-time music, and the youngsters would sleep on the floor. My mom would cook breakfast in the morning, and everybody would go home.

Our phonograph was one of the table models. In the wintertime my dad would let me set it down in the corner next to an old wood stove we had and give me some of the records that had become a little scratchy and that I couldn't do a whole lot of damage to! It had a governor on it, and I'd slow it down and try to understand some of the lyrics these guys were using. Later I learned that they were just going "dum-de-dum-dum" when they couldn't remember the words! They weren't saying them too clearly because they only had one chance to record them. But I remember well songs by Charlie Poole, Riley Puckett, and the Carter Family. If any of these groups would come to our little country school, my mother and I would usually go. There were three or four youngsters fairly close together and it was difficult for all of us to go. But I was the oldest so I would go with her, and my dad would babysit the rest of the youngsters.

My mother was quite an avid fan and knew quite a few old songs. She would listen to the radio and if they would sing a song that she thought I'd like, or that she liked, she'd write down a verse or two. Next week or so they'd repeat the song, and she'd get another verse or two. I have some eighteen composition books of those old songs in her handwriting that are just absolute treasures to me.

I'd been singing and collecting these old songs for as long as I can remember. I was about twelve years old when I first started to play a bit. I literally did order the $3.95 guitar job from Sears. Absolutely everybody says that, but I did it. It came in a cardboard box, and that was the only case I ever had for it. It was well over a year before I could get it in tune. Then a traveling preacher who could play a little bit tuned that guitar for me, and I managed to halfway keep it in tune. The first song that I ever got my mouth and hands together on was "Empty Cot in the Bunkhouse Tonight." I was sitting beside a kerosene lamp one night with an old songbook and, after much frustration, I managed to anticipate the chord changes enough in advance so that I was there with my fingers when my voice got to it. I think they had to drive me to bed that night, because when I got the first one, then I could apply what I'd learned to anything. I sat there with the book and just sang and sang and sang!

Among the old records we had were songs like "Train 45" and "Don't Let Your Deal Go Down." I don't always recall which artists did which songs, but I do remember "Don't Let Your Deal Go Down" by Charlie Poole, and I tried, as near as my memory would serve me, to go back and do his lyrics. I believe my mother was the first person I heard sing "Little Rosewood Casket," although I also remember it from Bradley Kincaid and from a songbook that I ordered from a group called the Tobacco Tags who used to perform over WPTF out of Raleigh, North Carolina. I took two or three different versions and tried to put together the whole story.

My first experience with what I considered big-time radio and show business was working for Molly O'Day from the fall of 1946 until the spring of 1947 at WNOX in Knoxville, Tennessee, on the Tennessee Barn Dance and Mid-Day Merry-Go-Round. She hired me as a solo act within her group, what would be referred to to-day as an opening act. We'd all go onstage and open up together, do a couple of up-tempo things, and then they'd introduce me. I'd do a fifteen-minute set with the fiddle and the dobro and participate in some of the comedy skits that were a big part of the shows then.

I first heard "Poor Ellen Smith" from Molly, although I've since heard Wilma Lee Cooper and others do it. It's supposed to be about a real event that happened around Mt. Airy, North Carolina. Again, I combined several versions and tried to get the entire story told. I think that the version here is quite possibly the most complete version that's ever been recorded.

"Kentucky" comes from Karl Davis and Harty Taylor, who I remember from the Suppertime Frolics over WJJD out of Chicago. They contributed a lot of songs to what we now know as bluegrass. I also loved the way that Merle Travis did "Kentucky." I don't know if he ever recorded it, but he used to pick and sing it. I first remember hearing "Salty Dog Blues" by the Morris Brothers, Wiley and Zeke, over an Asheville, North Carolina, station. After I left Molly O'Day in the spring of 1947, I went to work on WCYB in Bristol, Tennessee. At that time Wiley Morris was work-ing with the Sheldon Brothers, Jack and Curly. They'd come in and do guest spots on WCYB, and in the early '50s, after I'd left, they became a regular part of that show.

I first remember "Dust on the Bible" from the Bailes Brothers. I used to hear them on early morning radio shows, and they later joined the Grand Ole Opry. Molly O'Day was also singing this when I was with her in 1946, but I don't believe that she recorded it.

"It's Mighty Dark to Travel" is one that I sang many times with Bill Monroe. One of my most embarrassing moments came the night I hired in with Bill. Lester Flatt and Earl Scruggs had become familiar with me when I was on WCYB, and when they left Monroe in the spring of '48, they contacted me, wanting to know if I'd be interested in organizing with them. I became one of the charter members of the Foggy Mountain Boys and worked with them about a year, until Christmas of '48.

Cedric Rainwater, who had also been with Monroe, was the bass player with the Foggy Mountain Boys. The band did a lot of songs that Lester had recorded and sung when he was with Bill, and Cedric sang the tenor part on these. But in the mean-time Lester was very, very busy writing new songs, and I did the tenor on all of these new things.

Now, Monroe had offered me a job while I was with Flatt and Scruggs. In the spring of '49, after I'd been gone from the Foggy Mountain Boys for about a year and had been working on WSB in Atlanta, I gave him a ring and asked him if the offer was still open. He said it was, so I met him in Alabama, and came on to work with him around Easter 1949. We were in the dressing room in a little school in Huntsville, Alabama, and he said: "Well, what are we going to sing tonight?" And the blood absolutely drained out of me! I was hiring in, and I didn't know any of his songs! I was familiar with all of them, but I had never sung them with Lester, because Cedric always had. I learned 'em in a hurry! He never made any comment; he knew right away, I'm sure, what had happened. But I felt so foolish.

"Old Camp Meeting Time" I associate with Grandpa Jones and the Browns Ferry Four. The Delmore Brothers were part of that group, and I believe that Red Foley sang bass on some of their numbers.

"Streamlined Cannonball" comes from Roy Acuff. I never had done it much before recording it for this album, although I recorded "Fireball Mail," another Acuff number, for Dot Records, and I've opened my shows for years with the "Wabash Cannonball" which is probably his most famous song.

Charlie Monroe was also at WNOX when I was there with Molly O'Day, and he's the first person I remember hearing sing "Red Rocking Chair," although I understand that it pre-dates him. When I was working on the Bristol station and driving back up in the country to do personal appearances, I would see the old ladies sitting in their rockers on their front porches stringing what they called "leather britches." These were green beans that they'd put on twine and then put up in the air to dry and later reconstitute in water to have green beans in the heart of winter. But I used to hear these old ladies sing "Red Rocking Chair" and other things a cappella—wouldn't have a bit of music going, just sit there in their rockers, stringing those beans on that card and singing this real shrill, mournful stuff! That's where the "high, lonesome sound" that you hear about in bluegrass comes from, right out of those mountains.

Jimmie Skinner is another one who contributed a lot of songs to bluegrass. He was around in Knoxville when I was back there in the early '50s, and I remember him singing "Doin' My Time." He played guitar and had a mandolin player named Curly Lunsford, I believe, with him. They both played out of time, but not together! Jimmie would come in and then Curly might come in after a little while. But it was unique; it was so unusual that it became very identifying. Skinner sang quite low, a little reminiscent of Ernest Tubb. Did most of his numbers slowly.

"I'm Just Here to Get My Baby Out of Jail" is another one from Karl and Harty. It was among the old songs that I used to do on the early morning radio shows. If you're doing an hour a day, five days a week, you burn up a lot of material; that's really where I built a lot of my repertoire.

I associate "Wait for the Light to Shine" with Roy Acuff. I remember him doing it after he'd added an accordion player to his band. On this number, the accordion fit very well, gave it kind of a churchy sound. But when I first heard him use an accordion, I thought he'd absolutely lost his mind. I was working in Maryland at the time, must have been around 1944, and was coming home after working a Saturday night gig. I was listening to the Opry, and he came on with that accordion. To me the world just about ended. I thought "Somebody has held a gun on this dude!" But I thought the same thing when I heard Hank Williams do "Kaw-Liga" so maybe my judgment isn't the best.

"(Beneath That) Lonely Mound of Clay" is another Acuff number, although Molly O'Day also recorded it and I played bass on the session. At Thanksgiving time in 1946, we traveled to Chicago and recorded sixteen sides for Columbia, with Uncle Art Satherley producing. Since then that's been my claim to fame, that I played bass on the first sixteen sides that Molly recorded! Those were my first recording sessions.

I first heard "Short Life of Trouble" from Mainer's Mountaineers. I met Wade Mainer when I was at WNOX in Knoxville in 1946 working with Molly. And then in 1951 or '52 when I was on a little station in Mt. Airy, North Carolina, J. E. Mainer was there with a band. And boy, I used to pick his brain! He was something. Very colorful, strictly a mountain man. You couldn't have changed him if you'd held a gun on him!

"Cryin' Heart Blues" is from Johnnie and Jack, who were also at the Louisiana Hayride when I was there in 1951, while "Don't Give Your Heart to a Rambler" is another Jimmie Skinner song. Jimmy Martin later did this and gave it more of an up-tempo bluegrass treatment.

I never hear "I'm Using My Bible for a Road Map" but what I think of Don Reno and Red Smiley. Reno was quite a prolific songwriter. He was from northern South Carolina, and Hank Garland and Buck Trent came from the same area. It was quite a little spawning ground for country musicians.

I used to work with the Stanley Brothers on WCYB in Bristol, but I don't recall them doing "How Mountain Girls Can Love" at that time. When they first entered bluegrass, all they did was what Monroe did. They'd listen to him on Saturday nights, and Monday morning they'd do his Saturday night show. They just idolized him. But Bill, instead of considering it a compliment, took it the other way and it upset him no end. He ended up leaving Columbia Records because they'd signed the Stanleys, although I heard Uncle Art Satherly try to explain to Bill that he'd signed them out of self-defense. He said: "Bill, if I've got them on Columbia I can control them." But Bill thought that Columbia had done him wrong, and that they liked the Stanleys better than him.

I've always been a big Carter Family fan, and "Sailor on the Deep Blue Sea" is one of their numbers. When I first went to WCYB, old Mr. A. P. Carter came in every day and did a little five-minute segment around 1:00. He sold little testaments on the air. He had a bit of palsy at this time, was a little shaky, but he would sing a couple of songs and pitch his little testaments. I had been doing some of the Carter Family songs for several years, and we struck up quite a friendship. I treasure that memory! He knew I was genuinely interested in what he did and what he had done, so he talked very freely to me. I wish now that I'd been more bold and asked him more point-blank questions, but I didn't want him to think I was becoming a bore and run me off! And later I became acquainted with Maybelle and all the girls and toured with them.

I never heard anybody except Carl Story do "Light at the River." He was another one who was in Knoxville in 1946 when I was there with Molly O'Day, and I've worked with him a lot over the years. In the late '50s I was working for Dot Records in Gallatin, Tennessee, and Carl was on a little station up on the Cumberland Plateau in Livingston, Tennessee, near Cookeville. He called and wanted to know if I wanted to do some shows up there in the coverage area of his station. He lined up a couple of musicians to work with us, but they didn't show up so we did three or four of those towns up there, just he and I. Carl would sing a little while, then I'd come up with the guitar and sing a little while. Then we'd do some duets and Carl played the fiddle a little bit.

I'm pleased to finally get the chance to record some of these old songs that have been a part of my life for so many years—especially since I had such a fine group of musicians to work with. If you already know these songs, maybe listening to this album will bring back pleasant memories for you, as recording it did for me. On the other hand, if these old things are new to you, I hope that at least one or two of them will become your favorites as well.

<hr>

Liner notes for *From Grass Roots to Bluegrass*, CMH Records CD-9041 (1990). Reprinted by permission of the authors and CMH Records.

Bobby and Sonny Osborne (born in 1931 and 1937, respectively) remain one of the most accomplished and hard-hitting bluegrass acts performing in the early 2000s. Born in Hyden, Kentucky, the brothers started their professional teaming in 1953. By that time, mandolinist Bobby had performed with the Lonesome Pine Fiddlers, Jimmy Martin, and the Stanley Brothers; Sonny had worked as a teenaged banjoist with Bill Monroe. Neil Rosenberg's perceptive look back at their career to date ran in two parts in *Bluegrass Unlimited*. The section included here captures their critical move from the regional Gateway record label to MGM, which lately had recorded Hank Williams and was where Williams's associate Wesley Rose was to work with the Osbornes. While at MGM, Rosenberg shows, the Osbornes made major moves toward developing a sound that would compete on the commercial country charts. Just a few years later, however, the brother team encountered another force that would change bluegrass: the college audience and its insistence that musicians feature more down-home offerings.

7

"The Osborne Brothers—Part Two: Getting It Off"

NEIL ROSENBERG

At the start of 1956, Bob and Sonny Osborne were once more at home in Dayton, Ohio, playing the local clubs. Enos Johnson, who had worked with them in Knoxville during 1953–54, and in 1952–53 with Sonny in the Dayton area, was their guitar player. One night Red Allen, like the Osbornes, a Kentuckian living in the Dayton area and a former Gateway recording artist, was asked to substitute for Enos. The upshot was that Red became the regular guitarist in the group. Fiddler Art Stamper, who had recorded with the Stanley Brothers and was at that time working with Red Allen, also joined the group at this time. In February or March of 1956, they recorded eight instrumentals for Gateway records. This was their last session for that company and musically the most interesting.

Bobby: "We messed around, played a few clubs (in Dayton), and Tommy Sutton helped us get a contract with . . . MGM Records. He was a disc jockey at WPFB at the time—early morning show and the afternoon."

Bill Emerson's recent very interesting interview with the Osborne Brothers which brings up a number of details not covered in my first installment, lists WONE Dayton as the station with which Tommy Sutton was affiliated at the time of the MGM audition.[1]

In April 1956, Tommy Sutton took an audition tape with him to Nashville and played it for Wesley Rose of Acuff-Rose Music. The tape included "Ruby," and it led to a recording contract with MGM.

This contract came at a time when country music was facing intense competition from rock 'n' roll. Elvis Presley's records were number one on the *Billboard* country singles charts through most of 1956. Country music recording executives were frantically looking for new sounds that could compete in the new context created by Elvis. That a group playing country music of the older style—in 1956 "bluegrass" was a word known to few people, and bluegrass musicians thought of themselves primarily as country musicians—could land a recording contract with a major label such as MGM spoke well for the quality of the group. The music of the Osborne Brothers and Red Allen was conservative in contrast to that of singers like Elvis Presley, Marty Robbins and Sonny James, big sellers on the country charts at that time. Nevertheless, the group was still evolving musically, and the very first MGM recording session introduced innovations in bluegrass style which have become the stylistic trademarks by which the group is still known.

Bobby had been singing "Ruby" since his first days as a professional in 1949. When he recorded it for the first time in 1956, a new dimension was added: twin

1. Bill Emerson, "The Osborne Brothers: Getting Started," *Muleskinner News* 2 (July–Aug. 1971): 2–11.

banjo accompaniment, in the style of twin fiddles. The idea of multiple instruments playing voicelike parts was not new to bluegrass—Mac Wiseman had introduced twin fiddles on his early (ca. 1951) Dot recordings.[2] And long before that, in the thirties and forties, they had been used in the western swing bands of Bob Wills, Milton Brown and others. Bluegrass musicians had been experimenting with twin banjos during the early '50s, but it was not until the Osborne Brothers and Red Allen's "Ruby" that the sound was introduced on record.

Originally Sonny had asked Noah Crase to accompany them on second banjo at that first MGM session in Nashville on June 21, 1956, but at the last minute Noah could not make the trip, so Bob ended up playing the second banjo on "Ruby."[3]

"Ruby" was released in the early fall of 1956. This led, indirectly, to their return to WWVA, as Sonny explained: "While we worked at Wheeling with Charlie Bailey ... I ... became very good friends of Paul Meyers, who was the program director or program manager at Wheeling ... I knew he was manager of the Jamboree ... When 'Ruby' was released we called and got a date up there." They did a guest appearance and were signed on as regular members of the WWVA World's Original Jamboree in October 1956. Art Stamper did not accompany the group in its move to Wheeling. The band on WWVA in the first year and a half consisted of Johnny Dacus, fiddle (he later played fiddle with Jimmy Martin); Ricky Russell, dobro; and Ray Anderson, bass. This band did not appear on any of the Osborne Brothers and Red Allen recordings, but those who have heard recordings of their shows or remember their WWVA broadcasts can testify to the brilliance of the group.

At their second MGM session in November 1956, three of the four songs recorded were twin-banjo efforts which attempted to repeat the success of "Ruby." But by this time, because their instrumental ability was established, the band was more interested in their vocal trio. Bluegrass enthusiasts sometimes forget (or resent) the fact that the average country music fan pays much more attention to the vocal aspects of a song than to the fine points of instrumental style. The Osbornes saw this clearly, and felt that it was in the best interests of their career that they turned increasingly to the development of a unique singing style. It was at the third MGM session, in July 1957, that they recorded the song which was to establish their special trio sound.

"Well, Dusty Owens had written the tune 'Once More' while we were working in Wheeling, and me, Bobby and Red ... actually, where it started was in the car. We were coming back from Wheeling to Dayton and we started rehearsing ... you know, singing it, 'cause we like the tune awful well and that's where the top lead and that came from. Actually, I think in Zanesville or Cambridge—Zanesville I guess it was ... finally we just parked the car and set there and learned the tune ...; That's where it really started. .... The harmony that we do now is much more complicat-

2. Flatt and Scruggs made the first twin-fiddle recordings in bluegrass, on October 24, 1951, as Everett Lilly and Howdy Forrester teamed up on "I'm Lonesome and Blue" and "My Darling's Last Goodbye."

3. The brothers' first MGM sessions took place on July 1, 1956, December 29, 1956, and October 17, 1957, according to Tom Ewing (personal communication, 2003).

ed. Back then we just used a regular high lead (sung by Bobby) and the two lower parts, the baritone (Sonny) and a low tenor (Red)."

The group was excited about the new sound of "Once More," convinced that they had a unique commercial sound that would sell records. However, the MGM a&r man Wesley Rose was not convinced. It took some talking for them to get the song included in the recording session instead of another "Ruby"-type song with twin banjos.

This session was also significant in that it was the first bluegrass recording session in which drums and dobro were used together. Sonny: "They sold us on it . . . I guess that's the first time we'd ever used drums . . . and it . . . gave the music such a lift." Bobby: "We were the first ones to use a dobro and drums together on a session too . . . The dobro [was] a popular instrument at that time. We only did about three sessions with it and we let it go."

This July 1957 session was for a number of reasons the Osbornes' crucial one. Having established themselves as masters of the art of classic bluegrass, they were successfully introducing their own musical elements to their sound, adding techniques and instruments not being used by other bluegrass groups. In this session as in others to come, some of the innovations were suggested by the record company. Others were their idea, but at each step since then the Osbornes have maintained what they considered the important part of their sound while experimenting with various aspects of it. It is at this point, then, that their style began to diverge from that of "hard-line bluegrass."

In devising a trio in which the lead voice was the highest, the roles and images of the singers in the group were significantly altered. In modern country-western music the lead singer is, in effect, the center of attention for the audience; the star. When Bill Monroe, who had never sung lead, started his own band in 1938, he had to deal with this fact. He solved the problems it presented by singing lead on the verses and tenor on the choruses. In this way he preserved the reputation he had earned as a tenor singer and developed a new reputation as a lead singer. Bob Osborne, too, switched parts this way sometimes, especially with the Lonesome Pine Fiddlers. With the high lead harmony, Bob Osborne solved the same problem Monroe had solved earlier, but in a different way—by singing lead throughout the song and at the same time singing the highest part. Moreover, Sonny, singing the baritone, had the middle voice in the harmony, which was the next most prominent. Thus this shifting of musical roles freed the Osborne Brothers from dependence upon the reputation of any single guitarist/lead singer, since the guitarist was now singing the lowest and generally least discernible part. From this time on, changes in band personnel with the Osborne Brothers became more manageable and, in terms of the band's overall sound, less significant.

Early in 1958 the Osborne Brothers recorded for the last time with Red Allen; he left the group in April 1958. After this point the group was to be known simply as "the Osborne Brothers" and other members did not receive billing, although their guitarists have been given publicity on record labels and jackets, as well as at personal appearances. After Red Allen's departure succeeding guitarists played more straight rhythm and less bass-line runs. Some listeners (especially in the early '60s) saw this as a lack of technique on the part of guitarists, but this in fact was due to Bob and Sonny's feeling that guitarists who threw in "fancy" runs all the time often did not keep good rhythm.

From April 1958 to early 1959, the guitarist and third voice in the trio was Johnny Dacus, who had been their fiddler. Dacus left the group just before their next recording session in February of 1959. Ira Louvin filled in for him on the one trio recorded at this time ("Give This Message to Your Heart"). Two other songs featured the unusual sounds of Ray Edenton's tiple.[4] An out and out rock attempt, "There's Always a Woman" marked this session, like the preceding one, as one of experiments.

During the middle of 1959, the guitarist and third voice in the trio was Ray Anderson, a disc jockey from Washington Court House, Ohio, who had earlier played bass with the group. Bob and Sonny had previously recorded a number of songs for the Mountaineer label with him in October of either 1957 (according to Red Allen who played bass on the session) or 1958 (according to Bob and Sonny). Anderson did not record with the Osbornes on MGM. The October 1959 issue of *Esquire* magazine carried an article by Alan Lomax entitled "Bluegrass Backgrounds: Folk Music with Overdrive." Among the illustrations by artist Thomas Allen (who later did most of the Flatt and Scruggs album covers) was a picture of Bob, Sonny and Ray Anderson on the WWVA stage.

In the fall of 1959, Benny Birchfield and Jimmy Brown, Jr., joined the group as bassist and guitarist respectively. The next MGM session reflected the solidarity of the new trio sound on three songs; Jimmy Brown, Jr., was to remain with Bob and Sonny longer than any previous singer-guitarist they had worked with to that point.

In February of 1960 this band played what is generally considered the first college concert played by a country bluegrass band. The time was ripe; Earl Scruggs played at the Newport Folk Festival the previous July; Flatt and Scruggs had been featured on a national TV show entitled Folk Music 1959 the same summer, sharing the spotlight with Joan Baez and John Jacob Niles.[5] For several years curious folk music fans had been attending bluegrass shows such as those at New River Ranch in Rising Sun, Maryland, and bluegrass bars like the Crossroads, near Washington, D.C., where the newly-formed Country Gentlemen were appearing nightly. But the interest was largely "underground" and when the Osbornes arrived at Antioch College in Yellow Springs, Ohio (only a few miles from Dayton), they were prepared to play rock 'n' roll. They were very much surprised to find an audience requesting bluegrass standards of the kind they had stopped performing regularly when they left Gateway Records—songs such as "Molly and Tenbrooks," "Earl's Breakdown," and "Little Maggie." The audience was enthusiastic about the vocal and instrumental ability of the group which was obviously much more professional than the two

---

4. Edenton, a staple of Music Row sessions for decades, was playing a tiple, a "ten-string mini-guitar from Argentina." Jim Washburn and Richard Johnston, *Martin Guitars: An Illustrated Celebration of America's Premier Guitarmaker* (Emmaus, Pa.: Rodale Press, 1997).

5. *Folk Sound USA* actually aired on CBS in July 1960.

college groups who shared the billing. The audience was also somewhat confused by the presence of what they considered "corny" country songs like "Pick Me Up on Your Way Down" and the down-home comedy routines. Some even giggled at Bob's serious announcement of "Hymn time." As other bands were to discover, college audiences liked bluegrass better when it was presented to them as "Folk Music" rather than a kind of "Country Music."

Nevertheless, it was a successful concert, and following the Antioch concert, the Osbornes played other college concerts, and appeared before "folk music" audiences at the Newport Folk Festival, Boston's Club 47 and other similar places. However their basic audience was, and continues to be, the mainstream country music audience. This reflects economic facts—the "Folk" audience is both more fickle and smaller in number than the country music audience. It also reflects esthetic preferences, for the Osbornes were not then interested in doing other people's tunes and bluegrass "oldies," which seemed to be one of the requirements of the "folk music" boom. Their next recording session, in the fall of 1960, indicated quite clearly their continuing interest in developing a distinctive personal sound.

The four songs recorded for MGM in October 1960—"Fair and Tender Ladies," "Each Season Changes You," "Black Sheep Returned to the Fold" and "At the First Fall of Snow"—were all trios, and were recorded, for the first time in the Osbornes' career, with pedal steel and electric guitar backing.[6] Sonny explains, "that was our idea . . . 'cause we needed more—in 'Fair and Tender Ladies' we all three sang all the way through it. There was no background. Bobby couldn't play background on the mandolin, I couldn't play background on the banjo. We needed something to fill it up on that so we used Hank Garland . . . and . . . Pete Drake."

These recordings, especially the single of "Fair and Tender Ladies" and "Each Season Changes You," were well received. "Fair and Tender Ladies" was one of their most requested pieces through the '60s. Thus, not only was the session successful musically, it also seemed to do well with record buyers.

On February 15 and 16, 1962 the Osbornes recorded an instrumentals album for MGM. On the 17th was a singles session. Later in 1962 Jimmy Brown, Jr., left the group. He was replaced by Benny Birchfield, who had been playing bass and second banjo on the double banjo tunes since 1959. The trio sound that the group was able to get with Benny was outstanding; the next and last sessions for MGM, on January 9–11, 1963, featured a number of interesting performances, some of which were released on their MGM album *Cuttin' Grass.*

It appears that at this time MGM was uncertain about the proper way to market the Osbornes. Their LP jacket notes stressed the popularity of bluegrass in colleges, etc., but in an inept sort of way which made MGM sound rather "out of touch," since they had no idea (apparently) why college kids were digging bluegrass.

---

6. This session actually took place on November 15, 1960; the February 1962 sessions took place on February 14 and 15; the next and last sessions noted took place January 8–11, 1963, with "Mule Skinner Blues" recorded on January 9 and "Lovey Told Me Goodbye" on January 10.

Their singles, on the other hand, were in large measure novelty numbers which didn't really get off the ground. The good ones, like "Poor Old Cora," got poor distribution and were not issued on LP. The one single from the last MGM session was a coupling of Boudleaux and Felice Bryant's "Lovey Told Me Goodbye" the (A side) with "Mule Skinner Blues" (the B side). As happens so often in the world of popular music, the B side was the one that sold the record. It was during "Mule Skinner Blues" popularity that the Osbornes left WWVA and the World's Original Jamboree, where they had been members for seven years.

Originally published in *Bluegrass Unlimited* 6 (Feb. 1972): 5–8. Reprinted by permission of the author and *Bluegrass Unlimited*.

M ore than perhaps any other of the founding-era acts, Jim and Jesse illustrated the tension between tradition and the need to make some money and explore new musical directions. As mandolinist-journalist-scholar Jack Tottle shows, Jim and Jesse took a number of musical paths—the brother-duet sound, cowboy music and gospel harmony—before settling in a countrified bluegrass direction under the direction of Capitol Records producer Ken Nelson. And that approach was far from the end, as Jim and Jesse roved the pastures of straight bluegrass, hard-hitting truck-driving songs, adventuresome instrumentals and a notable early experiment in mixing bluegrass and rock and roll. In a way, their far-reaching excursions were both a mirror and an extension of the eclectic approach Bill Monroe took in melding several different styles to produce bluegrass. As Tottle also points out, the McReynolds brothers were unlikely revolutionaries, always immaculate in appearance and in musical performance. Since Jim's death on New Year's Eve 2002, Jesse has continued to lead the Virginia Boys band on the Opry and elsewhere. The editor's note appeared along with the original article.

8

"The Grass Is Greener in the Mountains"

JACK TOTTLE

Editor's note: For a long time we have wanted an article that would give our readers a better understanding of the tremendous impact Jim and Jesse and the Virginia Boys have had in making Blue Grass the varied, exciting style it is today. To write this article, we needed someone who has been around a long time, listening and constantly absorbing Jim and Jesse's influence. Who better to write the article than

Jack Tottle, himself a mandolin player and singer? Many of you will remember Jack from the Lonesome River Boys who played in the Washington area and recorded a fine album over ten years ago. Today Jack lives in the Boston area, where he plays with Don Stover and the White Oak Mountain Boys, teaches mandolin and guitar, and is writing a mandolin instruction book for Oak Publications.

Jack recently met with Jim and Jesse at Shindig in the Barn in Lancaster, Pennsylvania, and reacquainted himself with their music by listening to a great stack of albums and tapes. We think you'll enjoy the results.[1]

In the late 1940s two young boys from the little town of Coeburn in southwestern Virginia were getting into music. Jim McReynolds played guitar and sang a lovely, clear tenor. His brother Jesse sang and played the mandolin. They experimented freely in their music, searching constantly for a musical style that would suit them and yet be "different" from what had gone before.

Like all young bluegrass musicians, they listened carefully to Bill Monroe's music, but the brothers were also drawn to other styles. They paid close attention to the mellow sounds of old-time country duets including the Bailes Brothers, the York Brothers, the Delmore Brothers, and the Blue Sky Boys. As time passed, Jim and Jesse also discovered the Chuck Wagon Gang, the Louvin Brothers and the Browns. These varied influences pointed the McReynolds' vocal style onto a path quite distinct from that simultaneously being explored by a couple of close neighbors—Carter and Ralph Stanley.

Just as the Stanleys did, Jim and Jesse first worked on their own in Norton, Virginia, and nearby West Virginia, calling their band "the McReynolds Brothers and the Cumberland Mountain Boys." Around 1949 they went with Hoke Jenkins and Curly Seckler to Augusta, Georgia, where they tried a conventional Blue Grass format. In 1951, feeling a need to test something different, they put together a western-style band including steel guitar and went to Kansas. There they did a "Sons of the Pioneers"-type show featuring numbers like "Cool Water" and "Home on the Range."

Later that same year Jim and Jesse got their first chance at recording. As it is with many musicians the first time around, the situation was less than ideal. They were to do a set of gospel songs for a small and financially shaky company whose owner seemed chiefly interested in the distribution of risque party records. Uncertain as to how the whole thing would go, the boys decided to adopt the name "the Virginia Trio" in case things didn't work out well.

As it turned out, the sessions were a great musical success. Joined by Larry Roll on the vocals and Dave Woolum (or Wooleram) on bass, the group produced a lovely collection of sacred trios, including "I Like the Old Time Way," "Camping in Canaan's Land," "I'll Fly Away," "On the Jericho Road," and several others. And there, one step behind some inspired vocal work, took place the stunning debut of Jesse's original mandolin roll, later to be dubbed "crosspicking."

---

1. This version omits a section that provides a "mini-lesson."

Though these recordings were available as singles for several years and were later re-released on various albums, the musicians involved did not realize much in the way of monetary encouragement.

Musicians, like the rest of us, do not live by bread alone and a certain minimum sustenance is required to keep even the most dedicated picker's body operational. It was thus an event of considerable importance when Ken Nelson of Capitol Records approached the brothers with a contract. In 1952 the group's name was again changed, this time to "Jim and Jesse and the Virginia Boys," and a series of recording sessions shortly ensued. Hoke Jenkins and Curly Seckler participated as did fiddlers Sonny James, Tommy Jackson and Tommy Vaden.[2]

Throughout their careers, Jim and Jesse have demonstrated a remarkable talent for attracting excellent but relatively unknown musicians. Their record in this regard is matched only by Bill Monroe and Jimmy Martin.

Curly Seckler is probably best known for his tenor singing on some of Flatt and Scruggs' classic recordings. Tommy Vaden played on some of Hank Snow's best releases. Tommy Jackson went on to become a successful Nashville sideman and recording artist. Sonny James, of course, has turned into one of Nashville's top country and western vocalists.

The resulting tunes quickly established Jim and Jesse as a major Blue Grass band with an unmistakable and compelling sound. "Are You Missing Me," "Too Many Tears," "Air Mail Special," "Just Wondering Why," "Memory of You," "My Little Honeysuckle Rose," and many other classic cuts featured the McReynolds' high, sweet vocals, Jesse's astounding mandolin and a characteristic tight yet airy instrumental underpinning. (All of these recordings are now available on a double Capitol set.)

Every silver lining, unfortunately, seemed to have its cloud. No sooner had the Capitol releases begun to hit the market than Jesse received his draft notice. Unable to follow up their new records with personal appearances, the band lost a good deal of momentum in the next two years, a momentum which was hard to recapture when Jesse returned in 1954.

The next blow hit Jim and Jesse along with everyone else in bluegrass. Writhing and moaning with sufficient sensual abandon that TV dared not show his lower half (my, how times do change!) Elvis Presley exploded almost simultaneously across the pop and country music scenes. Anything that resembled "Hound Dog" or "Heartbreak Hotel" became red hot, and nearly everything else cooled right down.

"No one (in the recording industry) was interested in bluegrass then," recalls Jim, "except Don Pierce of Starday Records. We ended up producing our own recording sessions and leasing the tapes to him." By 1959 when their first Starday singles were released, Jim and Jesse had a completely new band with a noticeably different sound from their Capitol days. Don McHan, a talented songwriter and singer,

---

2. Born James Hugh Loden, future country star Sonny James took his stage name in 1952.

played electric bass. Bobby Thompson (whose success in Nashville studios was chronicled in last month's *Muleskinner News*) was on banjo and Vassar Clements played fiddle. The Starday sides included, "Hard Hearted," "I'll Never Love Anybody but You," "Let Me Whisper," "Dixie Hoedown," "Border Ride," and a 45–rpm extended play record with six gospel songs. The approach on these recordings was perhaps a bit more aggressive and polished than on the Capitol releases, though they still featured the same striking harmony singing and fine mandolin work.

A further lift was provided when Martha White Flour signed Jim and Jesse for a TV series. By 1961 they were back with major label distribution. Two talented new discoveries, Allen Shelton on banjo and Jim Buchanan on fiddle, contributed immensely to the band's sound. Their new tunes, released on Columbia, included "Diesel Train," "Flame of Love," "Beautiful Moon of Kentucky," and "Gosh I Miss You All the Time." The group was still well within a bluegrass format, but seemed to be pushing slightly toward a commercial Nashville sound.

About this time the folk music boom of the early 1960s was getting under way and providing a much-needed lift for bluegrass. Though other bands which relied on more traditional folk material probably benefited more, Jim and Jesse were invited to the Newport Folk Festival (they appear on one of the Vanguard Newport sets) and felt a general salutary increase in the demand for their music.

During 1962–64 they returned to a sound more like the Starday cuts with Epic albums—*Bluegrass Special, Bluegrass Classics,* and *Y'all Come.* These contain outstanding renditions of "Blue Bonnet Lane," "Sweet Little Miss Blue Eyes," "Standing on the Mountain," "Salty Dog," "The Grass Is Greener in the Mountains," "Stoney Creek" (Jesse's popular mandolin tune), and much more flawless and exciting Blue Grass. The period also brought their release of two gospel albums and a series of singles. The single releases were, over all, less successful musically than the better album cuts, which may have reflected experimentation to see what would produce the best airplay results. On some of the singles such as "Better Times a-Comin'," "It's a Long Long Way to the Top of the World," "Don't Let Nobody Tie You Down," and "Cotton Mill Man," however, the experimentation produced excellent results. The latter two contain imaginative use of minor sections within songs in major keys. The repeated fiddle and banjo riff in "Cotton Mill Man" is particularly tasteful and catchy.

Following a number of guest appearances filling in for Flatt and Scruggs on the Grand Ole Opry, in March of 1964 Jim and Jesse were invited to become permanent members. This milestone, viewed by many as the ultimate in country music, was a well-deserved recognition of Jim and Jesse's ability and perseverance.

By 1964, however, the folk boom was beginning to falter, and electricity, this time personified by the Beatles (and their scandalously long hair) was again making things tough on bluegrass pickers. Bluegrass festivals, which would in later years provide a major source of work for the top acts, had not yet appeared. Promoters for country shows when approached for bookings wanted to know "What have you got on the charts?" As Blue Grass wasn't receiving much notice in the trade magazines, Jim and Jesse decided to try their hands at something that might. First they decided to play some rock and roll.

Their next album, *Berry Pickin' in the Country,* consisted of Chuck Berry's rock and roll tunes given a bluegrass treatment, still using acoustic mandolin, banjo and fiddle. Forced as the idea sounds, the results were extremely enjoyable music, especially on "Maybellene," "Memphis," and "Johnny B. Goode." Sales were respectable but still not enough to put them on the charts.

By the following year Jim and Jesse were ready to, as Jim says, "take a stab at country music." Their first stab, it turned out, was pretty deft. The album *Diesel on My Tail* featured an energetic Nashville sound with prominent pedal steel and dobro. The material leaned heavily on C&W standards like "Thunder Road" and "Sam's Place" with a spicing of country novelty tunes like "Diesel on My Tail," "Give Me Forty Acres to Turn This Rig Around," and even "The Girl Wearing Nothing but a Smile and a Towel in the Picture on the Billboard in a Field Near the Big Ol' Highway."

And lo and behold, both the album and the title single from it sold like nothing they had ever released before. In short order both were listed among the top ten tunes on the nationwide country music charts.

Throughout the remainder of the 1960s, Jim and Jesse's recordings were basically country, though traces of bluegrass came through from time to time. Albums of this period included *The All-Time Great Country Instrumentals, Saluting the Louvin Brothers, We Like Trains,* and *Freight Train.* Within their country format there is plenty of excellent singing, perhaps most notable on the *Freight Train* album, and some fine instrumental work as well. On the *Country Instrumentals* album, Jesse plays an electric mandola (a mandola is to a mandolin what a viola is to a violin, it is slightly larger than a mandolin and tuned a fifth lower to C G D A), which must be a first in country music. The overall effect on this album is a bit bland by bluegrass standards, but his musicianship is as astonishing as ever.

By the 1970s, however, bluegrass festivals had emerged as an important force in the music world, and acoustic music was again showing considerable appeal in radio airplay. For a time Jim and Jesse did some country shows and a syndicated TV show with an electrified band and, alternatively, took a straight bluegrass instrumentation to the festivals. Finally, with bluegrass festivals comprising 90 percent of their work, the group phased out the electrified country sound completely.

Today, the Virginia Boys feature Jim Brock (who first worked with Jim and Jesse around 1963, replacing Jim Buchanan) on fiddle and Vic Jordan (previously with Bill Monroe, Lester Flatt and Jimmy Martin) on banjo. Keith McReynolds, Jesse's son, plays bass. Their show is a relaxed mix of their great old tunes with some of their newer numbers.

Their current live sound is reflected on several recent albums, including the *Jim and Jesse Show* on Prize, *Mandolin Workshop* on Hilltop and *Superior Sounds of Blue Grass.* Jesse is also heard on recent albums by the Lewis Family and Carl Jackson. Jesse's versatility comes through on a recording he did with the Doors (a rock group) and "Me and My Fiddles" on Atteiram, in which he plays fiddle with considerable skill.

Jim and Jesse have not forsaken experimentation in their return to Blue Grass; their new singles for the Opryland label feature what Jim calls a "Blue Grassfolk" sound. "Three flat top guitars, dobro, Vic Jordan on banjo with piano and drums just for the bottom," he explains.

Asked which current artists have influenced their thinking in working on their new recorded sound, Jesse thinks of John Denver; Jim mentions George Hamilton IV. In the final analysis, it's pretty sure to sound a lot more like Jim and Jesse than anyone else, and to be well worth paying attention to.

Originally published in *Muleskinner News* 5 (March 1974): 6–10. Reprinted by permission of Carlton Haney.

Then a young folklorist and picker, Mayne Smith did bluegrass an unparalleled service with this comprehensive academic article on the style. Smith possesses both the scholarly credentials and the up-close acquaintance with bluegrass to offer chapter and verse on the style while placing it in accurate context along with other American folk and popular music. Smith's writing, although sometimes weighted by academic convention, gets close to the bone. He even notes, with wry understatement, that "financial reward for bluegrass musicians is not generally substantial." The piece, appearing in the scholarly *Journal of American Folklore,* was a revision of Smith's Indiana University master's thesis on bluegrass. The commercial and folk-revival connections of bluegrass made it a tough sell at authenticity-conscious IU, Rosenberg writes.

As the following article shows, Bill Monroe had plenty to say about Smith's piece; he must have been struck in its first paragraphs by the claim that bluegrass didn't begin until 1945. In addition, subsequent chapters of this book will make clear many changes in bluegrass since Smith outlined the characteristics of bluegrass: The music is no longer the sole province of Southern men. In addition, some bands have used more than four vocal parts, and bluegrass is in some instances dance music. More than thirty-five years after his breakthrough article, Smith remains active as a musician in California.

9

"An Introduction to Bluegrass"

L. MAYNE SMITH

The word BLUEGRASS has been used since about 1950 by musicians and disc jockeys to designate a style of hillbilly music performed by bands which most commonly include bass, guitar, banjo, fiddle, and mandolin. [*Note:* This article is partially drawn

from an unpublished master's thesis, "Bluegrass Music and Musicians: An Intro-
ductory Study of a Musical Style in Its Cultural Context" (Indiana University, 1964)
in which many of the points found here are elaborated. Portions of the article have
appeared as "Bluegrass as a Musical Style," *Autoharp: Organ of the Folksong Club of
the University of Illinois,* February 8, 1963, n.p. I owe considerable thanks to Alan P.
Merriam and Neil V. Rosenberg for advice and encouragement.] Building on earlier string band styles, Bill Monroe and his Blue Grass Boys played the first bluegrass
music in 1945. Since that time a total of more than three hundred Southern musicians have performed regularly with about sixty commercially recorded professional
and semi-professional bluegrass bands. They call their manner of performance
"bluegrass" in contradistinction to other strains of hillbilly music such as country-
western, western swing, and rockabilly.

It is the purpose of this article to describe the most important musical and be-
havioral phenomena associated with bluegrass, concentrating first on a concise description of the music and then dealing with its stylistic derivation and physical-cul-
tural context. Bluegrass has behind it a long history of folk and hillbilly styles of
performance, and it draws from many of them. The present task, however, is to describe the contemporary style rather than to trace its historical roots. Indeed, only with
detailed knowledge of separate performing traditions in folk and popular music can
historical relationships between them be adequately understood. The study of musical styles lies outside the perimeters of most scholarly treatments of American song.
Since precise academic knowledge is lacking, a brief discussion of the stylistic influences on bluegrass will have to suffice. Similarly, the increasing significance of bluegrass in the Northern urban "folksong revival" is only peripherally treated.

Although bluegrass was built upon and has absorbed elements of other styles,
it can be treated as a discrete entity. Though it may be theoretically impossible to
define a musical style in logical terms, it is at least possible to specify those characteristics of a style which, taken together, distinguish it from all others. This latter
task is difficult in the case of many musical styles—particularly those of non-liter-
ate peoples—but bluegrass musicians are surrounded by music from which they are
constantly distinguishing their own, and their distinctions provide important guide-
posts. Following the ideas of the musicians themselves, here are the defining traits
of bluegrass:

1. Bluegrass is hillbilly music: it is played by professional, white, Southern musicians, primarily for a Southern audience. It is stylistically based in Southern musical traditions.
2. In contrast to many other hillbilly styles, bluegrass is not dance music and
   is seldom used for this purpose.
3. Bluegrass bands are made up of from four to seven male musicians who play
   non-electrified stringed instruments and who also sing as many as four parts.
4. The integration of these instruments and voices in performance is more for-
   malized and jazz-like than that encountered in earlier string band styles.

Instruments function in three well defined roles, and each instrument changes roles according to predictable patterns.

5. Bluegrass is the only full-fledged string band style in which the banjo has a major solo role, emphasizing melodic over rhythmic aspects. The basic bluegrass banjo style was first played by Earl Scruggs in 1945 when he was one of Bill Monroe's Blue Grass Boys, and is named after him. Every bluegrass band includes a banjo played in "Scruggs style" or some derivative thereof.

The last three items are the most important in this list of the distinguishing characteristics of bluegrass. The instrumental and the vocal composition of bluegrass bands separates the style from all but a few white gospel groups and string bands. Though the manner of ensemble integration links bluegrass with jazz-oriented hillbilly bands, it excludes almost all pre-bluegrass string bands, in which instruments seldom varied their roles. The use of Scruggs-style banjo playing serves mainly to distinguish bluegrass from the sound of the Blue Grass Boys before 1945, though it is often seen as the principal unique element of the style and is the most easily verbalized trait that distinguishes earlier bluegrass performance from earlier string band music.

In capsule form, bluegrass is a style of concert hillbilly music performed by a highly integrated ensemble of voices and non-electrified stringed instruments, including a banjo played Scruggs style. This skeleton description of bluegrass provides a framework for a more thorough examination of the style.

Instrumentation in bluegrass bands involves various combinations of six instruments. The five-string banjo, mandolin, Spanish guitar (with steel strings), fiddle, and string bass compose the usual group. The steel guitar is denied true bluegrass status by some (who use the Blue Grass Boys as the criterion of judgment), but it has been employed more and more widely since its addition to the band of Lester Flatt and Earl Scruggs in 1955. This instrument, in the form used by bluegrass bands, is called the "dobro" after the brand name of an especially resonated guitar manufactured by the three Dopera brothers, principally during the 1930s. [*Note:* John Duffey, "The Dobro," *The Country Gentlemen Song Book* (N.p., N.d).] The Spanish guitar and banjo are the two instruments essential to the style, but at least one of the other four instruments must be added, and few bands include fewer than four musicians.

Many bluegrass bands have added drums, electric guitars, and other instruments on at least a few disc recordings. On rare occasions the autoharp, mouth harp, Jew's harp, accordion, and electric organ have also been used. The fact that such instances are much more common in the recording studio than on the performing stage suggests that the influence of recording companies is largely behind the deviations. Many musicians express disapproval of them. The addition of these extra instruments does not affect the interrelationship of the standard instruments in the ensemble; rather, it is addition without integration.

Played in bluegrass style, the instruments of the ensemble combine with each other in three distinct roles: a lead part, produced by an instrument or voice as the central melodic interest; one or several instruments which "back" the lead, contrasting with it melodically and rhythmically but never threatening its domination; and an underlying, unvarying, and sharply accented rhythmic and harmonic base. All of the instruments function at times in all three of these roles, but each tends to emphasize one or two.

The fiddle, banjo, and dobro are primarily lead instruments which also produce counter-melodies and rhythmic figures to back other lead parts. The mandolin is equally important as a lead instrument, but when not performing that role it is crucial as a percussive-sounding rhythm part: its single notes have come to be regarded as too quiet for effective backing when not very near the microphone. Not all bands include these four lead instruments, and the relative importance of each varies from group to group and from piece to piece; the banjo has most consistent prominence. The functions of the guitar and bass, on the other hand, seldom vary; both instruments are essential elements in the rhythmic background and serve to balance the higher-pitched tonal range of the lead instruments. The guitar also takes a backing role by playing short melodic runs between major phrases of the lead parts; in some bands, the instrument has recently been employed for lead.

The overall impression produced by a bluegrass performance is one of multiple parts in continual interaction. Except when four voices are singing lead, the fiddle and banjo in a standard band usually play complex backing patterns while the guitar, bass, and mandolin maintain the rhythm; these functions are preserved when fiddle or banjo has the lead. When the mandolin is leading, the banjo tends toward a less melodic, more rhythmic function to compensate for the lack of mandolin rhythm. Without a mandolin to accent the up-beats, the banjo usually assumes a strong rhythmic role unless the band uses a dobro or second guitar to add to the background. Conversely, bands that include a dobro tend to understress or eliminate the role of one of the other lead instruments. On slower songs this may be the banjo; on fast songs, it is likely to be the mandolin. When the dobro plays lead, other instrumentalists simplify their music, since the dobro is relatively quiet and does not stand out clearly against a complex background. Sometimes lead instruments play duets; most common are double banjos or fiddles, and fiddle-banjo duos.

Just as individual instruments are chosen for their volume and brilliance of tone, bluegrass voices are typically high-pitched and tense. Singing parts sometimes reach more than an octave above middle C, and keys for songs are generally chosen to pitch voices as high as possible. There is considerable variability in vocal timbre within performances, since singers often stress the peculiar characteristics of each mountain-accented vowel sound; final consonants are often obscured. Particularly high notes may be sung in falsetto or a head-tone. The use of vibrato is rare, and most of the highly reputed singers perform in a loud and piercing fashion, not unlike shouting. A slight flatting of held pitches, rising attacks, falling releases, and grace notes are common ornamental devices. Bluegrass singing is often syncopated, with stress and durational preference given to words that receive these accents in normal speech, though never at the expense of the tempo of the song.

The combination of voices in two, three, and four parts is a salient aspect of bluegrass music and relatively rare in country-western (though duets are now becoming fairly common in the latter). The parts are called "lead," or melody; "tenor," almost invariably sung above the lead; "third," which may be sung above the lead or tenor ("high tenor") but is usually sung below both ("baritone"); and the lowest part, "bass." Voices are added to the lead in the order named, so that two-part harmony is always a combination of lead and tenor, and three-part harmony is always lead, tenor, and third. These parts are conventionalized to the extent that a good singer can usually join in with songs he has not previously heard. The tenor has some flexibility in duet singing, but in three and four parts the voices are expected to fill in all the notes of each triad in ways that predetermine their eventual pitches; at most cadential returns to the tonic chord, the lead comes to rest on the tonic pitch with the tenor a major third above him, the baritone on the fifth below, and the bass singing the tonic pitch, lowest of all. These relative levels of pitch are generally maintained with little crossing of parts. Anticipations, passing tones, and ornamental slides often create dissonances that dispel the impression of complete and predictable homophony. The occurrence of antiphony between various single voices and the other parts in many performances of religious songs is another device that adds variety.

On the level of melodic structure, bluegrass does not differ radically in most respects from Anglo-American tradition. Melodies are sometimes based on gapped-pentatonic (c, d, f, g, a) scales, but most are diatonic. As in other Southern musical styles, the use of neutral thirds, fifths, and sevenths (varying between the major and minor intervals) in the context of the diatonic scale is common. Most melodies seldom go far below the tonic pitch, the occasional use of 5 or 6 below 1 being the most common exception. The fifth tone in the diatonic scale rivals the tonic for designation as the duration tone in many songs; such melodies tend toward this pitch at mid-phrase points, returning to the well defined tonic note for final and many phrasal cadences.

Harmonic accompaniment in bluegrass most commonly involves the use of the three major triads: tonic, subdominant, and dominant, without the seventh. The most common progression of chords is I, IV, I, V, I, which is identical with the basic twelve-bar blues progression (though not always in the number of beats allotted to each chord). The relative minor of the tonic is almost the only minor chord used; it may be stated or only implied by introducing the sixth tone of the scale. In melodies that are apparently close to the gapped-pentatonic scale, the triad built on the lowered seventh degree is added to the tonic and dominant to provide harmonic backing. The progressions I, III, IV, and I, VI, II, V are sometimes used as well. Passage to the dominant chord is, in fact, often accomplished by transition through the super-tonic.

The general rhythmic traits of bluegrass are neither complex nor varied. Two basic meters are used, each at several characteristic tempos. Triple meter, used more often for ballads and religious songs, is notated best as $\frac{3}{4}$. Duple meter can be notated either as $\frac{4}{4}$ or $\frac{2}{4}$, depending usually on the tempo rather than on any basic change

in stress patterns. The examination of 125 bluegrass pieces performed on disc recordings by ten different bands reveals the following tempo patterns: *triple meter:*
tempos most often moderate, about 115 beats per minute, or fast, about 190; *duple
meter:* tempos center at points around 160, 250, and 330 beats per minute.

Though tempos in the lower range of triple meter and the middle range of duple
meter are the most common, the speed of bluegrass performance as a whole is greater than that of other hillbilly styles. The impression of speed is enhanced by the use
of accented up-beats in duple meter, off-beat melodic phrasing, and changes in pitch
to accent the rhythm. Even at tempos of 330, banjo players play mainly eighth notes,
which means that they are producing about eleven notes per second. On pieces that
are used as demonstrations of virtuosity by banjoists and fiddlers, the tempo may
suddenly be increased (at the end) to the point where only the down-beats or even
first beats of measures are played by accompanying instruments. Some bands (notably Bill Monroe's) tend to vary tempos slightly, speeding up at the beginnings of
phrases to give a subtle surging effect; this device seems largely unconscious and is
difficult to gauge.

Interesting rhythmic devices are also used at the endings of many bluegrass
pieces. Most slow songs, especially those in $\frac{3}{4}$ time, end with a few measures of ru-
bato; some songs, in fact, slow to a full stop in the middle, after which the original
tempo (but sometimes a new meter and tempo) is resumed. Almost all relatively
fast songs in duple meter end with a seven-beat rhythmic pattern that corresponds
to the "shave and a haircut—two bits" melodic cliché of nationally popular music.
The phrase begins on the first beat of the measure simultaneously with the singing
or playing of the last note of the melody, and ends with a heavily stressed final beat
on the third pulse of the succeeding measure.

The structural form of bluegrass songs is always strophic, employing one or two
large melodic units (strains), each composed of two or four phrases repeated in
sequence to make up an entire piece of music. Phrases are commonly combined in
such units as: a, b, a, c; a, b, b, c; and a, a', a, b. In vocal pieces, one of these units is
usually the setting for the stanzas, and another for a textual burden which follows
each stanza. Instrumental pieces sometimes have three major units instead of the
usual two and may involve one strain of indeterminate length, performed as an
improvisatory solo passage by the fiddle while the other instruments keep up a
constant rhythmic background on a single chord.

Pieces are performed with voices and lead instruments taking turns at the melody part or some variation upon it. Usually there are about eight repetitions of the
full two-unit sequence in each piece; most lyric songs, for example, involve four vocal
passages interspersed with solo passages from three lead instruments. The vocal
sections are often divided between solos for the stanzas and harmony singing for
the burdens. Pieces usually last about two and one half minutes; the earlier time
limitations of ten-inch 78–rpm discs probably caused the development of this pattern, which is seldom broken.

The textual characteristics of bluegrass songs are not as distinctive as the musical style in which they are performed, but they deserve some attention as we move away from strictly musical analysis. In subject matter, texts range widely through the kinds of emotion and situation dealt with in Anglo-American folksong—religious experience, love, and death. In religious songs, existence is generally pictured as a vale of tears; the dead have passed on to a better lot and death itself is a time of reward for earthly misery. Lyric songs usually express sorrow or anger over the loss of a lover, but many bewail the singer's nostalgia for his rural home or parents. This latter type of song derives from earlier popular and hillbilly material, but today is more common in bluegrass than in any other style; religious themes are often mixed with such nostalgic ones. Similarly, the relatively few light-hearted songs usually celebrate joy in religious experience or the memory of life "back home" in the mountains. The most common subject of ballads is violent death, in which a love relationship is usually involved: one lover kills another, or his rival, or commits suicide when rejected. The theme of impending execution or a lifetime in prison as punishment for murder is a common correlative.

The texts determine the identities of songs, since a large number of different songs have nearly identical tunes. (An informal count discloses over a hundred bluegrass songs that have at least one close tune-mate; many have more than five.) Yet the literal meanings of texts have relatively little importance to many bluegrass musicians. Interest focuses most often on the music to which the text is set and on the instrumental and vocal approach used. Musicians generally consider the mood suggested by the text in order to develop an appropriate musical treatment, but not often the poetic qualities of the words. It is indicative that many musicians can play—and admire—dozens of songs to which they cannot sing the texts. It is also significant that, as with most hillbilly styles, bluegrass texts are categorized only according to whether they are sacred or secular, serious or comic. The scholar's distinction between traditional and non-traditional items, and between ballads and non-ballads, is generally ignored and seldom made explicit.

About a fifth of bluegrass pieces derives from Anglo-American folk tradition and have become a part of the repertoire either through the folk background of musicians or through performances by non-bluegrass hillbilly groups. Since traditional pieces are more widely known and less bound by copyright laws than non-folk items, they tend to be repeated more than others. Though almost all bluegrass ballads derive from folk tradition, instrumental tunes and lyric songs, more common than ballads in the repertoire, are also the most common types of borrowed folk items. Among the ballads, most are of broadside origin and were first sung in the United States. Negro tradition is only slightly represented in the borrowing of specific items. Other songs are written by bluegrass musicians, who often adapt traditional tunes and words. Some of the songs are drawn from other hillbilly styles and still others come under the heading of nineteenth century middle-class parlor songs. The relative importance of these various song sources differs from band to band. The more affluent a band is, the more likely it is to avoid recording songs that other performers have already issued. This restriction does not hold for the public performances of most bands.

Taking performance patterns as a whole, bluegrass shares more stylistic traits with folk tradition than any other well defined category of hillbilly music now produced in quantity. Anglo- and Afro-American traditional styles have laid down the lines followed by bluegrass melodies, harmonic accompaniment, and phrasal organization. Bluegrass vocal style owes much to traditional ballad- and psalm-singing. Part singing derives from shape-note polyphony filtered through earlier stages of hillbilly music, and has also been influenced by Negro gospel performers. [*Note:* Gilbert Chase, *America's Music from the Pilgrims to the Present* (New York, 1955), 22–40, 183–206; Charles Seeger, "Contrapuntal Style in the Three-Voice Shape-Note Hymns," *Musical Quarterly* 26 (Oct. 1940): 483–93.] Negro performance patterns are also represented in the use of blues tonality and song structure.

On the other hand, bluegrass clearly shows stylistic links with Northern popular music and jazz. The marked rhythmic stress of the up-beat, the use of improvised solos whereby single musicians dominate the total sound, and the general pattern of ensemble integration are at base African musical practices; but they have reached bluegrass through jazz, at least partially with the mediation of western swing, a hillbilly style that was flourishing in the early 1940s when bluegrass was being developed. Since 1955 some bluegrass bands have been reflecting developments in country-western music, particularly of electric Spanish and steel guitar styles; exchanges in song repertoire occur as well. In the past several years, both the repertoire and the pop-based style of some "folksong" groups have been drawn upon by a few bluegrass bands.

Examined in cultural context, the commercial, popular nature of the style grows even more evident. Bluegrass was developed by professional musicians, and professional musicians are the ones who define and change the music in their paid performances. The style requires a degree of instrumental virtuosity and a type of ensemble integration seldom found among folk musicians in the United States. Though the composition of the bands derives partly from amateur and semi-professional square dance ensembles, the basic performing tradition behind bluegrass is that of medicine shows, radio programs, and disc recordings. In these contexts, singing, performances of religious songs, showmanlike "arrangements," and very fast tempos have always been more important musical features than with rural dance bands.

At the same time bluegrass is closely related to folk tradition on an extra-musical level. Unlike many performers of art, urban-popular, and country-western music, bluegrass musicians very seldom employ written music notation and have not developed a technical jargon to describe the sounds they produce. They learn their music aurally, whether from radio broadcasts, disc recordings, or personal contact. Though commercial discs permit bands to imitate past performances closely, both conscious and unconscious improvisation account for a considerable amount of variation, even between supposedly identical renditions of pieces. Thus, if transmission is not always oral (from mouth to ear), bluegrass nevertheless shares with folk tradition the elements of aural communication and relatively informal modes of repetition and change. [*Note:* Charles Seeger, "Oral Tradition in Music," *Funk and Wagnalls Standard Dictionary of Folklore, Mythology, and Legend* (New York, 1950), 2: 825–29, especially 826, 282.] Furthermore, bluegrass musicians are in constant contact with folk tradition. Over 90 percent of the professional musicians are Southerners and about 80 percent are Appalachian-bred; most of them carry numerous traditional items. Not only are many professional bluegrass performances carried to rural audiences by records, radio, and personal appearances, but amateur bands are found in many communities where folk tradition is still an important part of musical culture.

A general treatment of the cultural context of any musical phenomenon is ultimately concerned with the individual musicians whose experiences and attitudes determine and thus explain the nature of their products. While it would be impossible to discuss each prominent bluegrass musician, a brief history of the four most renowned bands can give considerable insight into the bluegrass style and lead the way to broader cultural considerations.

The dominating figure in bluegrass is Bill Monroe, who was born in Rosine, Kentucky, in 1911. His mother and her brother, a fiddler named Pen Vandiver, were both accomplished musicians who taught Monroe much of his early music; he was also influenced by a Negro fiddler and guitar player named Arnold Shultz; and he learned shape-note polyphony at local singing-school gatherings. By 1925 Monroe was traveling around the countryside with his uncle accompanying him on the guitar at country dances, but about this time he began to concentrate on the mandolin as his major instrument. [*Note:* Ralph Rinzler, "Bill Monroe—'The Daddy of Blue Grass Music,'" *Sing Out!* 13 (Feb.–March 1963): 5–8.]

In the 1930s Monroe played mandolin professionally with his guitar-playing older brother, Charlie, and the duo became well known throughout the South. In many ways the pair was similar in style and repertoire to the equally well known Blue Sky Boys (Bill and Earl Bolick). Nevertheless, special characteristics of Bill Monroe's music stood out already in this period: his technical virtuosity on the mandolin, the unusual speed and drive of his rhythm, and the high, tense vocal quality he achieved singing tenor over his brother's lead. The influence of Monroe Brothers recordings on bluegrass repertoire and style has been strong.

In 1938 the brothers stopped performing together and Bill formed his own band, the Blue Grass Boys. This group has been gradually changing in composition and sound ever since, but the 1945 band was the first to include all the key traits of bluegrass style; since 1945, Monroe has only augmented, rather than relinquished or greatly modified, the essential performance patterns of his band, though the personnel has changed scores of times.

The new and crucial element in the 1945 band was the banjo playing of Earl Scruggs, of Shelby, North Carolina, who came to the Blue Grass Boys with little professional experience. While with Monroe, Scruggs refined a style that modified earlier three-fingered (thumb, index, middle) banjo-picking methods to attain greater speed, clarity, and melodic flexibility. [*Note:* The question of how much of

"Scruggs style" is actually Scruggs is thorny. *American Banjo "Scruggs" Style,* ed. Ralph Rinzler, Folkways Record FA 2314, presents much relevant data.]

Other instrumental innovations were the flowing, often bluesy and sometimes swiftly moving melodic lines of the fiddle player, Chubby Wise, and the strong, clear bass runs of the guitarist, Lester Flatt, of Sparta, Tennessee. As with Scruggs's banjo playing, the instrumental approaches of these two musicians coupled with the increasingly choppy and jazz-like mandolin of Monroe to become basic to the developing style.

Flatt, a musician with some professional background, often sang the solo lead with the Blue Grass Boys. As time went on, however, Monroe came to pitch his voice higher and sing most of the solos himself. The salient feature of the vocal sound of the early band was the high harmony singing, with Monroe on the tenor above Flatt.

In 1948 Flatt and Scruggs left Monroe to form their own band, the Foggy Mountain Boys, which has become the most popular and financially successful of all bluegrass groups. Their music was based on Monroe's, but the mandolin soon took a less important solo role until, in 1962, it was dropped entirely in favor of a second guitar. [*Note:* Flatt and Scruggs added mandolin again for a brief period in the summer of 1964.] In 1955 the Foggy Mountain Boys added a dobro guitar played by Buck Graves. The instrument had been common in the hillbilly music of the 1930s and, in its electrified (pedal steel) form, in the later country-western music. It now became a part of bluegrass style, emphasizing a more relaxed, less "hot" approach which was further reflected in the increasing smoothness and lower pitch of Flatt's singing and the greater importance of slow and moderately paced tunes in the Foggy Mountain Boys' repertoire. Even with these changes, it is clear that the music of Flatt and Scruggs derives directly from the Blue Grass Boys, conforms to what most bluegrass musicians accept as the essentials of the style, and must therefore be considered a part of bluegrass. Many of the younger bluegrass musicians, in fact, are now more influenced by Flatt and Scruggs than by Bill Monroe.

Ralph and Carter Stanley began playing together professionally over Norton, Virginia, radio in 1946. By 1948 the Stanley Brothers and the Clinch Mountain Boys (the band being named after the brothers' home region in Virginia) were approximating the sound of the Blue Grass Boys. Though Ralph had learned from Scruggs's banjo playing while the brothers were living in Nashville, Tennessee,[1] and Carter was to play guitar for Monroe briefly in 1951, they were less bound by the personal influence of Monroe than Flatt and Scruggs, and thus may be said to have made bluegrass a proper style rather than a "sound" played by a single band and its direct offshoot. The harmony singing of the Clinch Mountain Boys came to place new emphasis on trios, and has been much emulated by other musicians. [*Note:* Neil V. Rosenberg suggested to me the points that the Stanley Brothers made bluegrass a full-fledged style and created new interest in trio singing; he also provided infor-

---

1. Ralph Stanley was exposed to Scruggs's playing when Flatt and Scruggs started broadcasting over WYCB in Bristol but also claimed to have learned from Snuffy Jenkins. Neil V. Rosenberg, *Bluegrass: A History* (Urbana: University of Illinois Press, 1985), 83–84.

mation about Ralph Stanley's relation to Earl Scruggs.] The group has close stylistic links with pre-bluegrass string band music, and a high proportion of traditional songs in its repertoire. Since about 1960 the band has often performed with a second lead guitar instead of a mandolin.

Soon after Flatt and Scruggs left the Blue Grass Boys, a young South Carolina banjoist, Don Reno, joined the band. Monroe has usually encouraged his musicians to imitate the styles and even the most successful recorded solos of their predecessors, and thus Reno played much as Scruggs had done. In 1951, however, Reno left Monroe and joined with Red Smiley, a guitarist and lead singer from Asheville, North Carolina, forming a band which now rivals the Blue Grass Boys and the Flatt and Scruggs group in reputation. Reno's banjo style began to incorporate rhythmic and harmonic ideas from western swing electric guitar and electric steel guitar, and the band has emphasized unusually polychordal instrumentals led by Reno and fiddler Mac Magaha. The group is called the Tennessee Cutups, and earns its name by presenting some of the most elaborate comedy routines among bluegrass acts. Since performances have also included an electric-guitar player who sings in country-western style and Reno's virtuoso exhibitions as a lead guitarist, the Tennessee Cutups are one of the most diversified bluegrass bands in business.

No account of influential bluegrass musicians can fail to mention several other individuals who have introduced innovations that appear to be permanent additions to the style, such as Jesse McReynolds, whose mandolin playing with a single straight pick vaguely approximates Scruggs-style banjo; Sonny Osborne, whose banjo playing has increasingly used elements of pedal-steel guitar from country-western music and whose singing with his brother Bobby similarly reflects the smoothness and flowing quality of country-western style; and William (Brad) Keith, a Boston-bred banjoist whose sojourn with the Monroe band (1963) marked the new importance of the North to bluegrass and introduced a banjo style in which nearly every note had a melodic as well as rhythmic and harmonic relationship to the others.

This short discussion of the most influential bluegrass musicians indicates both the varying emphases placed on different aspects of the style and the decisive role of Bill Monroe in the development of bluegrass. Nearly all of the musicians named above, as well as Jimmy Martin, Mac Wiseman, and members of other important bands such as the Country Gentlemen, the Lonesome Pine Fiddlers, and the Kentucky Colonels—all of these have worked with Bill Monroe for varying periods of time. Monroe himself consciously acknowledges this tutorial function, as do most of his alumni.

Just as the interrelationships of bands and musicians indicate much about bluegrass style, so also do the economic, social, and physical conditions under which the music is performed. Though bluegrass has established its viability through about twenty years of existence, financial reward for bluegrass musicians is not generally substantial. The major bands cited above are the only Southern bluegrass groups whose members can even hope to live exclusively on their earnings as musicians.

The great majority of bluegrass musicians hold non-musical jobs of all kinds, mainly blue-collar, and look up to the fortunate few who can live by their music-making.

One of the main sources of income is the commercial recording industry. But hillbilly records in general account for only 5 to 15 percent of total national record sales, and bluegrass recordings, though in many cases they sell steadily and lose popularity slowly, comprise only a small proportion of the hillbilly segment of the market. A July 1964 compendium of the active sales lists of all but the most peripheral recording companies in the hillbilly field includes about 350 separate performing groups, but only about thirty bluegrass bands. Between January 1945, and September 1964, only twelve bluegrass recordings placed on the weekly listings of the "top ten" hillbilly hits. [*Note: Billboard,* Nov. 2, 1963, sec. 2, 190; *The Billboard Encyclopedia of Music, Eighth Annual Edition: 1946–1947* 1: 548–50; Thurston Moore, ed., *The Country Music Who's Who* (Denver, 1964), pt. 3, 1–22.]

Though the South is far above the nation as a whole in sales of bluegrass records, only a small percentage of the people in any locality can be expected to pay to see or hear bluegrass. Most of the best known bands are therefore situated near large urban centers in the South. No single city, however, can fully support a band that makes only personal appearances, and most of the important bands therefore have heavy schedules of radio and television shows. These are often taped for distribution in many areas, and generally are presented early in the morning when the rural population is a significant proportion of the listening audience. Occasional or weekly appearances on large evening shows similar to the Grand Ole Opry (broadcast from WSM, Nashville, Tennessee) can be important sources of income and publicity.

Though personal appearances are usually less lucrative than time spent in recording or radio-television performance, they are necessary as a further source of publicity and income. Some bands, usually the least successful, play regularly in bars and road houses. County fairs and programs sponsored by various local organizations are further occasions for bluegrass shows. Bands' agents arrange for performances at school auditoriums, outdoor bandstands, and race tracks throughout the South and lower Midwest. In recent years bluegrass bands have performed for audiences in large Northern cities and universities as well. Such appearances, which often necessitate constant traveling by car or private bus, augment income from records and radio and help to provide the rather meager pay of most bluegrass musicians.

Wherever bluegrass bands perform, one factor, the microphone, is nearly always present. In the outdoor bandstand, the auditorium, and the recording studio, most of the audience must hear each instrument and voice through the microphone or not at all. An important part of any bluegrass musician's skill is his ability to maintain the proper relationship, spatially and thus aurally, with the rest of the band and the microphone. A bluegrass band carefully gears its movements and its music to the microphone, and its techniques of integrating voices and instruments as a unified ensemble depend on the use of that device, for without the microphone to give it prominence, the lead part cannot stand out.

Of all the various scenes of bluegrass performances, the most fitting and common seem to be the outdoor park bandstands. These showplaces share some traits with the settings of religious revival meetings and early traveling medicine shows. They are large tracts of land which provide parking areas, roofed stages, and sometimes large, barnlike structures to hold audiences on rainy days. Shows are usually given on Sunday afternoons and evenings during the late spring, summer, and early fall. Families pay approximately one dollar per person to come and spend the day, eating picnic meals or buying food at stands between shows. The performances usually involve several bands and singers representing different branches of hillbilly music and different degrees of polish. To head the bill there is often a well known performer from Nashville, the center for hillbilly music.

When a bluegrass band goes onstage, the leader introduces each musician, and the music quickly begins. Usually, songs follow one another with little talk between them, except when pre-set comedy routines are allowed to interrupt. The band's business is clearly to play music. The first songs performed are often the ones the band has recently recorded. Then follows a selection of the most popular of the group's older songs; some bands, like Monroe's, proceed entirely from this point by answering shouted and written requests from the audience. After they leave the stage, band members often sell record albums and song folios or souvenir programs which contain photographs and song texts. They sign autographs and pose for pictures with those who ask these favors. After the crowd has thinned out following the afternoon show, musicians—local and visiting, good and bad, bluegrass and rockabilly—form groups to experiment with new ideas, show off, renew old musical pleasures, and compare instruments (which have an important prestige function) until the next show goes on stage.

Within the almost ritually consistent framework of such scenes of bluegrass performance, elements of varying cultural derivation can be observed. Flood-lit stages, public address systems, special costuming, and sales pitches are all a part of the pattern. But with bluegrass performances there is less conscious showmanship than in other kinds of hillbilly acts, and dress is usually more subdued. Though the status positions are held by the performing musicians, particularly band leaders, there are few overt manifestations of this fact. The participants, be they general audience, special *aficionados* of bluegrass, or professional musicians, conceive themselves to be members of essentially the same, rural-and-blue-collar, Southern-based social group. This is much less true of country-western music, to which the glamour of Hollywood and million-dollar incomes has become attached. Similarly in contrast with country-western performances, few women participate. The value of the music itself, rather than the personalities of the performers, is primarily affirmed. Applause greets the start of a well known song, as well as its conclusion; and the audience claps at the beginnings of instrumental solos and harmony passages rather than at the ends, indicating its anticipation of the renewal of old pleasures, rather than a considered appreciation for a unique solo just completed. An informal atmosphere predominates, in which the shouts of playing children and joking youths, raucous applause, and casual conversation during performance are usual. Thus is maintained the aura of a gathering of peers ("friends and neighbors") for the sharing of musical and social pleasures common to all and based in a long cultural past.

From both musical and extra-musical evidence, bluegrass is a nexus of many different cultural factors. Since about the turn of this century, four wars and the often traumatic processes of industrialization and urbanization have swiftly displaced millions of Southerners both geographically and culturally, and there has been increasing economic and political pressure upon the South to conform to Northern urban ways of living. Bluegrass is both a symptom of and a reaction against this pressure.

Like Southern culture as a whole, hillbilly music has moved away from its traditional origins and increasingly incorporated elements of national popular music. As Paul Ackerman has noted, "More and more, the so-called traditional country singer has become a victim of the rockabilly—the archetype of which is [Elvis] Presley. . . . Instead of the sour sounding fiddles and guitars, there are lush violin arrangements. . . . Pop-styled vocal choruses are also common in records by present-day country artists." [*Note:* Paul Ackerman, "What Has Happened to Popular Music?" *High Fidelity* 8 (June 1958): 188.]

Since 1945 there has been a steady reduction of non-electrified hillbilly string music available over the air and on disc recordings. Of this diminishing amount of tradition-oriented music, bluegrass has come to comprise a dominant proportion. Fewer than half of the non-electrified professional hillbilly groups recording regularly today are non-bluegrass; and this minority is divided among a number of styles and individual approaches that, unlike bluegrass, are clearly receding in commercial importance. Thus bluegrass has acted as a decisive agent for the preservation in commercially viable form of musical performance values that have hardly survived in the rest of hillbilly music. The jazz-like rhythmic elements and ensemble integration of bluegrass function as a vehicle for the continued use of small non-electrified string groups, relatively simple harmonies, traditional vocal styles and repertoire. Bluegrass thus represents a reaction against the movement of hillbilly music—and perhaps of Southern culture—away from the traditions of rural Appalachia; and the appeal of bluegrass, its means of livelihood, must partially derive from this negative role.

In any case, the musicians are fully aware that their music is less akin to the music of national mass culture than other hillbilly styles, and, of course, that it is less popular and financially successful. Yet they take pride in being bluegrass musicians, and have adopted a set of esthetic standards distinctly their own. They rejoice in the increasing popularity of their style, not only because it enhances their opportunities for making money, but also because they identify closely with the kind of music they play. Whether or not the musicians are conscious of being engaged in rebellion, preservation, or adaptation in performing bluegrass, they clearly feel a need to uphold and affirm their special performance standards. Such attitudes have been implicitly expressed by Bill Monroe:

> A lot of the people down on the Grand Ole Opry kid me about bluegrass. They tell it to me . . . like I really started something. . . , when I started bluegrass, that can't be stopped. I'm really proud of the bluegrass music, and I'm glad to see people play it. You always play it the best way you can. Play it good and clean and play good melodies with it, and keep perfect time. It takes really good timing with bluegrass music, and it takes some good high voices to really deliver it right. [*Note:* Transcribed from a tape of a live performance at Worcester, Massachusetts, November 11, 1963.]

Originally published in the *Journal of American Folklore* 78 (July–Sept. 1965): 245–56. Reprinted by permission of the author.

After "An Introduction to Bluegrass" ran in *Bluegrass Unlimited,* Mayne Smith felt moved to write what newspaper editors would call a reaction story for the magazine about both what general readers may have thought and how one particular reader, Bill Monroe, had greeted the article. The short piece that resulted illustrates Monroe's irritation with the idea that Earl Scruggs was somehow equal with Monroe as a creator of bluegrass. Monroe's insistence that Flatt and Scruggs were merely tangential figures in his creation continued throughout his professional life. He told me in an interview in the 1980s that the duo simply "had a job" with him and that bluegrass was well on its way when they showed up in the Blue Grass Boys. Continuing contention on the issues shows the vitality bluegrass and its history hold for legions of fans. (I've trimmed a short section on Don Reno at the end of this piece.)

10

"Additions and Corrections"

L. MAYNE SMITH

Editor's note: These additions and corrections refer to L. Mayne Smith's "An Introduction to Bluegrass," which appeared in four installments in *Bluegrass Unlimited,* Vol. 1, Nos. 3, 4, 5 and 6.

Now that *BU* readers have had a chance to read my article, I welcome the opportunity to add a few remarks. My guess is that most bluegrass fans will think the article quite dry, and wonder why I sometimes used such fancy language to say such simple things. The main reason for these faults is that I was not writing for blue-grass fans, but for the academic world. Most folklorists and ethnomusicologists have never heard any bluegrass and wouldn't like it if they had. I was trying to show them that such a thing as bluegrass can be studied academically with great profit. I was also indicating to folklorists—who don't usually know music very well—that there is a way to use precise musical data, as well as history, sociology, anthropology, eco-nomics, etc., to extend the meaning and value of studies beyond the narrow inter-ests of traditional folklore scholarship. Not long after the article was printed in the summer of 1965, I turned up at the first Bluegrass Festival at Roanoke. I (perhaps foolishly) brought a copy of the article with me, hoping to learn from the reactions of bluegrass musicians. Before the first day was over, Bill Monroe had looked at the article. Here is the meat of the notes I wrote down right after our subsequent con-versation:

9/2/65—'TALK' WITH BILL MONROE CA. 9:45–10:20 P.M.

BM read my JAF article this afternoon and was quite upset by it. This evening—having been faintly warned of his displeasure—I broached the sub-ject and he quickly showed considerable anger. . . . BM felt I had overstressed Scruggs' importance and underrated his own by saying that bluegrass started in 1945.

From BM's point of view, the "timing" is the essential element in bluegrass ("the same beat as in rock and roll today")—and thus bluegrass existed from 1940 onwards. [Later I heard Bill call "Mule Skinner Blues" the first bluegrass recording.] It was Bill's choice to add banjo. Earl learned along with Don Reno, who joined him in watching radio sessions—from Snuffy Jenkins. Further, Earl, according to BM, hardly knew banjo when he came to the BGB. He could only play "a little roll" and knew only "Cumberland Gap" and "Lonesome Road Blues" in three-finger style.

Other musical elements not stressed to Monroe's satisfaction: the predomi-nant function of the fiddle as *the* lead instrument, ahead of banjo and mando-lin. Bill went on to point out that he has worked hard with his fiddlers. He also did not think the dobro should be called a bluegrass instrument, and thought I implied in my article that the mandolin is "dying out of bluegrass." (I had not meant to say that at all, of course.)

Bill did not stay mad at me long; he knows that I respect him tremendously, and that I had only been trying to tell the truth as I understood it. Even though I was very sorry he got angry, I think I profited greatly from the discussion. After talking it over with others who knew Bill, I think there's not really a serious disagreement between us—especially now that I have taken his suggestion to pay more attention to the fiddle, and the special rhythms of bluegrass.

But I still would not change much of my article if I were to write it again today. The reason is this: in the article I was talking about bluegrass as a phenome-non involving thousands of fans and hundreds of musicians—good, bad and indifferent. While I made it clear that Bill had started the whole thing and is still the greatest bluegrass musician, I also wanted to talk about bluegrass as it is played by all musicians. For Bill, bluegrass is an *idea,* a personal creative impulse. I can see it that way, too—and seen that way, we have to take it from Bill that bluegrass started with "Mule Skinner Blues"; he's the one who knows.

But if you look at bluegrass as a social phenomenon, then you also have to agree that the sound that was copied and changed by all the other bands was the sound of Bill's music from 1945 on. Along the same lines, if you name as "bluegrass" all those instruments that are often used by bluegrass bands, then you have to include the dobro. You may not like the dobro (I'd hate to hear one in Bill's band); but "bad" bluegrass is still bluegrass—at least to me.

Originally published in *Bluegrass Unlimited* 1 (Jan. 1967): 4–6. Reprinted by permission of the author.

N eil Rosenberg's revealing piece on the history of the word *bluegrass* appeared several years before his definitive *Bluegrass: A History.* The essay not only sheds light on how bluegrass got its name but also illuminates the different urban and "true-vine" approaches to the music. An introduction reads, in part, "Neil V. Rosenberg was born in Seattle, Washington and raised in Olympia, Washington, Los Alamos, New Mexico and Berkeley, California. He attended Oberlin College in Ohio and did graduate work at Indiana University. He currently teaches at Memorial University of Newfoundland in St. John's, Newfoundland, Canada. He has been playing Blue Grass music since 1957, and won first prize in the banjo contest at the Brown County Jamboree, Bean Blossom, Indiana, in 1963 and 1965."

11

"Into Bluegrass: The History of a Word"

NEIL V. ROSENBERG

In the March 4, 1974, issue of *The New Yorker,* on page 85, is a cartoon showing a hip-looking young couple in earnest conversation over a record player. The cartoonist, William Hamilton, has the young man saying: "For heaven's sake, Amanda, at least be honest with yourself. I was into bluegrass back when you were still on Vivaldi." Like most of Hamilton's cartoons, this one deals with the snobbery of upper-middle-class urbanites.

It is significant to bluegrass fans for several reasons. *The New Yorker,* one of America's most prestigious literary weeklies, would print a cartoon using the word *bluegrass* only if its editors thought the word was currently in wide enough usage that the cartoon would be comprehensible and funny to a large number of its readers. The cartoon itself comments on the way in which music consumption patterns operate among the trendy young and middle-aged folks who read the magazine. One person was "into" (in other words "consuming"—buying records, going to concerts, etc.) the music of an eighteenth-century Italian classical composer, while the other was "into" the music of twentieth-century southeastern American hillbillies. We can be pretty sure that such striking changes of musical taste reflect a limited amount of involvement, and that within a short time the two characters in the cartoon will have moved on to a new musical favorite—an exotic form like cajun music, a "camp" music suddenly taken seriously, like polka music, or the music of some newly discovered serious composer like Scott Joplin.

Perhaps the vitality of American culture is reflected in the omnivorous way in which urban Americans embrace the musical artifacts of exotic cultures. There are other, less optimistic explanations. Some say that this seeking out of other peoples' traditions is the result of a lack of tradition at home. And others see it as an aspect of capitalistic imperialism and colonialism, leading the richest people on earth to buy and sell and make money out of the music of less affluent peoples. Whether you accept these social or political theories or not, they do remind us that bluegrass is at its present state of popularity because the word *bluegrass* has taken on a special meaning for a large number of English-speaking people. Many of these people would not have purchased records of attended festivals of "hillbilly" or "country" music in the fifties or early sixties, for those words had negative, pejorative meanings to them. "Bluegrass" on the other hand has a positive meaning, because this music has been introduced to them as an art form, a kind of country jazz. How and when this happened has never been studied carefully. But it could only have happened after someone started referring to his favorite hillbilly music as "bluegrass."

At one time, the word *bluegrass* had no musical association whatsoever. It seems quite certain that people were playing the music we now call "bluegrass" before they were calling it "bluegrass." The musical style existed before the word was used to describe it. How and why did that word get hitched to that music?

First of all, the word describes a kind of grass which *The Wise Garden Encyclopedia* tells us is "Poa pratensis, also called June Grass, the standard lawn grass in temperate regions." [*Note:* E. L. D. Seymour, ed., *The Wise Garden Encyclopedia* (New York, 1970), 156.] Native to Europe and Asia, it came to North America with early European colonists. The grass thrives in moderately alkaline soil, and in proper circumstances develops naturally into a lush meadow (the word *pratensis* means "of meadows" in Latin). The first settlers in Kentucky found that the region around what is now Lexington had excellent soluble limestone soil which nourished blue grass. This part of Kentucky with its good meadowland was, from the end of the eighteenth century on, a particularly good place for raising fine horses and also for a number of kinds of agriculture. This was one of the most prosperous sections of Kentucky and became known as "the blue grass." And when it became fashionable for states to adopt nicknames, Kentucky became "The Blue Grass State."

It would be interesting to know which hillbilly group first adopted a regional or state name or nickname to identify itself. I suspect that a search for such information would lead us back into nineteenth-century vaudeville. Whatever the origins, it's clear that by the twenties a number of groups were identifying themselves in this way. Charlie Poole and the North Carolina Ramblers, Henry Whitter's Virginia Breakdowners, the Lone Star Ranch Boys and the Hoosier Sod Busters are a few examples of groups which used state names and nicknames to identify themselves. Such names reflected performers' pride in their home region or state, and helped radio listeners, record buyers and hillbilly show patrons identify and select the music of their region. Usually the name used had either romantic or comic overtones which appealed to both performers and audiences and, in a sense, told the audience: "these musicians are good old country boys from Texas or Indiana or North Carolina; not city slickers." Probably the performers who chose such names did not stop to think about why it would be wise or profitable to use them—they just picked something they liked that fitted both their own origins and the strong hillbilly music tradition of using regional or state names.

So it was hardly surprising that, when Bill and Charlie Monroe decided in 1938 to go separate ways, each chose a name for his group that involved his home state. Charlie called his group the Kentucky Partners and Bill called his the Kentuckians. Bill used this name for only three months, though. He probably dropped it because it was too close to the name Charlie was using, but whatever the reason, when he formed his second band in Atlanta during the winter of 1938–39, he named them the Blue Grass Boys.

Bill Monroe was not the first country musician to use the name "Blue Grass." At least one other person, Blue Grass Roy, had used that name, and I suspect there were others. But because Bill Monroe was on a powerful radio station and recorded for a series of nationally distributed record labels, the name "Blue Grass Boys" became very closely associated with him during the forties. He strengthened the association by naming a number of his compositions after the band—the first was "Blue Grass Special" recorded on February 13, 1945, for Columbia Records. Again, such a practice was not strange or unusual—for instance, Bob Wills and his Texas Playboys had recorded "Playboy Stomp" for Vocalion on June 7, 1937, and Bill Boyd and his Cowboy Ramblers recorded "The Ramblers Rag" for Bluebird on August 7, 1934. Many similar examples could be cited. Between 1945 and 1950 Monroe recorded five instrumentals using the words *Blue Grass*. He used the same words to identify his band's limousine (listen to the words of "Heavy Traffic Ahead," recorded in 1946 for Columbia), and the professional baseball team that traveled with his show in the forties was called the "Blue Grass Ball Club." By the late forties, Monroe had established "Blue Grass" as his trademark, his corporate image.

During the forties a number of groups began to copy the sound of the Blue Grass Boys, and to play the tunes that Monroe had recorded or featured on the Opry. Again, there is nothing unique about this—every musical act that achieves some degree of success is bound to have its imitators. Many musicians playing similar styles were borrowing parts of Monroe's sound in the late thirties and early forties—people like

Carl Story, Roy Hall and the Morris Brothers. I have sketched elsewhere the events that led to the first recorded copy of the Monroe sound, the Stanley Brothers' recording of "Molly and Tenbrooks." [*Note:* Neil V. Rosenberg, "From Sound to Style: The Emergency of Bluegrass," *Journal of American Folklore* 80 (1967): 143–50.] In 1948–49, a musical style based on the music of Monroe and his Blue Grass Boys was being performed on records, on radio and in live appearances in a number of places in the Southeast. Monroe's reaction to this stylistic borrowing is seen in his move from Columbia to Decca Records following Columbia's signing of the Stanley Brothers, because he felt they sounded too much like him. In 1949 Bill Monroe was more concerned with the competition these groups represented than with the flattery their imitation also represented. In view of these facts it seems unlikely Monroe was using "Blue Grass" to refer to anything other than his own band at this time.

How then did the present usage originate? About ten years ago I started asking people how and when they heard that word *bluegrass.* It was already a bit late to start asking, I found. Most of the older fans of the music, those who listened to Monroe on the Opry in the forties, knew exactly what the word meant when they first heard it. This instant identification (which accounts for the rapid spread of the word) led to a situation in which many people confused the sound of the music with the name they had come to associate with it. So they answered my question by describing the first time they heard the music. This kind of response was not unexpected, for we usually are not aware of the way in which new words and phrases slip into our vocabulary. Words are tools that we use in a very un-self-conscious way. For example, try to remember when you first heard or spoke the phrase "No way!" It has been around for only a few years, but already its origins are obscure.

The earliest date I have found for the use of the word to describe the music comes from the late Marvin Hedrick of Nashville, Brown County, Indiana. A native of Brown County, Hedrick had grown up listening to the Opry and other country radio programs in the thirties and forties. He played the guitar and was known to local musicians for the weekly jam sessions he held in the workshop of his radio-television shop. He occasionally played at local square dances. During an interview with me in December 1965, he told about the early fifties in Brown County, when Bill Monroe purchased the Brown County Jamboree in nearby Bean Blossom. Marvin got to know Birch Monroe who was managing the Jamboree, and he put pressure on Birch to book his favorites—the Stanley Brothers, the Lonesome Pine Fiddlers, and Mac Wiseman. "Bluegrass or old-time, what I was interested in," he said. I asked, "When did you start hearing those terms used—bluegrass and old-time?" He replied: "You know, I guess, bluegrass, the first guy I remember [using] that was Harold Lowry [a local musician]. It was in 1953, and Harold said, 'Why don't we come out some night and we'll pick a little bluegrass?' That's the first time I ever heard the term used. I think the term come into being right about that time." I asked about disc jockeys using the word, and he said, "I can't remember hearing disc jockeys use it until maybe five years ago, any to speak of." Did he remember Monroe or any of his musicians using the name, I wondered? "No, I don't think Monroe—I think Monroe just kinda sits back and lets the rest of the people say it." For Marvin

Hedrick and others around Brown County in the fifties, the word definitely referred to the kind of music Monroe was playing. I asked if the music had to have the banjo to qualify as bluegrass, and he said, "Not necessarily the banjo. I'd say that it's the general beat and feel of the music rather than the instruments." He continued by saying that "old-time" had been used ever since he could remember to describe music connected with square dancing.

Thus, from 1953 onward, "bluegrass" was a term used in southern Indiana by the small group of local musicians who listed to Bill Monroe, the Stanley Brothers, the Lonesome Pine Fiddlers, Mac Wiseman and others. They were aware of many of these groups only via radio broadcasts (which Marvin Hedrick and some others occasionally tape-recorded) and records. They listened to country radio stations in hope of hearing their favorites. None of them listened solely to this kind of music; it was just their favorite country music style.

This music has been especially popular in the region around Washington, D.C., since the early fifties. Don Owens was one of its supporters; he was a disc jockey on WEAM in Arlington, Virginia, as early as 1952. For a while he had his own band that at one point included Buzz Busby, and he later owned a record company, Blue Ridge. There are strong indications that he was a very influential promoter of the music in this region. When did he start using the term *bluegrass?* I don't know, and unfortunately Don Owens was killed in an auto accident in 1963.

Another active promoter of bluegrass in this region during the fifties was Michael Seeger, whose 1959 notes to the Folkways LP, *Mountain Music Bluegrass Style* (FA 2318) were the first detailed description of the style. When I asked him where he first heard the word, he said he thought he'd first heard it from Peter V. Kuykendall (Roberts). In fact, he suspected that Kuykendall made it up! Kuykendall, who is now editor of *Bluegrass Unlimited,* was a well-known local banjo player and disc jockey in the Washington area during the fifties. In the sixties he became a producer of bluegrass recordings. He could not remember where he'd heard the term first, but thought it might have been from Don Owens. Here, as in Brown County, local musicians and fans were using the word to refer to their favorite music. In both places, the word was the special property of what sociologists would call an in-group.

There was one such group of young urban people who were listening to the music at this time. Ralph Rinzler told James Rooney:

> There were a few of us from the city who were following Bill—Mike Seeger, myself, Ray Forshag, Jerry and Alice Foster. Mike and I would go to various parks sorting out who we liked—Bill, the Stanley Brothers, Grandpa Jones, Don Reno—but bluegrass had not got into the folk revival. But for me it was like going into another world. I was fascinated by the totally different lifestyle— dinner on the grounds, different speech patterns—a whole different way of life. The whole idea of it really astounded me—that this existed. That was in fifty-four and fifty-five.

These were people for whom bluegrass and other kinds of country music had previously existed (if they knew about them at all) only on record. They were not country music fans; they were the advance guard of the folksong revival—a new group of listeners who perceived bluegrass as a separate and distinct musical art form. Educated in American folk music via Folkways and Library of Congress recordings which emphasized Appalachian folk music traditions, they quickly recognized the folk elements in bluegrass repertoire. And they discovered the five-string banjo was alive and well in bluegrass. At this time, the only person outside country music using the instrument was Pete Seeger. He had a number of imitators within the folksong revival, but at this point in time—before the Kingston Trio—the folksong revival was probably a much smaller phenomenon than bluegrass.

The folksong revival was, in the United States, the product of left-wing political theorizing during the middle and late thirties. But the openly political goals of its leaders—Woody Guthrie, and Almanac Singers, Pete Seeger and the staff of *Peoples' Songs* (which became *Sing Out!*)—were not so important for many of the followers. These folksong enthusiasts, most of whom lived in the New York City region, were excited by the music which was an appealing alternative to the insipid pop music and the difficult-to-follow jazz of the period. Leadbelly (Huddie Ledbetter) brought the twelve-string guitar to young New Yorkers; Pete Seeger brought the five-string banjo. Even in the late forties Pete Seeger had a number of disciples in Greenwich Village. One of these early disciples, Roger Sprung, remembers being told about Earl Scruggs by another early disciple, Billy Faier, at a party in Greenwich Village in 1947 or 1948. In the early fifties, Pete Seeger published a five-string banjo instruction book. In 1955 he revised it and prepared a record, *The Five-String Banjo Instructor,* to accompany it (Folkways FP 303), which included a section on "three-finger picking (Scruggs' style)."

"Scruggs' style" banjo was popular with the young five-string banjo fanatics who congregated every Sunday afternoon, from spring to fall, around the fountain at Washington Square in New York City's Greenwich Village. Folkways Records was aware of this when they released, early in 1957, the first bluegrass LP, *American Banjo Scruggs Style* (Folkways FA 2314). Recorded by Mike Seeger, the record included a brochure with an introduction written by Ralph Rinzler, who described how, in 1945, "a well known mandolin picker and singer in Kentucky, Bill Monroe, organized a different type of band from those already in existence." A brief description of Scruggs and his style followed, and then a bit more history:

> Scruggs worked with Monroe for a short time before he and Lester Flatt, then Monroe's guitar picker, organized a band of their own. Before long this type of music was becoming popular in the South. The banjo, along with many of the "old-time" songs, had been revived and numerous "bluegrass" bands, patterned on those of Scruggs and Monroe, were soon doing performances and making recordings for well-known companies.

Here, as far as I can tell, is the first time that the word *bluegrass* was used in print to refer to a musical style. Rinzler continued with an explanation of how the word became attached to a style of music:

The term *bluegrass* refers to that section of Kentucky where Bill Monroe originally lived and where the music was most popular at the outset. It was applied to this music by disc-jockeys and is descriptive of a band usually consisting of a guitar and bass, used for backing, and one or two fiddles, a banjo and a mandolin used for lead or solo playing. The songs themselves, if not actually folk or "old-time" songs, generally are closer to that tradition than to the modern tradition of popular Tin Pan Alley or hillbilly songs.

We can overlook the several obvious inaccuracies in this description, for Rinzler himself has since corrected the account in his articles and liner notes on Monroe. The lasting importance of the statement lies in the way in which it defines "bluegrass." Emphasis is placed on instrumentation and the roles of instruments, and the closeness of the songs to folksong traditions is stressed. The fact that both Monroe and Flatt and Scruggs were Grand Old Opry stars is not mentioned, and the songs are carefully differentiated from popular "hillbilly" songs. The message is: This is a kind of modern folk music, defined largely by its instrumentation. Contrast this with the definition that I quoted before from Marvin Hedrick, who had been using the word since about 1953: "it's the general beat and feel of the music rather than the instruments."

What this early, perhaps first, appearance of "bluegrass" in print signifies is that by 1957 there were two ways of looking at the same kind of music—as a special kind of country music, and as a special kind of folk music. Debates about the definition of the term became possible once it spread beyond the oral traditions of those early die-hard fans who knew what the word meant when they heard it. By having a name, bluegrass was automatically defined as a special style, even though there might be disagreements about what made it a special style.

The word popped up frequently in print during 1957. The bimonthly *Cowboy Songs* issue number 50 for February 1957 included pictures and write-ups on two bands using the word *bluegrass* in their names. On page twenty was a story about the Bluegrass Champs, winners the previous year at the Warrenton (Va.) country music contest and on the *Arthur Godfrey Show*. The article called them the "Stoveman family" but in fact they were the Stoneman Family, then playing at dances and bars in the Washington, D.C., area. The article does not mention that the Family could be heard on Folkway FA 2315 *The Stoneman Old-Time Tunes of the South*, edited by Ralph Rinzler, or that Veronica Stoneman Cox appeared on Folkways' *American Banjo Scruggs Style*. Conversely the notes to these records do not mention that the Stoneman Family was calling itself the "Bluegrass Champs."

On page 24 of the same issue was an article on Curley Parker and Pee Wee Lambert, who called themselves the "Bluegrass Pardners." They were currently appearing on WJEL in Springfield, Ohio. This group had been together since at least December 1951 when they were appearing as "The Pine Ridge Boys" on WHTN radio in Huntington, West Virginia. Lambert had been mandolin player for the Stanley Brothers during their formative years, and was the person most responsible for moving their style closer to that of Bill Monroe. This was because he was an ardent fan and student of Monroe. So it's logical that when the word *bluegrass* became a generic term Pee Wee Lambert and Curley Parker would be among the first to adopt the word for a band name.

Also in 1957, the Grand Ole Opry published an updated and revised edition of *WSM's Official Grand Ole Opry History-Picture Book,* Vol. 1, No. 2. In it was a brief description of Flatt and Scruggs which included the following, "A simple and solid presentation of grass-roots entertainment, this pair is known in the trade as sincere salesmen of 'blue grass music'" (page 20). The same book included, on page 33, a description of Bill Monroe that did not use the phrase *blue grass music,* even though it did mention the name of the band!

Perhaps the best indication of the spreading popularity of the word came in Charleton publications' *Country Song Roundup,* issue number 52 for October 1957. On page 29 of this magazine was a full page ad for the Jimmie Skinner Music Center in Cincinnati, Ohio. This shop had been running ads in *Country Song Roundup* since the February 1956 issue (number 42). From the outset they had included Sonny Osborne record specials, advertised as "Featuring Five-String Banjo." On several occasions during 1956 the Skinner ad included a special section of five-string banjo instrumentals. Now, in the October 1957 issue, the ad read: "Best Selling Blue Grass Type Records (featuring five-string banjo, mandolin, etc.)."

With both the Skinner ad and the Flatt and Scruggs description in the Opry book, the term *blue grass* was used to identify the music for potential consumers. The in-group term had been adapted for marketing purposes by the country music industry, just as it was adapted for educational purposes by the folksong revival. In 1958 and 1959 the first LPs with "bluegrass" in their titles appeared; and articles on bluegrass were published in the *New York Times, Esquire, Sing Out!* and *Caravan.* The word spread rapidly after 1957, once it had gotten into print.

As it became fashionable to know about "bluegrass" and profitable to sell music as "bluegrass," non-fans began to misuse the word. In 1959, *Sing Out!* labeled the New Lost City Ramblers' music "bluegrass," prompting reader protests which forced an editorial retraction in the following issue. By the early sixties Starday Records of Nashville was marketing "Bluegrass Samplers" which included performances by people such as Stringbean, and *Time* even went so far as to describe Buck Owens' music as "electric bluegrass." The word took on a life of its own in print, separate from that of the music.

It would be interesting to know just how early that word was being used to describe the musical style. The earliest date I have encountered is 1953, but I'm hoping that some of the older fans of the music who read *Muleskinner News* can remember where and how they first encountered "bluegrass" in the early fifties. Perhaps it's only a question of historical detail, but my personal feeling is that the person or persons who started calling their favorite hillbilly music "bluegrass" really gave the musical style a life of its own because they gave it a name.

Editor's note: Publishing of this article provides an opportune occasion for us to explain our somewhat controversial policy of always spelling "Blue Grass" as two capitalized words rather than the more common "bluegrass."

It seems logical that if Kentucky is the "Blue Grass" state, and Bill Monroe named his band the "Blue Grass" Boys, then the music should be "Blue Grass" music. I've talked to Neil Rosenberg about this, and he feels "bluegrass" has become a common usage, somehow illustrating the trend taken by the style away from Bill Monroe's personal sound to a more diffused public domain.

I feel "Blue Grass" is not only more dignified, but a proper tribute to the music's origin. Sure, it's a minor point, and I know we're swimming against the tide. "Blue Grass" somehow just seems more correct. Your comments on this point are welcome.

Originally published in *Muleskinner News* 5 (Aug. 1974): 7–9, 31–33. Reprinted by permission of Carlton Haney.

T he country music scholar Charles Wolfe pointed out to me not long ago how efficiently Mike Seeger honed in on the basic touchstones of bluegrass in these pioneering liner notes for the Folkways LP *Mountain Music Bluegrass Style* (1959). Seeger looks at both sociological and musical influences as he details the picking and singing styles, natural habitat, commercial environment, and increasingly diverse audience for the music. Born in 1936 in New York City, Seeger grew up in the Washington, D.C., suburbs and started taking an active interest in traditional music in the early 1950s.

As a member of the New Lost City Ramblers, he became a leading champion of a wide range of pre-bluegrass styles. One of the very earliest musicians to come to bluegrass, so to speak, from the outside in, Seeger has remained a leading exponent of traditional music of several sorts through a half century of performing, record producing, and journalism.

12

"Mountain Music Bluegrass Style"

MIKE SEEGER

Bluegrass, the term, came into use in the early 1950s, originally referring to the music of Bill Monroe, from Kentucky, the Bluegrass State, and his Blue Grass Boys, a group that for twenty years has appeared on the Grand Ole Opry in Nashville and made records for Bluebird, Columbia, and Decca. Bluegrass describes a specific vocal and instrumental treatment of a certain type of traditional or folk-composed song. Vocally the style is characterized by high-pitched, emotional singing. In duets, Monroe's high tenor voice is dominant in volume and interest in harmony above the lead part using unorthodox, often modal and minor sounding intervals, prob-

ably influenced by his childhood church singing as well as by early country musicians such as the Carter Family. Often a third, or baritone, part is added, usually
below the lead voice and in gospel songs there is often a bass singer. Harmony in
parallel thirds, popular in more formal music, is rarely used, and Monroe's tenor
(harmony) often seems to be a separate and superior melody. The singers are also
the instrumentalists.

Instrumentally, Bluegrass music is a direct outgrowth of traditional hill music
styles, its two most distinctive features being that it has no electrified instruments
and that it uses a five-string banjo for lead or background in all songs. The guitar
player, most commonly also the lead singer, supplies the band with an open (not
"slap" [or rhythm] style) chord background, much like the Carter Family style, with
a few melodic runs such as Flatt's famous G run, but rarely takes an instrumental
lead. The five-string banjo is played in a style like that of Earl Scruggs who introduced his new style on Monroe's early Columbia records. See Folkways record
American Banjo Tunes and Songs in Scruggs Style FA 2314 for more on this. The fiddle
player uses odd double stops and slides that vary from breakdown to country blues,
a smooth style initiated largely by the Florida fiddler Chubby Wise, also on the early Monroe Columbia records. Monroe's mandolin playing is driving and syncopated
and like the fiddling is influenced by both blues and breakdown styles. The string
bass supports the guitar by picking on the downbeat with an occasional lead, and
the bass player usually is dressed in a ridiculous costume and provides the comedy
skits and songs. The songs themselves are mostly built on traditional patterns, four-
line verse, three or four chords and in simple $\frac{2}{4}$ or $\frac{3}{4}$ time; instrumentals are usually
in a breakneck $\frac{4}{4}$ time and like the songs are performed with great skill. Often new
songs are made from the old with a change of words, harmony, treatment, or pace.
The subject matter is most usually unsuccessful love but also covers home, mother,
catastrophes, religion and almost anything else under the sun. Monroe has written
a large number of his own songs, as do many other artists.

Bluegrass is directly related to the old corn-shucking party banjo and fiddle
music as well as the ballad songs and religious music of the southern mountains.
With the influx of the guitar, mandolin, and string bass from the cities of the Deep
South in the early 1900's, mountain people such as the Carter Family, Blue Sky Boys,
and especially in this case, Bill and Charlie, the Monroe Brothers, began adapting
old songs previously sung unaccompanied or with banjo and fiddle to the new instruments (with likewise new singing styles) and made these songs acceptable as a
performance. There were several other bands in this era that could also be called
pre-Bluegrass: the Mainers with their four-piece band and (sometimes) smooth
singing, and Byron Parker, who even had a banjo-picker, Snuffy Jenkins, who played
a style much like Earl Scruggs and came from the same area in North Carolina.

But not until Bill Monroe, Earl Scruggs, Lester Flatt, and Chubby Wise came
together after World War II did the Bluegrass band take its classic and most competent form. When the records of this group were released, old-time music and
especially five-string banjo-picking were in decline and the early Monroe Colum-

bias plus his show on the Opry brought new attention to the old-time music. Several groups such as the Stanley Brothers who had been playing old-time music with thumb-style banjo started working more towards Bluegrass.

Lester Flatt, a singer and guitar player, and Earl Scruggs, the five-string banjo-picker, formed a five-piece band, the Foggy Mountain Boys, with a style much like Monroe's but more polished, and featuring Earl's banjo-picking and Lester's singing. Mac Wiseman sang revised old sentimental songs with his clear tenor voice; Jesse McReynolds picks the mandolin somewhat like Scruggs style with a flat pick; Jimmy Martin features novelty songs; the Osborne Brothers specialize in smooth, close, trio singing and their own banjo and mandolin styles; Don Reno plays an expert, jazzy, harmonic plectrum banjo style (as opposed to Earl's melodic style) which is also more suited to their slow dance songs and has gained many converts; the Stanley Brothers feature good old-time Bluegrass music.

By about 1953 Bluegrass music reached its height of popularity, with no less than ten different bands on commercial records. And many smaller amateur bands sprang up through the South, perhaps one in every town of a thousand population. With such competition and with advanced recording techniques Bluegrass changed more quickly. "Bluegrass" became more a means of distinguishing any type of traditional music from the run-of-the-mill performance by the steel guitars of the Nashville Philharmonic and later, hillbilly rock 'n' roll. Bands are now called Bluegrass that contain one element of the original style, for example, the Louvin Brothers' singing and playing (but not their electric and Hawaiian-style guitars) or Charlie Monroe's singing (despite his electrified band members) or any number of combinations of less than the five main instruments such as banjo-fiddle duet, two guitars, a bass and banjo duet, etc., etc. . . . Bluegrass, like other types of music, is constantly changing and searching for combinations that will give them something new and put them a step ahead of the competing groups. Flatt and Scruggs now include in their band a Dobro guitar, fretted Hawaiian-style with a steel bar, unelectrified and often played like a banjo. Other bands have experimented with duets on instrumentals and instrumental breaks and with adding mouth harps, pianos, organs, tiple, or accordion but so far only the Dobro and instrumental duets have been accepted into the style. The trend in singing is away from the country twang towards smoother, more widely acceptable harmony. One of the greatest changes brought about in Bluegrass is the new method of "hi fi" recording and pressing of records and the use of the echo chamber, which gives it the full orchestra sound, destroying the home-made effect.

Also changing is the Bluegrass audience. Old-time hill music has always appealed to the individualistic mountain people since it is deeply rooted in their tradition and they feel that it is an expression of their preserving that tradition. But many of these have come to prefer the more sophisticated music of the commercial country music bands, or even rock 'n' roll. Many city-bred people however have been hearing and buying records by the Bluegrass artists, this being part of the urban revival of folk music. It is mainly a musician's music and is appreciated even by many commercial musicians (including Presley, whose first release was Bill Monroe's composition "Blue Moon of Kentucky"), who consider it a desirable part of all country music.

The main outlets for the six or so larger bands are on T.V., radio, theatres, school auditoriums, barn dances, summer amusement parks (such as New River Ranch and Sunset Park), country music jamborees like the Grand Ole Opry and the Wheeling W. Va. Jamboree, and through their records, on the many disc jockey shows on small radio stations throughout the South. The most successful of these touring bands, Flatt and Scruggs, can draw huge crowds of five or ten thousand as far north as New York City, as well as having a contract for daily radio and T.V. shows with a large dependable sponsor that even provides for them a bus that carries them thousands of miles weekly on well-organized tours. Their record sales, like other bluegrass bands, though not of "hit" proportions, are long and steady and many people are still buying their records that were issued five or ten years ago.

The smaller bands don't have quite such an easy time of it and play occasional shows or depend upon a job at a cabaret or night club which affects them musically and psychologically. The musicians themselves often hold factory and mill jobs in addition to their music playing at night, and some of the best give it up altogether in their early twenties rather than "go commercial" or play in a club.

The decrease in opportunity for the smaller bands is due to a great number of factors, the greatest being the development of the "D.J." shows on radio which replaced the small, locally originating live music programs with a large amount of recorded commercial country music and created at the same time a demand for local shows by these same large bands, usually from the Grand Ole Opry. The juke box and rock 'n' roll have also done their part, along with the fact that few Bluegrass musicians are good businessmen, an all-too-necessary quality in today's country music field.

Despite all this to the contrary, Bluegrass does not appear to slowing down at all and probably won't in the near future. It will certainly change, become smoother and technically more difficult, but young people will continue to play and sing, and make up songs for fun and hope for the day that they might go professional.

Liner notes for *Mountain Music Bluegrass Style,* Folkways FA 2318 (1959). Reprinted by permission of Smithsonian/Folkways Recordings.

M uleskinner News contributor Joe Wilson contributes the firsthand memories of a fan to this account of a historic radio station, even if his admitted lack of detail on some points does not meet the highest standards of precision. It's clear that Wilson was writing for a tuned-in audience; he didn't feel it necessary to tell readers basic information about Bill Monroe or Flatt and Scruggs. As Wilson's list of performers who held forth at the station shows, WCYB was an important cradle of the bluegrass movement. It started operations in December 1946 and reached listeners not only in Tennessee and Virginia but also in West Virginia, and Kentucky.[1] Radio stations such as WCYB and WPTF in Raleigh, North Carolina, served bluegrass acts both as employers and as far-reaching devices for publicizing records and live performances.

13

"Bristol's WCYB: Early Bluegrass Turf"

JOE WILSON

Bristol has two of everything: two mayors, two police chiefs, two post offices, two city councils, two large high schools. The middle of State Street, main street for the city, is the Tennessee-Virginia border and lane-swapping drivers can enter and leave a state with a twitch of the wheel.

The two-of-everything consistency of Bristol holds even for part of the musical history of the city. It was on the Tennessee side of State Street forty-five years ago that pioneer recording engineer Ralph Peer made the first recordings of two of the greatest acts of old-time music a few days apart—Jimmie Rodgers and the Carter Family.

A short distance away, on the Virginia side of State Street, is another site of importance in musical history. There's not much to see there, but this was the site of WCYB. During the late 1940's and 1950's many Blue Grass and old-time musicians gathered at the WCYB microphones; and some of the best still playing can trace their professional beginnings to this spot.

Lester Flatt and Earl Scruggs came to WCYB after leaving Bill Monroe; and the Farm and Fun Time announcer usually introduced Flatt with a line so bad that I can still remember it—"Here's the man with the hat, Lester Flatt." Listeners of the daily program supported and sustained Flatt and Scruggs and other early groups during the formative years of the sound, before the term *Blue Grass* was known. In turn, Flatt and Scruggs were the most influential band to play there; and they set the stage for much that happened there later.

Mac Wiseman came to the station at least twice. He had a band of his own there in 1947 and returned in '48 to do some memorable singing with Lester Flatt, Earl Scruggs and the Foggy Mountain Boys. He stayed briefly, then drifted on. Everett Lilly also joined Flatt and Scruggs for a short stint there.

The Stanley Brothers certainly equaled, and may have even surpassed, Flatt and Scruggs in local popularity. With daily programs heard over what was at best an area

---

1. Neil Rosenberg, "From Sound to Genre: 1946–1949," in *Bluegrass: A History* (Urbana: University of Illinois Press, 1985), 80–82.

within a hundred miles of the station and with limited distribution of a few records, they enjoyed an artistic and financial success that would be enviable today.

Once I saw the Stanleys fill an auditorium that would seat 450 people to capacity twice on a single Saturday night. (I know the capacity because it was the auditorium of the high school I attended.) This was in a town of 1,200 in a county of ten thousand. Forced to leave after the first show so that people outside could get in for the second show, I examined the shiny new Cadillac they had parked near a rear door. Then I joined others who had gathered at the open windows to hear more good Blue Grass until the second show ended; they emerged, still dripping sweat, and signing the song and picture books they had sold.

From the beginning they combined the graceful vocal harmonies of a "brother" act with hard-driving instrumentation to produce a music with power and depth. I thought then that it was the best music I'd heard, and time has had very little effect on that opinion.

The Stanleys were at WCYB early, beginning about 1948 for a stint of two or three years, and then returned later in the fifties. They were one group that could make frequent reappearances in the towns of that area. Even their comedy was good—far better than the "rube" comedy used by most groups at that time. At one point they featured old-time musician Clarence (Tom) Ashley doing portions of his act "Rastus Jones from Georgia." The old-timer had perfected his wildly funny routines in thousands of medicine show and stage appearances and Carter Stanley was a convincing actor in his parts. Ashley had many talents but his talent for comedy was probably his greatest gift. He was later caught up in the folk revival of the early sixties as a musician, but his comedy skills were probably last seen in his appearances with the Stanleys.

Bill and Earl Bolick, the Blue Sky Boys, were at WCYB shortly before they ended their career.[2] Like the Monroe Brothers, they influenced other "brother" acts of the area. One of the best of these, and one that was surely influenced by the Bolicks, later came to WCYB. Even then they called themselves "the Virginia Boys." But Jim and Jesse McReynolds were a mandolin-guitar duo then, and unless my memory is playing tricks with me, one of them played fiddle on some numbers.

Most of WCYB's live programming of Blue Grass and old-time music was confined to the two-hour daily Farm and Fun Time show, beginning at 12 noon, Monday through Saturday. An exception was the hymn programs that a few bands had on Sunday mornings at various times in the history of the station. Usually only one band had a Sunday morning "hymn time," and it was early, beginning at 7 or 8 A.M.

I recall hearing Carl Story first on "hymn time" programs; though he was also a Farm and Fun Time regular. At the time Story called his band the "Rambling

---

2. Bill and Earl Bolick retired from the music business in 1951 but then regrouped for performances and recordings in the 1960s. Bill C. Malone, "The Blue Sky Boys," in *The Encyclopedia of Country Music: The Ultimate Guide to the Music,* comp. by the staff of the Country Music Hall of Fame and Museum, ed. Paul Kingsbury (New York: Oxford University Press, 1998), 39.

Rumbling Mountaineers." He featured the mandolin "turn-arounds" between verses that have since become common in Blue Grass gospel singing. I'm sure that Bill Monroe started this, but Story's band adapted it and has in turn been widely imitated by others. I seem to recall that "Little Red" Rector was behind that mandolin, but since it has been twenty-odd years, and I was ten or eleven at the time, I'm inclined not to trust my memory about specifics of that sort. I do recall that Red was at WCYB and that his mandolin playing was excellent.

Bob Osborne was another mandolin player found in front of the WCYB microphones for a brief period. He came there with Jimmy Martin in the early fifties. Still another mandolinist who served time there was Curly Seckler. From the early days with Earl Scruggs and Ralph Stanley until live programming ended in the late fifties, there were good five-string men at the station. I first heard Larry Richardson and Porter Church on WCYB. Naming all the fiddlers who played there would be almost as difficult as naming all of the fiddlers who drink hard liquor, but I can recall a few: Leslie Keith, Chubby Anthony, Art Wooten and Lester Woodie with the Stanleys, Ralph Mayo, Charlie Cline, Curley Ray Cline and Bob Slone were there. Yes, the same Bob Slone who now plays bass with J. D. Crowe. He was a teenager at the time and was billed as an "upside down" (left-handed) fiddler in a band that Buster Pack fronted at WCYB.

Remembering "Fiddlin' Ralph" Mayo and Porter Church there brings to mind one of the good unsung bands that played at WCYB. This group was called the Southern Mountain Boys and was fronted by the Kingsport fiddler. There were personnel changes over a period of two or three years (Mayo stayed longer than most musicians), but among the best musicians with Mayo were Church and blind guitarist Jack Cassidy. Cassidy provided a piercing tenor lead and joined Mayo in tasteful duets. Mayo took the lead at times and had a pleasing voice of unusual timbre, especially in gospel singing. The group was always paced by a driving banjo, and Mayo's droning fiddle lent an archaic flavor that was very appealing to me. Although Mayo recorded a few cuts with the Stanley Brothers and also made a few 78s using the Southern Mountain Boys name, I've yet to hear a recording that captured this band at its best.

Bonnie Lou and Buster Moore had a long run at the station with Lloyd Bell. Buster played mandolin and frailed the banjo as he does today; and the group toured with the "cowboy" act of Homer Harris for a part of their stay. Bonnie Lou, Buster and Lloyd were a trio throughout their WCYB stay and had an old-time flavor. They didn't add steel guitar and other electric instruments until they moved to WJHL-TV in Johnson City, Tennessee in the early fifties.

A few novelty acts toured at times with WCYB musicians. "Suicide" Jones toured ball parks and other outdoor shows with Mayo's group. The "suicide" act consisted of Jones climbing into a plywood "coffin" and placing a stick of dynamite a few inches from his head and detonating the charge. For these festivities "Suicide" very judiciously donned a football helmet and placed a thick sheet of steel between his head and the charge. Mayo also carried a "hell driver" automobile act with him at one point. But of all the novel acts that passed by the WCYB microphones, bass-player "Lindy" Clear of Hansonville, Virginia, had one of the most unique. "Lindy's" forte was rural sound effects and his ability to vocally re-create complex sequences of sound was amazing. He reproduced the starting of a wheezy Model T from the first spin of the crank and futile hiss of the motor through several false starts until he finally sent the weary farmer backfiring and spluttering over a hill. His "dog meeting a dog" contained all of the growls, sniffings and explorations of two tough mutts meeting for the first time and the inevitable dogfight that followed. His ear-splitting mule bray punctured many instrumentals, and even a long-legged jarhead calling for some hay had to be in good voice and enthusiastic in order to match it.

On the air WCYB musicians sold feed for farm animals, rat poison, flour, soft drinks, laxatives, headache powders, chewing tobacco, snuff, fertilizer, insecticides, menstrual tension remedies, baking powder, "overhalls," used cars, chain saws, farm tools, and—you name it. Recently a friend asked what song was most associated with Charlie Monroe: I remembered his Wildroot Cream Oil jingle first and "Rose Connolly" second. This is just an example of how effective some of the radio selling was.

Originally published in *Muleskinner News* 3 (Oct. 1972): 8–10. Reprinted by permission of Carlton Haney.

The Monroes and Flatts and Scruggses of the world made their names on creativity and star quality. But from one point of view, they made their marks in large part through the contributions of the legions of side musicians who made up their bands. *Bluegrass Unlimited* contributor Wayne Erbsen's evocative portrait of fiddler Jim Shumate shows how a musician in the hinterlands can have his life changed forever by one telephone call from a major figure in search of a new player. In turn, Shumate's fiery fiddling affected the course the newborn music would take. The piece also offers an interesting, if brief, look at life on the road for one of the first female bluegrass musicians, Wilene (Sally Ann) Forrester. Erbsen follows the sound journalistic practice of letting Shumate, a good talker, talk at length.

14

"Jim Shumate—Bluegrass Fiddler Supreme"

WAYNE ERBSEN

It's a long drive from Raleigh, North Carolina to Nashville, Tennessee. Before Interstate 40 was cut through North Carolina, driving west from Raleigh meant winding through such towns as Siler City, Mocksville, Statesville, Hickory, and Old Fort.

Bill Monroe is no stranger to that road. In the forty odd years he has been performing, he has worn out many a set of tires driving that road. Being a bluegrass musician has meant accepting show dates spread out all over the country; it never seems to matter how many miles lie between. To pass the time, Monroe has often tuned in the nearest radio outlet in hopes of catching a country music station. One day in early 1943, while driving near Hickory, North Carolina, Monroe chanced to pick up WHKY, broadcasting from downtown Hickory. It was noon time and Don Walker was doing a live show with his Blue Ridge Boys.

The program presented by Don Walker and his group was typical of many country bands during that period. There were two guitars, a mandolin, fiddle and banjo. Along with the usual comedy routines and skits, their show featured both sacred and secular songs interspersed with fiddle tunes like "Katy Hill" and "Grey Eagle." It was the fiddling that especially caught Monroe's ear as he was traveling down Highway 64 and 70 headed toward Nashville. Before the program was over, Walker had introduced all the band members, and Monroe did not forget the name of the fiddler: Jim Shumate. It was not long after Monroe reached Nashville that he put in a call to the twenty-year old musician.

Howdy Forrester, who had been Monroe's fiddler, had just given his notice. It was war time, and the Navy had plans for Howard Forrester. Suddenly needing a fiddle player, Monroe chose Shumate. "One day I got a call from Bill Monroe. 'Course all my life I'd always wanted to be at the Grand Ole Opry. That was my idol. I'd listened to those guys ever since I first started playing the fiddle, but never dreamed I'd ever be there. So the telephone rang and a voice said, 'This is Bill Monroe.' That shook me up, you know. He said, 'Now you play the fiddle, don't you? You've got Howdy Forrester, Tommy Magness, and three or four others all mixed up together. If you play that type of fiddle, that's what I want.'"

So Monroe offered Shumate the job as fiddler with the Blue Grass Boys. Within days, Shumate packed his bags, tucked his fiddle under his arm, and caught the bus to Nashville. Although Monroe had only heard Shumate fiddle a few tunes over the radio before hiring him, he knew that he'd found the fiddler for the job. But he was mistaken in thinking that Shumate had learned from Howdy Forrester or Tommy Magness. Shumate's real influence was Fiddling Arthur Smith. "I learned off of Arthur Smith and The Dixieliners, the king of the fiddlers. He was what enthused me to want to play the fiddle. I fiddle a lot of his tunes today; I never have gotten away from it."

"I never got to see Smith in person but one time. It was at the Grand Ole Opry when he was playing fiddle with Jimmy Wakely. I admired him all of my life, from the time I was a little shaver on up. He was considerably older than I was. I didn't even get to talk to him. The dressing room was so full, so many people crowding around. Jimmy Wakely was a pretty big movie star at that time, and I just got close enough to see Smith. He was a genius, a flat genius, when it comes to playing the fiddle. He fiddled stuff like nobody else, like nobody you ever heard. Smooth he didn't fiddle a whole lot of fancy stuff, he was flat, down to earth. Like Earl (Scruggs) on the five string. Earl don't play a lot of fancy banjo, but what he plays is right; it's there. And that's the way Smith's fiddlin' was. He didn't do a lot of fancy, show-off, kick-up-the-dust stuff, but when he fiddled a tune, it was fiddled just like it ought to be.

"When I got to the Opry, Curly Fox helped me a lot too. Curly Fox was a real good fiddler, one of the best. Curly Fox and Texas Ruby had a program in Nashville at the same time we did. We had a program on the Checkerboard Jamboree. It was a network thing. He (Fox) and Forrester and myself—we'd all work together, and naturally one would show the other what we knew. I learned a lot from Fox. Anything like 'Buckin' Mule' or 'Lee Highway Blues' and stuff like that I needed to know, why during the program I'd say 'Get back here, Fox, I want you to show me something.' And he was very gracious to do it. He's a splendid fellow, and he'd help you in any way he could. Now some people will and some won't. Some of them say, 'Now I'm Mr. Big, and you can learn like I did, the hard way.' But not Fox, he is a splendid fellow. That's what it's all about, one helpin' another. I don't care who you are, somebody can fiddle stuff that you can't fiddle."

In addition to Bill Monroe and Jim Shumate on fiddle, there was a comedian and banjo player in the Blue Grass Boys named Stringbean (the late David Akeman). "When I sang bass on the gospel numbers," Shumate recalls, "String would sing the baritone. String and me also did a comedy act together—I worked [as the] straight man. People used to come up to Stringbean after he'd left Monroe and say 'you know that Earl Scruggs can really pick a banjo.' String would say 'Yeah, but you ought to hear both me and him play at the same time.' He never would let himself down, and he never would say that Earl could pick. String and I used to room together in the hotel. We buddied around together quite a bit. He was a card. We used to rib him about being stingy. I came in one day, and I guess he'd heard me coming. There was a trash can sittin' there beside the door. Just as I opened the door he had his pocket book out shuffling out one dollar bills out into this trash can. He said 'How in the dickens did all them ones get in there?' As I started walking toward the trash can, he dived in there to get 'em."

Playing guitar with the Blue Grass Boys was a young musician and singer from Tennessee by the name of Lester Flatt. Shumate recalls that "Lester had just started working with Bill when I joined the band. He'd been with Bill two or three weeks. He'd been singing tenor with Charlie Monroe. So he left Charlie and went with Bill at the Grand Ole Opry. I had met Lester when he was working with Charlie, so I was glad he was with Bill. We were both rookies. I remember that Lester always had a funny run on the guitar, and we used to kid about that run. I accused him of doing it just to let people know that he was still there. That's about the truth, because we'd be going so fast, he'd just hit one string here and there and then every chance he'd get, why he'd run something in there."

The fifth member of the Blue Grass "Boys" was Sally Forrester, Howdy's wife. Shumate remembers that "we always called her 'Sally Ann.' She did a solo sketch on each program as well as doing the books for us; she was the bookkeeper. Everybody thought that Sally Ann and me were brother and sister. Where ever we went, old boys would get to aggravating us and she'd say 'I'll call my brother and straighten you out.' I remember walking in a cafe one night and some old guy was harassing her, and she said 'Here comes my brother, and you better level off, hear?' He came running over, and man, you should a heard him apologize. I said 'I suggest you stay just as far away from her as you can, old friend,' and that was the end of it." Rounding out the Blue Grass Boys was Andy Boyett, from Florida. Boyett was a comedian and worked a blackface act along with Stringbean.

Like many fiddlers before him, Jim Shumate was surprised to discover that Bill Monroe does not often sing in the keys in which most musicians are used to playing. While most singers stick to the keys of G, A, D, and C, Monroe prefers B, B-flat and E. Shumate recalls his experiences playing with Monroe: "Oh my! That was the first time I'd ever hit B, B-flat and I'd never played anything in E till I got on the stage of the Opry. The one thing about Monroe, you didn't know what to expect. Sometimes when we was getting ready to play a tune, he'd whisper over to me 'This is going to be in B-flat or B natural.' With Monroe, you had to be set and ready for anything. But one thing about him he'd never let me down. He'd always kick it off with the mandolin, which gave me a chance to feel out the first verse and be ready, 'cause he'd always expect me to come in to kick off the second break. I had to do the second break, always. If there was any doubt in my mind, why there was a look I'd give him, and he'd take it himself, because he knew I wasn't ready. On some of those ones I'd never played, me being a rookie to start with, why sometimes he'd have to make two rounds before I'd have it figured out.

"I'll never forget the time when I was a rookie with Monroe, new at the job. After we finished the Opry, we was going to play a show in Evansville, Indiana, not too far from Nashville. We loaded up and started out from Nashville. Bill had one of those twelve passenger buses, a forty-one Chevrolet. It would really run. We were sailing along down the road and had a flat tire, so we got out to fix it. It was dark as the dickens. We didn't have a flash light. I got the extra tire out of the trunk and started to roll it around the bus, and it was heavy. There was some trees chopped down there where we had pulled off the road. And I thought it was a log that I rolled the wheel up against. I pushed and pushed, and that old wheel was heavy. I finally got it on over the log, and just as it got on the other side Bill yelled from under the bus, 'Who in the dickens is that rollin' that wheel over me?'

"The one thing, about it, you didn't practice with Bill. He'd check you out, I reckon, before he hired you. The only practicing we did that I can remember, was one time when there was this particular tune that we were going to do on the Opry on Saturday night. He and Lester worked one out one night, I remember. Ernest Tubb had recorded one during the war that was going pretty good, 'Are You Waiting Just for Me.' Bill and Lester did it on the program one night out on a show, they kicked it up bluegrass-style. And it was real good, real pretty. So we went to the hotel room to brush that one up a little bit and use it on the Opry on Saturday night."

After Bill Monroe and the Blue Grass Boys' success with "Are You Waiting Just for Me" on the Opry, it wasn't long before other Opry performers started doing the song too, according to Shumate, "The one thing about it, we set the pattern up there. Everybody did it after we started doing it on the Opry."

In addition to introducing new arrangements of country songs to Opry audiences, Bill Monroe and the Blue Grass Boys also added new techniques in playing the songs. In fact, it was Jim Shumate who introduced what is now the standard fiddle kick-off to songs. "Nobody kicked off a tune with the fiddle till I started doing it. Lester Flatt got me to kick 'em off with the fiddle. Why after that, all over the country, we was settin' the pace up there. I remember the first one I kicked off, 'Daisy Mae.' That was one of Ernest Tubb's numbers too. So I kicked it off with the fiddle, and from then on, everybody started kickin' off solos with the fiddle. I guess I must be the originator of that fiddle kick-off. I never heard nobody do it before. Flatt said he never had either, and after we did it, everybody started doing it. I was talking to Sonny Osborne not long ago, and he said 'You boys were the originator of that, I never heard nobody do it before.'" It was in one of the rare practice sessions that Shumate came up with the fiddle kick-off.

"Lester had a funny lick on the guitar. Bill would kick it off with the mandolin, but he couldn't turn him in. When Lester would come in to pick up the rhythm to sing, somehow or another they'd miss a beat. I kept standing and listening and I knew right off the bat what was happening, 'cause one of them was coming in a lick ahead of the other. Flatt turned around and said, 'Jim, see if you can kick that thing off with the fiddle.' He'd been hearing me in the background, I was kinda kickin' it off a little. So I just kicked it off and when I wound it up and turned him in, he hit that thing right on the button. So we kicked it off three more times before we hit the stage, and man, it was right. From then on, we kicked off everything with the fiddle; everything that we did, of course. If Monroe had something that he wanted to kick off, he did. If Lester had one he wanted to sing, Monroe left it usually up to the guys, because he was straight with us, Bill was, all the way through. If he thought we could handle one better the way we wanted to do it, why that's the way he let us do it. After all, if we flubbed, he was the one that took the rap."

The life of a Blue Grass Boy in the 1940's often meant being out on the road all week and getting back to Nashville just in time to play the Opry on Saturday night. On one trip out with the Blue Grass Boys, Shumate had borrowed Bill's violin while his was being fixed. Shumate explained that "When we were packing up after a show, we'd take turns loading up the music in the bus. My fiddle was small, and it was the last thing to be put in the truck. I'd always just lay it on the bumper. When Bill stuck in his mandolin, he'd always lay my fiddle in with his mandolin on top. He had a little compartment there on the side just for those instruments. I laid Bill's fiddle on the bumper as usual, and Bill was busy doing something else. We got loaded and started to leave. I got in the bus to drive, and see-sawed around. We had a short place to turn, and I had to back up a little. When I backed up I felt the bus hit something and then I heard it. It made a racket. I said to Bill 'Did you put my fiddle in the back?' He said 'No, didn't you put it in?' I said 'Ah, you gotta be kidding.' We was always ribbin' one another, and hiding instruments. He said, 'No, I swear, I didn't put it in.' So I told him we better look to see what I run over back there. So, sure enough, when I started moving the bus, it just pushed Bill's fiddle off the bumper and I ran right over the middle of it. It ground that fiddle up. As luck would have it, Birch Monroe was traveling with us, and he had a case that had two fiddles in it, so I finished out the week with one of his. My fiddle was in Nashville. This old fiddle-maker in Nashville put that fiddle back together, and man, you couldn't even tell it. It didn't hurt the tone a bit."

During this period of the early forties, Bill Monroe and the Blue Grass Boys were playing the Opry on Saturday nights, during the week there were appearances at school houses, theaters, clubs and radio stations. In the summer, Monroe put on tent shows in little towns all over the South. Shumate explained that "There was a tent crew that went along ahead of us. When we got there, everything was ready to go. We had a big tent that held about three or four thousand people, plus bleachers and chairs. They'd put the chairs down out front. They were reserved, and the bleachers were different prices. It was like a carnival, so to speak, except it was under one big roof, one tent. They had a popcorn machine, and all that stuff. Lester Flatt's wife [Gladys Stacey Flatt] operated the popcorn machine. She was one of the Stacey sisters that used to be with Charlie Monroe years ago."

As many a former Blue Grass Boy can testify, working with Monroe meant a lot more than making music. In the forties, Bill Monroe and the Blue Grass Boys were not only a bluegrass band, but also a baseball team. Shumate explained how this worked. "We had quite a ball team back then. We'd get to town early, usually around three or four o'clock. I'd go to the pool hall or somewhere where I could find some young guys and ask them if they had a ball team there in town. Most of them did, and I'd tell 'em who we was and that we had a bluegrass team and we'd like to challenge 'em. Oh man! They'd get busy and get their gang together and meet us at the field. Sometimes they'd meet us in an hour. We did that all over the country. Sometimes we had good crowds just for a ball game. We had a lot of fun. We played for keeps and had a good team. We had uniforms and everything. I played shortstop and was a pretty good hitter too. I could lay the timber to that ball. String pitched, he was a good pitcher. I believe Lester played third base. We had two or three of the tent crew boys that were good ball players. Bill played pitcher, but he was a better hitter than anything else. I've seen him just bust bats and break 'em wide open. They'd just splinter when he'd hit 'em."

What with working tent shows, keeping a bluegrass band and a baseball team together, plus doing his own booking, Monroe did not find time to make any recordings in the period from October 1941 until February 1945. Unfortunately, this was when Shumate was working with the Blue Grass Boys.[1]

"We did cut a lot of transcriptions that we used when we'd go out in the towns to ballyhoo the shows, but we never did release anything. I guess it was because he

---

1. Shumate only played with Monroe in 1945.

was just so busy. He wrote a lot of stuff and I guess he was just getting it all together. He never did give no reason for it. He was propositioned to record time and time again when I was with him, but we just never did. We really didn't have time, I don't reckon. We had our session up to be cut when I left, but it had never came through."

By 1945, the members of the Blue Grass Boys had been working together steadily for over two years. To add variety to the show, Monroe hired Lew Childre to work the tent show circuit with them for one season. The hiring of Childre was the catalyst that led to other changes in personnel in the band which resulted in a dramatic change in Monroe's sound. Many people argue that this event would mark a major turning point in the history of bluegrass. Shumate, who was a central figure in this episode, put it this way: "We hired Lew Childre to work with us on a tent show one season. He was an actor, a good musician, dancer, this, that, and the other. He and Stringbean got to fishin' together and they decided to come up with their own outfit—just the two of them working together as a team. So, Stringbean quit. Bill told me that Stringbean was quittin' and asked me if I knew anybody in North Carolina that could play the banjo. I said, 'Yeah, I know a fella, but he don't play Stringbean-style.' He said, 'Who is he?' I said, 'Earl Scruggs, lives in Shelby.'"

Shumate had met Earl Scruggs in Hickory, North Carolina, some years before. "We used to have a thing in the city auditorium in Hickory called the Carolina Jamboree. Earl came up there one night with a bunch of boys from Shelby and Earl was back in the dressing room picking banjo with a fella named Grady Wilkie, who was singing and picking the guitar. And that's where I met him. I liked his banjo-pickin' and I hadn't forgot it. I remembered how good I liked it, and that's how come I knew where he was.

"Bill asked me if I knew how to get in touch with him, so I called Earl. His mother said he was in Nashville then, working a tour with a fella by the name of Lost John (Miller). So I called the radio station [WSM] and they said he was doing an early morning radio program. I went up to the station and caught him. I was living in the Tulane Hotel, had a room at that time, and asked Earl if he'd be interested in playing with Bill Monroe at the Grand Ole Opry, and he said, 'Yeah.' I said, 'Well, come on down to the hotel and I'll call Bill and have him come on over and listen to you,' and he said, 'Alright.' Earl came down to the hotel room, I called Bill and he came over there and brought his mandolin. We took the mandolin, fiddle, and banjo there in my room. Earl was as nervous as all get out. Boy, he really laid the timber to that banjo. Bill had never heard nothin' like that. I said, 'What do you think?' Bill said, 'Gosh, that's good, I'm gonna hire him.' So he went ahead and hired him. So that week I come back to North Carolina and I tuned in the Opry on Saturday night to see if he really hired him, and there he was, he hired him. When Earl hit the stage, he really tore that place up."

When Earl Scruggs joined Bill Monroe and the Blue Grass Boys, a new chapter in bluegrass history was opened. In Scruggs' first appearance on the Opry, it happened that Jim Shumate was no longer playing fiddle with the Blue Grass Boys. The month just before Scruggs was hired marked another period of personnel changes for the Blue Grass Boys. Jim Shumate had originally been hired to replace Howdy Forrester who had been drafted into the Navy.[2] According to the rules established during the war, a returning veteran can have the job back that he gave up to join the service.

"I found out that Howdy was back and wanted his job, so I turned in my notice. I knew it wouldn't have been fair for me to have stayed. When Howdy joined up, that left Bill with three fiddlers: Howdy, Birch Monroe, and myself. Birch had been singing bass on the gospel songs, and fiddling old-time hoedown numbers. I had a job waiting for me in North Carolina, working in the furniture business, and had been wanting to quit anyway. I could have kept on working if I'd a wanted to, but I was glad and it worked out fine. I wanted to come back to North Carolina anyhow; I'd had me 'nuff of it. I believe I only stayed a week after Howdy came back. During that week, we all played together on stage. If there was a song, sometimes Howdy would break it, and sometimes I would. And sometimes both of us would play it together. We twin fiddled some, but not much. I never was too good at twin fiddlin'. Now Howdy was, so I'd take the lead and he would second it."

Even though Jim Shumate had left the Blue Grass Boys and had returned to North Carolina, he was still very much active in country music. It wasn't long after returning to Hickory that he joined up with Dwight Barker and the Melody Boys who had a regular television program on WSJS. He also managed a country music park and had his own bluegrass shown on radio WHKY. By 1948, Lester Flatt and Earl Scruggs had both left Bill Monroe and were putting together their own band. Their first choice for a fiddle player was Jim Shumate. Shumate recalled how it happened: "Lester, Earl, and Cedric Rainwater, (Howard Watts) came over to the house and said they'd pulled out from Bill and were organizing their own show and were going to call it the Foggy Mountain Boys. They said they were going to use "Foggy Mountain Top" as the theme song and they needed me to play the fiddle. I debated around a while because I really didn't want to but I thought well, since they went to all this trouble I may as well. So we decided to just split down the board. Lester said they were going to need one more man so they were going to hire Mac Wiseman. I'd never met Mac. So we got set up and did our first program over WHKY in Hickory. I think we worked a week there. We went from there to WCYB in Bristol, Virginia, and there we set the woods on fire. Everywhere we went, we turned them away. We played everywhere—at school houses, ball parks, auditoriums, and airports. Wiseman kind of acted as our agent. He could type and was a pretty good bookkeeper. The letters would come in from people wanting us to come to so and so, and Mac would answer back and give them the terms and open dates, and there'd come back a contract, and we would sign it. That's all there was to it in those days."

Lester Flatt, Earl Scruggs and the Foggy Mountain Boys seemed to be taking the country by storm. Their days of hustling for jobs were well in the past. As Shumate recalls, "We had no trouble at all getting work. Goodness gracious! If we did any-

---

2. Shumate actually replaced Chubby Wise in Monroe's band. Wise was to return, of course.

thing, we turned 'em down." Before long, Lester and Earl were signing their first contract together to record for Mercury Records.

In their first recording session held in a radio station in Knoxville, Tennessee, they recorded "Cabin in Caroline," "We'll Meet again Sweetheart," "God Loves His Children," and "I'm Going to Make Heaven My Home." Shumate fiddled on the first two cuts. He tried singing baritone on "God Loves His Children," but as he admits, "My baritone was so weak, it wouldn't come out. Earl, he'd never sung baritone much, but he did it on that one. It sounded good; they got a good cut on it. Earl picked the guitar Merle Travis–style."

When Lester, Earl, and the Foggy Mountain Boys were in their first recording session, Shumate remembers that "Everybody was very calm; we knew what we were doing. We'd done it time and time again on radio, and we knew how we were going to do it. Some people come to a session not knowing what they're going to do. It's not a good idea to practice on a record. You should know what you're going to do. I don't mean you should try to play the same break over and over every time. Every time I'd take a break I'd try to play it a little bit different. I never did try to play it the same way over and over. I like to try to add a little something to it, or take something away, to give it a little contrast.

"I did the fiddle kick-off to 'Cabin in Caroline.' When I was playing that song when we were on stage, I'd pull the bow on the kick-off. But on the record, I pushed the bow because I couldn't take a chance of squeaking the bow. You are subject to screech on the fiddle when you're going both ways. If you go the same way all the time, you ain't going to screech. It'll come out smooth. When we went to record, we did have a problem with 'Cabin in Caroline.' My fiddle is so loud. The boy at the controls stopped us a couple of times after we'd got started. He came in there and said there's something making a noise. They had me on a microphone all by myself with the fiddle. I was kicking it off. Directly, he came steaming out of the control room and said 'I know what it is.' He said, 'Shumate, hold your fingers off the strings, you're touching them.' I was a little nervous, you know, watching the cue card and the clock on the wall. They said it sounded like horses walking. They had the thing set high. They have to have the masters set high. He said 'Hold your fingers off of that fiddle. That's the loudest fiddle I ever heard.' So I thought, 'Uh, oh, I'm in trouble, 'cause I've got to have my position on the fiddle.' But I'd played it so much, naturally, I dropped right in. I just held my fingers up till he gave me the cue."

As a veteran bluegrass fiddler, Jim Shumate had the opportunity to influence the many young fiddlers he came in contact with. "I've taught a lot of young guys over the years. One I remember was Lester Woodie. He used to fiddle with the Stanley Brothers. I sort of started him off. He used to come to my radio show when he was just a kid and hang around with me. I got him to get his fiddle and helped him. He'd just play 'long with me and first thing I knew he was just a splendid fiddler. The Stanley Brothers came down to Hickory and wanted me to play the fiddle for them. I told them I wasn't interested in playing the fiddle at that time and they asked me if I knew anyone that might be interested. I told them I knew a fella that could cut the mustard with you boys if he's interested. I told them he lived in Valdese, North Carolina, at that time. They got hold of Lester and he just fell right in there with them. He fiddled with them a long time; he made a good fiddler."

Although Shumate had passed up a chance to work with the Stanley Brothers, he did eventually work with them for one week, on one of his vacations from his regular job. Playing fiddle with the Stanleys up until the time that Shumate joined them was Leslie Keith. Shumate had met Keith some years before while Shumate was fiddling with Flatt and Scruggs.

"That Keith was some fiddler. But the worst I ever saw Keith hurt was when I beat him in a fiddlers' convention. He'd take that 'Black Mountain Blues' and win every convention in the country. He could do that thing. When a man writes a song, it's his, you know, and he could handle it like nobody else. So we did a show at the National Fiddlers' Convention at Richlands, Virginia, in 1949. We had Buck Ryan on the program who was playing fiddle for Jimmy Dean at that time, Leslie Keith, who was doing a show out of Bristol, Chubby Wise, who was working with Hank Snow in Nashville, and myself. I was fiddling with Lester and Earl. There was a huge crowd, about nine thousand best I can remember. They run a fiddlers' convention sort of like a beauty contest. They started off and matched to see who was going to go first, and I came out last. I usually like to get in the middle, or pretty close to the first. That gives you a chance to pick your tune. I would have picked 'Orange Blossom' if I could have got on first. But Chubby Wise got to play first, so he played 'Orange Blossom.' Keith came up next and he did the 'Black Mountain Blues.' Then Buck Ryan came up and did 'Listen to the Mockingbird.' He really laid the timber to that thing. He could really play it. So I said, 'Cedric, what in the dickens am I going to play? They've done played everything.' He said 'Play the 'Lee Highway Blues,' and them fellows can't touch you with a ten-foot pole.' That made me feel more confident, because those boys were good fiddlers—they were the best. So I played 'Lee Highway,' and just laid them boys in the shade. So the first round the judges dropped off Keith. The next round they dropped off Chubby. The next one they dropped off Ryan, and that left me standing there. That made me feel good. I'd taken that thing by a landslide.

"I remember that Mac Wiseman backed up all of us on guitar. That way, they'd be no feudin'. Nobody could say 'If I just had so and so behind me I could have won.' The only disadvantage I could see to those guys was that Mac was working with us at that time, and he knew that 'Lee Highway' up one side and down the other. Every time I'd turn, he'd be right there. So that was a lick in my favor too."

Jim Shumate is long overdue to receive credit for the changes he helped create in bluegrass music. At fifty-six, he still resides in Hickory, North Carolina, and can fiddle even better now than he could in the earlier years. He is without a question— bluegrass fiddler supreme.

Originally published in *Bluegrass Unlimited* 13 (April 1979): 14–23. Used by permission of the author, Native Ground Music, Inc. <http://www.nativeground.com>, and *Bluegrass Unlimited*.

Listening to Rudy Lyle, the great banjo man, talk about his early days of playing with Bill Monroe makes it clear what a different world bluegrass was then. In the twenty-first century, there's an infrastructure of sorts for this music: festivals, Web-sites, record companies, magazines, and even some million-selling acts. Then, it was an off-beat branch of music that existed somewhere between minstrelsy and the Opry, with Monroe's band seemingly spending more time pitching the tent and pitching baseballs than performing bluegrass. There's also a glimpse in this story of the titanic force that was to transform popular music, Elvis Presley. Lyle's is a familiar name to generations of fans, although to a broader public he might be known only by the crackling energy of his banjo on some classic Monroe records. Lyle was fifty-four when he died on February 11, 1985.

15

"Rudy Lyle—Classic Bluegrass Banjo Man"

DOUG HUTCHENS

In any conversation about the great musicians in the formative years of bluegrass music one name always comes up, Rudy Lyle. Rudy played the banjo on many of the classic Bill Monroe recordings, including "Raw Hide," "On and On," "Sugar Coated Love," and probably his most noted performance on "White House Blues."

Rudy grew up on the Black Water River near Rocky Mount, Virginia. He lived with his grandfather Lomax Blankenship who was a noted local fiddler. At the age of nine he began to learn to play the five-string banjo.

"Lawrence Wright, he lives close to Rocky Mount. He was the first man I heard play rolls and I picked it up from him, I also learned a lot from Paul Jefferson," Rudy recalled.

In a few years Rudy met two boys from Rocky Mount that played music and began picking with them on WPAQ radio in Mt. Airy, North Carolina.

"We had Wilber Turner on guitar and Lefty Hall on the fiddle. They told my granddad that they would take care of me and they talked him in to letting me go with them." During the time they worked at WPAQ they worked with Uncle Joe Johnson and Pretty Little Blue-eyed Odessa. The band included Uncle Joe on the Dobro, Wilber Turner on the guitar, Lefty Hall on the fiddle, Pretty Little Blue-eyed Odessa singing and Rudy on banjo. It was during this time that Rudy first met Bill Monroe.

"I was in Mt. Airy working with Uncle Joe. Bill came through there with a show at the high school. It was on a Friday night that we weren't working so we all were there. We had announced on our radio program that he was going to be there with his show. At that time Bill's band had just broken up. Don Reno had just left. He didn't have too many people working with him. He had two boys called the Kentucky Twins and another fellow named Bill Myrick but didn't have a banjo player so I tuned up and went out there with him. That's where we got together. After the show I told Bill that I'd sure like to work for him and he said that he would like for me to but didn't want to take me away from Uncle Joe. Bill didn't want to hire me on the spot. I respect Bill for that.

"About three weeks later we were working a show in Radford, Virginia at the theatre. The manager came back stage and said I had a long distance call. It was Bill. He was in D.C. and asked me if I wanted to come to work. I said yes, I was ready.

"I got into Nashville and I didn't know anything about the town. I had rode a Greyhound bus in. Back then everyone wanted a car but everyone didn't have one. We had been using Wilber Turner's car in Mt. Airy. Cars were kind of scarce. I got into Nashville early Saturday morning. I spent the whole day walking around the block down around the station. The Grand Ole Opry was on the next corner. I didn't know where to go or what to do. Bill had said to be there Saturday night for the first show; the R.C. Cola Show. I was there in the alley when Bill and all the guys came around the corner. We went in and did the R.C. Cola Show. The first tune I did was 'Cumberland Gap.' I think the R.C. Cola Show was network then like the Prince Albert Show, so it was getting out pretty good. Bill told them that he had a brand new banjo player from over in Virginia—Rocky Mount, Virginia. Then he told them what I was going to play. I played, then Grant Turner came in. Boy, it was great, it was something else.

"When I got to Nashville Bill had Chubby Wise, Mac Wiseman, Jack Thompson, me and him (Bill). Joel Price was playing comedy. Jack Thompson was playing bass and he left to work with Lew Childre and Stringbean, to play rhythm guitar for them. Then Joel started playing bass. After Mac left, Jimmy Martin took his place. I brought Jimmy Martin in the back door of the Opry. Jimmy was standing out in the alley one Saturday night. Old Sergeant Edwards, the policeman on the door, had turned him away two or three times. Sergeant Edwards was a big old heavyset mean-looking policeman. He could just look at the people trying to get in the back door and they'd run. There was all kinds of people trying to get in that back door.

"I had heard Jimmy play a little bit and I told him to put his guitar back in the case and let's go inside. We came on through. I told Sergeant Edwards that Bill wanted to try this man out. Bill liked Jimmy's guitar playing because he played good guitar—solid rhythm. He also liked Jimmy's singing, Bill could tenor him good. They had a good close duet that was very close to Bill and [Lester] Flatt."

Rudy stayed with Bill from mid-1949 until late summer of 1951. During this time he saw other personnel changes. Red Taylor replaced Chubby Wise, then Vassar Clements took Red's place.

During this time, "Bill had the baseball team, the Blue Grass All-Stars. They were made of a group of guys that played good baseball. I mean good baseball. Some of them went on to the majors. Bill had a booking agent that would book these towns and book the local ball club against the Blue Grass All-Stars ball club plus the show. We would always open it up with the music and then after that the game would start.

"Bill would always let Stringbean start out pitching. Then if they got too hot on him and start beating us he would call in his other pitchers like G. W. Wilkerson. They called him Ziggy, he was great. G. W. was the son of Grandpappy George Wilkerson, the fiddle player with the Fruit Jar Drinkers.

"One of the other pitchers was Roy Pardue from there in Nashville. There was Stringbean, Ziggy and Roy Pardue. They were all great. String was really playing ball. He was a super pitcher but he lacked a little bit of the speed that Ziggy and Roy could put on it. He was a good straight honest pitcher and loved baseball.

"I love baseball too and a lot of times me and Bill would go out to Long Hollow and pitch.[1] He would say, 'Rudy you're pretty good but not good enough,' and I'd answer him back saying, 'Yes, I know, but I'm better than you.'

"Bill would manage [the team]; he didn't miss anything going on. He watched every little thing. He would work a lot with the catcher and pitcher to make sure they'd change up their pitches. We had a super ball club. We were easy on the other teams when we knew we could win. Sometimes Bill would put Stringbean back into pitch. The hardest team we ever played was in Des Arc, Arkansas. They had a super good team there. They really had some good pitchers; a good team, and good players, but we beat them by a couple of runs. The game was so good, the people enjoyed it so well that we re-booked it right there on the spot for another game to follow it up the next month."

During this period, the Blue Grass Boys were in great demand. "We did a lot of package shows—Hank Williams, Hank Snow, Ernest Tubb and Bill Monroe. Those were the big names on the Opry at that time. Hank Williams used to prank with us a lot, especially at the Friday Night Frolic up at old WSM on Seventh Avenue. There used to be a dummy elevator that they used to bring up food in. Every Friday night Hank would always be sitting in that elevator, signing autographs and having his boots shined and talking crazy. He talked to everyone, he never met strangers. He used to always kid Bill about where he got his banjo players."

During this time the Shenandoah Trio was formed. "The Shenandoah Trio was Joel Price, Red Taylor and me. Bill would use us as a break from himself on the show. We used to do things like the 'Rag Mop' song and tunes like that. There were also many songs written during this period. He wrote 'Uncle Pen' in the back seat of the car up on the Pennsylvania Turnpike on the way to Rising Sun, Maryland. On that same trip to Maryland, we were traveling in a Hudson Hornet and had a rack on top of the car. We had all our instruments up on the rack. We were going down the Pennsylvania Turnpike and the rack blew off. I mean just blew off. There were all our instruments scattered all over the highway. It broke the neck out of Chubby's fiddle and skinned up Bill's mandolin case pretty bad but my banjo wasn't even out of tune."

The banjo that Rudy played while he worked with the Blue Grass Boys was a RB-3 Gibson Mastertone (with wreath inlays). "I bought that banjo from a fellow

---

1. "Long Hollow," as Tom Ewing points out, refers to Monroe's farm in Goodlettsville.

close to Mt. Airy. I can't remember his name. [Johnny Vipperman, a noted local musician, thinks it was probably Early Jarrell.] Uncle Joe advertised that I was needing another banjo; I was having problems with mine—I had been playing a Bacon. This guy came over and said 'you can have it if you want it for $150.' I bought it and wasn't ever sorry." Rudy traded that banjo to Tom Morgan's brother in the 1960s; the banjo was severely damaged and its current whereabouts are not known. In those days of the skin banjo heads, the banjo player had to not only play the banjo but be a technician also. The skin heads were very responsive to climatic changes and you would have to change heads whenever one broke.

"We didn't have room to take two instruments so I'd carry extra heads with me. I kept eight to ten with me all the time in my suitcase. A lot of times I'd get to a job and the head would be busted so I wouldn't work that job. I'd be busy putting a brand new head on. There was only one way to get them on. They were calfskin heads, I mean real calfskins. You had to soak them in water and get them real loose to even put them on. Then after you'd get them on, you had to wait for the drying process for it to set up and not get too tight or it would bust again. You just had to work with it. I've put them on everywhere; in hotel rooms, in the car going to shows. I even put one on backstage at the Opry one night. Banjo players have it good these days with plastic heads.

"We worked a lot of theaters, one-nighters; on weekends we'd work matinees. One time we had Johnny Mack Brown, one time Max Terhune, the old Western Cowboys. They'd do shows with us. Max Terhune would come out with his doll Elmer. Me and Jimmy Martin would hide behind the stage and aggravate him. He would talk back there through the screen and say, 'Boys, now don't start that stuff.' I remember once we had been up in Charleston, West Virginia, and Bill had this fine race horse he'd bought, trailer and everything. We had that trailer on the back of the car coming around those mountains in West Virginia heading back to Nashville. If I'm not mistaken it was Chubby Wise driving and he said, 'I think I hear a horse running' and he really did. When we got back there we found the whole trailer floor had fell apart and the horse had kept up with the car.

"Once we played a show at Meadows of Dan, Virginia, and on the way out we stopped in Wytheville, Virginia. Bill bought this dog from a man there. It was the best dog this man had, a 'lemon walker' he called him. We had to be in Poplar Bluff, Missouri, the next day so Bill put that dog in the trunk of the car. We had all the instruments in the rack on top. We went all the way to Poplar Bluff, Missouri, with that dog in the trunk of the car. We were afraid to open the trunk afraid he'd get out and run. When we got there, there was a big fox chase. The old dog won the chase; he caught the fox. He had rode halfway across the country and still won the race."

Rudy was no different than many of the other young men when it came to the service. Rudy went into the Army on August 3, 1951, and was replaced in the Blue Grass Boys by the young Sonny Osborne.[2] "If I hadn't went in the Army I'd have probably stayed with Bill. I'd have been another Oswald."

2. Two banjo players, Joe Drumwright and James Ora Bowers, came between Lyle and Sonny Osborne.

During the time Rudy was in the Army he pulled duty in Korea. "On my way back I was in Japan. I was in the PX one day and at the table next to me I kept hearing this guy talking and I kept thinking, I know him. Come to find out it was Dale Potter, he was on his way back home. Dale was one of the finest fiddlers in Nashville."

After he got out of service he returned to his old job with the Blue Grass Boys. "When I came back from the Army, Flatt and Scruggs were doing the morning Martha White Show at WSM. They were in one studio and we were in the other. Me and Earl was good buddies. He would come by ever so often. I remember one Sunday they were working Dunbar Cave in Clarksville and Carter Stanley and me went up there with Earl."

There had been a lot of changes during the time Rudy was in service. One was an especially bright star on the horizon. Rudy remembers the beginning of another legendary artist. "We done the Phillip Morris Cigarette Show with Elvis. It was the T. D. Kempt circuit out of Charlotte, North Carolina. They called it the 'Chittlin Circuit.' It started in Florida and went all the way to Pennsylvania. It was one-nighters—theatres, mainly. That was when Elvis was first starting in '54–'55. We had Carl Smith on the show plus Hank Snow, Bill Monroe, of course Elvis was an added attraction. Tom Parker was bringing him out first and it got to where when Elvis got through doing his show no one else could go on stage. I remember that Hank Snow was trying to follow him one night and there was no way, so Hank just threw up his hands and walked off. They were all hollering, 'We want Elvis.' So Tom Parker changed it around and put Elvis last."

After returning from the service, as Rudy put it, "Things weren't the same." Many young servicemen probably suffered those same experiences returning home after a period of turbulence such as the Korean conflict. So in 1954 Rudy left the Blue Grass Boys.

"I went up to D.C. and worked for a while. Jimmy Dean had a TV show up there so I went up there. I was a little mixed-up. I just got back from Korea. Everything wasn't the same. My brother, dad and mother had moved up there. There was three of us brothers and I have one sister, her name is Patsy. My brother Bobby still works around D.C. playing music five nights a week. He plays the Chord-O-Vox (accordion). Nelson my other brother doesn't play much anymore, he just plays for fun.

"I was working up there with Jimmy Dean, working package shows with him. Roy Clark was working at the Dixie Pig on Bladensburg Road. I worked some with him. I had started switching back and forth from lead guitar to five-string. Hank Garland is the one that got me to switch. We all used to live together over on Boscobel Street (in Nashville). There was a rooming house over there, Mom Upchurch's. So I moved in and at that time Hank used to come around there a lot and we always got along real good together. I used to really enjoy to listen to him and watch him play. He was always so accurate, everything was so perfect and in my mind I felt like I could do it too.

"I worked a while with Claude King, he had the hit song, 'Wolverton Mountain.' I worked with Patsy Cline while she was with the Jimmy Dean Show." In the late '50s Rudy moved to the Knoxville area. "I worked for Cas Walker there and with a friend of mine at a car dealership."[3] It was while selling cars he met his wife, Mary. "I met Mary when I sold her a car, that was in 1963. I was working some with Red Rector and Fred Smith about that time. They had an act equivalent to Homer and Jethro. That's where Homer and Jethro and Jamup and Honey came from, too."

After a few years in Knoxville, Mary and Rudy moved outside Nashville where for a time they ran a restaurant and he began working for the Tennessee Department of Corrections in Nashville.

Much of Rudy's time in recent years had been filled with his hobby of building and flying airplanes. "I've always liked airplanes. Back when I was living down on Boscobel Street, years ago, me and Randy Hughes, who was with Cowboy Copas when they had their accident, learned to fly together.[4] We would go over to Comelia Fort Air Park there in Nashville and go flying.

"I bought this airplane, it was all to pieces and put it back together and I restored it. I've been everywhere in that plane. I worked on it for five years and I've been flying it for ten years. It's a EAA Sport Biplane with a 85 Continental engine. It cruises a little over a hundred miles an hour. I have a buddy who's an aircraft engineer who's got one just like it. We'll get up early and go out early on weekends and fly—the Dawn Patrol.

"I built a couple of airplanes there in my garage. I helped a doctor here in Franklin build one. I went ahead and got all my ratings then I got my FAA rating to do annual inspections on the aircraft, the A & P License. It's something I enjoy doing."

Rudy occasionally got together with some local musicians around his home in Franklin, Tennessee, and as Rudy said, "I'll never retire from my music. I'll keep on writing songs and playing my music and working on my airplanes."

All bluegrass musicians owe a great deal to all those musicians like Rudy Lyle who blazed the trail for the music we now know as bluegrass. And Rudy was a trailblazer, as Bill Monroe recently said: "There was Earl Scruggs, then Don Reno, they were wonderful banjo players but when Rudy Lyle came in there with me even Earl and Don was listening to Rudy. He could really roll that banjo and he was powerful."

Originally published in *Bluegrass Unlimited* 19 (April 1985): 44–49. Reprinted by permission of the author and *Bluegrass Unlimited*.

S unset Park, an outdoor concert site in rural Pennsylvania, and New River Ranch in Maryland became early spots for cross-fertilization between "true-vine" blue grassers and the small band of young urbanites who were musically and culturally

3. Walker was an influential east Tennessee grocer, political figure, and broadcaster who helped advance the careers of several early bluegrass acts.

4. Hughes, Copas, Hawkshaw Hawkins, and Patsy Cline were in a fatal airplane crash in March 1963.

fascinated by the sounds of Monroe and others. Mike Seeger's 1959 article on a banjo contest there, written for the early folk newsletter *Gardyloo*, provided an on-the-ground account of one such intermingling. Scattered among the locals and other pickers mentioned were the names of Sam Hutchins, who played banjo with Jimmy Martin; Gloria Belle Flickinger, an early female performer in several bluegrass settings; Roger Sprung, a key figure in the banjo-fixated New York City bluegrass scene; Eric Weissberg, who years later recorded the version of "Dueling Banjos" that became known as the *Deliverance* theme; and Seeger himself, who knowledgably performed the tune he had selected to play in both bluegrass and old-time styles. Seeger seemed, at least in retrospect, to take in courtly good spirit his loss to a sixteen-year-old local banjoist.

16

"Late News Report from Sunset Park, West Grove, Penn. Five-String Banjo Picking Contest"

MIKE SEEGER

For almost ten years there have been annual banjo contests at either Sunset Park, West Grove, Pa., or at New River Ranch at Rising Sun, Md., initiated originally by Alec Campbell of New River Ranch. In their earlier years many professional banjo-pickers such as Donny Bryant, Smitty Irwin, Sam Hutchins, Larry Richardson, and others, would vie with one another for the Gibson Mastertone five-string banjo that was to be given away. Several times both Don Reno and Earl Scruggs and their bands would be booked in on the same date and they played some of the best unaccompanied banjo duets ever picked.

But professionals such as Bryant and Irwin rarely won, since the contests were based on audience applause rather than a cold appraisal of ability by banjo-picking judges. In one contest a sailor playing Dixieland on a tenor banjo won mostly because of his uniform; the following year a somewhat inebriated man approached the contest microphone, held up his thumb and a forefinger and said, "I've only got two fingers but I'll pick the best I can." He flailed at the strings to little musical advantage but had the audience and therefore the contest. In following years one boy nearly won who had had trouble remembering the tune he was going to pick; another almost-won was a boy who brought his own cheering section to counteract the always-powerful local favorite. Incidents like these brought bad will toward the promoters of the contests and year by year more rules have been applied to the contest.

All of this is meant to be background on this year's banjo contest on July 4th at Sunset Park, sponsored by Sunset Park and Don Reno, with a prize of a Gibson Mastertone or $200. The rules of the contest have been tightened up considerably so that only five-string banjo players above age sixteen are now eligible, and furthermore not allowed to say a word into the microphone, must pick their own announced tune, draw lots to determine their order of appearance, and must not let any other instrument in their band (if they do have backing) take the lead.

At about 3:30 the contest got underway and all banjo-pickers were called on-stage where they were to remain until the end of the contest. As Eddie Matherly, the announcer, read off the name of the banjo-picker, his or her hometown and the name of the tune that was to be played, each would step up to the microphone and play his tune, usually a variant of Scruggs' style and nervous as a result of a thousand or two people in the audience.

First off was Joe Kaskell of New Jersey, playing "Banjo Signal" (Don Reno), followed by Eric Weissberg of NYC with an excellent arrangement and performance of several old-time tunes, then Andy Philips of Sinking Springs, Pa., playing "Tower Mountain Twist" (with breakdown pegs); Gloria Flickinger, Hanover, Pa., "Dixie Breakdown" (Don Reno), the only girl in the contest this year and better known for her Molly O'Day-style singing and mandolin playing; Phil Trump, Sheridan, Pa., "Clinch Mtn. Backstep" (Ralph Stanley); Burrill Kilby, Oxford, Pa., "Home Sweet Home" (Don Reno, Allen Shelton); the other Trump brother played "Hard Times" (also by Ralph Stanley); James Brooks of Rising Sun, Md., "Bugle Call Rag" (Earl Scruggs); J. Holbrook, Phil., Pa., "Bluegrass Breakdown" (Bill Monroe); Pete Huey, Balt., Md., "Home Sweet Home"; Mike Seeger, Washington, D.C., "John Hardy" (in minor both Scruggs and thumb styles); Carl Chatsky, NYC, "Foggy Mtn. Breakdown"; Sam Hutchins, Balt., Md., "Cumberland Gap" (Earl Taylor's lead singer and guitar player who won last year's heated contest against a rock 'n' roller who played "Milk Cow Blues," with his version of "Kicking Mule"); Roger Sprung, NYC, "Paddy on the Turnpike" (played well, Scruggs- and frail-style—also exhibited Pegram-style stage presence);[1] French Zahn, Alexandria, Va., "Farewell Blues" (Earl Scruggs); Kenneth Hurley, Wilmington, Del., "Hamilton County Breakdown"; Sonny Miller, Delaware, "Dear Old Dixie" (Earl Scruggs)—Sonny is one of the best banjo and especially fiddle players in the area; Gerald Flaharty, age sixteen, Woodbine, Pa., "Beer Barrel Polka" (Don Reno); Rick Churchill, Arlington, Va., "Dixie Breakdown"; Elvin Burkheart, Lancaster, Pa., "Foggy Mtn. Special" (Earl Scruggs); Stuart Klavens, Balt., Md., "Wildwood Flower" (plectrum-style); Sonny Bowers, Williamsport, Pa., "Banjo Strut" (McCormick Bros.).

After all of the twenty-two players had finished their tunes, each was called back, [Arthur] Godfrey Talent Scout–style, to play a short part of his tune after which the audience applauded and the three judges, audience volunteers from Delaware, Md., and Pennsylvania, judged the applause and came up with five semi-finalists: Weissberg, Seeger (Mike), Sprung, Miller, and Flaharty, all of whom were to appear in the finals at 8:00 that night. It was fairly clear who had won and that the Park was just trying to give a better show and have people stay at the concessions.

At the evening show the five were first trimmed of Weissberg and Seeger, then Sprung and Miller. The winner, Gerald Flaharty, has been playing in this area for

---

1. Presumably a reference to old-time banjo player George Pegram, known for his showmanship.

more than two years and until this year had been frustrated by the sixteen-year-age minimum ruling and the audience knew this. His father (who was fiddling at a dance this night) and his mother had helped in his wish to play and had driven him to other contests in which he'd developed stage presence which in addition to his good banjo-picking showed up many of the older contestants at Sunset Park. It was a good balance of picking, presence, and local appeal that won him this contest on July 4th.

Originally published in *Gardyloo* 4 (Jan. 1959): 23–24. Reprinted by permission of the author.

The stars of bluegrass have led lives of relative obscurity compared even to mainstream country acts, let alone to the giants of pop music. Several steps below that were hardworking acts like Earl Taylor and Jim McCall, subjects of an incisive profile by the insightful, Kentucky-based journalist (and musician) Jon Weisberger. Appearing in the alternative country publication *No Depression,* Weisberger's article drew an implicit contrast between Taylor and McCall, who beat out public-domain tunes in a rough-and-ready Cincinnati studio, and Monroe and others, who used top-flight sidemen to record many of their own tunes in major-label studios in Nashville.

17

"Earl Taylor and Jim McCall:
Twenty Bluegrass Favorites, Rural Rhythm"

JON WEISBERGER

Old habits die hard, and one of the hardest to shake is the tendency to assign bluegrass to the Appalachian hills and hollers. Though understandable, it's inaccurate; almost as quickly as Bill Monroe's brand of country music turned into a genre, it found a home in the smoky nightclubs that served thousands of hillbilly transplants in the industrial centers east of the Mississippi. Performing in this milieu called for the ability to play hard and sing loud, and to do both for hours on end; the musicians up to the task sometimes made a (barely) sufficient income, but almost always inspired an undying devotion among their fans.

Among the most enduring of these was Earl Moses Taylor, a native of Tennessee, who worked for a short while with Jimmy Martin before putting his own band together in Baltimore in the late 1950s.[1] Briefly sponsored by folk revivalist Alan

1. Earl Taylor was from Rose Hill, Virginia, and had played clubs in Baltimore starting in 1953 before joining Martin in 1955, according to Mike Seeger's liner notes for *Mountain Music Bluegrass Style* (Folkways FA 2318).

Lomax, the Stoney Mountain Boys were the first bluegrass act to appear at Carnegie Hall and one of the first from outside of Nashville to record for a major label, but Taylor was no businessman, and so wound up spending most of his career playing working-class bar gigs in and around Cincinnati, Ohio, while a succession of musicians passed through his band, often on their way to bigger, though not necessarily better, things.

Earl worked best with a lead-singing partner who could match his piercing tenor, and none fit the bill better than Jim McCall, a guitarist with a powerful right arm and a vocalist squarely in the "rear back and let 'er fly" mold. Though their volatile relationship regularly caused the two to work separately, they teamed up long and often enough to record several albums of hard-core, traditional bluegrass that is no better described than by the word *stout*. *Twenty Bluegrass Favorites* is one of these, released on Uncle Jim O'Neal's California-based Rural Rhythm in 1967, but recorded in a Cincinnati backroom studio. With an eye to keeping royalty payments at a minimum, most of the songs were public domain; with an eye to keeping studio time at a minimum, the arrangements were unvarying: kick off, sing a verse and chorus, take an instrumental break, repeat as necessary, then out. This approach put a premium on straight-ahead picking to keep things moving along and sheer force of personality to put the songs over, and Taylor, McCall and company had plenty of both.

The music here isn't for the faint of heart; it's raw, and not in a mountain sense, but in an industrial one, made to appeal to the homesick tastes of migratory factory workers over the hubbub of a hard night's drinking. The album itself was thrown into the market with little regard for the niceties of music-as-art, and that's almost as true of the reissue as of the original release, which is probably why a misidentification of the supporting musicians remains uncorrected (for the record, the banjo was supplied by Vernon McIntyre Jr., not Tim Spradlin, and the bass by his father, "Boatwhistle" McIntyre, not Charlie Hoskins; the occasional fiddle most likely comes from Scotty Stoneman).[2] Forget all that, though; it's not important. What shines through here is a spirit as powerful as it is indescribable.

Originally published in *No Depression* 16 (July–Aug. 1998): 88–89. Reprinted by permission of the author.

As hard-core country music and the budding rock and roll sound vied for prominence on the charts, the duo of Don Reno and Red Smiley used creative means to keep their bluegrass act vital. In addition to having brilliant singing and musicianship, they offered a memorable, often funny, stage show and new songs that showed the influence of the honky-tonk style. This excerpt from a chapter on Reno

---

2. The fiddling was by Moon Mullins.

and Smiley comes from Bob Artis's book *Bluegrass* (1975), a full-length treatment that detailed all the pioneering acts as well as the budding progressive movement. Artis, a picker and educator as well as a writer, remains active in bluegrass in the Pittsburgh area.

18

"Don Reno and Red Smiley"

BOB ARTIS

King was an important label of the postwar years; it had the Delmore Brothers, Grandpa Jones, Clyde Moody, Cowboy Copas, Hawkshaw Hawkins, and several other important names. Syd Nathan was looking for a bluegrass band in 1952.

It seemed to be the thing in those days—every major label had at least one bluegrass band on the payroll. Monroe was at Decca; the Stanleys were at Columbia and would soon join Mercury; Flatt and Scruggs were at Mercury and would soon join Columbia; the Lonesome Pine Fiddlers were at RCA. Nathan had hopes of hitting the then-new bluegrass market when he recorded the classic few cuts by Jimmy Martin and Bob Osborne in 1951, but things didn't seem to work out. Most of the backup group consisted of the Lonesome Pine Fiddlers, and shortly after the records were cut Osborne was drafted into the marines and Jimmy Martin returned to play with Bill Monroe.

Nathan signed Don Reno and Red Smiley and their band, the Tennessee Cut-Ups. The group included Red's old friends Jimmy Lunsford and Red Rector as well as the legendary bluegrass bassist John Palmer.

King was doing well in the gospel market with various quartet groups (usually including people like the Delmores and Grandpa Jones), and it was decided that Don and Red would record some religious material. The result was some superior bluegrass gospel, sixteen cuts of excellent music on which Reno sang a variety of parts and played not only banjo but lead guitar and some remarkable finger-picked mandolin. Many of the songs were Reno's own compositions, and these stand as some of the very finest material ever done in bluegrass: "Get Behind Me, Satan," "The Lord's Last Supper," and the best known of the early King material, "I'm Using My Bible for a Road Map."

"Road Map" was a big seller for King, but, ironically, the group just couldn't make a go of it on the road. Their career had just begun when they had to make the painful decision to disband.

Reno returned to Arthur Smith and in 1954 helped Smith record the original "Feudin' Banjos." The number featured Reno on the five-string and Smith on the tenor banjo in a simulated duel for musical supremacy. This classic cut, recorded and released on the MGM label, is still musically interesting after twenty years, better than the many versions that followed it under the title "Duelin' Banjos."

King continued to record and release the music of Don Reno and Red Smiley, even though they weren't really a band anymore. The recordings made during that period are some of the best: "Springtime in Dear Old Dixie," "Talk of the Town," "Dixie Breakdown," "I Know You're Married, but I Love You Still," "Charlotte Breakdown," and many others.

The sound Reno and Smiley were developing through the early 1950s was totally different from that recorded by Monroe and the others. They seemed to be aiming at a different market. That era in county music was marked by the switchover to electric instruments. Drums hadn't yet found their way to Nashville, but songs were geared more and more to the honky-tonk crowd, songs about honky-tonk angels, cheatin' hearts, neon signs that flashed into sleazy motel room windows, and the problems encountered by hillbillies moving into urban culture. Hank Williams and Ernest Tubb were the kings of the barroom tear-jerker, as fans in country music roadhouses all over the county danced and drank to songs like Tubbs' "Walkin' the Floor over You," and Williams' "Honky Tonkin'," "Hey, Good Lookin'," and the classic "Your Cheatin' Heart."

This was the music Red Smiley had been performing as a featured country vocalist in Ohio. Now Reno and Smiley were turning it into bluegrass, and it sounded great. They both had enough show business savvy to know that not everyone was going to identify with songs about cabins in the hills, so they added a dance-floor beat to their music and began singing dance-type country tunes like "One Teardrop and One Step Away."

They had more than enough talent and ability to pull it off. Red had the most appealingly commercial voice in bluegrass, and Reno's smooth tenor blended with it perfectly. In addition, Reno was an extremely sophisticated musician, able to play an imaginative banjo break on anything. He added elements of electric and steel guitar technique to his banjo work. On the slower tunes, his full-chordal style, almost like plectrum banjo playing, added an entirely new dimension to bluegrass five-string banjo.

Reno was considered the best writer of new, original bluegrass tunes through most of his career, and the majority of the top songs recorded by Reno and Smiley in their heyday were Don Reno compositions.

The King records sold well through the early 1950s—so well, in fact, that requests for personal appearances began coming on a basis regular enough to cause them to reorganize. For their reactivation they hired their old friend bassist John Palmer. A good show fiddler was needed, and Mack Magaha got the job in 1955. This band stayed together for many years and is remembered as the classic vintage of the Tennessee Cut-Ups.

One of the most important Saturday night radio "jamborees" was the Old Dominion Barn Dance, broadcast from powerful WRVA in Richmond, Virginia. Like WWVA in Wheeling, the beam went all over the Northeast, bringing the sound of country music to a huge audience. Mac Wiseman was a regular, as were Flatt and Scruggs. In 1955 the premier bluegrass act of the Barn Dance was the Reno and

Smiley group. They also secured an important spot on television, the Top o' the Morning show at WDBJ-TV in Roanoke. They were getting more television and radio exposure than any group outside Nashville.

In the time of their greatest popularity, the Tennessee Cut-Ups were considered the greatest show band ever assembled in the field of bluegrass. Not only did they exhibit vocal and instrumental superiority, but they were polished and capable showmen. Other musicians could play flashy licks all day long and never really reach the crowd. Reno and Magaha made listeners know they were hearing something special, made them sit up, pay attention, and love what they were hearing.

Not the least of their stage appeal was their great country comedy. They would stage elaborate skits, using ridiculous hillbilly outfits and names like Chicken and Pansy Hotrod (Don and Red), Mutt Highpockets (Palmer) and Jeff Dooly Tater (Magaha). The riotous routines would sometimes last ten or fifteen minutes, and it was the kind of comedy the country audiences couldn't get enough of.

It was largely their comedy that made them unique in bluegrass music through the late 1950s. Monroe and most of the others were already aware that bluegrass was developing its own audience and had gone "serious," feeling that they no longer had to sell a product to a large, general market. Bluegrass musicians, following the lead established by Monroe, became known as sullen, dour-faced individuals who would rarely laugh, smile, joke, or give any indication of enjoying what they were doing. Most bluegrass band relegated their comedy to the bass player, and even that tradition was eventually dropped as the country market became more sophisticated. But Reno and Smiley were determined to give folks an enjoyable, entertaining performance for their money, and that's exactly what they did.

They were stylists, showmen, songwriters. But the most lasting contribution of the Reno and Smiley sound to the ever-broadening field of bluegrass was the phenomenal banjo playing of Don Reno. His active mind restlessly searched for something new. New licks and songs seemed to pour out of him, and he was, without question, the most creative and imaginative instrumentalist of the years before 1960. He was a musician's musician, his left hand all over the fingerboard as his right hand executed roll after endless roll. It was improvisational playing, and his complete knowledge of the instrument and fertile imagination produced sounds that ranged from dazzling to unbelievable. Reno and his school of jazzy, spontaneous bluegrass banjo playing was responsible for the eventual elevation of the idiom to the status once enjoyed only by classical music and jazz. It started an upward trend in bluegrass that still thrives.

Almost every banjo tune Reno did became standard fare for the many flashy banjo players coming into their own, especially after the folk music revival brought the five-string banjo into the limelight after years of obscurity. The Reno tunes were the essence of instrumental showiness, and numbers like "Little Rock Getaway," "Double Banjo Blues," and "Dixie Breakdown" became standard bluegrass showpieces.

Reno and Smiley and their band were among the fortunate ones. The daily television show in Roanoke was steady employment and enabled them to keep the same musicians year after year. It meant they didn't have to be on the road continually to make their living. The Old Dominion Barn Dance spread their name across most of the East, and their King records were being widely distributed and sold. Then, at the zenith, the act broke up.

The bluegrass world was shaken by the news that one of its best-loved acts would no longer be making the circuit. Reasons were sought for the breakup, and gossip-hungry insiders were disappointed to learn that the two men parted friends. The Old Dominion Barn Dance had closed its doors in 1964, depriving them of one of their principal means of exposure. An attempt to revive the program on television was unsuccessful, and Reno felt a need to take his music to wider markets and new territory. Smiley, in failing health, was unable to go along with it. It was an amiable parting, and they would eventually reunite, but the glory days of the old Reno and Smiley bands were over.

Excerpted from *Bluegrass: From the Lonesome Wail of a Mountain Love Song to the Hammering Drive of Scruggs-Style Banjo, the Story of an American Musical Tradition* (New York: Hawthorn Books, 1975), 62–66. Reprinted by permission of the author.

Alan Lomax, son and collaborator of the famed folk music collector John A. Lomax, struck a mighty blow for bluegrass with this now-famous profile of the music that appeared in *Esquire* in 1959. Taking square aim at the magazine's presumably sophisticated readers, he manages swipes at that era's jazz and pop music before making a good case that bluegrass was ripe for the sort of widespread acceptance that Dixieland had enjoyed decades before. The phrase "folk music in overdrive," appearing in the body of the story, has appeared widely as a shorthand description of bluegrass. Although it may have oversimplified the music, the phrase offered people entirely unfamiliar with bluegrass an easy conceptual road. Summing up the developments since Monroe's emergence as an Opry star, Lomax largely paved the way for the next two decades of bluegrass, when city slickers and country folk combined to take the music to new levels of broad public acceptance.

19

"Bluegrass Background: Folk Music with Overdrive"

ALAN LOMAX

While the aging voices along Tin Pan Alley grow every day more querulous, and jazzmen wander through the harmonic jungles of Schoenberg and Stravinsky, grass-roots guitar and banjo-pickers are playing on the heartstrings of America. Out of

the torrent of folk music that is the backbone of the record business today, the fresh-
est sound comes from the so-called Bluegrass band—a sort of mountain Dixieland
combo in which the five-string banjo, America's only indigenous folk instrument,
carries the lead like a hot clarinet. The mandolin plays bursts reminiscent of jazz
trumpet choruses; a heavily bowed fiddle supplies trombone-like hoedown solos;
while a framed guitar and slapped bass make up the rhythm section. Everything goes
at top volume, with harmonized choruses behind a lead singer who hollers in the
high, lonesome style beloved in the American backwoods. The result is folk music
in overdrive with a silvery, rippling, pinging sound: the State Department should
note that for virtuosity, fire and speed our best Bluegrass bands can match any Slavic
folk orchestra.

Bluegrass style began in 1945 when Bill Monroe, of the Monroe Brothers, recruited a quintet that included Earl Scruggs (who had perfected a three-finger banjo
style now known as 'picking Scruggs') and Lester Flatt (a Tennessee guitar picker
and singer); Bill led the group with mandolin and a countertenor voice that hits high
notes with the impact of a Louis Armstrong trumpet. Playing the old-time mountain tunes, which most hillbilly pros had abandoned, he orchestrated them so bril-
liantly that the name of the outfit, "Bill Monroe and His Blue Grass Boys," became
the permanent hallmark of this field. When Scruggs and Flatt left to form a powerful group of their own, Don Reno joined Monroe, learned Bluegrass, departed to
found his own fine orchestra, too. Most of the Bluegrass outfits on Southern radio
and TV today have played with Monroe or one of his disciples—with the noteworthy exception of the Stanley Brothers, who play and sing in a more relaxed and gentle
style.[1]

Bluegrass is the first clear-cut orchestral style to appear in the British-Ameri-
can folk tradition in five hundred years, and entirely on its own it is turning back
to the great heritage of older tunes that our ancestors brought into the mountains
before the American Revolution. A century of isolation in the lonesome hollows of
the Appalachians gave them time to combine strains from Scottish and English folk
songs and to produce a vigorous pioneer music of their own. The hot Negro square-
dance fiddle went early up the creek-bed roads into the hills; then in the mid-nine-
teenth century came the five-string banjo; early in the twentieth century the guitar
was absorbed into the developing tradition. By the time folk-song collectors headed into the mountains looking for ancient ballads, they found a husky, hard-to-kill
musical culture as well. Finally, railroads and highways snaked into the backwoods,
and mountain folk moved out into urban, industrialized, shook-up America; they
were the last among us to experience the breakdown of traditional family patterns,
and there ensued an endless stream of sad songs, from "On Top of Old Smoky" to
"The Birmingham Jail." Next in popularity were sacred songs and homiletic pieces
warning listeners against drink and fast company; and in the late thirties, the favorite theme for displaced hillbillies was "No Letter Today."

---

1. As noted elsewhere in this volume, Carter Stanley worked briefly with Monroe in 1951.

Talented mountaineers who wanted to turn professional have had a guaranteed income since the day in 1923 when Ralph Peer skeptically waxed an Atlanta fiddler playing "The Old Hen Cackled and the Rooster's Going to Crow," and Victor sold half-a-million copies to the ready-made white rural audience. Recording companies sent off field crews and made stars of such singers as Jimmie Rodgers, Uncle Dave Macon, Gid Tanner, the Carter family and Roy Acuff.

Countless combinations of hillbillies have coalesced and dispersed before radio microphones since WSB in Atlanta began beaming out mountainy music on its opening day. Grand Ole Opry has been broadcasting from Nashville for thirty-three years;[2] the WWVA Jamboree has gone on for twenty-seven.[3] In the beginning, performers sang solo or with one accompanying instrument; but before microphones they felt the need of orchestras, which, while originally crude, developed with the uncritical encouragement of local audiences.

By now there has grown up a generation of hillbilly musicians who can play anything in any key, and their crowning accomplishment is Bluegrass. When the fresh sound of New Orleans Dixieland combos hit the cities some fifty years ago, it made a musical revolution first in America, then the world. Today we have a new kind of orchestra suitable for accompanying the frontier tunes with which American has fallen in love. And now anything can happen.

---

2. Lomax was imprecise in this number. The Opry's precursor, the WSM Barn Dance, started in 1925 and received the "Opry" name from George D. Hay in 1927.

3. The WWVA Jaboree started on January 7, 1933. *The Encyclopedia of Country Music: The Ultimate Guide to the Music,* comp. by the staff of the Country Music Hall of Fame and Museum, ed. Paul Kingsbury (New York: Oxford University Press, 1998).

2

The Reseeding
of Bluegrass

1960–79

R eared in New Jersey and educated at Swarthmore, Ralph Rinzler played several key roles in the move of bluegrass to a wider audience in the late 1950s and
early 1960s. He played mandolin with one of the first New York–based bluegrass acts,
the Greenbriar Boys. In addition, he brought Doc Watson out of the North Carolina mountains and managed Bill Monroe for a few key months in 1963. During that
period he wrote this piece on Monroe for *Sing Out!*—the influential folk magazine.
Rinzler's aim was to take the spotlight away from Earl Scruggs and put Monroe in
what Rinzler perceived as his rightful place as creative godfather of bluegrass.

20

"Bill Monroe—The Daddy of Blue Grass Music"

RALPH RINZLER

Blue grass music does not come from the Blue Grass region of Kentucky, but from
the Western region of the state known as the "Pennyrile" (folk pronunciation of
"pennyroyal," a type of mint which is evidently found in great abundance in that
area). Nonetheless, the entire state is known as the "Blue Grass State," and it was
with the thought of identifying his music with his state of origin that Bill Monroe,
the man known as the "father of bluegrass music," chose to name his band the "Blue
Grass Boys."

The term *bluegrass music* came into popular usage in the early 1950's, taken up
by disc jockeys and country music fans to describe the music of string bands which
were following a trend established by Bill Monroe in the early 1940's and maintained
by him on the Grand Ole Opry since that time.[1] (For those who are not familiar
with the sound of bluegrass and/or its development and currency, an excellent discussion of the subject has been presented by Mike Seeger in his notes for *Mountain
Music Bluegrass Style*, Folkways FA 2318.)

The music itself has been criticized by some city folk music enthusiasts as being nothing more than mere commercial hillbilly music. Others take from it the
instrumental techniques (banjo, guitar and mandolin—few citybillies tackle the
fiddle) and overlook the subtle and equally unusual vocal styles. Most are unaware

---

1. Both time elements in this sentence are open to question. On the history of the word *bluegrass,* for the timing of its first usage, and for when bluegrass took its "classic" shape, see various
writers, including Neil V. Rosenberg, *Bluegrass: A History* (Urbana: University of Illinois Press, 1993).

of the wide variety of different traditions, folk and otherwise, on which innovator Bill Monroe drew when establishing "his music" on the Opry some twenty-three years ago.

Perhaps a glance at a few of these traditional elements will clarify this point. The fiddling style characteristic of blue grass music blends the Scots-Irish with the little-known Negro fiddling tradition. The song repertoire draws on the Anglo-American ballad and folk song tradition, on the urban commercial tradition of "heart" (or sentimental) songs of the nineteenth and early twentieth centuries, and on the recently established tradition of White and Negro commercial country music (generally dated from Ralph Peer's first recording of Fiddling John Carson in 1923). The vocal style developed by Bill Monroe reflects childhood influences: listening to songs and styles of neighbors and family and singing in Methodist and Baptist churches; and it reflects a long-established feeling for both Negro and White blues singing. The banjo style generally identified with Earl Scruggs is actually a development of the three-finger style of picking first popularized on records by Charlie Poole (North Carolina Ramblers) and Dock Walsh (Carolina Tar Heels) in the twenties and thirties, later improved upon by Fisher Hendley (Aristocratic Pigs) and Snuffy Jenkins and brought to its final form and current prominence by Scruggs himself when he started his professional career with Bill Monroe in 1944.[2] In contrast to this, the style of mandolin picking associated with blue grass music is radically different from any approach to the instrument which existed prior to Monroe's appearance.

Bill Monroe, the youngest child in a family of eight (six boys and two girls) was born in Rosine, Kentucky, September 13, 1911. His father, James Buchanan Monroe, was of Scots ancestry—a descendant of James Monroe, fifth President of the United States.[3] He farmed, cut and hauled timber, operated his own saw mill and mined coal on his six-hundred-acre farm located between Beaver Dam and Rosine, Ohio County, Kentucky. Although his father did not sing or play music, Bill recalls that he was a fine dancer and enjoyed doing a local dance known as the Kentucky backstep. Bill's mother, Melissa Vandiver Monroe, sang old songs and ballads in a clear, pure voice, and also played the fiddle, harmonica and accordion. As a young boy, Bill learned to read music from shape note hymnals while attending singing schools. Bill recalls learning the essentials of guitar and mandolin at eight or nine years of age, but it was not until he was twelve or perhaps thirteen that he took a serious interest in learning music.

There are two distinct influences which Bill Monroe recalls from this period of his life, and both of these are clearly manifested in his unique musical style. His mother's brother, Pen Vandiver, was a fiddler of considerable talent and local reknown. It was he who taught Bill the essentials of the guitar, fiddle and mandolin, and from the age of twelve, Bill would travel riding double with his Uncle Pen sometimes as often as twice a week to play the guitar behind the older man's fiddling at country dances.

---

2. Scruggs actually joined Monroe in 1945 and had worked with Lost John Miller previously.

3. Research cited by Tom Ewing in *The Bluegrass Reader* (Urbana: University of Illinois Press, 2000) shows that Monroe was not directly descended from President James Monroe.

At one such dance, Bill met a Negro fiddler and guitar picker, Arnold Shultz, a man whose name is almost legendary in that country. (Shultz influenced Kennedy Jones who in turn influenced Mose Rager, the man from whom Merle Travis learned to play the guitar during his boyhood.) Shultz played the fiddle in a "bluesy," syncopated fashion, getting notes and sounds that were not commonly heard in country fiddling. His guitar style also set forth a musical language which Bill was not to forget; the young boy would frequently play guitar behind Shultz fiddling at dances. Shultz did not sing but Bill recalls he could "whistle the blues" better than anyone around.

There were many opportunities that young Monroe found to stand by and listen to Negro workers "whistle the blues" while they plowed fields, lined track and did other forms of labor in the area of Rosine and Beaver Dam. Surrounded by these sounds in his daily life, Bill Monroe resolved, at the age of thirteen, to play the mandolin in a way that nobody else had ever played it and to play his music cleaner and better than anyone. The few people around home who did play the mandolin simply chorded it as an accompaniment to singing.

Bill and his older brother Charlie played and sang around home, finally winning a singing contest with the song "He Will Set Your Fields on Fire" (*Monroe Brothers*, Bluebird 71451; *Bill and His Blue Grass Boys*, Decca 29196). In 1927 they formed a band with their older brother Birch playing lead on the fiddle, Charlie singing lead and picking the guitar, and Bill chording the mandolin and singing tenor (he was then sixteen years old). After touring for three years, they settled in Hammond, Indiana, in 1930 and for several years performed on radio stations in the area. When Birch left the group in 1934, Charlie and Bill worked at various radio stations as "The Monroe Brothers" (WAAW, Omaha, 1934–35; WBT, Charlotte, 1935–36) gathering considerable reknown and polish.

When Victor first approached them to make records they refused, thinking the returns would be slight. After their second refusal they received a wire from Victor Bluebird representative Oberstein saying "MUST HAVE THE MONROE BROTHERS," and he would not take "no" for an answer. In Charlotte on February 7, 1936, Bill and Charlie recorded ten songs (among them "Nine Pound Hammer," "You've Got to Walk That Lonesome Valley," "Darling Corey," and "This World Is Not My Home"), and within a few weeks their first record, "What Would You Give in Exchange for Your Soul," sold a hundred thousand copies. They continued recording for the Bluebird label until January 28, 1938 (thirty-one records were released, some of which are soon to be reissued on the Camden label).

During these years, Bill and Charlie worked at radio stations WFBC, Greenville, S.C. (1936–37) and WPTF, Raleigh, N.C. (1937–38). In 1938 the brothers separated, and Bill went to Little Rock, Arkansas, forming his first band, the "Kentuckians." They played for station KARK for three months, but Bill felt this would lead to nothing significant, and went off to Atlanta, home of the Crossroad Follies (a popular country music show), put an ad in the paper indicating that Bill Monroe was recruiting musicians for a band, and subsequently chose Cleo Davis (guitar and lead voice), Art Wooten (fiddle), and Amos Garren (string bass).

It was at this time that Bill began to sing lead on some songs. He rehearsed this band with great care, and after six weeks the "Blue Grass Boys" made their first radio appearance in Ashville, S.C. Soon after this Bill set out to establish himself with a permanent spot on a leading radio station, and his first stop was at WSM, Nashville. He was auditioned by the Stone Brothers and George Hay ("The Solemn Old Judge," initiator of the Grand Old Opry), and was hired with the words, "If you ever leave the Opry, it'll be because you've fired yourself." The following Saturday night (in October, 1939) Bill Monroe and His Blue Grass Boys played their first show on the Opry, starting with a song which is still one of Monroe's most popular, "The Mule Skinner Blues." In time a banjo-picker was added to the group, and with this addition the blue grass band took its final form. Stringbean, Monroe's first banjo-picker, played old-time, two-finger-style banjo and did comedy as well.

In the ensuing years Bill Monroe and the Blue Grass Boys were heard on the Opry every Saturday that they were not touring, and the sound of bluegrass music was heard on radios, jukeboxes and phonographs throughout the country. Bill has always trained the musicians who worked for him with the result that, regardless of the change in personnel over the years, the driving rhythm and characteristic fiddling style (which Monroe imparts to his fiddlers) have been ever-present in the music heard on records and in performances of the group. Most of the leading musicians in blue grass music have at one time gone through their period of "apprenticeship" with Monroe: Flatt and Scruggs, Carter Stanley, Don Reno, Mac Wiseman, Jimmy Martin, Sonny Osborne and Gordon Terry, to mention a few.

In conversation as well as in performance Bill Monroe's respect for and belief in his music are immediately apparent. It is this conviction, as profound as a religious belief, which has enabled Monroe to resist the trends of Nashville and to retain his remarkably unique musical style throughout more than twenty years of constant exposure. This same conviction, imparted to other musicians and to audiences, is responsible for the endurance and significance of the traditional folk strain in commercial country music.

At this point it is an easy task to evaluate the contribution of Bill Monroe. It was the combination of musical traditions, both the Anglo-Scots and the Negro, meeting as they did in that area of Kentucky, which enabled Monroe to blend these two powerful strains in his own instrumental and vocal style. In his choice of instrumental treatment and repertoire, it was Monroe who set the trend to play traditional songs on traditional instruments, and this he did at a time when the trend in commercial country music among performers of his generation was directly opposed to him. The searing tenor harmonies dependent upon intervals of the fourth and fifth which Monroe features are reminiscent of those found in the old shape note hymnals from which he learned his sacred songs as a child.

Monroe pioneered mandolin virtuosity and forged the driving rhythms and

tempos (characteristic of his music from the time of his first recordings with Charlie in 1936: "My Long Journey Home," BB 6422, "Roll in My Sweet Baby's Arms,"
BB 6773, for example). Bill Monroe is still the most dynamic and subtle singer in
the field of bluegrass music, exhibiting a vocal style which could only have developed from a background of rich and varied musical styles.

But more important than his function as an instrumentalist, vocalist, creator
and preserver, Bill Monroe is a spiritual force. It is his ability to sing and play with
the fire and inspiration characteristic of only a great musician that draws people to
him and to his music. In the fashion of the best traditional folk singers, Bill Monroe never sings a song the same way twice; each performance is a creative challenge
and thus his songs never lose the excitement which is the burning soul he has imparted to his music.

"If you're singing a song to satisfy your heart and feeling, you won't sing it the
same way every time."

(I should like to acknowledge with gratitude the contributions and assistance of
Bessie Lee and Bill Monroe, Ed Kahn, D. K. Wilgus and Richard Rinzler.—R.R.)

Bluegrass journalists, by definition, almost always have a day job. Tom Teepen
has written perceptive and entertaining pieces about bluegrass for decades
while maintaining a distinguished career in mainstream journalism. He retired in
spring 2000 but has continued to write a column for Cox Newspapers that runs in
New York Times–affiliated newspapers. He previously served as editorial page editor of Dayton's *Daily News*. "For a few years I wrestled with a banjo, but it won, two
falls out of three," Teepen says. "It is hard to retool a high school tympanist into a
grown-up banjo-picker." Teepen's evocative reminiscences of Dayton's vibrant
music scene were written for a 1989 reunion of the area's pickers and fans.

21

"Dayton Bluegrass"

TOM TEEPEN

They came down off the mountain sides and up out of hollows of Appalachia, and
they caught us city kids by surprise. For more than a few jumped down from the
Greyhounds and Trailways, anxious, into an alien cityscape, with an old Silver-

tone mandolin or guitar from the Sears and Roebuck catalogue among their be-
longings.

Drawn by rumors of top-dollar jobs at Frigidaire, Chrysler Airtemp and the
NCR and by the siren song of radio stations that seemed to promise stardom, they
brought with them a music, in some ways as old as the hills of their ancestors' Scotland and Wales, that would become charged with urban energy and reshaped by new
experiences.

Who could have known that these eager young men came as the bearers of an
ancient bardic tradition—and the creative geniuses of a new one? Typical, I think,
of my time and type, I backed into bluegrass music from folk music. First delighted by the irresistible Uncle Dave Macon and moved by Mother Maybelle Carter's
strong guitar line, which somehow seemed to match eternity's own gait, I eased
forward to the Stanley Brothers and Bill Monroe.

And in the company of friends, I learned what musical riches lay close to hand
for those of us around Dayton who were willing to keep an ear tuned for any hint
of a teardropping banjo and who would follow to wherever the music swelled. At
first a music of stoops and porches, played around linoleum-top kitchen tables,
bluegrass soon enough slipped out of the house to begin a long honky-tonk career.
It was a shifting, restless scene in the 1950's and 60's, with a band here one night
and gone the next. Few made a good living at their musical work, and many didn't
make any kind of living from it at all. Yet, incredibly, they made art.

Off and on through what were their most formative years, Sonny and Bobby
Osborne, as I remember it, drove cabs in Dayton, but on weekend nights at Ruby's
White Sands, there they were, Sonny's virtuoso banjo flat tearing up ground his
elders had only scuffed and Bobby's new "Rube-e-e-e-e" keening through the smoke
like a cry across a distant valley.

What a treat when young Larry Sparks landed that rarest of bluegrass boons, a
steady gig, at Tom's Tavern. Saturday night by Saturday night over an exciting winter, he pulled together his classic band with Wendy Miller and Mike Lilly. At the
Mermaid on East Third, Gene Sweet plucked as pretty a "Great Speckled Bird" from
his dobro as you'll ever hear. And dear Art Wydner, the bass player who always knew
where the good "shine" was but would never tell, would cut delicate shapes out of
folded napkins between sets to please the kids who had been dragged along by their
parents.

There were shows now and again at local schools or at small festivals in woody
groves, and there were a few live radio programs (Mike Lilly surfaced as an eleven-
year-old banjo prodigy on one sponsored by a cut-rate furniture store), but you
pretty much had to take your bluegrass where you could find it—and your bluegrass records, too. Jack Lynch wove through it all, selling amazing recordings from
the crook of his arm and the trunk of his car.

Over the years together, we had become a family—musicians, hangers-on, audiences, bookers and DJs. The family took a daring risk and grew dramatically in

1960 when the Osborne Brothers played the first bluegrass concert on a college campus, at Antioch, a bold step beyond the Appalachian circles to which the music and its people had until then largely been confined. And the music took another new turn when Red Allen's four remarkable sons enriched the rural tradition and drew a new, young audience with harmonies and styles that picked up something of the beat and hippness of the counterculture '60's.

As in any family, there were rivalries, sulks, even anger now and again. But when we felt challenged by outsiders, we pulled together for one another. And we did that, too, when tragedy struck. When the so-talented Neal Allen died, little more than a boy really, the memorial concert at Loews Theatre brought together players and fans in a close bond of sorrow and celebration.

Dayton, over a period of twenty-five years or so, sat at the center of the northern arc of the bluegrass circle that looped around the Blue Ridge, Smokeys and Cumberlands and the smokestack cities of the lower Midwest. The city's extraordinary collection of musical talents combined, broke up, and recombined in shifting patterns, perfecting old ways, creating new. It was a period of extraordinary invention and excitement, a once-in-a-lifetime intersection of opportunity and ability, and the words and the music went forth, honed and bright into a nation that had little notion of where they had come from—and no idea what great good fun it had all been.

Originally published in the program book for the Dayton Bluegrass Reunion, April 4, 1989. Reprinted by permission of the author.

Like many other bluegrass and traditional musicians, Hazel Dickens has often had a day job. She was working in retail sales in a building that also housed the Washington, D.C., alternative newspaper *Woodwind* when she met Richard Harrington, a journalist and *Woodwind*'s publisher, in the 1970s. "I knew Hazel as a saleslady before I knew her as a musician," Harrington said during a 2002 interview from his *Washington Post* office. A *Post* contributor since 1978 and a staff member since 1980, Harrington has poured out a high-quality stream of articles on every kind of music "except classical" and has proved a dependable mainstream voice for traditional music. "With bluegrass, the only thing I always try to do is not make it seem like it's a weird, outside kind of music. People hear the word *bluegrass* and get scared for some reason," he said. The estimable singer/songwriter Dickens received the full treatment from her long-time friend Harrington in this *Post* profile. Historical perspective and insightful comments from Naomi Judd and others make the article compelling both to Dickens fans and the general readers Harrington had also to consider.

22

"In Harmony with the Hills: Bluegrass Pioneer Hazel Dickens Struck a Rich Vein of Music That's Being Mined Still"

RICHARD HARRINGTON

If it weren't for Hazel Dickens and Alice Gerrard, there might not have been a Judds.

The Judds won't be here today as the Smithsonian's Festival of American Folklife honors Dickens, the West Virginia singer, songwriter and labor activist who has lived in Washington since 1970. But country music's award-winning duo always credited Dickens and long-time partner Gerrard as the musical and spiritual roots of their partnership. It was in 1976 that Naomi Judd found a three-year-old album, *Hazel and Alice,* in a used record store in Berea, Ky., and took it home to play for her young daughter.

"The harmony was so bold," Naomi Judd recalls over the phone from her home outside Nashville. "Their whole sound was so unpolished, so authentic, they were unabashedly just who they were—it was really like looking in the mirror of truth. We felt like we knew them, and when we listened to the songs, it crystallized the possibility that two women could sing together.

I will never forget—Wynonna was twelve years old, I was putting myself through nursing school, and we were living on a mountaintop without TV or telephone," says Judd. "We listened to [the album] together, standing over our little $40 phonograph player . . . and we were silent for the longest time, transfixed."

Dickens will be the featured performer as well as the subject of a tribute from other performers in the second annual Ralph Rinzler Memorial Concert on the Mall.

It's an appropriate setting. Rinzler, the Folklife Festival co-founder who died in 1994, was an early and consistent champion of Dickens, as well as a long-time friend. And it was at an '80s Folklife Festival that singer Lynn Morris, of Winchester, Va., first heard Dickens.

"I was really moved by what she did and wanted everything she'd ever done," says Morris, whose devotion has paid off in unexpected ways. Her rendition of Dickens's heart-wrenching ballad "Mama's Hand" has been the No. 1 bluegrass single for the last three months, as has the similarly titled album. Morris, Gerrard (whom Dickens has played with infrequently since the duo split up in 1977) and Laurie Lewis are among the artists participating in this evening's concert, which runs from 5:30 to 9:30.

Rinzler, says the shy, soft-spoken Dickens, "always made me feel good about myself and what I was doing." That included frequent invitations to the annual Folklife Festivals.

It was at one of the festivals that New York filmmaker Barbara Kopple first heard Dickens in the mid-'70s.

"I thought she was so incredible," Kopple says, so much so that she asked Dickens to provide the closing theme for a documentary she was making. Dickens wrote "They'll Never Keep Us Down" for *Harlan County, U.S.A.,* a film about the deadly struggle to unionize a Kentucky coal mine that won the Academy Award for best documentary in 1977. "Hazel's work was so profound, her voice so beautiful, her a cappella so piercing, that it made the images in the film really come alive," says Kopple.

Clearly, Dickens means many things to many people. In the late '50s, Hazel and Alice was the first women-led group to infiltrate the boys' club of bluegrass music, which made them role models to musicians and, later, inspirations to the women's movement. Both remain leading advocates for old-time music, and Dickens has been heralded around the world as a social and political songwriter in the working-class tradition of Joe Hill, Aunt Molly Jackson and Woody Guthrie.

A shy, modest woman, Dickens is transformed when she sings. She's possessed of a high, raw, intensely emotional voice that is perfect (though hardly pitch-perfect) for what Dickens herself calls "hard-core singing."

"Oh, I never hit the right pitch," Dickens says with a laugh while sitting on a chair in her small apartment in Glover Park. "I go for that feel, I go for the jugular. I can't even think about [the pitch]. When I'm singing, I'm thinking about the real things."

For Dickens, "the real things" are rooted in Montcalm, a tiny coal-mining community in West Virginia's Mercer County. Just as there is a severe, mountain beauty to the sixty-one-year-old Dickens, there is an Appalachian finality to her childhood. The eighth of eleven children, Dickens left school after the seventh grade. Most of her brothers went to work in the coal mines. Her father was a timber hauler as well as a Primitive Baptist preacher. It was in his church that Dickens first explored hard-core, unaccompanied singing.

Dickens left home at sixteen and moved to Baltimore, where she cleaned houses, worked in textile mills, factories and department stores. In the mid-'50s, Dickens got her start as a Kitty Wells/Wanda Jackson–style singer in that city's hillbilly bars, but, she says, "My heart wasn't in it."

Her prospects changed when she connected with the city's nascent folk scene and particularly musician and folklorist Mike Seeger, who had been taking care of Dickens's oldest brother, Robert, at a local tuberculosis clinic. One of Hazel Dickens's most powerful songs, "Black Lung," is a tribute to Robert, who died of the disease, as did two of her brothers-in-law and "countless cousins." Two other brothers died of mining-related illnesses.

> Black lung, black lung, oh your hand's icy cold
> As you reach for my life and torture my soul
> Cold as that water hole in that dark cave
> Where I spent my life's blood diggin' my own grave.

Alice Gerrard recently recalled her first encounter with Dickens. "My husband told me, 'There's this little girl with a great big voice that you've got to hear.' I had heard this type of singing with an edge before, but I remember thinking it was fantastic. I just sort of listened for a long time."

Eventually, they gravitated to each other despite very different backgrounds. Gerrard had been raised in California listening to classical and pop music, embracing traditional folk music as an Antioch College student in Ohio. One thing that connected them was a love for the old-timey duet tradition in which the vocal interplay was complex and the harmonies anything but sweet.

With her low voice, Gerrard often sang a man's part while Dickens sang "over" it, like a tenor—a startling new sound for women, what Dickens once described as "mountain soul."

The two began performing together in 1962 and recording a year later. Smithsonian/Folkways has just released *Hazel Dickens and Alice Gerrard: Pioneering Women of Bluegrass*, which includes two albums the duo recorded for Folkways in 1963 and 1965. The later wasn't released until 1973, the same year Rounder released the *Hazel and Alice* album that so impressed the Judds.

But in 1977, just as the follow-up album was completed, and just as the duo stood to benefit from the critical acclaim that had been building for several years, the two went their separate ways. Dickens embarked on a solo career that has produced four critically acclaimed albums, the last being 1987's *A Few Old Memories.* Gerrard, who continues to work in traditional music and, for the last seven years, as editor and publisher of the quarterly *Old-Time Music Herald,* didn't release a solo album until 1994.[1]

But after having done vocal workshops together over the years and a reunion performance at the Merle Watson Festival in April, there is talk of a reunion tour sometime next year.

While they were still together, Dickens began to reveal the songwriting craft that had quietly bloomed in the '60s.

"I was becoming more aware, like a sponge, just taking in all the stuff—the social scene, how women were treated, how men were treated, how they were treating each other in those bars," says Dickens, who began to explore her personal and class history on such albums as *Hard Hitting Songs for Hard Hit People* and *It's Hard to Tell the Singer from the Song.*

Melding contemporary issues to the sounds of traditional music, Dickens has written about many types of struggles and how they've impacted people's lives. Among her better-known songs are "Don't Put Her Down, You Helped Put Her There," "Working Girl Blues," "Long Black Veil," "My Better Years," "Which Side Are You On" and "Pretty Bird" (Dickens's haunting a cappella recording recently showed up in the climactic finale of the Jason Patric film *The Journey of August King*).

"There's a pure emotion that comes out in Hazel's singing and writing," says Takoma Park folk singer Cathy Fink. "She's been writing real stuff about real people's lives that real people identify with, sometimes because it's been their experi-

---

1. Gerrard founded the invaluable Durham, North Carolina–based *Old-Time Herald*. She resigned as editor in 2003.

ence or because they learned to appreciate somebody else's experience through her music."

"Hazel can write about loss, about love gone wrong, without the sense that the woman is this helpless, hopeless victim," says Lynn Morris. "She writes from the perspective of a strong woman with a lot of feeling, and it's really hard to find material like that."

In conjunction with the tribute, the American Film Institute at the Kennedy Center will screen *Matewan,* John Sayles's fictionalized film about the struggle to unionize West Virginia coal miners in the 1920s. Dickens, who not only sang but acted in the film, will attend. Excerpts from an upcoming Mimi Pickering documentary on Dickens will also be shown. (The tribute starts at 1 P.M. tomorrow.)

Even in their prime, Hazel and Alice never received much airplay but their sound, and commitment to tradition, can be heard today in such progeny as Alison Krauss, Laurie Lewis, Iris Dement and in the Judds catalogue. Naomi Judd insists that the thought of two women singing together "had never occurred" to her before she took home the duo's first Rounder album.

After learning the Hazel and Alice version of the Louvin Brothers' classic "The Sweetest Gift, a Mother's Smile," mother and daughter sang it for Naomi's mother as a Mother's Day gift. "My mom's not a crier—she's been through such hardships in her life—but I'll never forget sitting under the tree in her front yard and how she was transported."

Last year at Nashville's annual Fan Fair, Naomi Judd was herself transported by Dickens and Gerrard's surprise appearance singing "The Sweetest Gift."

"I can guess what people are giving me for my birthday and Christmas and I can smell a surprise party a mile away," Judd insists. "This is the only time Naomi Judd has ever been totally surprised."

It's not that she hadn't wanted to meet them before; it's just that Hazel Dickens had always thought she wasn't dressed for the part.

"I had turned down opportunities because Naomi might be all dressed up," Dickens explains. "I don't buy anything like that to wear and would hate to have to do that just to go visit." When the long-awaited meeting took place, Dickens and Gerrard weren't about to change.

"We didn't get all dolled up. We looked good—but it was our kind of good."

By 1965, when he wrote this piece for the folk music bible *Sing Out!,* Pittsburgh-born Samuel Charters had already produced his groundbreaking *Country Blues.* The 1959 volume's examination of performers such as Lonnie Johnson and Muddy

Waters set a standard for succeeding generations of blues and traditional-music chroniclers. Charters is also a novelist, poet, record producer, and label owner. West Virginia–born brothers Everett and Bea Lilly had twenty-five years of touring and performing behind them, including Everett's tenure with Flatt and Scruggs, at the time of this piece. Charters offers a vivid, although somewhat sentimentalized, portrait of the Hillbilly Ranch (the following article profiles the bar's more raucous side).

23

"The Lilly Brothers of Hillbilly Ranch"

SAM CHARTERS

When I called Everett Lilly's wife, she said that he had already gone down to the club with Bea, so I'd better go there if I wanted to talk with them. The club was in downtown Boston, across the Charles River from Everett's house in Cambridge. "You won't have any trouble finding it. It's just by the bus station." It wasn't difficult to find: a low, dark building behind the Trailways Bus Depot, on the corner of an alley and one of the small squares that help to snarl Boston traffic during business hours.

"Hillbilly Ranch." There was even a painting of steer horns on the end of the sign. Forty years ago, when country music was beginning to take its place on the American musical scene, someone might have been perplexed at the idea of a hillbilly ranch (a cattle drive up the Appalachian Trail? using a sickle to get enough grass to run a still in Kansas?), but in cities like Boston, the country people have drawn together in a vague defensiveness against the rush of American life that tries to drag them with it.

Virginia, Florida, Wyoming, Orange County, California, just as long as you don't come from a city. Even some cities—Nashville, Louisville, Dallas, Fort Worth. It's an attitude, not a place. Northern Florida raises more cattle than North Dakota. There's more coal under Wyoming than there is under Kentucky. (And the attitude is never forgotten. One night in Berkeley, Jack Elliott and Derroll Adams and I, drunk and noisy, had a man and his wife come up to us, good suit, obviously money, a half-forgotten mountain scent to the voice, and she said in a small voice, "My cousin used to sing before he died; I'd like you to come to our house so I could show you some of his songs," and when we got to the house and sloped down to the floor with a drink, she went to a drawer and brought back all her family pictures of Jimmie Rodgers.) So, "Hillbilly Ranch." Also a good commercial name for a bleak Northern city with dirty snow heaped along the sidewalks and a thin layer of blackened ice along the gutters strewn with torn newspapers, cigarette butts, gum wrappers, and a lost, forlorn, trampled mitten.

It was a hillbilly ranch inside. Paintings of mountain cabins on the walls and the dance floor inside a corral fence. The bandstand was against one of the side walls, with dozens of small tables with red-and-white checkered tablecloths in front of it. The music itself was a mixture of the Eastern mountains, of the Western fiddling styles, of Southern singing, of the blues, of country ragtime, of Elizabethan balladry and Salvation Army hymns. Almost the definition of Bluegrass. Everett was playing the mandolin and singing, his older brother Bea was backing him up on the guitar, Don Stover was playing the five-string, and there were three or four musicians alternating on bass and second guitar.

I'd never seen them before, but I knew them from their pictures. Everett blond and chunky, when he wasn't smiling, just ready to smile. Bea shorter and thinner, serious and always concerned. Stover behind them with his banjo, red-haired, energetic, hardly looking at his fingers, turning to talk to someone leaning against the side of the bandstand as he played. The music was ragged and haphazard, but it was suited to the Ranch and its audience. Couples got up to dance to an old-time duet version of the ballad "The Butcher Boy," and sailors at the tables whistled for Don Stover's "Bluegrass Breakdown." I knew that Everett and Bea had been working six nights a week at the club for more than twelve years, and I could understand their relaxed attitude. The audience isn't the same night after night, but it seems the same. The couples get up for the slow tunes, the lonely sailors sing along with the ballads, and everybody stamps on the floor for the breakdowns. Nobody dances them any more so they've gotten faster and faster, like Bill Monroe with his mandolin specialties. Once during their set, a couple set out to do a confused polka to one of the breakdowns, and everybody in the room stood up silently to watch. It was music that reflected this withdrawal of the American country scene. It had lost its regional flavor, but it had become an expression of a deeper rootlessness in America, and there was a wildness in its appeal to the people in the room, drawing them together into a mood that reflected more than the simple words of the songs or the rhythms of the dances.

I looked at some of the faces around me in the dim light. The girls looked like waitresses or store clerks. Sweaters or carefully ironed blouses and simple skirts. They were pale from their jobs, their arms muscular, their faces serious. They accepted an invitation to dance with the seriousness of William Faulkner accepting the Nobel Prize. The men's faces reflected their loneliness. Most of them were young servicemen, there were a few truck drivers at the end of a run away from home, some seamen. When a girl came through the door, they turned and watched her walk to a table. When a couple got up to dance, their eyes followed the movements of hips and legs, imagining themselves dancing with her. A few noisy ones moved through the room, leaning over each table of girls, their eyes going from one to another, looking for the one that would go with them to one of the nearby hotels for the night. It was everything I'd seen in my years in the Army, in the back end of Salinas or on the main street in Anchorage, Alaska. Sitting at tables, drinking flat beer and listening to the noises and the music around me. It was always the same. Just as rhythm-and-blues is the same from clubs in Tupelo, Mississippi, to Spokane, Washington; Dixieland sounds the same in New Orleans and Portland, Maine; and hotel dance bands are as relentlessly bad in Costa Verde, California, and West Lebanon Springs, New York. In America, you can pick your attitude and you find it somewhere in every city and town. Once, I drifted into a bar in San Francisco to listen to a sailor play mountain breakdowns on a tenor banjo and heard him again in a bar in Seattle three weeks later. The noisy ones? They always find someone to go home with. I could see the girls in the Hillbilly Ranch covertly watching the men move around them, trying to decide what they'd say when one of them got to their table. (I would come back from some art film that I'd found in the back end of Carmel, California, tired of pretentious talk and old French movies, and the noisy ones would come stumbling back to the barracks, loudly bragging and gloriously drunk. "I had eight-and-one-third girls this weekend," the man who had the bunk under mine told me unsteadily. "One-third?" I said. "Well, there was three of us took this little girl out," he answered, trying to untie his shoes and falling over a foot locker.)

Everett and Bea were just like their music as we stood and talked at the bar after the set. The quality that sets the musician apart from the instrumentalist: Bill Monroe's pride, Roscoe Holcomb's intense sincerity, Charlie Mingus's rage, John Hurt's quiet sweetness. They were instinctively polite, with the sincere courtesy that you find only among country people, and they were both uncomfortably pleased that there were people seriously interested in their music. Bea is quieter, and usually leaves the talking to Everett; so, after a moment, he excused himself and went to sit on the other side of the room. Everett stayed to talk. In their long years of playing together, it's always been the same: Bea letting Everett do the talking for them. He's the older brother by a year and a half, but Everett is more restless, in his way more ambitious, although he would never change the music that they've grown up with since they began singing together in Clear Creek, West Virginia, in the late 1930s.[1] In the music, too, it's Everett who is always pushing to entertain the audience with something a little different. Manny Greenhill, their manager, told me the next day of a concert that they'd done. After they had sung their old duets and country songs and played some of the Bluegrass favorites, Everett had gone offstage and come back with a fiddle and played an "Orange Blossom Special" that had gone on for nearly ten minutes. (I heard him do it later at the club, and I have never heard an "Orange Blossom Special" with so much music in it.) Then, Everett had gone offstage and come back with his pants rolled up, lipstick on his nose, and a five-string banjo under his arm. For twenty minutes, he did claw-hammer banjo solos, told country jokes, and even danced a little on one of the breakdowns. This is one of the reasons why Everett sometimes gets hired away from the club for a year or two with one of the top Bluegrass bands, like Flatt and Scruggs. The other reason, of course, is his mandolin playing. There are city musicians who rate the more colorful mandolin players like Frank Wakefield higher than Everett, but Everett has a beautifully clear tone and a consistent melodic inventiveness. In the recording studio a few

---

1. Bea Lilly, born on December 15, 1921, is actually about two and half years older than Everett, who was born on July 1, 1924. Ivan M. Tribe, "The Lilly Brothers," in *The Encyclopedia of Country Music: The Ultimate Guide to the Music,* comp. by the staff of the Country Music Hall of Fame and Museum, ed. Paul Kingsbury (New York: Oxford University Press, 1998), 298–99.

weeks later, he did take after take with consistent taste and ingenuity. Bea, with his quietness and stubborn sincerity, is a good counter to Everett's impulsiveness. He spent a year carving a guitar out of a piece of wood with a penknife and sandpaper, put strings on it, and uses it every night at the club, without feeling any necessity to tell anybody about it.

Standing with Everett at the bar, I found that there was another side to him which had nothing to do with music. It was like the Greek legend that I only half-remember from my reading book in the third grade. The gods visit an old man and his wife in the country, and every time the old man tries to give them some wine the vessel fills itself again. With Everett, it was Budweiser. The glass was always full. My glass was always full. I even walked to a booth and sat down, and the glass filled itself as we talked. I spent the rest of the intermission with my hand nervously covering the top of the glass. When the relief band left the bandstand and it was time for the Lilly Brothers to go on again, I could only lean heavily against the back of the booth and watch Everett with a new admiration. As he stood up, the young musician who had been playing bass at the end of the set came over to talk to us. "This is my son," Everett said. "I'm making him go to college so he can make something out of himself, but I've been letting him play a little music, too, since it seems to come in our family." Everett Allan, Jr., short-haired, good looking, nervous, looked away uncomfortably. He was pleased, but he wasn't sure of what he should say. Bea was back on the bandstand and was tuning up. Don Stover was standing to one side of the room with some friends.

I stayed for most of the next set. Nervous young sailors asked the silent girls to dance, a drunk truck driver got too friendly with a waitress and had to be helped into the night air, a recruit in an unpressed Army uniform played a number with the band and did a fast version of a banjo tune he'd learned from a Flatt and Scruggs record. Through all of it, Everett smiled and sang, sometimes turning to Bea, who nodded gravely to what Everett was saying. For some numbers, they stood aside on the little stage and let Don Stover have the microphone to sing and to play. As I sat listening, drinking the last of the Budweiser that Everett had managed to get into my glass, I realized that the folk audience, with its emphasis on social identification on one side or showmanship on the other, would probably never understand Everett and Bea. The city people never really understand the country people. Each uses the other, uncomfortably and unsuccessfully, but there is no real understanding between them. I left the Ranch with the music still swinging around inside my head. It was dark on the little square. Dark, cold, and windy. A wind sweeping in off the Atlantic and chilling the bare hands that I had jammed into my pockets. I stood in the middle of the street and looked back at the club. Hillbilly Ranch. I began to worry about the people I knew in Kentucky trying to manage a spring roundup, and, with my head bent into the collar of my coat, I walked slowly through the lonely wind looking for my car.

Michael Melford, who in 1965 gave the musician's side of working at the Hill-billy Ranch, wrote me in 2000—from his Cambridge, Massachusetts, law office—that he wasn't proud of his warts-and-all portrait of the Boston club. But he agreed in the end to allow use of the piece, which appeared, after slight editing of the version here, in the mimeographed folk newsletter *Autoharp*. It seemed to me that the story, particularly read in conjunction with Sam Charters's *Sing Out!* story on the Lilly Brothers, offers an invaluable contemporaneous look at the way city and country audiences met and the way musicians provided the soundtrack for that cultural intermingling. The portrayals of the Hillbilly Ranch by Charters and Melford aren't necessarily mutually exclusive, but they are certainly different.

24

"Working the Hillbilly Ranch"

MICHAEL J. MELFORD

Our correspondent, Michael J. Melford, is a native of Tennessee and a bluegrass mandolin picker who has worked professionally for several years. At the request of the editor he has set down his experiences as a working musician in one of the East Coast's largest country-music bars and his impressions of the various types of people who come to listen to the music in such places. His reminiscences quickly took on the character of an exposé, and the editor delightedly spit on his hands and began cutting stencil. In a movement filled with every sort of cant imaginable, the following comes not only as a shock, but as a beautiful revelation.

Fritz asked me to write something about working the Hillbilly Ranch in Boston, Massachusetts. This place has three claims to fame: It is the biggest country house in New England, seating maybe four or five hundred people; it's the only place where you can hear live country music seven nights a week; and, according to the United States Navy, more contact with V.D. are made here than anywhere else in the area. I guess I worked there about seven months with Alabamian Bill Phillips and Kenny Brown, a banjo-picker from Pennsylvania, as well as a number of other musicians, including Herb Applin and various fiddlers and singers, both locals and transplants from the South. The Lilly Brothers, Everett and B and Don Stover were the headliners at the place. I have to wrack my brain to say anything good about the establishment. Rather than give you the usual promotional nonsense I was expected to hand out while employed there I try to tell you what working there was actually like.

Our audience consisted mainly of sailors and truck-drivers from the South, and these were our best fans. The rest were the dregs of Boston society and college students who were, with a few exceptions, a pain in the ass. What we played is mostly so-called Bluegrass music with some modern country and western songs thrown in. Also "Happy Birthday" about once every two hours. The sound system is terrible, so we had to practically lift the strings out of the bridge and sing at the top of our voices to make ourselves heard above all the shouting and fist fights. Once in a while we got applause if there wasn't a good fight or something more interesting to watch. But we knew they were paying attention to us because we were always getting more requests than we could fill, and a lot of fine people bought us drinks, the fuel you need in order to work in a dive of this type.

For diversion we had the truck-drivers chasing the waitresses around the place, only to be thrown out by the two reputed Mafiosos who owned the place, assisted by a goodly number of Boston's finest, who keep a paddy wagon outside the door for this purpose, and the folkies from Harvard Square, who were funnier. Fritz has asked me to say something about them. We never saw them on the dance floor (another diverting area of the establishment), and they mostly sat and nursed one coke all night, to the disgust of the management. They came armed with instruments and pads of paper to write down what we were doing, which especially annoyed Kenny, who, like all paranoid banjo-pickers, had nightmares about having his licks copped (he has plenty of good original ones, incidentally). Once in a while these people would climb up on stage and attempt some songs or instrumentals which never failed to end disastrously. This included just about all the professional entertainers from Cambridge, who for some reason insist on playing Bluegrass music (a mistake) for what they call the folk music in it. Some of them have played the Newport Folk Festival and have recorded for the folk labels, but when they got up before a country audience they seemed to get rather shook up and often forgot the chords to whatever they were playing. Then they would come over to the bar side with us when the relief band came on and allow us to buy them beers while they spent half an hour telling us how much they knew about country music and all the country entertainers they had met. This is very fascinating to listen to. We usually got along with them unless they asked to get up on the stage. We didn't mind listening to them (they were also interesting to look at) except when we had some women in to see us, when we ignored everything else. Maybe I should tell you that we worked six hours a night, seven nights a week, and even though we had a few hundred songs we just performed them over and over again, and some, like "Tennessee Waltz," "T for Texas," "Alabam" or other songs with state-names, we did about every set, depending on where the clowns in the audience were from.

We also had a number of local fags that the management allowed to get up and sing Kitty Wells songs at each other ("Meanwhile," "Down at Joe's," "I'd Like to Be the Winner of Your Heart," "Lonely Side of Town," etc.). They had the boss's permission. The owners were straight though, unlike the situation at other joints around Washington Street, which is known locally as the "Combat Zone," although it was as tame as Green Street compared to Calumet City, Illinois, and Columbus, Mississippi, where we have worked some pretty tough joints.

Until I started working professionally I used to wonder what the performers were thinking while we sat there looking at them. Were they as wrapped up in the music as we were? I can tell you that they spend most of their time comparing the physical attributes of the women in the audience and seeing who they can put on, except when they got a really good, hip audience, which is when the music really gets good.

To answer Fritz's question, the folkies wanted to hear songs like "Katy Dear," "Mary of the Wild Moor," other old antiseptic "Blue Sky Boys Songs" and fancy, emotionless instrumentals like "Devil's Dream" and "Blackberry Blossom," which have lots of notes and tricky runs and which are fine for limbering up your fingers. The country people wanted "I Know You're Married, but I Love You Still," "Heartaches by the Number," "Detroit City," "Miller's Cave," a few oldies like "New River Train," and for instrumentals they liked to see Kenny put some hurtin' on something like "Foggy Mountain Breakdown," "San Antonio Rose" or "Fire on the Mountain." I guess I don't have to tell you which type we prefer. What we really like is stuff like "Somebody Loves You, Darling," "Thinking about You," "Over the Hills to the Poorhouse" (written by Everett or his mother) [*Note:* I find this throwaway line (which is highly typical of the writer) so intriguing that I promise to worm its explanation out of Melford at our next session of cork-popping, and I likewise promise to pass the story on to our readers. Ed.], "Drink Up and Go Home," some songs I wrote, old Flatt and Scruggs, Reno and Smiley, Ray Price and Lefty Frizzell songs.[1] We don't really like instrumentals very much, except for Kenny, who, like all banjo players, can't sing.

We had our good nights and bad. Usually we played better earlier in the evening and enjoyed it more later as we progressively drove the blood from our alcohol streams. Almost all country performers drink, incidentally, to excess. We were at our best when people like Bill Monroe, Webb Pierce, Frank Wakefield and others came in to jam with us. The last-named came and stayed about a week with us, and we had a great time. But usually it was pretty boring.

Plous wants me to write more, but I have to go to work now, so I'd like to thank him for showing me how to use a typewriter.

Originally published in *Autoharp* (Campus Folksong Club, University of Illinois at Urbana-Champaign), no. 27, Dec. 18, 1965, 1–3. Reprinted by permission of the author.

Years before his glory days as the prime exponent of gonzo journalism, Hunter S. Thompson did a fair amount of writing about music, including this highly opinionated piece on the Greenwich Village bluegrass scene. He pitched it unsuc-

---

1. Written by George L. Catlin and David Braham in 1874, "Over the Hills to the Poorhouse" was suggested as a 1951 recording by Flatt and Scruggs by Everett Lilly, who learned it from his mother. Thanks to Tom Ewing for pointing this out; Neil Rosenberg had unearthed this information for his liner notes to the Bear Family Records boxed set *Flatt and Scruggs, 1948–1959*.

cessfully in late 1961 to an Illinois-based magazine, *Rogue,* where science fiction mainstay Harlan Ellison also labored at the time. Thompson's Kentucky background gave him a different perspective on the fine line that bluegrass revivalists faced. Even songs they genuinely loved, such as "Amelia Earhart's Last Flight" (here given an incorrect title by Thompson), often came off as condescending kitsch to the urban listeners at Gerdes Folk City. To Thompson, the Greenbriar Boys—guitarist John Herald, mandolinist Ralph Rinzler, and banjo player Bob Yellin—were simply "fraudulent farmers" who had no Kentucky connections deserving of the name bluegrass. The "Irv Weissberg" mentioned as a musical guest appears to have been Eric Weissberg, a long-time staple of the New York City bluegrass and country music scene.

25

"New York Bluegrass"

HUNTER S. THOMPSON

New York City—The scene is Greenwich Village, a long dimly lit bar called Folk City, just east of Washington Square Park. The customers are the usual mixture: students in sneakers and button-down shirts, overdressed tourists in for the weekend, "nine-to-five types" with dark suits and chic dates, and a scattering of sullen looking "beat-niks."

A normal Saturday night in The Village: two parts boredom, one part local color, and one part anticipation.

This is the way it was at ten-thirty. The only noise was the hum of conversation and the sporadic clang of the cash register.

Most people approach The Village with the feeling that "things are happening here." If you hit a dead spot, you move on as quickly as you can. Because things are happening—somewhere. Maybe just around the corner.

I've been here often enough to know better, but Folk City was so dead that even a change of scenery would have been exciting. So I was just about ready to move on when things began happening. What appeared on the tiny bandstand at that moment was one of the strangest sights I've ever witnessed in The Village.

Three men in farmer's garb, grinning, tuning their instruments, while a suave MC introduced them as "the Greenbriar Boys, straight from the Grand Ole Opry."

Gad, I thought. What a hideous joke!

It was strange then, but moments later it was downright eerie. These three grinning men, this weird, country-looking trio, stood square in the heartland of the "avant garde" and burst into a nasal, twanging rendition of, "We need a whole lot more of Jesus, and a lot less rock-n-roll."

I was dumbfounded, and could hardly believe my ears when the crowd cheered mightily, and the Greenbriar Boys responded with an Earl Scruggs arrangement of

"Home Sweet Home." The tourists smiled happily, the "bohemian" element—uniformly decked out in sunglasses, long striped shirts and Levi's—kept time by thumping on the tables, and a man next to me grabbed my arm and shouted: "What the hell's going on here? I thought this was an Irish bar!"

I muttered a confused reply, but my voice was lost in the uproar of the next song—a howling version of "Good Ole Mountain Dew" that brought a thunderous ovation.

Here in New York they call it "Bluegrass Music," but the link—if any—to the Bluegrass region of Kentucky is vague indeed. Anybody from the South will recognize the same old hoot-n-holler, country jamboree product that put Roy Acuff in the 90 percent bracket. A little slicker, perhaps; a more sophisticated choice of songs; but in essence, nothing more or less than "good old-fashioned" hillbilly music.

The performance was neither a joke nor a spoof. Not a conscious one, anyway—although there may be some irony in the fact that a large segment of the Greenwich population is made up of people who have "liberated themselves" from rural towns in the South and Midwest, where hillbilly music is as common as meat and potatoes.

As it turned out, the Greenbriar Boys hadn't exactly come "straight from the Grand Ole Opry." As a matter of fact, they came straight from Queens and New Jersey, where small bands of country music connoisseurs have apparently been thriving for years. Although there have been several country music concerts in New York, this is the first time a group of hillbilly singers have been booked into a recognized night club.

Later in the evening, the Greenbriar Boys were joined by a fiddler name Irv Weissberg. The addition of a fiddle gave the music a sound that was almost authentic, and it would have taken a real aficionado to turn up his nose and speak nostalgically of Hank Williams. With the fiddle taking the lead, the fraudulent farmers set off on "Orange Blossom Special," then changed the pace with "Sweet Cocaine"—dedicated, said one, "to any junkies in the audience."

It was this sort of thing—hip talk with a molasses accent—that gave the Greenbriar Boys a distinctly un-hillbilly flavor. And when they did a sick little ditty called, "Happy Landings, Amelia Earhart," there was a distinct odor of Lenny Bruce in the room.

In light of the current renaissance in Folk Music, the appearance of the Greenbriar Boys in Greenwich Village is not really a surprise. The "avant garde" is hardpressed these days to keep ahead of the popular taste. They had Brubeck and Kenton a long time ago, but dropped that when the campus crowd took it up. The squares adopted Flamenco in a hurry, and Folk Music went the same way. Now, apparently out of desperation, the avant garde is digging hillbilly.

The Village is dedicated to "new sounds," and today's experiment is very often tomorrow's big name. One of the best examples is Harry Belafonte, who sold hamburgers in a little place near Sheridan Square until he got a chance to sing at the Village Vanguard.

Belafonte, however, was a genuine "new sound." If you wanted to hear him, there was only one place to go. And if you weren't there, you simply missed the boat.

With the Greenbriar Boys, it's not exactly the same. I thought about this as I watched them. Here I was, at a "night spot" in one of the world's most cultured cities, paying close to a dollar for each beer, surrounded by apparently intelligent people who seemed enthralled by each thump and twang of the banjo string—and we were all watching a performance that I could almost certainly see in any roadhouse in rural Kentucky on any given Saturday night.

As Pogo once said—back in the days when mossback editors were dropping Walt Kelly like a hot, pink potato—"it gives a man paws."

Originally published in *The Fear and Loathing Letters*, vol. 1: *The Proud Highway: Saga of a Desperate Southern Gentleman, 1955–1967* (New York: Villard, 1997), 303–5. Reprinted by permission of Random House.

C harles Wolfe's voluminous writings on country music display scholarly grasp of detail and also employ an agreeably conversational writing style. His many books deal with subjects from the Grand Ole Opry's early days to the life of blues-folk legend Lead Belly. His look at the history of County Records and Dave Freeman ranges beyond the hard facts to the key notion that "the beliefs and philosophies of key record company owners and promoters can help us understand a lot about the state of bluegrass and old-timey music today." A long-time professor at Middle Tennessee State University in Murfreesboro and a widely heeded author and interview subject, Wolfe is a font of highly reliable information and opinion.

26

"Dave Freeman and County Records"

CHARLES WOLFE

It is possible that there are bluegrass fans living in the caves of West Virginia who have never heard of County Records. Unlikely, but possible. There may also be bluegrass fans who have never bought a bluegrass record, and have heard the music only in bars and at festivals. But even the most obtuse fan has heard of Bill and Charlie Monroe, Flatt and Scruggs, the Stanley Brothers, Bill Clifton, the Blue Sky Boys, Norman Blake, Larry Sparks—all artists whose music has found its way onto some sort of County Record. For over fifteen years, County Records and its mail-order component, County Sales, has acted as a potent force in promoting and developing both bluegrass and ole-time music. Without intending to, County has had a considerable impact on the way a couple of generations of fans have perceived the music, and on the way a lot of younger musicians have learned styles and repertoires. With any art form, the conduit—the way the art reaches the public—can have a lot to do with the way fans perceive the art; and a look at the beliefs and philosophies of key record company owners and promoters can help us understand a lot about the state of bluegrass and old-time music today.

The first thing anyone interested in Dave Freeman or his County label should realize is that the outfit includes several diverse operations. There is County Records itself, started in 1963, which has over one hundred bluegrass and old-time albums currently in print; County Sales, a mail-order retail firm started in 1965, which sends its monthly newsletters to thousands of fans around the world; and Record Depot, a distribution network set up to provide stores in Virginia, North Carolina, and Tennessee with bluegrass records. In addition, Dave Freeman runs an auction service for rare and out-of-print records and has recently taken over management of Rebel Records, a pioneering bluegrass label started by Dick Freeland, as well as Kanawha Records, a small label devoted to southeastern traditional music. Freeman is also involved with Barry Poss in the Sugar Hill label, a relatively new company which, to quote from its press release, is interested in documenting "all facets of country music with roots," and which has produced impressive and successful albums by Ricky Skaggs, The Country Gentlemen, The Seldom Scene and Buck White to mention only a few. All of these different facets influence each other in all kinds of subtle and complex ways, and an exact analysis of the way it all works together would require a computer; suffice it to say that all the activities have in common a long-standing and obviously sincere dedication to traditional and bluegrass music. No one who spends much time talking with Dave Freeman or the people he works with can doubt that.

In some ways, the early history of County reads like a classic American small business success story. It starts in 1963, in New York, with young Dave Freeman working at the post office and spending a lot of his spare time listening to the old pre-war country records that had been made in the 1920's by people like Charlie Poole, the Skillet Lickers, and Uncle Dave Macon. It was in the middle of the "folk revival," and among the hootenanny freaks who were getting off on the Kingston Trio and the Limelighters, there were a few young people who were going back to genuine roots of the music, and listening to the old records—when they could find them. In an attempt to remedy this situation, one record company started a series called Origin Jazz Classics, which included material reissued from old pre-war blues 78s. These reissue albums impressed Dave Freeman. "I had a pretty decent collection of old 78s," he recalls, "enough to make a decent choice as far as fiddle music was concerned. I felt I could do the same thing as these Origin things, and if I didn't someone else would, sooner or later. I checked a couple of stores in New York and asked them if they could use some if I put out something like that, and they didn't encourage it much, but I had a feeling I could sell a few, just enough to break even."

He had also been running mail-order auctions of 78s, and had a mailing list of about 120 people; many of these, he felt, would take such an album. The result was County 501, *A Collection of Mountain Fiddle Music,* an anthology featuring 1920s' recordings of Charlie Poole, Burnett and Rutherford, Crockett's Mountaineers, the Leake County Revelers, and the Blue Ridge Highballers—the semi-professional country string bands which laid the foundation for modern bluegrass and grass roots music.

"We pressed up about 440 of them; they actually came out in early '64. We printed the cover ourselves. My dad was in the printing business and he drew a little mountain cabin and designed the thing and we printed it on a press that he had used to print greeting cards on. We couldn't print them large enough for a wrap-around jacket, so we designed them the way they did those old Folkways jackets, stuck it on, then stuck a little strip on the back with the tune titles."

The decision to call the new label "County" did not come about casually. "I wanted something with a rural association. I kept thinking of the word *rural,* but there was already a Rural Rhythm record label. When I was travelling around the South looking for old records, part of what had fascinated me was the county system—each little county had its own personality in a way. We didn't have the equivalent of that in New York City . . . I hesitated in that I thought it would get mixed up and misspelled as 'Country,' which it does, but that's worth it, I guess." County 501 was not an immediate smash hit—it took Freeman "four or five years" to finally sell all his original 440 copies—but enough money was generated by sales to permit him to do three more reissue anthologies in the next year: 502 (ballads), 503 (more fiddle music), and 504 (*Mountain Songs,* the earliest County album still in print). All the early anthologies were pretty basic: stark covers, no liner notes whatsoever, and minimal discographic information. Part of this lack of liner notes was due to the fact that historical research in early country music was almost non-existent, and there was very little information about many of the early bands or singers. Some reviewers at the time complained at this, but Freeman later noted that, in those days, it would have cost him thousands of dollars in research expenses to have documented the albums as well as most historical albums are today.

Meanwhile, however, the company had taken off in another direction with the release of *Clawhammer Banjo* in 1964; this was a collection of new field recordings of four older Galax-area musicians played in a rapping, frailing, or downpicking style, styles predating bluegrass banjo by two or three generations. The album was numbered 701, to distinguish its new recordings from the historical reissues of the 500 series.

The album marked the start of Freeman's association with Charles Faurot, who was to become instrumental in developing County's "modern" catalogue. "I met Charley Faurot through Bill Vernon; they were both living in Brooklyn; I had known Bill since 1960 or '61. Charley is from a suburb of Chicago, was a contemporary of John Cohen at Yale, and that's how he got interested in old-time music. At Yale he had actually gone and recorded Buell Kazee and done a few things like that back in the mid-1950's. When I met him he was going out and recording these guys just as a hobby—he worked in a bank—and played a little banjo himself, and was interested in banjo, and had recorded ten or twelve banjo players from different parts. It wasn't on a big scale, but he had a few nice tapes, some things on Kyle Creed, and asked if I would be interested in doing an album of new things, and we did." The *Clawhammer Banjo* album did have notes—good ones, giving biographical information and even tunings—and the record became an important learning tool for a lot of young revivalist banjo players trying to pick up a pre-bluegrass style. It helped Freeman realize that there was a market for new recordings of southern string band music that was as strong as the one for historical reissues. Other 700 series albums soon followed.

"Charlie Faurot did most of the first fifteen albums we did in the 700 series; I think the only ones I did myself were the Red Allen and Janette Carter.[1] He arranged everything—in effect he brought me the finished product, as far as the tape goes." The early albums had a strong orientation to the music of the Galax-central Blue Ridge area, since both Freeman and Faurot were attracted to that style of traditional music. "I realize," recalls Freeman, "there was music all around at other places, but somehow I felt this was probably the best."

While many of the 700 series albums concentrated on old-time banjo and fiddle music, a significant number documented bluegrass. Freeman recalls that "in a way, I was more into bluegrass than old-time music then. As far as following current music, I was more into bluegrass." This interest was reflected in County 702, a hard-driving bluegrass album by Larry Richardson, a Galax-area guitarist and banjoist who was comfortable playing in both old-time and bluegrass modes. Did the bluegrass album have more sales appeal than the others? "Not really. The only thing was, a group like Larry's, they had a ready-made audience there. They were playing dates, they could take the record around, they could get air play, and some of the stores there in Winston-Salem would take it. Even then, it took ages to sell five hundred of them too." Other bluegrass albums soon followed, ones featuring Red Allen, Joe Greene, Kenny Baker, Red Rector, the Lilly Brothers, Buck White, and soon the 700 series was outstripping the reissue series.

Up until now County had been doing things similar to what companies like Folkways had been doing a few years earlier, and directing much of its product at a northern-based, even academic market. But by 1965–66, Freeman was finding that the southeastern mountain music also still had commercial appeal in the South as well. "I had been collecting 78s door to door in the South since '59 or so. The South appealed to me in all ways, not just the music, even though I was a New Yorker. In the course of doing that, people talked all the time, 'Gee I wish I could get a record of Gid Tanner now,' and it was obvious to me that a lot of people, especially the older people that remembered but even some of the younger bluegrass musicians, remem-

1. The records were *Red Allen* (County 704), released in March 1966, and Joe and Janette Carter's *Carter Family Favorites* (County 706), released in December 1966.

bered or were interested. I even felt the major companies like Columbia or Victor were missing a bet by not putting out a Skillet Lickers album. I became convinced there was still a market for old-time music in the South. I was also aware that there would be some from a city background or a college background that would be interested, but honestly at that time I didn't think there would be enough of a market to aim it at a college or a big city audience. If I felt I would have to sell five hundred copies that way, I don't think I would ever have put out the first record. Knowing a bit about the South, I felt I could sell a few in this town, fifteen or twenty in Galax, a few in Mt. Airy. I remember selling a few to a store in (East) Jenkins, Kentucky the first time I was there. I would carry County albums in my car as I drove around looking for 78s. At first, most of the sales—especially that Charlie Poole reissue—were down in the southwest Virginia area. In fact, that's how I got most of my distribution in Virginia, and indirectly how we came to later settle in Floyd and this area."

While County's individual records were successful enough, it was the creation of County Sales in 1965 that allowed Freeman to quit his job and devote his full time to the record business. County Sales originated as an informal mail order service to British readers of a magazine called *Country Music News and Views;* after three or four years, it had expanded to include domestic customers as well. By 1965 Dave had established a mailing list, and a *County Sales Newsletter.* Originally the *Newsletter* was designed to "meet the need for a good source for Bluegrass and Old-Time Records and information," and contained a good deal of miscellaneous information in addition to record notices. The information function of the *Newsletter* gradually dropped off with the establishment of *Bluegrass Unlimited* in July 1966, *Old Time Music* in 1971, and other similar publications. At about the same time, though, the record reviews began to gain in importance. In his *Newsletter* #50, dated March–April 1972, Freeman wrote: "In the past few years the picture has changed considerably with regard to the production of Bluegrass and Old-Time records. The great majority of such records are now issued by the smaller, little-known companies, or by the artists themselves." With this decentralization of record production, outlets such as County became even more important to fans who wanted records on obscure labels.

As Freeman's mailing list grew, he began to notice that he was sending lists out to rural addresses in the South and Midwest as much as to urban, northern audiences. Some of his customers, he found, were even able to offer him leads as to the whereabouts of older musicians that had dropped out of sight. Partially because of his success in selling his records to the rural audience that had originally generated it, Freeman moved his entire operation from New York to the small Blue Ridge town of Floyd, Virginia, in June of 1974. There he continued his mail order service and set up Record Depot, a distribution service now headquartered in Roanoke, which sells some thirty-five different labels, almost all bluegrass or old-time, to retail outlets in the region.

Meanwhile, County kept issuing its own records. The typical County release, either new or reissue, sold rather slowly but steadily. Still, "Best-sellers" developed: the clawhammer banjo albums, Kenny Baker, the Stanley Brothers ("You put 'em in any store and they sell; we just don't get any returns on them"), and most recently, the album by Senate Majority Leader Robert Byrd, which threatens to become County's all-time best-seller.[2] Among the reissues, Uncle Dave Macon and Charlie Poole sell very well. But by standards now used by major labels, many of these best-sellers would not be all that impressive. Says Freeman: "Nowadays I don't think the major companies would be interested in anything that sold less than twenty-five thousand copies. I heard that when Decca—MCA—cleaned house a while back, they used forty thousand as a bottom line figure. I really expected them to even cut Monroe." Unlike other companies, County does not really care all that much whether an artist sells a lot of the records himself or tours a lot: "There have been artists on our 700 series who have never sold a single record themselves. In the past, if I believed in a record enough to put it out, it never bothered me one iota if the group broke up the next day, or never sold one record on tour. That's beginning to change some now. In fact, one of the reasons we started Sugar Hill was to produce more active groups, groups that do get out and appear a lot, where we can afford to sink more into production and promotion."

Over the years, County developed a distinct image among record buyers: one that centered on hard, "pure," traditional bluegrass and mountain music. In one recent *Newsletter,* Freeman estimated that 60 percent of his audience still preferred the older, Monroe-Stanley forms of bluegrass to the newer, more experimental forms. In 1977 he refused to review the New Grass Revival album *When the Storm Is Over* in the *County Sales Newsletter,* explaining: "I felt the album to have no relation at all to rural or country music as I know it. The songs, style, and approach were all contemporary in nature (or rock oriented) and I just do not have the background in this type of music to be able to judge whether or not the group was successful in what it was trying to do."

Later, Freeman amplified these views. "I can never appreciate newgrass when they do bluegrass versions of rock songs, but if they're taking their own material or traditional material and experimenting with it, that doesn't bother me. But what I need before I can really get into it is the feeling that they've really assimilated whatever they're using as components and they're at home with it: that it's a natural evolution. I feel a lot of the younger people are forcing it, saying in their minds that they're going to come up with something new because they feel they have to. It's the thing to do, come up with something new and different. Even old-time groups are doing it: bizarre combinations of instruments, the most obscure tunes they can find. But when they can get up and do 'Soldier's Joy' and it comes out of their own thing, without having to say it's different because they did this or that, or because

---

2. Sen. Robert Byrd's *Mountain Fiddler* (County 769) was released in 1978.

of some obscure piece, then I feel they've got a point." Freeman's judgement seems borne out, at least, by his own sales; County's customers still buy more traditional albums than newgrass, and the fastest-sellers he has had in recent years have been some custom pressings of old Flatt and Scruggs' sides from the early 1950's.

Yet Freeman is aware that the music, within even the older bluegrass tradition, must develop. "A lot of the younger musicians are restless, they keep searching. I keep saying we're in a transition period. I don't know what it's going to lead to, in terms of a new music. It's obvious now that it can't keep up in the Stanley or Monroe tradition. I realize that now, and I'm not looking for that. I suspect that new groups that get on our label would be more likely to be contemporary groups rather than strictly traditional groups—though there are some new artists doing exciting things in the traditional mode. It can be done. The Dave Evans albums are a good example; we would have liked to have had them on our label, on County."

Such considerations were influential in the formation, in 1978, of the Sugar Hill label run by Barry Poss. Sugar Hill, which in no way is a subsidiary of County, is located in Durham, N.C., not Floyd, and has a entirely different philosophy as a company. Freeman: "The idea behind Sugar Hill was that it would free us to put out a more commercial type of music. I didn't want to put certain types of things on County; it has a reputation for acoustic, traditional music. Something that created a problem would be the music of Buck White. I wanted to work with Buck White, I like what they're doing. I believe in them; on the other hand, what they're getting into is not exactly any longer bluegrass. In their case, I agree, they're going in the right direction, I don't think bluegrass would be helping them anymore. And I don't think it would necessarily be doing justice to it either. We thought their new album should have been on a different label—like Sugar Hill." The recent releases on Sugar Hill, such as ones by Ricky Skaggs and John Starling, contain electric instruments, studio production sound, and are making a distinct impact on the commercial country market.

Another facet of County's image is that, unlike almost every other label, the company has never recorded any of the numerous young old-time "revival" bands heard so often at festivals today. This, coupled with Freeman's occasionally severe reviews of revival bands in his *Newsletter,* has led to charges that he is prejudiced against young, northern-based revival bands. He denies this. "I never had anything against revival bands as such. What I was objecting to, it was just a sort of gut feeling that they hadn't put in their time. It was like the city bluegrass groups, which I feel the same way about, ten to fifteen years ago in the north. They were interested, they had the enthusiasm, they'd heard a fair amount of the stuff, but they hadn't had enough time as a group to put it together. Now in the last couple of years, there have been some albums come out, where I don't think in terms of separating them, rural or urban group, anymore; that *Plank Road* (String Band) album, I enjoyed that for the music, I didn't care who was on there. I liked some of the New Lost City

Ramblers, such as that *Songs of the Depression,* because they did the tunes and didn't copy them note for note like the originals, and I don't see anything wrong with that, but even if you get it down perfectly, what's the point of putting that on a record?[3] Playing it on a show is a different thing. I've heard a lot of young groups today play on stage songs they learned off of County reissues—they did a great job, sometimes, but I'm not going to put that on record again."

In addition to his involvement with Sugar Hill, Freeman has recently been expanding his activities in still other directions. He recently acquired the rights to the Rebel catalogue, one of the first and most respected bluegrass labels, and plans on reviving the label; some of the original catalogue items will be reprinted, and new releases are out by Bill Grant–Delia Bell, Bill Harrell, and Larry Sparks. County has also recently been working with Columbia for more custom reissues of classic bluegrass like the Flatt and Scruggs; scheduled for release soon are two more LPs of early Bill Monroe material from Columbia's vaults, and somewhere down the line may be a vintage Roy Acuff collection. The County reissue program continues to develop, with new albums planned by Uncle Dave Macon, Fiddlin' Doc Roberts, and collections of Galax-area string bands and early gospel singers. The *County Sales Newsletter,* still written and edited by Freeman himself, continues to offer informative reviews and bits of information. In fact, all of the various activities surrounding Dave Freeman continue to whirl along, a fact which is reassuring for the music and its fans.

Originally published in *Bluegrass Unlimited* 15 (Dec. 1980): 50–55. Reprinted by permission of the author and *Bluegrass Unlimited.*

F rom the earliest days of the music, Bill Monroe and other bluegrass pioneers drew from a broad range of styles to create their heady and captivating sounds. In turn, performers such as Elvis Presley and Carl Perkins summoned up bluegrass as well as country and blues music when coming up with rock 'n' roll. So it should have made some kind of sense for string musicians to bring elements of rock back into bluegrass. But when mainline bands such as Jim and Jesse and northern exponents such as the Charles River Valley Boys actually recorded rock-based albums there were predictable howls from many hard-core bluegrassers. Reviewing two such releases for *Bluegrass Unlimited,* Neil Rosenberg took no particular issue with the choice of rock tunes but found the records to be generally undistinguished. The inroads of rock into bluegrass had only begun. What would those who objected to Chuck Berry tunes say of more recent bluegrass incursions into the music of AC/DC, Pink Floyd, and others?

3. The disc was *Songs from the Depression* (Folkways FH 5264), 1959.

27

"Rockbluerollgrass/bluerockandrollgrass Recordings"

NEIL V. ROSENBERG

Beatle Country with the Charles River Valley Boys
Electra EKL-4006 (stereo) EKS-74006

"I've Just Seen a Face" / "Baby's in Black" / "I Feel Fine" / "Yellow Submarine" / "Ticket to Ride" / "And Your Bird Can Sing" / "What Goes On" / "Norwegian Wood" / "Paperback Writer" / "She's a Woman" / "I Saw Her Standing There" / "Help"

Berry Pickin' in the Country   Jim and Jesse
EPIC LN-24176   EPIC LN-24176 (stereo) BN-26176

"Memphis" / "Johnny B. Goode" / "Sweet Little 16" / "Roll Over Beethoven" / "Reelin' and Rockin'" / "Maybellene" / "Bye Bye Johnny" / "Too Much Monkey Business"/ "Back in the U.S.A." / "Brown Eyed Handsome Man"

Rock and roll has often been contrasted with bluegrass by bluegrass fans, who see R&R as little more than noise aimed at mindless teenagers. While it is true that rock has a very different audience than bluegrass, it is also true that the roots of the two musical styles have much in common. Bluegrass is country music heavily influenced by blues; rock and roll is blues heavily influenced by country music. One of Elvis Presley's first recordings is a version of Bill Monroe's "Blue Moon of Kentucky," and Elvis is said to be a 'grass fan from way back.

But when the rock and roll revolution took place in the 1954–55 period, it spelled disaster for many bluegrass bands. The record industry was turned upside down in the rush to rock, and such popular groups as Jim and Jesse were out of a record contract. In such an atmosphere, not many bluegrass musicians were eager to record rock and roll hits bluegrass-style.

///

Recently, however, LP recordings of rock and roll tunes have appeared. The first, Jim and Jesse's *Berry Pickin' in the Country,* released in December, 1965, features "the great Chuck Berry songbook." The idea for the record is conceived by an A&R man; Jim and Jesse were skeptical at first, but when their arrangement of "Memphis" was so successful that it was borrowed by Flatt and Scruggs, they went along with the Berry album enthusiastically. Unfortunately, "Memphis" is by far the best song on the album (perhaps because its story line is so much more like that of a country song than most rock and roll songs); most of the other performances just don't have the spark that separates a great recording from a competent one. Allen Shelton's banjo is not up to par with his creative standard on the earlier Epic LPs; Jim Brock's fiddle breaks are too much stock country. Only Jesse McReynolds seems able to cope with the unusual songs, and the result is an album full of neat mandolin breaks. Vocally, the singing is good, but the band is handicapped by the nature of rock and roll song phrasing, which often packs many words into small musical spaces. The total of all this is a record which is interesting to listen to once but which does not wear well.

In November, 1966, the Charles River Valley Boys' *Beatle Country* was released. The motivation behind this album is, I suspect, rather different than that of *Berry Pickin'*. The Northern college and coffee house bluegrass musicians have always been more experimental and eclectic with their repertoire. (Two country bluegrass bands have been influenced by this experimentalism: Flatt and Scruggs and The Country Gentlemen). From 1965 on this eclecticism has included Beatles tunes. Thus, rather than an A&R man's brainstorm, this record represents a trend. The differences between this album and the Jim and Jesse one are on two levels—band and songwriter. The Charles River Valley Boys don't have the rock-solid sound of Jim and Jesse (although they do a good job most of the time), whereas the Beatles' songwriting shows more variety of sound and feeling than Berry's. The Beatles have (among other things) increased the amount of country music feeling in rock and roll (they even recorded Buck Owens' "Act Naturally"), and this makes it easier for a bluegrass band to interpret their songs.

To this listener, the outstanding feature of *Beatle Country,* is Joe Val's mandolin playing—clean, uncluttered, a distinctive style with great feeling. Val's breaks on "What Goes On" and "Help" are classics. The singing varies from the forced sound of "I Saw Her Standing There" to the high point of the album, "Norwegian Wood" (which is also instrumentally the best item). Studio sidemen Buddy Spicher (fiddle) and Craig Wingfield (dobro) add considerably to the cuts on which they appear; Bob Siggins does a good job of converting the Beatle humor of "Yellow Submarine" to Grandpa Jones–style, with the help of clever sound effects men at Elektra.

Once again, though, the total effect is a record which is more interesting than captivating. The J&J and CRVB LPs each offer one song which stands on its own as a great bluegrass performance: "Memphis" and "Norwegian Wood." But one feels that both albums show the strain of trying to find twelve songs by one writer which will fit the bluegrass format.

Two other fully successful performances of rock and roll tunes by bluegrass bands should be mentioned. One is the Cincinnati Bluegrass Partners' (Harley Gabbard, dobro; Benny Birchfield, bass; Jr. McIntyre, banjo; Jim McCall, guitar) "Haunted House" on a REM single—a driving trio performance with fine dobro of a mid-fifties hit by Jerry Lee Lewis. The other is a rendition of a recent Chad and Jeremy rock hit, "Yesterday's Gone," by the Osborne Brothers on their latest LP *Up This Hill and Down* (Decca DL 4767). In both recordings the singing is excellent and the style of the songs appropriate to the bands.

What does all this prove? Simply that some rock and roll songs can be done well bluegrass-style; that bluegrass musicians can expand their musical consciousness by turning on to groups like the Beatles, the Lovin' Spoonful and others. It also proves that doing a whole album of one songwriter's material is not likely to be successful. The main point is that too many bluegrass songs on record use the same old musical cliches—the antidote for this musical paralysis is awareness of what other people are doing.

Originally published in *Bluegrass Unlimited* 1 (April 1967): 5–6. Reprinted by permission of the author and *Bluegrass Unlimited*.

Many aspects and issues in bluegrass seem remarkably constant through the years. "Even with all the success that bluegrass is having right now, there is still a reluctance in the record industry, radio stations, etc. to support the music promotionally. Do you think bluegrass can ever be as big commercially as other types of music?" That was the question Doug Tuchman posed to the Country Gentlemen in this 1973 interview. But it could just as easily have been asked in the 1950s or in 2004.

The Country Gentlemen dealt with the problem of profitability in bluegrass, in part, by incorporating pop and folk influences and by taking some of the hard edges off the high lonesome sound. This in-depth interview with guitarist-singer Charlie Waller and his mates also reveals an unusual level of detail about bluegrass financial arrangements. Future acoustic-music superstars Ricky Skaggs and Jerry Douglas were merely hired hands in this edition of the Gents, we learn.

28

"The Country Gentlemen"

DOUG TUCHMAN

The Country Gentlemen are the most award winning band in bluegrass. In talking with Charlie Waller, Bill Yates and Doyle Lawson it is easy to understand one of the reasons why. Their approach to music is very carefully thought out and they are at home playing traditional as well as contemporary bluegrass in a commercial market which demands both. This interview took place December 13, 1973, in New York City.

Pickin': Charlie, where and when did the Gents first come together as a group?

Charlie: We formed July 4, 1957. There was John Duffey, Bill Emerson and myself in the beginning. I'm trying to think who played the bass fiddle at the time.[1] I

---

1. The band's bassist on July 4, 1957, was Larry Leahey.

was working with Buzz Busby at the time in (Washington, D.C.). He was in the hospital from an automobile wreck. In order to keep the job we were working Bill Emerson brought over John Duffey. We liked the sound and we stayed together.

Pickin': When did Eddie Adcock come in?

Charlie: Emerson wasn't with us very long—about a year. There was conflict between Emerson and Duffey—mainly just small things. It just didn't work out. We were on the lookout for another banjo player. We used Pete Roberts (Pete Kuykendall) for a long time, and we had Porter Church for a short time. We met Eddie Adcock and he had such a unusual style and with a lot of feeling that we asked him if he'd work with us. It worked out very well for a long time.

Pickin': Would it be fair to say that the best known early edition of the Gents would be John Duffey, Eddie Adcock, Tom Gray and yourself?

Charlie: Yes.

Pickin': The Country Gentlemen began as a four-piece group, without a fiddle. Now, after many years the band has added not only a regular fiddle player, but during the summer you have Jerry Douglas on dobro. Why the growth in the group?

Charlie: We came upon Ricky Skaggs back when Emerson got his arm hurt. I liked him so well as a person and liked his fiddle playing so much that he's still with us. We came across Jerry Douglas out at Warren, Ohio at one of the festivals. He just shocked us right off our feet. He played with us all last summer while he was out of school. We fly him in or go get him for the recording sessions.

Pickin': Bill, how long have you been a bluegrass musician?

Bill: I started out with my brother Wayne about thirteen years ago. We used to pick around the house all the time and sing. We enjoyed it. So we decided we'd get us a job and see if we couldn't make some money pickin'. We started out in a little club in Alexandria, Virginia. We worked for tips and it turned out very good. We advanced up to where we were getting paid to work. Porter Church started pickin' banjo with us and my brother-in law, Ferle Brown, (was) pickin' guitar. Later on, Porter left and Bill Emerson came with us. The name of the group at that time was the Yates Brothers and the Clinch Mt. Ramblers.

Pickin': How did you get to the Gents?

Bill: When Wayne got sick I decided I'd see if I could go on and get bigger things. I went to work with Jimmy Martin. About the middle of '69 I quit Jimmy and went with Bill Monroe. In the meantime, I had talked at different show dates about working with the Gents. Charlie and I had been friends for, I guess, about sixteen years. I knew him when the Gentlemen first started out. Eddie and Charlie asked me would I be interested if they ever got an opening. I told them I would. (One day) Eddie called me up from the New Jersey Turnpike—they were going south—and said, "Are you ready to come to work?" I said, "I'm ready." So he said, "Well, you're hired. You got the job." That was about the end of October, 1969. I worked out my notice with Monroe and on the 27th of November, 1969, I moved back to Washington, D.C.

Pickin': Were you playing upright bass all those years?

Bill: Yes

Pickin': Doyle, where does it begin for you?

Doyle: I started to play when I was about eleven years old.[2] I used to listen to the Grand Ole Opry ever since I was four years old. The very first time I heard Bill Monroe and the Blue Grass Boys I said, "Why, that's what I want to do." As the years passed I kept listening to that; and I decided I wanted to play the mandolin.

Pickin': When did you join the Gents?

Doyle: August 1971. I believe it was Bill Emerson who called me. They had talked to me earlier, that Jimmy Gaudreau might be leaving. I went to Jimmy and I said, "Well, I hear that you're leaving." He said he was thinking about it. I said, "Well, if you got any smarts you better stay where you are." In a couple of weeks Emerson called me and said Gaudreau was leaving. Would I want the job? I said, "I'll take it."

We got together at Gettysburg, Pennsylvania, at the festival up there. Oh! It was a disaster for me. I had laryngitis. What a time to try to sing tenor to the best groups in the business! But it worked out really good. I had enough voice in me that we knew it would blend.

Pickin': Charlie, any group in particular turn your head to bluegrass?

Charlie: I didn't dig bluegrass in the beginning because I had never heard that much of it. Basically, I'm a Hank Snow fan. I did hear some early Flatt and Scruggs songs, and I loved them. It wasn't something that I thought I'd be playing. But "The Tie That Binds" by Reno and Smiley—I had to stop the car. I couldn't drive; it tore me up.

I really got turned on to Ralph Stanley. We played a benefit for Carter, after he passed away, at the University of Maryland.[3] I sat out in the crowd and looked at Ralph on the stage. I just got bumps all over me because of what he was doing (and) the way he was doing it. That door opened, man, and that's when I really started digging bluegrass.

Pickin': Charlie, I've always had a personal liking for tunes such as "Make Me a Pallet on the Floor," "Katy Dear," "High Lonesome"—tunes which go back to early editions of the Country Gentlemen. They weren't super-fast-tempo bluegrass, but still good basic 'grass. Yet they never really made it as hits. Now they are more popular. Have you ever had the feeling the Gents were ten to fifteen years ahead of their time?

Charlie: Yes, I really have. We were kind of like Studebaker automobile. I thought its styling was very advanced for its years. I thought we were a breakthrough group. Enough people didn't get to like this kind of music because the minute they heard certain sounds they said, "Well, that's that ———— music." We overcame a lot of that by playing to audiences that didn't like it. We would do "Greensleeves." By doing that people would realize that these fellas were pretty good musicians. Then we'd throw "Jesse James" in there.

---

2. Lawson would have been hearing some powerful Blue Grass Boys on the Opry in 1948, when he was four. He was born on April 20, 1944.

3. Carter Stanley died on December 1, 1966.

I, like you, have always liked the song "High Lonesome." I thought that it was a very beautiful song. Actually a little too pretty to be a hit. There's a lot of them that way. But I think the world now, especially the kids, are a little more ready for it . . . more interested in good words.

Pickin': Many people thought that the departure of Duffey and Adcock, and then Emerson, would diminish the group's audience appeal. All three have had a lot of success in their own separate ways, and the Gents are as popular now, if not more so, than ever before. It must make you feel pretty good as a group to see something like this happening.

Charlie: Very much. I think that music is something that has to come from the heart. You haven't sung a song if it doesn't have heart. I believe that there's enough getting through that the people dig to see what we're doing. I'm very happy that it's come out this way.

Pickin': The basic Country Gentlemen sound has remained pretty identifiable since inception. How has this been possible?

Charlie: I would have to say it has a lot to do with my sound because I'm the only one that's still there. We've been lucky in that we went from John Duffey to Jimmy Gaudreau. Jimmy is very up on our material and it sounded much the same way with Doyle Lawson except he didn't have a northern accent. Duffey had a very dominating tenor voice. If you could see three people singing, you could look at him and see what part he was singing. He is much louder. Truthfully, it is just one of our characteristics which isn't there now.

I've always felt that it's a good harmony when you can look at three people singing and not be able to tell who is singing what. But I wasn't looking for our next mandolin player to be dominated because Duffey is just one in a million.

Pickin': Doyle, you have a southern voice, and Rick's voice has that lonesome quality. Would it be fair to say that the present Country Gentlemen group has more of a traditional sound than some of your previous groups?

Doyle: Rick and myself have the rural voice, which is very true. We both have what you might call a mountain tenor; and, of course, we can both double on baritone. He does most of the baritone stuff except on the old quartets. We're into this quartet thing pretty heavy because we love it. By having the rural sound we can adapt and do the earlier stuff as well as we can do our thing.

The biggest things we go back to do now are not "Uncle Pen" or "Roll in My Sweet Baby's Arms," which are things people do who stick to basic bluegrass. Instead, we go back and take tunes that Flatt and Scruggs and Monroe sang when they were a bluegrass quartet.

Charlie: Yeah. I think that's true more in the sound. But the material, it just mainly has to pass on me. If it's something that I realize isn't me, or I couldn't sing, then I'd have to say no on it. But most of the stuff, traditional or not, doesn't have to do with who's in the group.

Pickin': Vocally, then, you feel as a group that you are now in the strongest position to go in all directions?

Doyle: Absolutely. I have no doubt about it at all.

Pickin': How do the Gents put together arrangements of tunes?

Charlie: Mostly Doyle Lawson. He's pretty good at that. Much better than myself. I have to put most of my thought into singing the song with feeling. In the beginning, Duffey was the biggest part of the arranging. Adcock was very, very good at it. Later on, Emerson and Doyle Lawson fell right in.

Doyle: The first thing we do when we go to work up a tune is to get our vocals together. We hardly fool with the instrumentation at all until we get our vocals and harmony as close as we can get it.

Bill: If you work out your harmony and know exactly where to go; what harmony parts to drop, to raise, and switch, then there's no problem. You don't have to practice to pick your instrument.

Pickin': In other words, you won't have your instruments in your hands the first time you're working on a tune?

Doyle: No. A lot of things we do have a weird or different harmony arrangement. We do a lot of stuff where even the lead will switch to a baritone line and the baritone voice will go to a lead; or sometimes even the tenor will come down to a baritone line and the baritone has to go all the way up to a low tenor. It's very distracting if you're trying to frail away with your instrument when you don't know the song to begin with.

Pickin': Bill, I've noticed that you do very little slap bass and seem more content to stick to rhythm and a good bottom sound. Am I right?

Bill: This is correct. I never did like slap, to tell you the truth. You're getting just noise and really can't slap in perfect time. I'm not saying that a bass shouldn't take lead on some things. But you've got to have rhythm to sing, and my job in this band is to play rhythm.

Doyle: Very true. The bass bottoms out the whole rhythm section. In our case, we have four lead instruments: mandolin, dobro, banjo and fiddle. What do you need with another lead instrument? If you keep the beat with the bass and guitar, the lead instruments just can't hardly miss.

Pickin': Charlie, you seem quite content to play rhythm guitar, and leave lead work aside although you can flatpick "Under the Double Eagle", etc. Is this deliberate?

Charlie: In the beginning, no. I think I was capable of playing lead then except there wasn't that much need for it. Usually a song has two places for a break and we had the banjo and mandolin. Mainly, I've just never been a very pushy person to the microphone. Somebody always beat me there.

I've thought about it lately. I should really get on it and do more, but everybody goes through their learning years and my heart is . . . I just been playing rhythm so long now. I could still play lead, but naturally, I wouldn't learn as quick as kids coming up now.

Pickin': Doyle, you seem to experiment a lot with different chords that people don't normally associate with a particular tune.

Doyle: That goes right back to your rhythm section. If the rhythm's right, you could do a little lick that you didn't do on the record and feel fairly sure you can get it across. It's your fault if you screw it up.

Pickin': The Country Gentlemen do a lot of contemporary tunes which are written in different keys and have more than the usual chords and changes. Doesn't this automatically allow you to experiment?

Doyle: Absolutely. Really more so than ever with the Gentlemen. I don't play now exactly like I played before with other groups. I didn't ever have the complete freedom that I have now. I really dig this type of thing we're into, as well as the pure 'grass.

Pickin': Do you think then the person starting off in bluegrass is making a mistake by learning tablature and possibly getting hung up on notation?

Doyle: Well, Doug, that probably would be up to the individual. Lots of people do start with tablature and there's nothing wrong with it. Some people have a more sensitive ear, what they can hear, how they pick it up and how they deliver it.

I tend to think that you are more mechanical if you do start by tablature. You're just a little bit mechanical about your whole operation. Whereas if you learn to play by ear, you learn to play off the top of your head—you deliver better and you can feel it.

Pickin': Doyle, how much of J. D. Crowe's *Model Church* album is your thinking?

Doyle: To be very truthful about it, Doug, it is all really my idea. A lot of the material used on the album came from back home when dad had his quartet. We'd work out our trio first with a cassette tape player, and when we got to where it would shake the speaker then we'd say, "Well, that ought to do it."

Pickin': What do you think of the trend of some groups toward amplification and drums?

Charlie: Well . . . if that's what they want. I think if a lot of work and effort has been put into making a good guitar then it should be heard as an acoustical instrument. I think an electric bass is acceptable. However, it doesn't have stage appeal. I've always been able to go along with the sound of an electric bass, but I don't see having drums or at least carrying drums. I have nothing against slight help with drums on the rhythm side if you're making a record.

Pickin': Your first Vanguard album had drums and electric bass. Was it a decision of the group?

Charlie: Snare drums was. I got a little upset when I walked in and saw a full set of drums setting there. I thought, "Well, all I agreed on was snare drums." 'Course that's all we used. I don't want to make drum players mad at me, but that's just my own feeling.

Bill: A lot of people liked the electric bass. The diehards won't have anything that has a cord hooked out of it. That's just the way it is. If you believe in something, you believe in it.

Pickin': You're recording again now for Vanguard. Will you continue using an augmented group?

Charlie: I'm not sure. The last record was a little further out than I wanted it to be. This one is coming right back. I like it better, although I really liked the other one. I'm not a purist. I love singing "Casey's Last Ride" because I feel the song and I love singing the stuff on this new album, too. I can sing both as long as it comes from the heart.

Pickin': "Casey's Last Ride" is a Kristofferson tune. One of the things that typifies the Gents through the years is a search for new material.

Charlie: We're trying to find original material like everybody else. This is the most original album that we will have done.

Bill: It will be more on the order of what the Country Gentlemen have been known for . . . the sound of what we're trying to do now and what has been done in the past.

Doyle: I have the feeling that on the first album we were trying to please the record company instead of the people. All they want us to do on our upcoming album is be ourselves and record exactly what we want to record. We have complete freedom. As a matter of fact, I'm producing this next album.

Pickin': Even with all the success that bluegrass is having right now, there is still a reluctance in the record industry, radio stations, etc. to support the music promotionally. Do you think bluegrass can ever be as big commercially as other types of music? Or do you think lack of commitment and exposure are the problem?

Charlie: There's certainly a lack of exposure. I believe the reason it has never gotten to be as big is because people just can't hear it.

Doyle: This music can be successful in a very successful industry. But the first thing you have to have are record companies that want to spend money on a bluegrass artist. Second thing you have to have are radio stations that will air your music. Until we get that it's not ever going to be successful as modern C&W and rock.

Bill: The only time that bluegrass has really been able to do anything has been when the song has already been on its way. Then the record companies will try to put a little bit to it—like "Dueling Banjos." It is just a simple ordinary tune but it happened to be in a movie. People that would go see the movie would get interested in the banjo-pickin'.

Doyle: Unless you get to where people can hear your music, there's no point in getting frustrated about it. You've got to put up with it.

Pickin': I've heard people tell that they refuse to go to a big concert hall to hear a bluegrass concert. They said it didn't belong there because it would lose its intimacy. Do you agree with that?

Charlie: Nuts. I think anybody ought to be able to hear it anywhere. A big concert hall means it will hold more people. There's no place too good to put bluegrass music as far as I'm concerned. I wouldn't want to turn anybody against the music because it is in a big place, but I don't think they should feel it should be kept out. It doesn't help the artist to play small places all his life because it's just harder to make a living. There's enough things going on to keep the music down. The Country Music Association probably doesn't want too much of it on the radio.

Pickin': How do you explain the growth of interest in bluegrass around the world?

Charlie: The young people . . . it's their roots, their heritage. They're interested in it. I think the sound of a banjo is very intriguing and they want to go into it.

Pickin': Do you find it surprising that it's been the young people in the northern parts of the country—where bluegrass is least heard—who took to the music strongest over these last few years? You'd think it would be the other way around.

Charlie: You'd think so, but you're right. I know ten years we were able to play up this way to a lot more interested audience. It just didn't go over in Alabama, Nashville, etc. There's big interest now in the Carolinas and the music is just beginning to catch on in Texas. I think the festivals are the reason.

Pickin': Charlie, was there ever a point in your life when you thought the music would die because there wouldn't be any young people who would want to continue the music, and be capable enough?

Charlie: Yeah. There was a point when I first started. I had played a long time on the Louisiana Hayride. It just seemed that I had seen so much of the other stuff making it—stuff I thought was trash—that I almost went into "crying in your beer" songs in order to make a living. But I got off of that pretty quick because I just couldn't put myself into it.

Pickin': Am I right that the Country Gentlemen are incorporated?

Doyle: To make a business you have to make it work like a business; and you've got to do everything that you can do once you get to the top or working toward the top. We felt a year or so ago that it would be to our benefit to incorporate. Bill Emerson was still with us at the time. We formed a corporation, The Country Gentlemen of Virginia, Inc. Emerson left so now it leaves Charlie, the original Country Gentlemen, Bill and myself as the three partners. Rick Skaggs and James Bailey and Jerry Douglas work for us. Len Holsclaw is our manager, booking agent and president of the corporation. And I would like to mention that he's doing a tremendous job for us.

Bill: Go back to when we were talking about the progress of bluegrass music. Most of the entertainers that have a band, they pay them so much a day when they work. We pay our guys a salary every week whether they work or not. They can go home and go hunting and still get their money. I think this is a big part because it doesn't make any difference how much you love the music, you gotta eat. That's run a lot of good musicians out of the business because they couldn't make a living as sidemen. You take fiddle players like Vassar Clements and Jimmy Buchanan and Buck Ryan. They love the music but I know a couple of times they've gotten out of it because they couldn't make a living. Who can go out on his own with a fiddle? Very few do. Most of the guys that go out on their own are guys that's got voices and can play guitar. This is why I believe our group is run so smooth. We do pay a salary every week for the group and we don't ask any one of the guys to do anything that we wouldn't do ourselves.

Pickin': Do you think the future of bluegrass lies as a traditional idiom, a contemporary one, or both?

Charlie: I think both. I don't like to have any boundaries you can't go over. We've done things that are way away from bluegrass. We do it our way, and with bluegrass instruments. It's just new material: "Exodus," "Greensleeves," etc. It'll all fit.

Doyle: I definitely think that there's a trend away from the hard rock and acid rock. I won't even classify it as rock; it's electric instruments and the loud music that they've heard for ten years. People are getting away from that. They are going back to their roots; their American heritage, so to speak. That's why in the last three years bluegrass is beginning to come on again and come into its own—where it should have been years ago.

You hear some of the country singers—modern country, and even some rock singers that are trying to get into bluegrass . . . I don't feel that it's going to do it because people can recognize the fact that it's a warmed-over commercial-type approach and it doesn't come from the heart like it does us guys that has been beatin' down these roads for years.

Pickin': That is, once they hear the real thing. If they don't, then they may just stop at that point.

Doyle: Well, I don't think they will stop at that point. The biggest thing that will interest them is going to be the five-string banjo. Anybody that does anything to do with bluegrass, man, you've just got to have a banjo in there. Once they hear that banjo they're gonna want to know where it comes from. They'll do a little research and find out that there's some honest, good, down-to-earth American music left.

Pickin': All you're saying is that you just want to get your foot in the door and you'll take care of the rest.

Doyle: Absolutely.

Originally published in *Pickin'* 1 (March 1974): 4–12. Reprinted by permission of Roger Siminoff.

Pete Kuykendall had already been a banjo player—with the Country Gentlemen and others—record producer, songwriter, and record collector when he and a small band of compadres started *Bluegrass Unlimited* in July 1966.[1] Through nearly four succeeding decades, the magazine has promoted, prodded and praised several generations of bluegrass artists and fans. Articles from it make up a large share of the bluegrass journalism in this volume for good reason: *BU* has probably produced more bluegrass journalism than any other source.

1. Neil V. Rosenberg, *Bluegrass: A History* (Urbana: University of Illinois Press, 1985), 224–26.

Kuykendall's clear-minded history of the Kentucky Colonels offers mostly just the facts but never conceals the writer's undying enthusiasm for the fine points of his story. "The process was cyclical and magnificent," he writes of a chain of musical influence within the band. On July 15, 1973, a little more than four years after this piece ran, the brilliant guitarist Clarence White was killed in a street accident in California. Roland White has enjoyed a long and successful career with acts that have included Bill Monroe, Lester Flatt, the Country Gazette, the Nashville Bluegrass Band, and his own New Kentucky Colonels.

29

"The Kentucky Colonels"

PETER V. KUYKENDALL

One of the most significant of the urban bluegrass groups of the 60s were the Kentucky Colonels or the Country Boys. They were known under both names. Though the groups disbanded in 1965, their music is still talked about today.

Their home base was the Los Angeles, California, area and they, along with the Dillards, were amongst the most respected groups of the newer bluegrass generation.

The groups started as a family unit in 1952, composed of the White children, Roland, Clarence, Eric and Joann.[2] They started playing as a country band with a Louvin Brothers sound, and began doing bluegrass around 1954. They were all born in Maine, of parents who came to the U.S. from Canada. They moved to California in 1951. Their parents had country music backgrounds, and the family had uncles and grandfathers who played fiddle. The group [was] practicing one day and [was] heard by a neighbor who suggested they enter a talent contest held locally at a theater. They entered and won first prize, a TV appearance.

Roland White was the leader of the group. In 1958 they added Billy Ray (Latham) from Cave City, Arkansas on banjo. Roland had been playing banjo approximately one year prior to that but when Billy Ray came he returned to mandolin. In 1959 they added LeRoy Mack on dobro, and shortly thereafter made their first record on Sundown. They were mainstays on the West Coast TV shows Town Hall Party and Hometown Jaboree, even though their average age was only eighteen. By this time the group consisted of Roland White—mandolin, Clarence White—guitar, Eric White—bass, Billy Ray—banjo and LeRoy Mack—dobro. They also recorded some sides for Gene Autry's label for which there is no further information at this time. In early 1961 they added Roger Bush on bass fiddle and second banjo to replace Eric who had recently married and did not wish to travel. They recorded four appearances on The Andy Griffith TV show at this time. They also recorded four songs on

---

2. The family name was originally LeBlanc.

an LP with Andy Griffith, *Songs, Themes and Laughs from* The Andy Griffith Show, Capitol (S)T1611, which was released around November of 1961. Things were starting to pick up for them when Uncle Sam beckoned to Roland and called him to the Army from 1961 to 1963. The group functioned without a regular mandolin player and added a rhythm guitar player. Clarence White, after hearing Doc Watson at the Ash Grove in Los Angeles, started playing lead guitar and using mandolin-style breaks. Since Clarence's background was in bluegrass rhythm, he was able to take a lot of Doc Watson's lead picking technique and integrate it tastefully into a bluegrass band.

During Roland's Army service, thanks to the help of Joe Maphis, the Colonels made their first LP on the Briar International label, owned by Paul Cohen of Nashville. This LP marked the beginning of the "Kentucky Colonels." Briar did not want to release the record under the name of the "Country Boys" and phoned the group giving them a list of names to pick from. "Kentucky Colonels" was the lesser of several evils and from then on that was their name.

Before Roland returned in 1963, they added Bobby Slone on fiddle. Bobby was unique in his approach. He was left-handed, but played a standard strung right-hand fiddle. When Roland returned, the group became more active, touring in New York, Washington, Detroit, the Dakotas and Canada. They also appeared at the UCLA and Newport Folk Festivals in 1964.

Everywhere they played they drew acclaim as one of the most impressive current groups in the business. During 1964 their home base was the Ash Grove in Hollywood, California. Through its mentor, Ed Pearl, their recording activities increased, with their use as session musicians on Dick Bock's World Pacific label. World Pacific, thanks to the success of Glen Campbell's twelve-string guitar LPs, became active in recording West Coast bluegrass material. The Colonels made one LP and backed Tut Taylor on both of his. They appeared in a movie entitled *Farmer's Other Daughter* and as Roland put it: "it's a real winner, you might see it on TV sometime on the late, late, late, late show!"

One of the groups active on the West Coast at the time were the Stonemans. After Bobby Slone left the group, Scott Stoneman joined the Colonels playing fiddle. This combination of Roland White on mandolin, Clarence White on guitar, Billy Ray on banjo, Roger Bush on bass and Scott Stoneman on fiddle is one of the most exciting sounds to come along in quite a while. Scott's added impetus was the spark that really turned on each one of the individual members to their utmost. It is a shame that only tape recordings are available of this band. Their music was just unbelievable. Clarence inspired Scott, who inspired Billy Ray, who inspired Roland, who inspired Roger, who inspired Scott. The process was cyclical and magnificent.

When the group disbanded in early summer of 1965, Clarence became a studio session guitarist on rhythm and lead (electric and acoustic) around Hollywood, recording with Wynn Stewart and Ricky Nelson. He is now playing guitar with the Byrds, of rock fame.

Roland White, as most of the devotees of bluegrass know, is now playing guitar and singing lead with the Blue Grass Boys, adding a lot to the current sound of Bill Monroe.

Billy Ray (Latham) has returned to Arkansas and is working as comedian and banjo player on the Ozark Opry. Roger Bush has faded into obscurity and his activities are not known at the present.

Bobby Slone is now playing bass with J. D. Crowe and the Kentucky Mt. Boys around the Lexington, Kentucky area. If you are able to find any records by this fine group, do get them. You will be quite impressed with their contribution to bluegrass music.

Records by the Kentucky Colonels (Country Boys)

Sundown 45–131—"I'm Head over Heels in Love with You" / "Kentucky Hills"
Capitol (S)T1611—*The Andy Griffith Show:* "Flop Eared Mule" / "Sourwood Mountain" / "New River Train" / "Cindy"
World Pacific ST/WP 1821—*Appalachian Swing*
World Pacific ST/WP 1816—*Twelve String Dobro*—Tut Taylor with Roland White, Clarence White
World Pacific ST/WP 1829—*Dobro Country*—Tut Taylor with Roland White, Clarence White and Billy Ray
Briar-109—*The Kentucky Colonels*

Originally published in *Bluegrass Unlimited* 3 (April 1969): 3–4. Reprinted by permission of the author and *Bluegrass Unlimited*.

One important figure interviewed another in this piece. As has been seen throughout this volume, many bluegrass and old-time musicians are dedicated scholars and boosters of the music they love. Few have been more significant in this role than Alice Gerrard, who's achieved renown as the duet partner of Hazel Dickens, as a musical collaborator of former husband Mike Seeger, as a distinguished writer and collector of songs, and as the long-time editor of the North Carolina–based *Old-Time Herald*. Then married to musician Jeremy Foster, Alice interviewed one of Bill Monroe's favorite sidemen, Kenny Baker, and brought forth some resonant truths, among them the degree to which Monroe's music leaned on that of French jazzman Stephane Grappelli. Monroe might have been appalled to hear it, but the highly articulated, singing fiddle style he loved to hear from Kenny Baker stemmed in great part on Baker's love of Grappelli. Gerrard's piece also sets forth the sociological and historical context in which Baker developed his cornerstone fiddle style.

30

"Kenny Baker"

ALICE FOSTER

Kenny Baker plays fiddle with Bill Monroe. He is a coal miner, a Country and Western fiddle man, and is a very articulate person with a lot to say.

From Jenkins, Kentucky, he was born June 26, 1926. His family originally came from England and settled in North Carolina. "As a matter of fact this great-ancestor of mine slipped out of England . . . I think that knowing my people . . . they were fortune hunters maybe, or . . . you might say they were more or less explorers. They definitely didn't stay in one place too long. My mother's people as near as I can get back to come from maybe a Dutch descent. . . . My great-grandfather settled in Wise County, Virginia . . . I was raised in Wise County to a great extent. I used to stay with my grandparents quite a bit . . . the only reason in the world why Jenkins is my home is because that's the only public work they had there and my daddy bein' a miner, why that was it."

Jenkins was set up as a coal town by Consolidation Coal Company. They sold out to Bethlehem Steel somewhere along in the early fifties. "Now there's some wild stories can be told about the [union] organization. . . . The coal companies didn't recognize no union laborers at all . . . they bought the property, built the houses, rented you the house and any time they caught more than two or three men together they broke it up—they had these company police to come around and just break it up . . . they had to meet back in the mountains, and they just stole out here and there to meet and plan their labor moves . . . my father was very active in that."

///

Kenny started trying to play the fiddle when he was eight or ten years old by imitating the first person he heard play—his father. "Daddy played such stuff as 'Billy in the Low Ground,' '8th of January,' 'Forked Deer' . . . all old-timey tunes you know. I can remember hearing my great-grandfather, Richard Baker, play. He was ninety-six when he died." But Kenny gradually became discouraged. "I just give the fiddle up . . . my dad kind of criticized me . . . he said I'd never learn . . . well really and truly, he tried to teach me and . . . maybe I just didn't have enough interest or whatever it might be . . . and he just made a rulin' for me not to get that fiddle . . . and from there on every time I got in there I stole it."

He mostly played guitar until he was sixteen when he went into the Navy. The first time he played the fiddle more or less formally was for a USO show on a dare. "They just wanted to see if I really had the nerve I guess, and so—you know me— I just walked right up there." Later, when the Red Cross put on a square dance and didn't have a fiddler, Kenny volunteered because he knew some square dance tunes. They flew a fiddle in to the base and he worked on it to make it playable. "That's the last guitar work I did then."[1]

Back in Jenkins after his discharge he went to work in the mines as a coal loader—"130 pounds a day, man . . . averagin' about 8 dollars a day"—and didn't play fiddle for three or four years. He started up again by playing for local square dances with two other men, Virgil Mullins and Glenn (Slick) Gallion. "The same thing happened twice . . . they needed somebody to play the fiddle." He played locally for two or three years in addition to mine work. "Very rarely we would do some work [playing] for the local coal company there, if they had some kind of a big day . . . such as safety days . . . labor day celebrations.

"The biggest influence I ever had with the fiddle is Marion Sumner. Marion was a more up-to-date fiddle man that my father was . . . he started me wantin' to learn to play a fiddle . . . he was from Hazard."

Kenny's first real interest was more in jazz fiddle and he listened to guitarist Django Reinhardt and fiddler Stephane Grappelli, noted French jazz musicians. "The first fiddle playing that I studied at all . . . or even thought about is of that nature [jazz] . . . I took numbers like 'Darkness on the Delta' . . . from the Ink Spots . . . the Mills Brothers used to do that number . . . and I'd just play 'em the way I wanted to play . . . of course down in the country when I played that stuff I had to play it to myself. . . . It was a new sound and I liked it . . . just like eatin' a piece of bread at your mother's house . . . I was a great fan of Tommy Dorsey's and Glenn Miller particularly . . . he used to hit licks . . . I'd take my guitar—along at that time you know I didn't study what the guitar player was playin'—it was the licks he [Glenn] had . . . I used to listen to a lot of orchestras . . . you get your own ideas from stuff like that. . . . You take this 'Careless Love' thing that Bill recorded . . . the idea of the tune come to me in a movie . . . I think it was . . . Nat King Cole . . . and he did this number.[2] He did it real slow and it was the first time I ever heard the real chords . . . it's the first time I ever heard the real down meanin' of that tune and the melody, see—the lyrics—today I couldn't even think about them—but it is the music that he is getting' . . . and after I heard Bill sing—I didn't even know Monroe at the time I saw this movie . . . we was in this recording session one day and we was beatin' around tryin' to hunt another number and I happened to think about that number . . . I thought, well, if I show it to him just exactly like he done it, he'll not be interested but if I 'boost it up just a little bit he might' . . . so we tried it and we took one cut and right there and then we just recorded it . . . every note I hit, this man had it on the piano.

"I wasn't interested in the big band sound, but I liked the way they [the soloists] went about it . . . their notes are more distinct. Now that's gettin' back to this

---

1. Baker revived his guitar playing for recordings with Buck Graves on the Puritan label in the 1970s.

2. Monroe's recording was on November 23, 1962.

Grappelli and the difference in him and my daddy's playin' you know. . . . Now the difference that I made in the music, Grappelli played his music with a distinct sound and every note was there . . . every note he played meant something—he's not a mechanical fiddler. Now every day you hear somebody play tunes like 'Soldier's Joy' and this and that and nine old-timers out of ten when you hear one man play it you've heard 'em all. . . . Some might be a little smoother, but they all stick to the same notes, they never give or take."

About 1953 Kenny and a band went to WNOX in Knoxville to play the Saturday Night Barn Dance. Lowell Blanchard offered him a job but he turned it down because right then he didn't feel like playing music for a living. About a week later Don Gibson called him. "Just as things happened in the coal fields . . . they had made a new machine which took the place of about eight men on one section . . . a lot of people felt bitter about it . . . if you figure from both sides, the labor and the operator, why I think they were in their rights . . . they were in there to make the money . . . I was put off on Wednesday and Don called me on Thursday . . . so I said I'd try it with him."

Kenny said he learned a lot about playing a fiddle from being with Don Gibson.

"I learned to pick up notes that would sound to me like they would be a major maybe, and a minor, and I learned to pick up a lot of rhythm licks, you know, that I had never even dreamed existed . . . a very good teacher. . . . He don't play, but he's got enough know-how about him to where he can put his finger right on what he wants."

Kenny hadn't had much of any chance to play jazz fiddle until he went with Don Gibson. "When I got with him I found that the steel man that he had, and himself too, they were deeply interested in that stuff . . . we just kind of worked it all over." The new musical ideas that he developed "came from banjo-pickers and maybe a few licks I heard on a horn here and there—and this and that. It's just ideas that you drum up you know. Of course there's no use in me a-sayin' that I didn't listen to no fiddle players . . . about the only listenin' I ever did really, is to learn the melody but as far as takin' a recording . . . and just study it note for note, I never do that."

He worked with Don for about four years. Then toward the end of 1956 Kenny went with Bill Monroe.[3] Bill had originally heard Kenny in Knoxville and had spoken to him two or three times about working with him. "There wasn't no particular agreement really, he just asked me a couple of times and at the time I decided to go I felt I needed to go so I went. . . . When I went to work for Bill, the change I had to make in the music . . . you might say it was a big challenge . . . I decided before I ever went there I just knew I could play that kind of music without even thinking about it. I found that I didn't know near what I thought I did. Bill explained to me after I'd worked with him for a while that he felt that my fiddle would help his music

---

3. Tom Ewing notes that Baker first joined Monroe in 1957 (private correspondence, 2002).

some . . . I was trying to make myself believe that I couldn't play what he wanted and at that time what I thought he was wanting, I just couldn't put it in there, you see." At the time a friend of Kenny's was helping him learn some of the breaks and tunes. "The meter and the notes he was giving me to play, I just couldn't put 'em in there . . . I explained to Bill that I couldn't put the stuff in there . . . he said, 'now don't listen to what somebody else is playing, you play what you feel and what you hear, that's why I want you.'

"I found Bill very easy to work with in recording . . . he sets his music up and he tells you what he wants . . . he either let me get away with a lot or else we heard the same stuff . . . we would take a number and if it was a strange number to us they'd play it for us . . . and we would listen to it and each man would figure out his break . . . and then we would start with it and somewhere along the line some man's gonna make a boo boo then that gives you another chance to improvise this number as you go with it . . . four times most of the time we generally had a pretty good cut."

Kenny left Bill in 1958 or 59, returned after a short while, left a second time, went back again and stayed until 1963, when he left and went back to Jenkins to work in the mines.[4] "I've got to refer to Bethlehem Steel . . . that company is not a cutthroat outfit . . . they're deeply interested in your family . . . if a kid comes up and they see that he's got a pretty good head on him that company'll willfully send him to school . . . they're far ahead of the first company that was there . . . I went to school in the Safety Department for Bethlehem Steel . . . a program they had to eliminate accidents in the mines. . . . You go around and you check each and every machine that they had and make sure it is permissible."

Kenny stayed with mine work until 1968, when he went back with Bill. I was interested in some of his thoughts on the area of Eastern Kentucky—Kenny is a friend of Harry Caudill, author of the book *Night Comes to the Cumberlands,* and he is very aware and interested in the problems of that section of Appalachia.

"And no man after he gets up to the age of maybe forty or fifty years old and if he's dedicated his life in the mines and once he leaves there regardless of what kind of job he gets he'll never be satisfied away from the coal mines . . . you spend more time underground than you do outside . . . you learn to live with very abnormal conditions . . . once you get away from it it kind of bugs you just a little bit—I've had some of that, I know . . . that's home to them . . . and the mining part of it is just as much as bein' in their front room.

"Well here's the thing now. If they're so interested in the welfare of the poor people down there, why do they go down there and appropriate a lot of money and send it in there to a bunch of political leaders and the money never even got to the people that they need . . . as a matter of fact there's six men on trial now in Eastern Kentucky on that . . . $75,000 I believe was the government grant to them for that one particular county . . . they could only account for maybe 10 or 15 thousand

4. Baker worked with Monroe, "generally, 1957–1959, 1962–1963 and 1968–1984" (ibid.).

dollars . . . even the county judge is in on it, and the D.A. . . . so I hope they get their money's worth out of it."

While Kenny was in Washington recently, he listened to a tape of a Bill Monroe show made in 1957 at New River Ranch in Maryland. "I'm real proud that show is taped . . . I've often studied what I did sound like back in them days . . . you could tell . . . I wasn't no grass fiddle man in them days, you can tell it . . . real pitiful . . . I was searchin' that fiddle for the sound I was wantin', that's exactly what it was. . . . It was disappointing I'll tell you, but I could also hear some stuff in there that I was hearin' in them days that . . . I can put it in there today . . . I was tryin' and I was searching . . . I could hear it but I just didn't have the ability to put it to it . . . if you'll notice there was very few fiddle take-offs that we had there . . . but that just goes to show you now—I really thought I was pulling the wool over Mon's eyes there . . . I believe he thought, 'well how long is he gonna take him to get away from that other stuff he's been playing?' I guess that entered his mind—or else, 'you reckon he's lost his mind or what?'

"Let's say that Bill has, whether he knows it or not . . . fairly advanced his music . . . I think he's been very creative in the Nashville sound . . . he's the first man that ever used two fiddles down there[5] . . . and of course Pee Wee King and Redd Stewart and those boys they were there years ago . . . in western swing music two fiddles has been a pattern all the time—two and as many as three fiddles . . . but Bill was definitely the first . . . country artist that had two fiddles.

"It's just like this with his music. His songs don't change and the titles don't change but the music changes as the years go by because every year we change that music whether he knows it or whether he don't—I'm sure he does, and he himself has changed so much in the last four years it's incredible. The man's playin' a third more mandolin today than he was playin' four years ago . . . and he's more conscientious of what he plays. . . . He concentrates strictly on his sound—the sound is one thing, the melody is another. Now, you can play melody for Bill and as long as you play it clean he'll never say a word to you but if you play melody and maybe brush in a little something' extra, if it's good, fine, and if it's bad he'll not say nothin' to you right then and there, but you know . . . I think that Bill has changed his music as much as any man . . . you take tunes like 'Blue Moon' and 'Mule Skinner' and 'Footprints' . . . 'Uncle Pen' and all that . . . he has to stay in that same category of melodies and that don't give him the right to leave those numbers when every place he appears they want those numbers . . . so all that's left for him to do is to improvise the music, not the lyrics."

Kenny has lived in Nashville on and off for a number of years now—and we spoke some about the Nashville Sounds.

"When they added the strings . . . the orchestra [to Hank Williams records], this music that they put to his singin' there is strictly off sheet music and every note of that is there just like it should be and what I'm sayin'—now I don't know this to be

---

5. As noted elsewhere in this volume, Flatt and Scruggs first used twin fiddles in bluegrass.

exactly, I seriously doubt if Hank Williams could've took his guitar and played the exact notes that his orchestra is a-layin' down there . . . the feeling is something else.

"In every musician there's always the will to play more and get more out of one number . . . and I think that these boys, your guitar pickers . . . can look back to Chester [Chet Atkins] . . . he's not only played the melody but he had the chords a-comin' right with it . . . even your fiddle players and your banjo men are more conscientious about their melodies and their chord progression . . . I think that a lot of the boys was a-listenin' to a lot of artists like . . . Glenn Miller's band, stuff like that. I think they had a big lot to do with the advancement of country music . . . and Tommy Dorsey particularly.

"Now the Osbornes . . . I think they've advanced bluegrass music quite a bit . . . really and truly if you get right down to it you've got to give those boys credit because their harmony is so accurate . . . they've got a different sound to their music than anybody else but yet . . . it's grass . . . I think it [bluegrass music] will branch out into different sounds . . . There's no reason in the world why a bluegrass band can't get their own songs . . . I think that that's the way that people get their starts."

Originally published in *Bluegrass Unlimited* 3 (Dec. 1968): 8–11. Reprinted by permission of the author and *Bluegrass Unlimited*.

In 1957 Carlton Haney, a colorful, North Carolina businessman, had a vision that was to help bring bluegrass to a much wider audience. Haney, tapped by Bill Monroe to promote Monroe's concerts, grew increasingly fascinated by the history of bluegrass as personified by Monroe. Haney researched the music's progression through recordings, through contact with former Monroe sidemen, and in conversations with East Coast bluegrass figure Ralph Rinzler. In 1965 Haney started putting on bluegrass festivals that included an all-star performance that recapped Monroe's story.

By the mid-1960s, several other forces were at work that also brought bluegrass greater attention, but it's easy to argue that the festivals Haney pioneered have been a prime catalyst for keeping the music popular through the years. On his way to an influential position in country and bluegrass, Haney ruffled more than his share of feathers. For whatever it's worth, a full-scale 1977 profile of Haney in *Hustler* magazine called him "one of the most disliked men in the country music community."[1] In a long interview he gave to *Hustler,* Haney observed, "Those Nashville egos just couldn't stand me no more." Harvard-educated journalist Fred Bartenstein conducted this interview, which ran in Haney's own influential *Muleskinner News* magazine.

---

1. John Pugh, "Carlton Haney: The P. T. Barnum of Country and Western," *Hustler* 54 (Nov. 1977): 126 passim.

31

"The Carlton Haney Story"

FRED BARTENSTEIN

An interview with Fred Bartenstein, taped August 4, 1971, Ruffin, N.C.

Can you tell us where and when you were born?
Born in Rockingham County, North Carolina, September 19, 1928.
Did you hear much country music while you were growing up?
I didn't like it at all.
When did you first begin to get interested in it?
My brother Charles and a bunch of boys were singing "Rainbow at Midnight" about 1945 and I heard some of Ernest Tubb's records. I liked Ernest Tubb for a long time but I didn't particularly like country music.
When did you first hear Bluegrass Music?
Well, of course I heard it. My people would have the Bill Monroe shows, the Wall-Rite show on, on Saturday night, and I heard it, but it didn't mean nothing, and then about 1953, I wondered why they even allowed that kind of music on the Opry or on radio. Then I met Clyde Moody, met Bill Monroe, then went to work for him strictly for the money.
How did you happen to get a job with Bill?
I was at Clyde's house, and he come there, in Danville, Virginia. Then I met him and two or three months after that he called me and said he had some show dates cancelled and would I book four or five show dates for him and I did and they turned out real good and he said if I ever wanted to quit the job I was doing in a battery plant making automobile batteries, that I could go to work for him.
What made you think you could book a show?
I don't know, he just knew. He could tell if a guy could make a musician. . . . He could just tell.
How long did you work for Bill Monroe?
Oh, about a year and a half, I booked shows and travelled on all his dates, and then he sent me to Bean Blossom that summer to run Bean Blossom and I stayed up there from about June until September of 1955.
Was it during this period that you began to like the music?
Naw, I didn't particularly like it. I just did it because of being around Bill Monroe and doin' something I wasn't confined to eight hours a day. I'd heard of him, you know, and to say I was associated with him, you know, you could walk around with your chest out. And then we had square dances at Bean Blossom on Saturday night and somebody turned the radio on WRVA, that Dominion Barn Dance in Richmond, Virginia, and I heard a banjo player and asked somebody who it was and

they said it was a boy named Don Reno.[2] I'd never heard of him. Then after I left Bean Blossom I went back to North Carolina and found a group that needed somebody to book for them—Alan Shelton, Curly Howard, Roy Russell, Bill Phillips, called the Farm Hands. Alan and them would go into Richmond Saturday night and play on the Dominion Barn Dance. So I went with them to Richmond and somebody said "Yonder's Don Reno and Red Smiley" and it didn't mean a thing to me. The next week I went back with 'em and they come up and introduced theirself and they'd heard of me booking dates for Bill Monroe so they said what was I doing and all that and I told them I was home for while and they told me they'd love me to get some dates.

When was it that you first began to listen to the music and really like it?

Well, I liked Don's banjo playing because he could play any song. He'd get your attention and I liked their singing pretty good—they had a terrific show. But I was really booking 'em for the money I made. So in 1957 I carried them to Nashville to be on the Grand Ole Opry as a guest . . . and while we was backstage Don had the banjo and Bobby Hicks was there and Charlie Cline, Chubby Wise was in that dressing room 'cause Hank Snow was there and Jimmy Martin was there and I asked Jimmy Martin and Bill to sing a couple of duets like they used to, and Don was gonna play banjo and Red was there too with the guitar and they decided to do "Live and Let Live," Jimmy started it twice and Bill stopped it both times and said, "Let me start it," and when he started it, it was in entirely different time[3] than I'd ever heard music in and that must have been the first time that I really got interested in bluegrass.

Did you start listening a lot more then?

Yeah, I started finding out the difference between what the other groups was doing and what Bill Monroe was doing, and theirs had no excitement in it, it was just straight beat, but when he'd do it, it had . . . it'd make the hair stand up on your arm. And then I thought if I could get the ones had sung with him—who knew it—they were the only ones could play it. So I thought if I could get all of them, or some of 'em, back together and let people hear what I heard in the dressing room they'd buy tickets for it.

You first had this idea in 1958?

'57, October of '57.

How long did it take you to get the idea together of having a festival?

Well, I worked three years 'fore I told Bill, and he came to the house a lot in Roanoke and I told him what I wanted to do and asked him where we should have

---

2. The Old Dominion Barn Dance emanated from WRVA in Richmond, Virginia, between 1946 and 1957. Haney then started the New Dominion Barn Dance, also broadcast over WRVA, and kept it on the air until 1964. Walt V. Saunders, "Old Dominion Barn Dance," in *The Enclopedia of Country Music: The Ultimate Guide to the Music,* comp. by the staff of the Country Music Hall of Fame and Museum, ed. Paul Kingsbury (New York: Oxford University Press, 1998), 393–94.

3. Haney was using "time" in Monroe's sense of a rhythmic approach, in this case a driving beat, not necessarily in reference to tempo (personal correspondence with Tom Ewing, 2003).

it, and he said Roanoke would be the best place; and so I started looking for a place. I started work and then he brought Ralph Rinzler there and Rinzler started telling me things about the music that I would have never known, but even the average farmer in North Carolina or the South when they liked bluegrass didn't know these facts, they just knew they liked it. . . . So I told Ralph Rinzler what I was going to do and he was interested in it and said it would be nice if it could happen and I said, "It can, those guys still know those songs." So I worked seven years, from '57 to '64, and I then found a place where they were having country music shows called Cantrell's Horse Farm and I asked the man to let me put a festival on there and he said I could. So in '65 I hired the acts and did, Labor Day Weekend, I had Mac Wiseman, Reno, Smiley,[4] The Stanley Brothers, Jimmy Martin, Bill Monroe, Larry Richardson, Clyde Moody, and some more and the Osbornes were booked in Texas and couldn't be there. So on Sunday I walked onstage and said I was gonna do a story of his [Monroe's] music.

Had you made up the story?

No.

Where did you get the idea to do a story?

Well, that was the only way I could show what real bluegrass was, to start back at the beginning with those guys singing with him. You see they were having the *Hootenanny*[5] show on TV and all, calling everything that got on there with a banjo, mandolin, fiddle and a guitar bluegrass and it wasn't bluegrass and I knew that the only men who could sing bluegrass was men who had learned it from Bill Monroe.

Why did you always choose "Mule Skinner Blues" to start out your story?

Well, in all the records I'd heard I went back and "Mule Skinner Blues" was the first one that I heard with this driving time.

So in your opinion, bluegrass started with the "Mule Skinner Blues"?

Yeah, he put it in a different key from Jimmie Rodgers and that was what made bluegrass, was singing songs in a different key than what country was done in, in a higher key, and then you could do harmony and by his voice being unusually high he had to have high lead singers to blend with him and that's what created bluegrass music. Of course it was in Bill Monroe time.

How would you describe that time?

It's like the mandolin hits between all the other beats and fills it up and that way it keeps it moving, and it's perfect time, and then it's the feeling that every man, his individual feeling, he puts it into each song or each thing he's doing, to make the four or five things come together. But I believe Bill Monroe's the only one you can learn real bluegrass from. 'Cause he's the only man can make you sing in those keys and stay there. And you'll learn to sing true; you can sing off-key till you go to singing with him for about a year and a half and you'll sing just as true as a dollar. And

---

4. Don Reno and Red Smiley were fronting other bands at the time.

5. The ABC television show *Hootenanny*, which capitalized on the folk-music craze of the day, was on the air in 1963 and 1964.

you'll play an instrument just true as a dollar. He's only man in the world can make you do that. What Bill Monroe plays is bluegrass, and what everybody else plays is just a copy of him.

What would you say was the primary reason for putting on your festivals?

My only reason to put on a bluegrass festival was to let the world know that it all came from Bill Monroe, that's the only reason. I wanted to give him the credit before he died. I'll say after guys like Sonny Osborne or Reno or Jimmy Martin or any of 'em, after they learn the basic beat, the basic bluegrass, then they put their own stuff in it, but they still use his time and his keys and his sound . . . but they each put in their own thing individually into the music.

Has the purpose of your festivals changed any since the beginning?

Well, I've done proved my point, I think I've proved to everybody that Bill Monroe is to get the credit and then Chubby Wise and Lester, and Earl Scruggs and Charlie Monroe did a lot on the guitar. I think those five people created the basic fundamentals of bluegrass music. I think I've proved that, so now I want to teach as many boys to play it as want to play it. If I can help him with an opportunity to play it, that's the purpose of the festival and of my doing bluegrass.

How do you go about doing your festivals now?

Well, we use new groups, two or three on each festival, and we've got a lot of bluegrass contests and this gives them a chance to play. And they don't get much money yet, but they're artists, a lot of them will develop into great artists, and if we hadn't a'started the festivals, in another two years, by 1966 or 1967, there woulda been no more, nobody learnin' it, there was nowhere to learn it and nowhere to play it and enjoy it. The festivals gave 'em an opportunity to play it, and so the festivals now are for that purpose, also for the fans who enjoy hearing it now. They can hear some exciting music.

Well, now there seem to be quite a few new bluegrass festivals being put on every summer. Do you think this is a healthy development?

Yeah, I think if they create fans in the Troy area, they are coming to Camp Springs; if you create fans in the Cosby, Tenn., area, they'll come to another festival. It's just like somebody inventing a new style of clothes or food. If they like it, they're going to go after it.

Do you think bluegrass could ever be a nationwide, widely accepted style of popular music?

When they get to playin' it back, right. They're getting close now, but there's a little ways to go and they've got to get it perfect.

What do you think is the major problem today with bluegrass music?

No material, no new material. I mean, country music got material, so people wanted to hear it. Trouble with bluegrass is they've heard "Footprints in the Snow," and "Blue Moon of Kentucky," and I don't mean to pick two of Bill's songs. Now we're getting a few new groups supplying new material and if we can get material. It's like putting money in the bank—you can't write checks unless you put something in it.

Why do you think no strong new material has been created since the early period you talk about?

Same way a boy can't pick a banjo, he's just never learned to do it. He can learn to write just like he learns to play a banjo and now we've gotten 'em playing the instruments over the last seven years and now we've got to get on 'em and start telling 'em to learn to write.

Have you written songs?

Country.

What do you do now besides putting on the bluegrass festivals?

Well, we put on country music shows in coliseums and make some money at that and we've used a lot of that in the bluegrass. And the ironic part, it may be that bluegrass in another three or four years may make enough money that, now that country music has made its cycle, maybe bluegrass can help it.

What are your plans for Blue Grass Park?

Well, we bought that piece of land so that there could always be a festival on Labor Day and I hope there's always a festival every weekend if we can get enough people to like it and come to it. And so then we decided to develop into other things—we want to build a Hall of Fame to these musicians and want to fix a place where the tapes and records and biographies of these artists can be kept so that a hundred years from now, people could come and hear the original generation, the way they played. I think we're going into a second generation now and there's boys are going to do it a little different, but they can always go back and hear how the twenty original groups did it. So Blue Grass Park, we'll leave a building there with this stuff stored in it so that young boys that like the music fifty or a hundred years from now can come there and hear this time that I've been talking about and how Reno or how Scruggs or how Chubby Wise or how Mac Wiseman and those guys did it.

You are associated a great deal with the country music personalities. Do you find that many of them like bluegrass music?

They like it; they can't play it; they can't do it because their voices are not made for that high range, but Buck Owens' favorite group is Reno and Smiley, Merle Haggard loves the fiddle and is trying to learn to play it now, Porter Wagoner came to one of our festivals just to hear it. They all like it—any musician's got to like it that understands country music.

When the Reno and Smiley team broke up in 1964 and they left to go on their separate ways, which way did you decide to go?

Well, I stayed on booking shows for Red, but I started promoting country music shows in coliseums. That was not being put on in coliseums so I rented a coliseum in Winston-Salem, N.C., and hired some country acts and I also had the idea that something's got to happen onstage in any kind of entertainment and I had to make it happen, so I hired Ray Price and Porter Wagoner and Norma Jean and the Kitty Wells show and these were three entirely different shows and I got the idea that I could blend it all together and wind up with an ending that would make people buy tickets again and I did.

How do you go about making something exciting happen onstage?

Well, in the first place you get the entertainer backstage. You get him interested in the show and what you're doing and you get him sort of keyed up and so that when he goes onstage at my shows, he's almost at where he would be ending another show, then I want him to go from there, so I talk to him and tell him some of the songs I want him to do, let him know I'm interested in him other than making money at the box office. I want to hear him sing something ain't never been sung before, just like in bluegrass.

Can you make this happen anytime?

Anytime. I can make it happen anytime because I've studied every entertainer. I did the same thing in country. I've studied what makes him cry, and who he loves and what he likes to do—play golf, play ball, go fishing, so forth. Then I start talking to him about his children or his wife or some of those things and I may even talk to him about some of the things we did years ago. I get him to thinking, remembering, and then a lot of times I can make an entertainer cry, in the dressing room.

Maybe you could tell us a story about one time that this happened, maybe with some of the bluegrass people. Do you remember when something exciting happened on the stage at a festival?

Well, I'd been with the Osbornes two weeks before that second festival and I even kept on till I got them to the point where I told 'em that you'll hear (something) next weekend at Fincastle[6] you'll never forget the rest of your life, every time you lay down, close your eyes, you'll hear it . . . when you're laying on your deathbed, and they tell you you're dying, what'll come into your mind'll be what you hear at that festival. There's no way you can drive it out. And they thought I was silly until, course, I had 'em psyched out, and then when they went on the stage on the Sunday and they'd never sung together with Bill Monroe, the both of 'em, and we did a song called "I Hear a Sweet Voice Calling," there was harmony and the notes; sound come out of their mouth and made tones that had never been made before and Sonny Osborne cried and we had to take him offstage into a tent and Bobby Osborne cried and Bill Monroe—one tear came out of his eye, and I wrote a little story that said, "How many miles and how many years and how much work and how many heartaches had gone into making that one bluegrass tear," and from then on, we knew that we could do it every year, 'cause it was still inside of him and it was my job to get it out, and it was the people's job to buy a ticket to hear it.

Do you plan to stay with bluegrass?

I plan to develop Camp Springs[7] and Blue Grass Park, build a Hall of Fame, Library and Archives, and a recording studio so that all acts can record and leave that to the musicans and anything else they need me to do they can ask me and I will.

Originally published in *Muleskinner News* 2 (Sept. 1971): 8–10, 18–21. Reprinted by permisson of Carlton Haney.

6. Haney refers to his second bluegrass festival at Fincastle, Virginia, in 1966.
7. Beginning in 1969, Haney held his festivals in Camp Springs, North Carolina.

As *Muleskinner News* editor Fred Bartenstein recalls, the "festival lifestyle" was within its first years of existence when the magazine got started in 1969. Connie Walker, wife of bluegrass musician Ebo Walker, knew well her subject when she trotted out some excruciating details of life on the festival site. Her humorous account nonetheless reflected the budding feminist tone of the era. See Thomas A. Adler's "Is There a Link between Bluegrass Musicianship and Sexuality?" in this volume for more on the role of bluegrass festivals as an extended family for participants.

32

"The Plight of the Bluegrass Widow"

CONNIE WALKER

Well girls, it's happening again. Your husband has been vague since the first warm day, he has a glassy look about his eyes and his conversation all revolves around the family's summer festival schedule.

Yes, the summer of '72 is here and that brings joy to his heart and gloom to yours. For the bluegrass widow, summer means extensive grocery shopping, pulling out bedrolls and camping equipment, dusting off coolers and canteens, and relocating the first aid kit, calamine lotion, and all those maps which never seem to include places like Bean Blossom, Knob Noster and Camp Springs.

Once the notes for mailman and milkman are strategically placed, the whole family plus tent, plus dogs, plus those precious instruments are packed into the car, and you are on your way to—the Festival! Your weekend will go something like this:

You are wakened at 6:30 A.M., the kids clamoring for breakfast. Since daddy was up picking until half an hour ago, he can't be coaxed out of his sleeping bag to help you light the stove (or go out to borrow the kerosene you forgot), or manage the young'uns as you turn eggs with one hand and fight off flies with the other. As soon as the last breakfast utensil has been dried and put away, he's up. And what does he want!? Breakfast, of course! He trots off to the restroom telling you he'll be right back.

Three hours later he wanders in, explains how he was waylaid by his picking friends, and asks about breakfast. You're really too upset to complain, however, since the little monsters have disappeared! Oh well, they're either in the poison ivy or the river. (What's that song about "The Little Girl and the Dreadful Snake?") Your second meal of the morning completed, the old man's gone again. Now where are those kids? Here comes one with the first skinned knee of the season. While washing off the mud to get to the blood you notice that he has managed to acquire a half-inch layer of red clay top to bottom.

The other one is at the next camp, eating all their cookies. Finally together, it's up to the stage—and don't forget the suntan lotion. You sleep through the 7th and

8th groups only to be awakened by the unearthly screech "Rubeeeeee!" For the first time, it's not your husband wanting dinner. But the kids are hungry, so its back to the camp and that darned Coleman stove.

Several hours later, daddy dashes into the tent, eats, and dashes out again. The next time you see him is around midnight, out in the middle of the parking lot, lurching and sounding less like the Kentucky songbird and more like the Tennessee Hound Dog. Your shoes and hair are soaked from your mighty search, but at last you've found him. When the song you came in on finally wears out he explains that things are just warming up and he has no intention of turning in. You give up and head back across the field to bed down with the kids.

This summer can be different. Forget about big boy and start thinking about yourself. Join the Bluegrass Widows Association. This will be the greatest invention since Red Cross Shoes. What to do is this: After the morning meal, pack lunches, set the kids out with their toys, leave Him a note, and be on your way. Decked out in your jeans or bikini (no makeup) and carrying a cooler of your favorite refreshment, head for my blue Chevy van. You can recognize me by my big white dog and my little white dog.

Once gathered we can plan our agenda. We might take in some of the local color, visit antique shops, go to the movies (if the town has one), treat ourselves to a meal cooked by someone else for a change, and discuss something other than bluegrass music. For those who are soap opera buffs, I have a TV set.

All in all, I'm sure we can have an enjoyable time doing what our hearts desire. The men can do for themselves! See you this summer, girls.

Originally published in *Muleskinner News* 3 (May 1972): 60–61. Reprinted by permission of Carlton Haney.

T om Teepen, retired as of spring of 2000, has been the editorial page editor of the *Dayton Daily News* and the *Atlanta Constitution* and national correspondent for Cox Newspapers. He uses the eye for detail and writing skills of a news professional in this *Muleskinner News* piece on Larry Sparks.

As one of the most talented of the generation that followed the Monroe-Flatt-Scruggs-Stanley axis, Sparks emphasized that he wanted his band to develop its own sound while remaining in a traditional context. Teepen tagged along on a Sparks road trip and offered readers an inside look at what a traveling bluegrass band encounters—even a talented one that has a national buzz. The all-night drives, stays with relatives and friends, and exultation over hearing one's own record on the radio will ring familiar to anyone who's ever traveled a similar road.

Teepen also has enough background as a musician to catch details such as the pall that a banjo player's dropped fingerpick can cast over a show.

33

"Larry Sparks . . . on the Road"

TOM TEEPEN

It's an illusion you can get sometimes when you've been driving hard for a long while: that you are standing still while the unheeding road slips under you. Then you shake it off and things slip back into their regular order.

Larry Sparks is going places.

"Surviving. You could say that's all I was doing until this year—just surviving," Sparks says of the time since he left Ralph Stanley in early 1970. By then he had put in three years as guitar player and lead singer replacing the late Carter Stanley. It has been a long road back up.

This year, however, singing with greater assurance than ever and sporting the best version yet of his band, the Lonesome Ramblers, Larry Sparks has been on the move. By the season's end, he will have played about a dozen festivals, even head-lining a new one at Port Huron, Michigan. At each, public response has been strongly favorable. So has been the critical response to an album issued at mid-summer by the Old Homestead label.

The crowd's reaction at a Virginia festival brought an on-the-spot, three-year recording contract with Starday. Spark's first Starday LP, *Ramblin' Blue Grass*, was released in early September. Each festival has won additional bookings. Sparks and the Lonesome Ramblers expect to be even less lonesome next season. It looks as though they will be logged for at least twenty-five festivals. Bill Monroe has taken a paternal interest in the singer and guitar flat-picker as one of the young musicians whose style is rooted in traditional bluegrass.

Sparks bought a '66 Chevy station wagon for this summer's travel. The '63 had been run into the ground. Already, in the three months since, he has put eighteen thousand miles on the '66. The odometer is rolling toward 130,000 miles as Sparks drives into Nashville.

He is on his way to Bill Grant's festival in Hugo, Oklahoma. He and the band left the Dayton, Ohio, area at 4 A.M. Larry lives in Franklin, south of the city. Mike Lilly, the banjo-picker and Wendy Miller, the mandolin player, live in Dayton. They rendezvous at a truck spot on Interstate 75, and it is still before dawn when they pick up the band's bass player and resident senior citizen, Art Wydner, in Cincinnati.

There's a stop in Nashville at the Starday studio. Sparks and the band are to be photographed for the new album cover. The raucous humor, ranging down from ribald, is still running strong. Miller and Lilly tease the Starday secretaries shame-lessly and everyone, even the secretaries, rag Wydner. He'll take several minutes of it before harumphing a come-back that takes him off the hook for a while.

The photographer arrives and Sparks and the band change into their stage duds.

A four-hour photo session follows at the home grounds of Starday president Hal Neely. The musicians unload the wagon, take out their instruments, pose and then pack up and move to another location, each time repeating the loading and unloading. It's hot, and the session is work. A title for the album is gimmicked up.

"I signed him," Neely said, "because of the young groups in bluegrass, I think they've got the best shot. And because I had heard such good reports on Larry from the older hands, from Ralph Stanley and Bill Monroe."

Among the poses Neely had asked of Larry that afternoon was one under an American flag and one with a dog. A shot on a tractor, which is used for cutting the lawn at Neely's home, was considered but skipped because the tractor had a flat tire.

"We lived on a farm, and I worked there a little—very little," Sparks says. "I mostly picked, but I've been on a tractor a few times."

Sparks, twenty-five, was born in Lebanon, Ohio, and grew up in Ohio, though as a child he lived briefly in Kentucky.

"I picked up music from records and from my older brothers and sisters. Dad played the banjo around the house, the claw-hammer way. One of my sisters, Bernice, taught me chords—that was when I was five. I've still got some records we made in the house on one of those little machines that make their own records. I was five then too. I was singing on them."

The records he listened to were by the Carter Family, to whom his guitar style still pays dues, Don Reno and Red Smiley, the Stanley Brothers and Bill Monroe.

"I just kept listening and figuring it out. Once I had picked up that guitar, I never put it down. Me and my sister played in churches and on local radio shows. I never thought about other work."

In his early teens, Sparks held a few part-time jobs, one at a car wash, another at a gas station. He put in three days at a factory. "I didn't like it," he says.

"Daddy never did say either way about my playing, about what I should do. My mother, she always wanted me to get out and play."

Guitar is Sparks' basic instrument, but he also can play mandolin, banjo, dobro and bass, and he is learning fiddle now.

"I liked the banjo, but it's hard to sing lead and play the banjo the way it should be, to drive a band. When I was a kid, I tried all the instruments and thought I'd be good on them all, but I learned you can't do that."

Sparks got his first professional job in Blue Grass with the Stanley Brothers when he was seventeen.

"There's a friend of mine, Wilbur Hall, who plays banjo, and he told Moon Mullins about me." (Mullins is a bluegrass disc jockey at WPFB in Middletown, Ohio.) "Moon came up to the house and heard me. He told the Stanley Brothers about me when they came to Hamilton and needed a flattop player. Carter called me to come down to the nightclub where they were playing.

"I was early. Yes, sir. I was more nervous about just getting to meet the Stanley Brothers than I was about playing with them. Carter talked to me about some road work. They had a concert coming up at the University of Chicago, and the festivals would be starting. They said they'd call when they came through next."

The call came in about four weeks. Sparks already had quit school and was playing full time, though making little income, with local bands. From that spring in 1965, he worked part time with the Stanley Brothers, alternating with George Shuffler until Carter died in 1966. "Singing hadn't really become important to me until I had got older and started working with the Stanley Brothers. With them, I started singing baritone in the trio numbers.

"Ralph didn't do much after Carter passed away until about February 7th, I think it was, Ralph was playing Tom's Tavern in Dayton. I didn't know what he was going to do, but I thought I could do the job if he wanted it done. We sang some together there at Tom's and he hired me that night."

Sparks stayed with the redoubtable Ralph Stanley until early 1970, taking on the next-to-impossible job of being the first replacement for Carter and inevitably compared to him.

"Ralph never told me how to sing. I just tried to sing Carter's style as close as I could. I had always liked Carter's singing, and that's just the style I used. We worked hard to keep the Stanley Brothers' Sound. Ralph wanted to keep that sound."

Sparks put a lot of music, a lot of songs behind him in those years—and a lot of miles. "We traveled by car then. That gets rough on you. Rough; yes sir."

After a quick supper, Larry Sparks and the Lonesome Ramblers had driven on from Nashville, riding quieter through the dusk and crossing the Mississippi at Memphis and pushing through Arkansas and into Texas through the night. The driving chore was rotated, with two men sleeping in the back seat while one "rides shotgun" up front to keep the driver awake.

The destination is Dallas and the home of Sparks' brother, Lloyd. Sparks has a line on a used bus in Dallas at a good price. He'll check it out before heading up into Oklahoma for the Hugo festival.

It's 7 A.M. when the band pulls up at Lloyd's home. It has been a twenty-eight-hour day. You get those on the road sometimes. Wendy Miller notices that a knee he hurt on a factory job has cramped up from the long ride. Art Wydner flops in the closest bed and is immediately asleep. Sparks and the others, however, are eager to see the bus. The body is in good shape. Travel facilities easily could be built in or temporarily rigged until a full job can be afforded. But the engine will have to be replaced.

"A 431 Lincoln," Lilly observes. "High compression burns out pistons in something like this." He thinks the Ford 390, low-compression industrial engine would be better. Lloyd knows where a rebuilt one can be bought for a good price. "Wendy and me could put it in," Lilly says. Wendy agrees. Sparks believes he will buy the bus, then. They decide to drive back down to Dallas in a couple of weeks or so when the replacement motor is ready, put the motor in and then drive the bus back to Ohio. The rest of the day is spent sleeping. Mrs. Sparks bustles around keeping the kids quiet. The house seems virtually littered with musicians. Probably they wouldn't have heard the kids.

That evening some friends stop by to meet Larry Sparks. One brings a banjo, another a mandolin. Larry picks up his guitar. Art unsheaths his bass. Outside, Mike Lilly swears nothing and nobody could get him to pick tonight. He has been arguing amiably with a friend about whether the Dodge Charger does or doesn't look good with its rear end raised. The guitar hasn't been chording and the bass thumping from inside the house for more than five minutes when Lilly goes in and starts picking. Other friends and other instruments appear. The living room is crowded. Sparks sings a couple of songs, but not many. His throat is a little scratchy and the festival begins the next day in Hugo.

"You just never can tell about Blue Grass and people," Larry's sister-in-law says. "The last time Larry was here, the people next door told us they had heard him playing. We hardly knew them, even though they live right there, but they said they heard Larry and had heard about him. They said they like Blue Grass music, and their house is beautiful inside."

The picking this night lasts till midnight. Then, knowing Larry has to start early for Hugo, the friends pack up their instruments and thank Larry for letting them pick with him. It has been a pleasure and a privilege, they say.

"I just decided to try it on my own," Sparks says. "I felt I wanted more than just being a sideman. I figured I could do better and would get more experience by having to do it on my own. I didn't know exactly what I wanted. Blue Grass, of course, but it's hard to do much without sounding like someone. I knew I wanted to be myself but I didn't know what that was yet,"

Sparks left the security of Ralph Stanley's band and its sure bookings in early 1970. "At first I was working local clubs again. It was like starting out all over again."

Sparks brought out his first LP, *Ramblin' Guitar,* on the Pine Tree label from a Hamilton, Ohio, studio soon after he had left Stanley. A gospel album on the same label followed the next year.

The current band built slowly, with each new member leading to another.

Wendy Miller was first. "I got with him in late January of '71," Sparks says. "A friend of mine knew him and that I needed a mandolin player. It worked out fine." Mike Lilly was added next, in the late spring of that year. "I needed a banjo and a good one wasn't easy found. Wendy knew Mike and we got together and talked and picked. I had wanted a more driving banjo like his." Mike led sparks to Art Wydner early this year. He is one of the most seasoned and steadiest bass men in Blue Grass.

There had been a smattering of festival jobs, personal appearances and bar gigs last year. Over the winter of 1971–72 and through this spring, Larry and the band worked out their material, mostly in weekend appearances at Tom's Tavern in Dayton, where he had first joined Ralph Stanley full time.

"We just all matched up playing and singing," Sparks says. "We worked hard getting new material. People have liked it so far. We've got our own sound, a lot of new stuff. Mike doesn't play just like anybody else. We've all got our own ways. We're trying not to get too fancy or too far out, so we can stay near the old-time sound."

The group has developed a close harmony, and it carries the tradition logically forward into an exceptionally smooth sound. Lilly plays a hard-driving hard-picking banjo, and both he and Miller can pick full speed ahead without wobbling on the turns. They often surprise one another by improvising new licks and breaks on the stage. Sparks plays a steady, lilting rhythm, and because of his fluid, agile flat-picking, his guitar, unlike that of most lead singers, adds a strong instrumental solo voice to the group's playing. His singing has gained in authority and subtlety over the last year. He is building recognition as one of the best "lonesome" singers in Blue Grass.

"I knew I was lost for a couple of years," Sparks says. "I was really searching. After I did the album on Old Homestead and now the one for Starday, I knew I had what I wanted. But I have to keep working at it, working hard to keep it."

Hugo is shortly east of the Muddy Boggy River, and if you don't live there, it seems pretty near nowhere—and gaining on it. No matter. A crowd of several thousand has turned out for the festival in the pleasant wooded park.

Sparks backs the station wagon up near the large crowd. The card table is unloaded and the records taken out of their cartons for display. Larry himself takes the first stint selling. During the two days the band will be performing here, the members will take turns hustling the records between their two shows daily.

Other business will be conducted too. The promoters of an upcoming festival in Cleveland, Texas, renew their acquaintance with Sparks; they remember his success with the crowd at the festival in McKinney, Texas, earlier in the summer. Sparks would like to play the Cleveland shows. The organizers would like to have him but aren't sure it can be worked in.

There is some dickering and a contract is signed. It's a good break. The trip to pick up the bus can be combined with the festival in Cleveland, assuring some income where only out-go had been expected. Shortly, Sparks will be plugging the Cleveland festival from the stage here.

Later, Sparks also books a November show in Ardmore, Oklahoma. A couple from the area wants to found a Larry Sparks fan club. The singer is pleased and grateful but begs time to think about the proposition. The couple later provides a welcome chicken dinner.

"Fan clubs can be important," Sparks explains. "They can do you a lot of good getting bookings and working up interest for personal appearances."

Larry Sparks and the Lonesome Ramblers have prominent spots in the Saturday and Sunday shows. The crowd is attentive and enthusiastic, but it is not as demonstrative as many of the Blue Grass festival crowds back in the East. Yet the fans obviously are moved by Sparks' singing and, though it takes them a while to realize that here's a lead singer who also plays fine solo guitar, they warm up to the flattop when they do. Lilly's dramatic, aggressive banjo-picking wins excited applause.

Sparks has been doing a lot of writing lately. The haunting "Thank You, Lord," which Larry wrote with his former bass man Neal Brackett, goes over especially well during the Sunday morning gospel show. Miller's fresh, catchy "Kentucky Chimes" instrumental is popular. The gospel tune will help sell several copies of the LP it's on and it helps attract attention to the full gospel album. The 45s of "Kentucky Chimes" sell out; the tune is on the new Starday album and will bolster that.

Sparks finally hits the bed at 3 A.M. after the Saturday shows. Miller and Lilly have sworn they aren't going to get involved in any late-night jam sessions, but an exceptionally good one gets going. They pick in it until 5 A.M. The band is up, has had breakfast and is ready to play its gospel show by 11 A.M.

This festival, like most, drags on too long. The audience is worn out, if the musicians are not. Sparks' last set Sunday has to fight that but starts well anyway. Then, midway in a rousing banjo instrumental, a pick flies off Lilly's finger. He has to retrieve it and the band's rhythm breaks. It's one of those things, and the crowd understands but the good mood that had been building is never fully regained.

Sparks' part is over, but he hangs on until the picking ends at 11 P.M. in case anyone in the rapidly dwindling audience still wants a record. His table is the last to close shop. A couple from Texas invites the band to their camper for steak sandwiches. By midnight, Art Wydner has eaten his fill, no small accomplishment, and is ready to go. But the host has an old Gibson Mastertone banjo with a crisp, clear ring. "After a while," Sparks tells his bass man. "I'm picking banjo a little." He plays a half-dozen tunes, and it's 12:30 A.M. when the band files out of the camper.

The station wagon pushes out of the festival grounds and turns east. The drive is silent for a long while. Lilly and Wydner are asleep. Sparks has been adding up the record sales in his head. "I believe that we've bought ourselves a motor for the bus," he says. Some minutes later he adds, "I'd rather make $100 playing music any old day than make $300 in a factory." Miller says, "Yeah, buddy."

But it is hard work and a gamble, and even the success Larry Sparks has had this year, until it is secured by success in following years, will be haunted by the specter of the factory.

The wagon's radio is tuned to a Ft. Worth station. The wagon is whipping into Daisy, Arkansas—population according to the sign, eighty-six. Suddenly a recording of "Kentucky Chimes" by Larry Sparks and the Lonesome Ramblers is being played over the radio. Larry quickly turns it up. "That's a fifty-thousand-watt station, clear channel," he says. "You can get it up in Kentucky, Indiana, Ohio. How about that!"

It's 3 A.M. in Daisy, and Larry Sparks and the Lonesome Ramblers think, hope, almost know that they're going places.

Originally published in *Muleskinner News* 3 (Nov. 1972): 8–12. Reprinted by permission of the author and Carlton Haney.

Bluegrass Unlimited, in its articles and letters columns, has long served as a forum for the seemingly unending arguments of bluegrass. When did it really start? Did Bill Monroe really give birth to it single-handedly? And, perhaps the most pervasive and basic argument: What is bluegrass, anyway? Purists argue, naturally enough, for purity, for music that sounds very much like Monroe and the Stanleys. Another frequently heard position is that bluegrass should make room for innovation, both to keep it vital and to allow musicians to make a living playing it. An irate John Duffey, long-time mandolinist for the sometimes experimental Country Gentleman, offered this extensive prose rant in response to people who taped bluegrass instead of buying records and to critics of his band and his own playing. Elsewhere in the story, it's interesting to note that Duffey hit the nail on the head about vinyl as opposed to tape. Old audiotapes have indeed deteriorated in many instances, while well-preserved vinyl records still sound great.

34

"So You Don't Like the Way We Do It (or Damn Your Tape Recorder)"

JOHN DUFFEY

For several cycles of the moon my ears and eyes have been blessed with verbal and printed forms of slander upon our group [The Country Gentlemen] and anyone else for that matter who does not use "Molly and Tenbrooks" or "Uncle Pen" as a strict guideline for their music.

First of all, let me enlighten you to the fact that there are different ways to play other than the style of Bill Monroe. Do not be misled by this statement—Bill is the finest in his style and no one can surpass him at it! However, anyone in the business knows that no success or fame can be achieved by copying note for note an already established artist.

Next, let us go into why groups leave the so-called beaten path. One reason is to try and establish their own "sound" but still retaining the designated and accepted instruments. Another reason is the record companies who are interested in selling their little discs of vinyl plastic. This now brings me to one of my pet peeves—That damn tape recorder!!!!! It seems that too many dyed in the wool bluegrass fans would rather tape it than spend a couple of bucks on a record. They don't seem to realize that what they have on tape doesn't help the artist one damn bit. I talked to some of the people who were taping at the Bluegrass Festival in Roanoke last year who were complaining about the music we play now as compared to five years ago. One of them had purchased one of our records (we have seven albums and twenty some singles at present) and the others confessed that they don't buy records they "borrow someone else's and tape it." This same story is repeated over and over everywhere, and to this day I can't understand why. I am informed by electronics experts that a phonograph record under good care will last a hundred years, whereas a tape will deteriorate in twenty-five years. I recently talked with someone else who wanted to know when we would be playing in his area so he could tape us. He mentioned specific numbers he wanted—I suggested he buy the record, he replied, "I'm fascinated with the tape machine, I don't buy records."

Unfortunately, this taping mania seems to be confined to bluegrass. The proof of this being you don't see a mass of tape recorders at a concert by Frank Sinatra, The Beatles, or Ernest Tubb, but if there is a bluegrass band appearing it looks like the United Nations as far as microphones leading into tape machines. Why do you think Buck Owens for instance is always on the charts? People don't tape him, they buy his records! Record sales are the only thing the trade papers have to go by. This is one good reason why bluegrass will probably never be a tremendous commercial success. I can't figure out if bluegrass fans are unintentionally ignorant of the facts or if they are just a bunch of tightwads! Remember clods, in our dollar-minded society, if there is a demand, there will be a supply.

Now let me tell you why we (The Country Gentlemen) have tippy-toed into other realms of possibilities in our music. I think the preceding paragraph is somewhat explanatory. If we can't sell our straight bluegrass to bluegrass fans, then we have got to sell something to somebody else. Believe me, if you don't sell records, the company doesn't want anything to do with you. In 1961 we began venturing into the booming "Folk Field." Why? It's very simple, we would name our price and the concert promoter or the coffee house owner would say, "Great, when can I get you?" We would name our price to a hillbilly park owner or country promoter and they would say, "We don't pay that kind of money for bluegrass, we can get the Nashville Sound for half the price and a bottle of Old Crow." Going into other fields involved some change in material in order to give our audience what they wanted to hear. However, this alteration brought no change in our instruments or singing. It merely brought new material to the field. These slight deviations also made bluegrass music more palatable to many more people. I think I'm safe in saying that possibly other than Lester Flatt and Earl Scruggs, we have converted more people to bluegrass than any other group. The old saying "when in Rome, do as the Romans do" also applies in music. When you can make the snobs think you're one of them, pretty soon they are on your side. And they will take notice of what you are doing. This makes it easier for the next group who comes along. Before you scream commercialism, remember that everyone in the business whether it be opera or bluegrass is trying to make a living. You who scream the loudest have probably never tried to earn a living playing bluegrass music.

Let's take a look at the instrument which is always the #1 subject of controversy—the five-string banjo. To some of you, there seems to be only one way to play it, and that is "Scruggs Style." BOSH!! If you think a fast roll would sound good in the middle of "Bringing Mary Home," then your musical taste is in the part of your anatomy on which you sit! Necessity is the mother of invention, and when you need a banjo for other uses than breakdowns, then you need someone who has two hands instead of one. Eddie Adcock is more versatile and can do more things with a banjo than anyone within the realm of public notice. However, some people who have not outgrown childhood jealousies will beg to differ. Another point to be mentioned is if you can't do what the other guy is doing, then knock it—spread the word, tell the people it's bad, and if you happen to be the "big wheel" in your sewing circle you can probably convince some of your sheep that you are right. I also would like to give due credit to the banjo players who are very skilled in the Scruggs style. I have heard too many to mention but, in my opinion, the number one man in the category is Bill Emerson, who is unsurpassed for clean, straight, hard-drive playing. He has perhaps more drive than Scruggs himself. So you see, right here is a typical example. The inventor of a product does not necessarily make the best one! Also, we should not forget Bill Keith, who came up with a superlative new sound for the banjo. I've heard people knock him also.

In behalf of other groups such as Flatt and Scruggs, Jim and Jesse and The Osborne Brothers who have received much criticism, they have the habit of having to eat just like you. They got a little tired of driving five hundred miles to make a hundred dollars and decided it was time for a change. I for one admire every dollar they've made and I'm sure they cry all the way to the bank every time they hear a derogatory comment about their music. Apparently there are enough good supporters on the other side of the fence to make it worthwhile.

In answer to a snide remark in a recent article about The Country Gentlemen being conspicuous by their absence, I am well aware of how cheaply some groups sell themselves. It is appalling to know that one can make a better living sweeping streets than some well-known groups make playing music. We have no intention of saving up to go on tour, and therefore if it is not worthwhile, I would rather stay home and glue guitars together. Doesn't that make sense? And just in case you plan to make a case of it, I am in a position to back up every thing I say!

In summing it up, I'll give those of you who are just dying to say "he must be conceited" something to rave about. I've had lots of criticism about how I play my little mandolin. Well, it may be good or it may be bad, some like it and some don't, whatever style you want to call it doesn't matter, but remember, IT'S MINE! What have you contributed besides criticism, buddy boy?

In closing, one word of advice to bluegrass bands. Through the years it has been the policy for bluegrass musicians to stand upon the stage and look mad at the world or as if they died the day before. We have found that this is a bad policy. If you look like you are enjoying yourself and put a little "show" into your performance you'll be surprised at the amount of new faces you will attract.

EPILOGUE: To those of you who have never tried to make a living playing straight bluegrass music; get out and try, or keep your damn mouth shut!!

Originally published in *Bluegrass Unlimited* 1 (April 1967): 3–4. Reprinted by permission of Nancy Duffey.

R obert Cantwell came to Bill Monroe's Bean Blossom festival already commit-
  ted to bluegrass but left as a total convert. In a relatively mainstream-press
treatment of bluegrass, he used sociological and historical means to analyze the
music as it faced changes to its historical context. In 1984 Cantwell produced *Bluegrass Breakdown: The Making of the Old Southern Sound* (Urbana: University of Illinois Press), one of the first book-length treatments of the music.

35

"Believing in Bluegrass"

ROBERT CANTWELL

The themes of bluegrass music transcend simple otherworldliness, and at best they
are genuinely metaphysical.

Bill Monroe's Fifth Annual Bluegrass Music Festival last summer in Bean Blossom, Indiana, drew more people than even Bill Monroe could have anticipated. Bill
Monroe, in case you didn't know, is a direct descendant of President James Monroe and the man credited with the "invention" of bluegrass music. If you ask Bill
Monroe just what bluegrass music is, he will say simply that it is "the best music in
the world." I doubt that anyone at Bean Blossom much minded the hyperbole. Those
of us who love bluegrass love it obsessively. I got my money's worth right at the gate,
where Bill Monroe, who had never seen me before in his life, said "Howdy!" and
smiled like a senator.

When Bill Monroe thirty years ago began to sing and play the traditional string
band music of the Appalachian range, he was able, by a subtle and sensitive control
of immense exertions, to focus its diverse energies into a formal style as rich as the
blues in its powers of personal expression. His ringing, athletic mandolin-picking
and his unearthly tenor voice, which sounds something like the wind, have made
him a sort of Leadbelly or Bessie Smith of mountain music. And because his band
hailed from Kentucky, he called them "the Blue Grass Boys," and so named a renewed tradition of folk music which is, remarkably, still in the hands of its own folk.

We came to Bean Blossom to hear bluegrass music, and to see it. In the park
the commerce of guitars, banjos, fiddles, mandolins and tenor voices could be heard
from six o'clock one morning until three the next. Bluegrass bands are as exciting
to watch as hockey games, and cannot be fully appreciated except in person. I discovered at Bean Blossom that because I had never seen Bill Monroe in person I had
never really heard him. The most sophisticated recording instruments cannot reproduce the drama generated by the corporate creation of a tune. First, there is the

choreography of performance, the regularly changing relationship of each member of the band to the microphone—or simply to the foreground—which a group must master in order to render a piece coherently. The lead singer, who most often plays mandolin or guitar, lingers near the center and is joined by one, two, three, or all of the others for choruses in harmony. Meanwhile, a vastly complicated interplay of melodies is embroidered in the background by fiddle, mandolin, and banjo. At the end of a chorus the singer abruptly disperses to make way for the solo instruments—banjo, fiddle, mandolin, and more recently the guitar—on which the soloist displays his often incredible virtuosity with variations on the theme. At the end of his break he will sail away on a river of notes or suddenly swoon into a void behind the lead singer who has returned to the point of focus. All of this is done, by professionals at least, with fluidity and ease, but with scrupulous care as well. Part of the effect of the music is in the tension one feels between what is heard, with its energy and movement, and what is seen, the absolute concentration required of a performer in the execution of a break. While the music may make you want to jump out of your skin, the band itself, especially the banjo player, is stone-steady and poker-faced. For the musician, performance is an opportunity to be both wholly himself—to display his particular abilities and ideas—and to submerge himself wholly in the identity of the group.

Just what makes the "identity of the group" is an interesting question. One highly proficient professional group, the Country Gentlemen, who have been playing bluegrass for at least fifteen years, recently had a rather sweeping change in personnel; of the original quartet, three have been replaced. Yet they are, in some fundamental way, the same people that they have always been. Similarly, Bill Monroe's Blue Grass Boys, with whom practically every well-known bluegrass musician has played at one time or another, retains that quality which Bill Monroe once sought and obviously found. Like oral epic literature, if I may be allowed a somewhat academic analogy, bluegrass music is formulaic, being primarily a fund of instrumental licks and runs, traditional melodies and songs which are transmitted not only in live performance, as it was for epic in the days of Homer, but also by means of phonograph records. In fact, all songs and instrumental breakdowns, whether traditional or originally composed, enter the bluegrass "tradition" once they are recorded, yet change, grow and influence one another in authentic oral fashion.

At Bean Blossom perfect strangers could form bands and moments later be making fine music together. Even though a bluegrass musician develops himself largely in solitary, he cannot fully display or even realize his musical abilities until he participates with other individuals in a band. Thus he is not fully an individual, musically at least, until he is swept up in the operations of that tiny but very real community. I believe anyone who has ever played in a bluegrass band will testify that it can be a deeply satisfying and elevating experience, and at times—in those moments of transcendent cooperation—sublime. Consequently, the music is largely participatory, and those who came to Bean Blossom were seeking, I think, something more than diversion, stimulation or entertainment. I was astonished to find that even while Bill Monroe performed in the park pavilion, intrepid pickers and fiddlers, in and out of tents, campers, and house trailers, were making bluegrass.

On Tuesday, "Barbecue Bean Day" and the first day of the festival, there were flash floods forty miles away, where two inches of rain had fallen in forty-five minutes. In the remote areas of the park, now filling up as more and more people arrived, cars and pickup trucks with campers were settling complacently into the mud and declaring that spot their campsite. Not until the following day, when attendance began to exceed expectations, did it become necessary to move the automobiles and park them in neat rows to make room for newcomers, who were arriving at all hours of the day and night. In this mild crisis there was, of course, an elated conviviality as strangers cooperated to push out of the mud the most absurdly marooned Oldsmobiles, Buicks and Chevys—not all showroom iron. A brightly painted pickup with chrome wheel covers, two or three American flag decals on the back window, and a richly laden shotgun rack behind the driver's seat arose from the mud with the aid of four or five grunting, groaning, laughing hippies with shoulder-length hair, tie-dyed shirts, and mottled jeans, and a braless girlfriend standing by.

Through Wednesday and Thursday the society in Bill Monroe's Jamboree Park shifted and settled, each newcomer orienting himself to the somewhat elusive water supplies, to the geography of the park and to the IGA store a quarter of a mile down Indiana 135. Being neighborly seemed much easier in the more perfect democracy of a camping ground, where outward signs of social differences are minimized and unwitting judgments happily retarded. Nearly everyone was cooking on a Sears or Coleman cookstove, lighting his way with a Sears or Coleman lantern, sleeping in a Sears cotton-twill wax-finish cabin tent—what did it matter that some folks had campers with built-in stoves and real beds? It was a kind of circus, and it was difficult to feel anything but innocent delight.

Walking from one end of the camp to the other, perhaps from the phone booth out on the highway or from the grocery store back through the main gate, across the flat plain of the parking area, down the hill and into the woods, then onto the mud road leading back to a second, recently bulldozed clearing, one could hear, in fluid sequence, bluegrass bands, first one, then a hint of the next, then a new band several yards ahead, one band never interfering with another. Occasionally, one would stop to hear some exceptionally good fiddler or banjo-picker or to catch the last verse or two of a favorite song. I stopped once to listen to the sharp tenor singing of a man in a fishing hat, who leaned laconically against his camper where a sign read: "Business? Gone to Hell!" and strummed his mandolin. One morning we were attracted to an unusually large crowd in a grove of trees near the park pavilion. In their midst was a wholesome-looking family seated in lawn chairs making some breathtakingly clean bluegrass: father on guitar, sisters on bass and mandolin, and junior on banjo. Junior, a lad of about thirteen whose glasses kept slipping down his nose, was picking a series of riffs and runs and slides and chord changes that were literally beyond belief. "He's fantastic!" I said spontaneously to no one in particular.

"He shore is," a rather large man in front of me said dolefully, turning away and heading, I supposed, back to his banjo.

A few came to Bean Blossom, it seemed, only to say that they had been there. A squirrel-hunter from Indianapolis who nearly mowed down our tent when he arrived in the middle of the night hung around his truck, with a bottle of beer perpetually in hand, and never once for three days, went up to hear the performing bands. "This is mah fift yer at Bean Blossom," he said proudly. "Used t'be held up awn Birch Monroe's farm up chere the road about two miles. You know got too big fer thet." Birch Monroe was Bill's older brother and on the previous night he had fiddled his way through a veritable briar patch of old-timey tunes. "Ahm from Kentucky, originally," the squirrel-hunter added, redundantly.

On Thursday afternoon one of the first major events, the banjo-pickers' contest, was held in the pavilion. The youngest contestant, about nine, whose banjo was perhaps an inch shorter than he was, raced through "Reuben" as nimbly as a typist typing. A mustachioed college dropout who had built his own banjo, including the delicately cut mother-of-pearl inlays and the inlaid presidential eagle on the back, appeared onstage alone (the others brought guitar accompaniment) and played an original piece called, I think, "Fox Run."

Every bluegrass banjo-picker is ultimately indebted to the man who played banjo with Bill Monroe's original Blue Grass Boys—Earl Scruggs. Scruggs had developed out of the old "drop-thumb" style of banjo-picking a three-finger, syncopated style so compelling that audiences still bounce on their haunches listening to it, even youngsters nurtured on electric rock. At Bean Blossom, nearly every competitor played at least one tune worked into the style from traditional melodies by Earl Scruggs himself, and although the Scruggs style of banjo-picking has been much elaborated since the early days of the music, specialization having overtaken even bluegrass, it seemed to me that the contest was won almost solely on the winner's capacity—and it was considerable—to bring Earl Scruggs to mind.

Through Thursday, Friday and well into mid-afternoon on Saturday, people continued to arrive. Bill Monroe and his fiddler Kenny Baker, along with some volunteers, worked most of the day digging postholes and stringing new fence in order to expand the available camping space. By Friday at suppertime, when the park was filled with people and with music, a sense of rich purpose pervaded everything. A walk to the gate would show that the name bands—Ralph Stanley and the Clinch Mountain Boys, Don Reno, Bill Harrell and the Tennessee Cut-Ups, Jim and Jesse and the Virginia Boys, Jimmy Martin and the Sunny Mountain Boys—had begun to arrive in their lettered buses. All the young banjo-pickers, mandolin-chunkers, and the high lonesome screamers of the preceding three days took on the obsolescence of a just-read novel. Even the Brown County Boys, a group of fifteen-year-olds from five miles down the road who had astonished everyone with their cool skill, faded behind the presence of storied professionals, who might be seen walking about, or standing in conversation (often slightly plumper than record album covers showed) or signing autographs. Lester Flatt ambled by me wearing a red-white-and-blue, hand-painted tie. Don Reno, whom I had seen at the University of Chicago Folk Festival three years before with silver-white hair, now sported a wavy auburn pompadour. He still had those fancy white cowboy boots that I recall were the envy of a Blackstone Ranger who happened to be hanging around the university coffee shop.

The authentic beginnings of the festival took place that evening around the gate of the park. Bill Monroe had organized what in five years had become a tradition—he called it the "sunset jam session." Everyone who dreams of playing bluegrass with Bill Monroe here found his opportunity. In the confines of a small grassy area defined by a clothesline hung across temporary posts, Bill had gathered with upwards of one hundred and twenty guitar-, banjo- and mandolin-pickers, fiddlers and singers to play and sing, into three widely spaced mikes wired to a sound truck, songs and tunes from the Bill Monroe canon which *everyone* knew by heart. Knew, that is, in the absolute, liturgical sense. Clustered around Bill Monroe in his gleaming white jacket and white cowboy hat were the very young, amateurs and professionals, musicians who had learned under Monroe, played in his band, and had gone off to make their own reputations, and those who hoped eventually to record and carry on Bill Monroe's traditions themselves. Bill administered each number, singing and playing into one of the mikes, dropping behind and inviting a friend or a stranger to sing or play a bit, or with the palm of his hand gently prodding a shy and thrilled youngster to play a hesitating but thoroughly satisfying instrumental solo. "I call you all my children," Bill said and suddenly it became clear that this bluegrass festival was nothing more or less than an old-time camp meeting, an evangelical retreat of the very kind that rural folk a century ago waited all summer for, yet now somehow enlightened beyond dogma, hellfire and exploitation. And here was Bill Monroe the teacher, founder of all the brotherhood and sisterhood, standing among all the picking and singing like John Wesley on the green of an eighteenth-century English village. That night, when someone in the audience asked the highly talented mandolin picker for the Brown Mountain Boys to play "Raw Hide," an instrumental created by Bill Monroe and requiring incredible dexterity in both hands, the young man drawled, "Naw, let's leave that one for the Master."

And why shouldn't it be so? Is it the province of a religious teacher to restore a private and inward dimension to people whose lives have become dominated by outward forms and thus by the hypocrisy and cant which inevitably result—to freshen "the individual value of every soul"? This is, I believe, what Bill Monroe established for his people through the agency of their music, music being the most characteristic and most articulate mode of expression, the prime embodiment of the mountain imagination. Thus he became for mountain people, who, like other rural societies, have tended to move more slowly and deliberately through history than the rest of the world, the first modern man.

I hesitate to use the sociological term *subculture,* since the people out of whom bluegrass music originated and to whom it is addressed are not, in my opinion, subordinate to American culture as a whole (assuming there is such a thing as American culture as a whole). They are certainly a "people," however, with ties more fundamental than the music itself, though the music may be *like* a religion, that common body of knowledge, ceremony, and experience which makes their unity self-conscious and serviceable because it has been outwardly expressed. In the broadest sense, inclusive of the gospel and string music which preceded it, bluegrass is perhaps one of the largest surviving funds of traditional knowledge in the country outside of Indian lore and religion itself. As such it is bound up with larger attitudes and beliefs axiomatic with the people and especially with their special, almost heretical variety of protestant Christianity which, along with their music, reveals the unique way of appreciating life they as individuals hold in common.

Over fifty bands, amateur and professional, not to mention a great number of individual fiddlers, banjo- and guitar-pickers, appeared onstage at Bean Blossom. Many more performed who never stepped onto the stage but who entertained hundreds passing by. Every novice and amateur band, even some of the plodders, was received with enthusiasm. Bill Monroe's people are warmly hospitable and emotional, deeply appreciative of fellow feeling.

These emotional qualities are still more pronounced in bluegrass musicians themselves, who have a reputation for intensity and unpredictability. I heard of one accomplished guitarist who abandoned the instrument altogether when his guitar was stolen, insisting it would be a kind of betrayal to play a strange instrument, and took up mandolin. Another fine singer of my acquaintance refuses to sing anything but sacred songs. In short, there is a kind of mysticism in bluegrass music. In its subject matter, in its performers and their performances, even its most antic moods, it is pervaded by death. Often it is actually about death, in pious, morbid, or sentimental ways; murder ballads and tales of death on the railroad or highway are, of course, nearly synonymous with traditional music. One of Bill Monroe's most famous songs, "Footprints in the Snow," seems even to celebrate death, since it foretells of the reunion in heaven of a man with his departed wife, whom he met "when the snow was on the ground." The symbolic association of snow and death is, I think, lost on no one; yet the tune is lilting, joyous—confidence in the promised land is so lucid and steadfast that it is the implied subject of nearly every "sacred" number, and seems to underlie every serious treatment of life. Bill Monroe's voice, with its high lonesome pang, seems sometimes to come from beyond the grave, not from some dreary underworld, but from a bright, bucolic mountain paradise.

One seems most significant of all in this respect: Ralph Stanley. If Bill Monroe's voice sounds like the wind, Ralph Stanley's voice sounds like the woods. He and his brother Carter came out of the Clinch Mountains in the late forties playing and singing a style strangely steeped in an ancient mountain modality which persisted even after they had acquired the habits of bluegrass. Not long after a performance at Bean Blossom several years ago, Carter Stanley died; Ralph continues to play the music of the Stanley Brothers and the Clinch Mountain Boys, and has found a series of guitarists who can virtually duplicate Carter's singing and playing so that to hear Ralph's new band is to feel that Carter has been reincarnated.

But the queer phenomenon of calling up the dead past goes still further in

Ralph's band. Two young Kentucky musicians, aged seventeen and eighteen, who last year created a sensation by playing and singing in an absolutely perfect imitation of the early Stanley Brothers, are now regular members of the Clinch Mountain Boys. To hear the whole group then is to hear not only Ralph and Carter Stanley but also a kind of geological record of their career, collapsed into some of the most hair-raising and beautiful harmonies in any music. Ralph's voice is not perfect; there is a slight quaver in it, and a laurel twig. But it can stir up matter at the primitive floor of the soul with as much authority as a Navajo chant.

Ralph is an earnest man, showing the kind of steady watchfulness and complete absence of frivolity that we associate either with deep piety or with fear. In concert he makes much of Carter's grave, its situation on a hillside, the headstone, the epitaph—his interest is almost medieval in its fondness. At Bean Blossom he did a monologue about their musical life together, backed up by a weird reincarnation of the old Stanley Brothers singing a gospel song. Ralph seems to sing in the expectation of death, with dread nobly penetrated by creative necessity. Or it is possible that his zeal arises out of a slender doubt:

> As the years roll by, I often wonder—
> Will we all be together someday?
> Each night as I wander through the graveyard
> Darkness finds me as I kneel to pray.

At its worst, the death motif in bluegrass music acquires an effete morbidity. A most interesting and appropriately named group, James Monroe and the Midnight Ramblers, capture in their music a funereal quality highlighted by a range of imagery reminiscent of Petrarch's Tuscany. Replete with fields of lilies, bloodstained veils, and dark impulses, it is a world of the dead.

James Monroe has a corpselike pallor and shadowy eyes; his music has the eerie loveliness of an Easter basket or a funeral wreath. Unlike most bluegrass bands, his is unaggressive and obsequious, the fiddler offering mournful, sustained condolences, the banjo-picker politely lingering in the background. His lyrics are ambiguously situated between dream and reality and thus symbolic: virginal figures drift through in white, wanderers recline on green lawns or pause at crossroads. In one moving ballad called "I Haven't Seen Mary in Years," the singer is led after a life of profligacy to a meadow where a family reunion is being held. There he sees his father, who does not recognize him because of his changed appearance, and his mother, whom the singer cannot recognize, explaining in the concluding line of the song, "I haven't seen mother in years."

Mother! All along we have assumed that Mary is a lost *wife*, but now wife and mother are confounded with all the straightforwardness of a textbook in intermediate psychology. James Monroe's ladies are almost always named Mary, recalling Anglo-Saxon hymns to the Virgin; when we expect him to sing "my life," he sings "my dream," and in many respects he himself seems a dream, a ghost. Incidentally, he is Bill Monroe's son.

The deepest allegiances in bluegrass, then, are to Mother and Dad, to home, in a way that few of us have had the privilege of feeling. Some of the most frequent subjects in serious pieces are the death of parents and of children, the regret over having left home, the reunion in heaven. All are, of course, one, and together make a kind of rude cosmology. The imagination of a poor and isolated people ranges only as far as their own experience, so that the natural life provides material for their deepest insights. It is thrifty and practical, intellectually speaking, to associate eternity with the better world of childhood; the stories in traditional music of lost souls who return home only to find parents gone, pathways overgrown, and the fields turned brown make good figures for life itself, "life's railway to heaven," with its drift away from innocence. Death, being wholly dark behind, becomes a kind of twist in the fabric of things by which everything returns to itself. There is the less mysterious explanation, of course, that when life is wretched—as it no doubt was (and is) for many poor mountain folk—the mind clings to fantasy worlds. A sense of individuality also implies a sense of one's own finiteness. But the themes of bluegrass music transcend simple otherworldliness, and at best they are genuinely metaphysical. The same sentiments churned out in Nashville and hawked on the air by sincere-sounding disc jockeys can turn the stomach.

I suspect, however, that many of Bill Monroe's people are suffering a subtle death they can't detect, a gradual impoverishment different from the kind which, over the generations, they have learned to live with. As technology penetrates their isolation, and American prosperity, however hollow it may be, their poverty, the way of life which created the music and which continued to cultivate an imagination receptive to it eventually dissolves and disappears. They are dying as a people as they become assimilated into the great mass of middle-class Americans who crowd the roads and parks in the summertime and who have discovered that one way to relieve some of the pang of existence is to diminish the intensity of life. And as the scope and depth of their lives shrink, so will the music seem more distant: too emotional, too rigid, too . . . well, hillbilly. The ecstasy of which the music is often capable will be gone too.

The fact is that Bill Monroe's people themselves feel that they are preserving something of the past. They call it the "old-time music." Bluegrass musicians are constantly giving awards to one another for preserving it. Possessed in this way of a historical sense, death, time's instrument, becomes a matter of intense interest to them. As the late Johan Huizinga pointed out in *The Waning of the Middle Ages,* a consciousness of the past, awakened in the medieval mind by scholarship, produced a pervasive melancholy over the transitory quality in men and the world. Artistically this meant an obsession with death in its early physical signs and in the corruption of the flesh which follows. Bluegrass folk, surrounded by a civilization which advertises its material advantages and falsely represents its values as the same ones they hold dear, are secretly persuaded by it, and so indulge the waning habits like an old clock or a failing grandparent. The sublime becomes quaint. The essential becomes recreation, and it's a proud man who can make up a bluegrass band out of mere children, with a six-year-old on the five-string.

Yet in all this there is a massive contradiction. Though death is often present in the music, Bean Blossom was astonishingly alive. Bluegrass music is as fresh as if it had been born yesterday, and as full of surprises. In fact, it must be said that the show was deftly stolen by a brand-new group out of Louisville who call themselves The Bluegrass Alliance. More children? Nope. Hippies. Hippies, that is, with the one exception of Lonnie Peerce, a twenty-year veteran of the fiddle. "I suppose you folks wonder why Lonnie here is playing with a bunch of freaks," the bassist, Ebo Walker, asked the audience. Hoots, howls, and hollers. "I'm their social worker," Lonnie answered, and started fiddling. They all started in, banjo-picker picking, mandolin-picker picking and jiving around the stage, hair hanging to his shoulders, making it seem as though we were watching the Jefferson Airplane and not some bluegrass group. Finally the lead singer, who from a distance might have been a prim old maid with hair severely tied behind her head, opened up with a voice that was pure gold bullion, something like three trumpets blowing two octaves above middle C in a tiled shower room. The crowd went wild. "We'll be selling some albums back at our bus," Ebo said. "Bring 'em back if you have any trouble with 'em—they're on the Oral Roberts label, and we have a little problem with the holes healing up." Laughter, some muffled protests. "I see we got both sides here tonight."

The folks loved them on Thursday night, on Friday night; and on Saturday, when they were not originally scheduled to play, they brought the house, or rather the treetops, down with "One Tin Soldier," a song very different from most in bluegrass:

> Go ahead and hate your neighbor
> Go ahead and cheat your friend
> Do it in the name of heaven
> Justify it in the end.
> There won't be trumpets blowin'
> On the Judgment Day:
> On the bloody morning after
> One tin soldier rides away.

The point is that while some folks may be growing away from the music, others are growing toward it, and it may be that even those for whom it is a native idiom are beginning to awaken to their own traditions, the way blacks and American Indians are to theirs, to what they created while the business of living went steadily on. However at odds the members of the Bluegrass Alliance may be with their audience upon any other issue but bluegrass, on that one they have come to a profound agreement. Bluegrass music is the traditional life, a kind of knowing many of us have difficulty in understanding, and the traditional life is the sacramental life. We who live among dead things should wonder at a people who, though they dwell upon death, have not forgotten how to live.

Originally published in the *Atlantic Monthly* 229 (March 1972): 52–54, 58–60. Reprinted by permission of the author.

S ay the words "classic band" to a hard-core bluegrass fan and the first image would likely be that of the Blue Grass Boys lineup featuring Bill Monroe, Lester Flatt, Earl Scruggs, and Chubby Wise. But the early 1970s' version of Ralph Stanley and the Clinch Mountain Boys would also have to reside near the top of anyone's list of great bluegrass outfits. Stanley himself was in rare form, not only returning to and rejuvenating some of the classic Stanley Brothers material but also venturing into modernisms such as Jesse Winchester's "Brand New Tennessee Waltz." Meanwhile, Clinch Mountain Boys newcomers—and future country stars—Keith Whitley and Ricky Skaggs became standouts in a band full of top-level musicians. Long-time *Bluegrass Unlimited* contributor Walt Saunders aptly put all this in perspective in this featured review.

36

"Ralph Stanley and the Clinch Mountain Boys: *Cry from the Cross*"

WALT V. SAUNDERS

"Cry from the Cross" / "You're Drifting On" / "Will He Wait a Little Longer" / "Bright Morning Star" / "Death Is Only a Dream" / "Come on Little Children" / "Take Your Shoes off Moses" / "Stairway to Heaven" / "I Am the Man Thomas" / "Step Out in the Sunshine" / "Sinner Man" / "Two Cents"

Rating*****

For a quarter century now, the name Stanley has been synonymous with the finest in old-time gospel music. Although his current audiences have extended far beyond the Appalachian Bible Belt that produced this remarkable man, hymns remain as popular as ever with Ralph Stanley fans. This album is abundant proof why. It's truly an exciting experience, yet it's more than that, for it inaugurates some very significant firsts for him, which should be noted.

This is Ralph's first release on Rebel Records, a move that came as a delightful surprise to me. It's doubtful that many will lament his departing the King-Starday fold, as the improvement in overall quality is immediately apparent. It seems obvious that he will be given a free hand in selection and arrangement of material. Dick Freeland, Rebel's intrepid commander-in-chief, thoughtfully provided complete recording data on the back cover, and the mastering by Roy Homer Studio is very good.

This LP represents Ralph's first recording session since making some important band personnel changes. Only he and Curly Ray Cline remain of the group that cut those King albums, yet Ralph continues to preserve the famous "Stanley Sound." No small portion of the credit must go to Roy Lee Centers, who replaced Larry Sparks as lead singer/guitarist. Sparks was a good musician whose voice often bore some resemblance to Carter Stanley, but Centers is absolutely incredible. He sounds so close to the original that it's nearly impossible to detect a difference. Fortunately, Roy does much more than merely sound like Carter; he plays solid rhythm, and leads out on the songs in a calm, assured manner, yet with real feeling. Jack Cooke, who traveled and recorded extensively with the Stanley Brothers, now plays bass and sings baritone. Jack is also a former Blue Grass Boy and all around excellent singer/ musician, whose style blends wonderfully with the ensemble.

For the first time on a Stanley album, possibly the first time on any bluegrass gospel record, a cappella singing (no instruments) appears; "Morning Star" and "Sinner Man" and the effect is unbelievably beautiful. A cappella singing is found among many fundamentalist religious sects in the southern mountains. There are the slow modal chants, and the lined-out singing styles, used by the "Old Regular" and "Hardshell" Baptists. Ralph is well acquainted with these forms of music, but here he and the boys use a slightly modernized quartet style, more closely associated with the "Freewill" Baptists of southwestern Virginia.

This set also marks the recording debut of two unusually talented teenagers from Kentucky, Ricky Skaggs and Keith Whitley. Ricky plays mandolin/fiddle and sings tenor while Keith plays lead guitar and sings bass. Anyone who has seen these kids performing with Ralph know what hair-raising sounds they are capable of, especially on the older Stanley songs.

The abundance of highlights will make it hard to pick out favorites. The title tune, Johnnie Masters' powerful "Cry from the Cross," is back by popular demand, and it sounds much like the original 1957 Mercury cut, complete with some superb twin fiddling by Cline and Skaggs. Two noteworthy numbers are "Step Out," an old Bailey Brothers favorite, and "Will He Wait," cut by Ralph and Carter for Mercury but never released. My favorite is the stirring "Death Is Only a Dream," originally recorded as a quartet at the Stanley's first Rich-R-Tone session in 1947. Here it's done as a trio, a little slower yet with haunting beauty. A tremendous LP, and a moving testimonial from one of the great pioneers of traditional music. This album is indispensable; don't miss it.

Originally published in *Bluegrass Unlimited* 5 (May 1971): 14. Reprinted by permission of the author and *Bluegrass Unlimited*.

In this short 1969 article, musician-journalist Alice Foster offered not only a captivating portrait of the young Sam Bush but also a canny prediction of the musical course he was to take in decades to come. Foster, now known as Alice Gerrard, drew on her personal acquaintance with Bush, whom she met during her collaboration with singer-songwriter Hazel Dickens.

The musical open-mindedness Bush was already displaying as a teenager has carried him through a stellar career as a star instrumentalist, singer, band leader, and record producer. As Foster intimated in this article, Bush went on from his teen prodigy days to create memorable and compelling music that draws on folk roots as well as all the stimulating musical tumult of the last half-century.

Just a few examples of Bush's musical energy and range have been the *Poor Richard's Almanac* album with Alan Munde mentioned here; leadership of the genre-smashing New Grass Revival from 1971 until 1989; road and session work with rock master Leon Russell, vocal star Emmylou Harris, and others; instrumental partnerships with Mark O'Connor, Edgar Meyer, and others in classical-leaning music; and an increasingly vital solo career.

37

"Sam Bush"

ALICE FOSTER

A year ago at the Nashville DJ Convention in the hallway of the Sam Davis hotel it was party time, crowded and smoky. A sixteen-year-old boy with a fiddle and another older boy with a guitar walked in. They strode determinedly into the middle of the haze, opened their instrument cases and commenced without a smile, without a word, to play. The fiddler then proceeded to astound the crowd with one fiddle tune after another for the next few hours.

This was Sam Bush. While Hazel and I were in Bowling Green, Kentucky, on tour last April, Sam came to the concert and fiddled a couple of tunes with us. There was a party afterward where we had a chance to talk for an hour or so. Since then I haven't seen Sam, so this short article is based on that talk; it may be a little out of date in terms of what he is currently doing. But it is always relevant that a younger person is carrying on a tradition established generations before, albeit with a mind that is open to many different sounds and ideas. And it is relevant that Sam is an excellent musician.

Sam's grandfather played banjo and fiddle and his father Charles Bush played fiddle and was brought up on country music, schoolhouse shows, the Grand Old Opry, the Possum Hunters, Arthur Smith and the Dixieliners, records with fiddlers Clayton McMichen, Curly Fox, Natchee the Indian, Roy Acuff, Art Wooten, and later Howdy Forrester. When Sam was a boy there were plenty of musical instruments around the house—a Martin mandolin, two fiddles, a dobro and a Blue Comet banjo that belonged to his grandfather. He started playing the mandolin, which he claims is still his first love, when he was eleven, and he began to play fiddle when was thirteen or fourteen by listening mostly to Tommy Jackson records. Around 1965 he heard a recording by the Dillards with Byron Berline playing fiddle, and in this way became interested in Texas fiddling. And this is the kind of fiddle that he wants to play.

Sam has been to contests in Texas and Idaho. . . . "They're (mid-westerners) not as creative. They stick more to the straight pattern; Texans just make a complete new tune out of it . . . all they do is just sit around and play, and there's not a bad one in the bunch."

Like many creative people, he tends to feel stifled by lack of outlets for his talent as well as a certain feeling of being bound up in patterns he finds it difficult to break out of. Also, like many people, he feels that perhaps California is the answer. . . . "I like it out there—people listen to you more and they're not like Nashville . . . California's not afraid to accept new stuff and probably I'd be new stuff . . . I'd bum around till I starved and then come home." He feels that no matter where he goes or what he does, it is bluegrass music that he wants to play. He also feels that there is room for initiative and experimentation in the music although he knows where it came from and what the musical worth and integrity of those roots are. His friend and back-up guitarist, Wayne Stewart, put it this way. . . . "It's the young people who more or less want to establish themselves as having done something to contribute to the music. . . . Like Sam, when he's playing bluegrass fiddle he puts in little rock licks. And he's got mandolin licks that he stole from the Jefferson Airplane. It's new and it's not flashy—it fits in.

"There are some mandolin tunes when I hear them, I want to hear them the way they were done when Bill recorded them in certain tunes I don't think should ever change. And that's the trouble with some people—how they just seem to fit their ideas in at the wrong place when it should have that old trembly plain sound that it had. One of the reasons bluegrass has remained as pure as it has is because Bill (Monroe) has been around to fight for it. It will never die, it's established its roots like jazz, and it'll be here from now on."

Sam and Wayne and Alan Munde on banjo set up a homemade studio with blankets and tape and recorded twenty-five (some original) tunes, out of which they will pick twelve or thirteen and make up an album. They are going to pay to have it pressed and plan to put it out on their own label. Friends in Seattle, Washington, will help them distribute it.

Whether he goes to California, whether he finds a place for himself there or not, and no matter in what direction he chooses to go, I feel fairly certain that he will produce good and interesting music. It takes talent, it takes imagination, it takes a certain ambition and nerve, and with Sam it may take experimenting around— maybe with fiddle or mandolin, maybe with pedal steel or lead rock or country guitar. It will be interesting to see what happens.

Originally published in *Bluegrass Unlimited* 4 (Nov. 1969): 11–12. Reprinted by permission of the author and *Bluegrass Unlimited*.

Regional groups such as Kentucky's Bluegrass Alliance and North Carolina's New Deal String Band served as key breeding grounds for what came to be called "newgrass" music—a blending of hard-core bluegrass instruments and songs with a counterculture-inspired approach that brought tunes from other styles and freewheeling instrumental techniques. The band, as described in John Kaparakis's 1969 article, included flatpicking hero Dan Crary as well as bassist Ebo Walker (whose given name is Harry Shelor), a future member of the New Grass Revival. By the 1971 festival season the band included Sam Bush, a frequent band guest in 1969, as well as banjo player Courtney Johnson and guitar guru Tony Rice. The group released a self-titled album on American Heritage in 1970, but by late 1971 the core of Bluegrass Alliance had become the first edition of New Grass Revival: Bush, Walker, Johnson, and guitarist Curtis Burch.

38

"The Bluegrass Alliance"

JOHN KAPARAKIS

Mr. Webster, in his oft-quoted book, defines alliance as being "a union of interests," "any union by relationship in qualities" and "a connection for mutual advantage between any groups or bodies." They named themselves well, this band about which I am writing. The Bluegrass Alliance is certainly a union of members having many interests (ranging from paperhanging to preaching!) and including one of mutual interest in and devotion to performing and promoting bluegrass and old-time country music. The related qualities each member possesses which make up the union are talent, personality, dedication and a good knowledge of the music they play— as well as a fine spirit of teamwork. The Alliance and the audience for whom they play are the groups needed to satisfy the third definition—the mutual advantage is immediately apparent to anyone who hears them play: Great pickin' and great listening!

I have known of The Bluegrass Alliance since December of last year when they first were listed in *Bluegrass in the Clubs*. The Alliance opened up the Red Dog Saloon in Louisville, Kentucky, in October of '68 and have played there ever since. They also play for parties, country music shows and are available for all types of bookings. At this writing, they are considering offers for a recording contract and hope to have a single released by October and an album recorded in the near future.

I had the pleasure of seeing this great band in person at Reidsville, and they alone were worth the trip down and the price of admission. The Alliance wasn't formally scheduled to be on the festival. They played several times at the informal concerts and workshops held Tuesday through Thursday, and received such a warm (and well-deserved) response from the audience that the officials there hastily arranged for them to appear on the festival program. In my opinion, the Bluegrass Alliance was the most exciting and well-received new bluegrass group at the Festival, and ranked among the top four bands in over-all audience response and appreciation.

During most of their appearances as a band at Reidsville, the Alliance had a guest musician sitting in with them who is certainly deserving of recognition. Though he is only seventeen years old, he is already one of the finest mandolin and fiddle players in the country—I'm talking about Sam Bush from Bowling Green, Kentucky. It is Sam and other young musicians like him who will be maintaining the traditions of bluegrass and keeping the music alive for future generations to enjoy. Along with the established artists of today, these budding talents are fully deserving of our support.

For the next year or possibly longer, the Bluegrass Alliance hopes to keep busy playing as much music as they can. They are all fine singers, musicians and instrumentalists so they are off to a good start there. Their occupations range from skilled craftsmen making $400 per week to graduate students who don't make quite that much, and full-time music will necessitate a few adjustments in their lives, routines and probably their eating habits as well.

Their material is divided between standards and classics in the field, new and original songs and traditional tunes, some of which are seldom-heard numbers very well suited to their style. The arrangements and presentation by the band are both outstanding. They enjoy playing music and the audience is aware of this and enjoys listening to them a little more because of it.

To sum up, the story of the Bluegrass Alliance will be repeated wherever they go from now on as it took place in Reidsville. That story can be told in a short phrase from ancient history, slightly modified (with apologies to Julius, Baby): "They came, they were seen, they conquered."

Members of the Bluegrass Alliance

DAN CRARY—Dan is originally from Kansas City, Missouri, and is twenty-nine years old. Dan has been a disc jockey on several country music radio stations, and at present he is a divinity student working toward teaching theology later on. "Big Dan" sings baritone and lead, is the emcee for The Alliance, does the arranging for the group and plays lead guitar.

And does he ever play lead guitar! Dan has been playing for about fifteen years, and this has included all types of music. With this background, a great sense of timing, plus his amazing skill at flat-picking and cross-picking, he is nothing short of phenomenal. Dan is not just another note-for-note carbon copy of Doc Watson, as some lead guitar pickers strive to become. Dan puts his own ideas, interpretations and arrangements into his playing with beautiful and tasteful results. There are few musicians whose name I would mention in the same breath with that of Clarence White, the greatest bluegrass lead guitar player of all time. "Big Dan" is one of those few—he demonstrates the same kind of affinity for the guitar that Clarence has.

At Reidsville there was no guitar workshop scheduled, but because so many people wanted to hear Dan play lead and demonstrate his style, the officials quickly put together a workshop consisting of Don Reno, Clyde Moody and Dan. Very ably assisted and accompanied by Wayne Stewart, guitar player for Poor Richard's Almanac, "Big Dan" once again testified to his skill and accuracy on the guitar, and blew many minds in the audience!

DANNY JONES—Danny is the newest member of The Bluegrass Alliance and does a good job singing lead, playing the mandolin and also guitar. Grayson County, Kentucky was originally Danny's home, and he played with a band there for several years. He is also twenty-nine years old, and "Big Dan" introduces him by saying that Danny used to be a linebacker in professional football! He would make a fine member of any football team or bluegrass band, and the Alliance is happy he has chosen music.

BUDDY SPURLOCK—Buddy is twenty-eight years old and plays banjo. He has been playing about nine years. Before joining the Alliance, he played with several other groups locally. Buddy is originally from Dwarf, Kentucky, which is about ten miles north of Hazard on Highway 80. When he's not picking the five, Buddy seems to stay as busy as a one-arm paperhanger. That was an awful way to lead into the fact that Buddy is a paperhanger by trade. (Since Buddy has two arms, does this mean he is twice as busy when he hangs paper as the cat with only one?)

LONNIE PEERCE—Lonnie has been playing the fiddle for twenty years, and he must know nearly every fiddle tune ever invented. Lonnie is forty-two years old and is originally from Grayson County, Kentucky. He sings tenor and has played mostly old-time style as well as modern and country and swing fiddle before bluegrass.

Lonnie loves to play music, and is indestructible. On several occasions in Reidsville I was staggering around the grounds in the wee hours of the morning, getting ready to turn in for a few hours sleep, and I'd hear one last group picking in the woods somewhere. On investigating, sure enough—there was Lonnie, sawing away on his fiddle and enjoying every minute of it.

EBO WALKER—Ebo is the bass player—he started out playing washtub bass for backyard groups and switched to upright bass in September '68. Ebo is originally from Louisville, Kentucky, and he sings the bass part on the Alliance's quartet and sings lead on some novelty numbers. "Big Dan" affectionately refers to Ebo as the "Flower Child" of the group. In addition to being long on hair, Ebo is also long on brains—he is doing graduate study in college and is the business manager for the Alliance.

Originally published in *Bluegrass Unlimited* 4 (Oct. 1969): 12–14. Reprinted by permission of the author and *Bluegrass Unlimited*.

For all its down-home associations, there's a certain wildness and even eccentricity to bluegrass that has long given it links with America's counterculture. Bill Monroe and other founding figures found acolytes in the form of rockers such as Jerry Garcia of the Grateful Dead and Chris Hillman of the Byrds. Mandolinist David Grisman and guitarist Peter Rowan, both with rock credentials on their resumes, joined Garcia and fiddler Vassar Clements in the early 1970s in the adventuresome bluegrass band Old and In the Way. In these liner notes from a 1997 live CD, Rowan, Clements and Grisman reminisce about some golden times in which people "from different backgrounds" came together for the love of bluegrass. The CD release was on Grisman's Acoustic Disc label.

39

"Old and In the Way: *Breakdown. Original Live Recordings from 1973—Vol. 2*"

PETER ROWAN, VASSAR CLEMENTS, AND DAVID GRISMAN

In October, 1972 I arrived in the California promised land where I met up with David in the little seacoast town of Stinson Beach. Jerry lived up the hill on the golden flanks of Mount Tamalpais. Garcia met us at his gate under a sign that read "Sans Souci" ("No Problem"). He had his banjo strapped on and was pickin' Earl Scruggs' "Pike County Breakdown." We had our instruments out of their cases in no time and Old and In the Way was born!

When we needed a fiddle player for our first tour, I suggested Vassar Clements, who as a teenaged prodigy had helped Bill Monroe cut "New Mule Skinner Blues" (Feb. 3, 1950).[1] With Vassar on fiddle and Garcia Band stalwart John Kahn on upright bass, we were a full band.

Our rehearsals were hilarious and full of infectious spontaneity. Jerry was eager to play music at any hour. Each of us would go to different parts of the house playing a tune. We'd wander around and meet back in the living room in time for the next chorus. If we were still "in time" we were doing alright! We tried songs from Bill Monroe, Flatt and Scruggs, Red Allen, Frank Wakefield, The Stanley Brothers and The Country Gentlemen. I wrote "Panama Red," "Midnight Moonlight" and "Land of the Navajo" while David came up with "Old and In the Way" after Jerry named the band in a moment of inspired foolery. We even adapted "Wild Horses" and "The Great Pretender." I don't think we ever had a sense of our own "style"; we just tried to play it all as bluegrass. We felt instinctively that this robust style could

---

1. Born on April 25, 1928, Clements was twenty-one when he recorded "New Mule Skinner Blues" with Monroe on February 3, 1950.

handle any type of tune. If we could pick it or sing it, then it was ours. We became a "real" bluegrass band, singing duets, trios and quartets and picking hot instrumentals. Spanish guitar, African banjo, Italian mandolin and fiddle mixed with Celtic melodies, gospel harmonies and blues. As Bill Monroe once said, "There's a world of music in there, man."

Garcia gave us all nicknames and we would introduce each other onstage. I was "Red," John Kahn and his bass fiddle were both "Mule," and Vassar was "Clem," or "Clamp" if he was smoking his pipe. David introduced Jerry as "Spud Boy," and "Spud" introduced David as "the Dawg!" So here we are again folks, back in your living room just in time for the chorus! Join us as we venture forth one more time to tilt at the windmills of the "original bluegrass quest." Mule, Clem, Red, Spud Boy and the Dawg, we are once and forever Old and In the Way.

—Peter Rowan

Pete Rowan called me to start with, and he talked to my wife Millie 'cause I was gone. That's when I first heard of the band. We met the day before the first show in Boston, rehearsed that night and started playing the very next day. I hadn't met any of the guys—I didn't know what to expect. What's so funny was how we all became friends and everything before I even knew who was who! Actually, everything was funny. We got to San Francisco and we'd been out on the road I don't know how long. I saw a billboard sign and said "Garcia, that looks like you up there." It was a billboard of The Grateful Dead! They all cracked up over that. I was from a different world.

I do want to say something about the music; it was unique in the way that it used the instrumentation of bluegrass yet it's a different type of bluegrass. If you don't believe it, put on a record of The Stanley Brothers, Flatt and Scruggs or even The New Grass Revival—put on anything you want and then put this on. Now how do you explain the difference? I don't know what you'd call it really, but I know one thing—to me it was one of the most enjoyable playing experiences I've ever had. It was the type of thing where there's no pressure; you get up there and you have fun. It's good tunes, it's good music and it's different. I thought it was great, I really did. I knew it sounded different then and I still to this day don't know how to explain it. I used to say, "Well, people came from different backgrounds," but then I found out that Garcia loved bluegrass way back then too.

Not that many people would have heard Old and In the Way if it hadn't been for Jerry. I think that was a wonderful thing. Jerry, David, Pete, John—they all were an inspiration to me. And I'll tell you what—I've played in a lot of bluegrass bands and a lot of country bands and different things, and I've never had a better time. I don't know what kind of words to put it in—I just knew I loved it.

—Vassar Clements

Marin County seemed like a great place to be in 1970, so I traded my tiny Greenwich Village apartment for a room in Stinson Beach. Within a year, Jerry bought a house there and Pete Rowan showed up as well. We found ourselves gravitating to Garcia's living room, where we'd sit around playing bluegrass with Jerry picking his old Weymann five-string banjo. You see, once bluegrass music is in your blood, it never leaves. In a way, we were the perfect urban bluegrass combination of our generation: Jerry, the folk-rocker from California; Peter, the transplanted New England Blue Grass Boy/singer-songwriter; and me, the Jewish oddball mandolin-picker from New Jersey! Here we were, all three of us playing the music we'd recently left behind, just for fun! We casually became the now-legendary "hippiegrass" band Old and In the Way, and played local gigs with various fiddlers (Richard Greene, John Hartford and, finally, the great Vassar Clements) and Jerry's bassist John Kahn for most of 1973.

The live tapes made by Bear, our mad scientist/sound man, at San Francisco's Boarding House, stand up as high-fidelity documentation of our work in progress, and also the fun we were having. Recorded on two nights in October, these recordings represent the band at its peak. Our unique repertoire of originals (Pete's "Blue Mule," Jerry's "Old and In the Way Breakdown" and Vassar's "Kissimee Kid," among others) and bluegrass standards, both common ("Mule Skinner Blues," "Pig in a Pen") and less common ("Home Is Where the Heart Is," "You'll Find Her Name Written There") had expanded and evolved to a level that's ensured longevity for this informal group that played for less than one year. Of course, the musical talent, individually and collectively, of this singular combination was certainly formidable. For me, however, the key to our chemistry was the inspiration of playing with one of the great masters of the bluegrass idiom, Vassar Clements—like being a Yankee with Babe Ruth on the team. It was a true payoff for the time we'd all spent trying to play this music "right."

Looking back on it now, nearly a quarter of a century later, it's amazing what we managed to accomplish in that short space of time, both for ourselves and a whole unborn generation of future bluegrass adherents. Our legacy continues through these live recordings, and I'm pleased to present to you this third collection from two October nights so long ago.

—David Grisman

Liner notes for Acoustic Archives Series ACD-28 (1997). Reprinted by permission of Acoustic Disc Records.

Nashville *Tennessean* reporter Kathy Sawyer traveled to Marin County to offer readers loving detail about a bluegrass festival with a distinct hippie twist. Her news "hook" was the presence of a number of hometown musical heroes performing amid the likes of Jerry Garcia and the Nitty Gritty Dirt Band.

40

"Showing 'Em How It's Done"

KATHY SAWYER

San Rafael, Calif.: Shivering a bit in the blasts of acid rock, a group of music-lovers in the San Francisco Bay area reached out across the Mississippi last weekend and pulled the driving strains of an older and warmer music over them like a patchwork quilt.

The first Golden State Country and Bluegrass Festival here at the Marin County Fairgrounds was a kind of love feast for the quiet, straight, "real" pickers who came from the other side of the land—many from Nashville—to show them how it's done right.

The three-day event added the Bay area officially to the burgeoning roll of bluegrass strongholds. Though not nearly as large as others of the numerous bluegrass-oriented festivals being held now (the *Muleskinner News* listed 290 in 1973), this one was significant because, as one Nashville picker put it, "They usually like to make up their own things out here, but this time they're ringing it in from back home."

With tickets priced at $22 (or $8.50 a day), an estimated 1,200, mostly young and long-haired (and some older, some executives, some farmers, a few celebrities and intellectuals), gathered to hear the sounds that many Nashvillians take for granted in their own backyard—the sounds of the Opry's Jim and Jesse McReynolds and the Virginia Boys, of Mac Wiseman, Doc Watson and his son Merle, the Greenbriar Boys with Frank Wakefield, Tut Taylor and Ramblin' Jack Elliott, Norman Blake and Doug Dillard, Ralph Stanley and his Clinch Mountain Clan.[1]

The promoters dedicated the festival to Nashville fiddle virtuoso Vassar Clements—"not only for his astounding musical ability—and unbelievable versatility"—but for the time and energy he has devoted to helping aspiring musicians and the bluegrass movement.

"Get it ON, Vassar!" the young fans would yell and he obliged, sawing vigorously, lovingly on his fiddle for long hours and with various groups—both old-timers and progressive younger ones.

He first attracted his following in the Bay area last summer, when he performed as a soloist with Old and In the Way, a band which included Jerry Garcia of the rock group Grateful Dead, on banjo—the kind of cultural sharing that gives bluegrass its unique richness of creative tension these days.

A native of Florida, Clements came to Nashville in 1949 with 35 cents in his pockets. He eventually got a job with Bill Monroe's band and has done stints with Jim and Jesse, Faron Young, John Hartford and the Earl Scruggs Revue. Besides the fiddle, he has mastered the guitar, bass, mandolin, tenor banjo, cello and viola.

---

1. Sawyer meant the Clinch Mountain Boys. The Clinch Mountain Clan played with Wilma Lee and Stoney Cooper and with Wilma Lee after Stoney's death.

"Turn up the fiddle, Vassar!" they yelled.

Asked how he felt about the unexpected tribute, which was timed to coincide with his forty-sixth birthday, he grinned, his high cheekbones squeezing his eyes flat under his eyebrows. "It's embarrassing. But I love it."

Under hats of straw or of makeshifted Coors beer cartons, with dogs and kites and jugs of cider or red wine (or in at least one group, Jack Daniels Black drunk straight from the bottle), boxes of fresh strawberries, "authentic Southern" corn on the cob and ham and pecan pie from the concession stand, and all wreathed in the pungent smoke of another kind of grass, the crowd was an attentive sea on the carpet of golden straw laid for acres around the stage.

Rebel yells and whoops punctuated their enthusiasm for this or that number, and generally for the whole trip "home" to times and places and roots, to hazy blue mountains and ramshackle cabins, train wrecks, and little white churches that most of them had never known.

They heard a lineup which ranged from the downhome barn dance rhythms of local groups like the Homestead Act to the pop folk sounds of John Hartford and Maria Muldaur to the unfettered progressive sounds of the Great American String Band with black bluesman Taj Mahal.

The Nitty Gritty Dirt Band finished the festival by joining with Watson, Blake, Clements and Jimmy Martin for a partial reprise of their classic *Will the Circle Be Unbroken* album.

(Nashville's Merle Travis, one of the country's most influential pickers, was forced to cancel his appearance because of illness.)

The festival was designed as an educational as well as entertainment experience for Bay-area bluegrass enthusiasts. The musicians spent mornings when they weren't performing conducting workshops for up-and-coming pickers eager to learn from the masters.

The Bay area has a live bluegrass radio show Saturday afternoons, and bluegrass clubs are on the rise, featuring new groups with names like Skunk Cabbage and the Phantoms of the Opry.

"This idiom is influencing the whole music world in San Francisco and we wanted to give people a chance to hear the best, the ones from Nashville and that area," said Paul Lammers, who with his wife Judy, a Georgia native, organized the festival.

Despite the pop appeal of some of the younger performers, the emphasis and heart of the festival was with "pure" bluegrass, as played by the old-timers, featuring banjo, fiddle, mandolin, guitar and bass—the traditional instrumentation.

"I want to tell Doc Watson I hear drums on one of his albums!" grumbled one indignant young purist in the crowd, an American Airlines pilot from North Dakota. Purists abhor the use of piano or drums and demand their bluegrass be free of the electrical umbilical, of the electrified string which some see as a heresy in Nashville's country product. These people fear that success will spoil bluegrass.

Such points concern fans and critics more than they do the musicians.

"What if they built the Model-A and then stopped building cars?" was the re-action of Nashville's jovial, foxy Tut Taylor, one of the only flat-picking dobro players around.

Backstage between performances he ate barbecued chicken and interrupted his conversation occasionally to do a little business with fans. The Milledgeville, Ga., native is proprietor of the Taylor Instrument Co. on Nashville's 2nd Ave., which, he will tell you proudly, is the outfit that made the dulcimer that was presented to Mrs. Richard Nixon at the opening of the new Opry House. His public appearances now are a sideline, "just for fun."

"Uh, what'll you take for that mandolin?" inquired a young bearded man in a Yamaha T-shirt. "I got a 1924 A-4 to trade."

"Six hunned dollars with the hardshell cover, son."

The young man went off to consider. An hour later the deal was concluded.

Taylor agreed with other old-time pickers that West Coast bluegrass talent is improving, as is the sophistication of the audiences.

"But a lot of what we were playing went—zit—right over their heads," he said, with a planing motion of his hand. "I mean the technique. They still kinda look for the heavy beat. 'Course, there are more young people in this crowd than you get at the festivals back East. But I don't see any problem in what's going on. I'd never conform to what anybody told me I should be playing. I play the way I play."

"The people are the governors," said Mac Wiseman, the master flattop guitar-ist and singer. "If you get too far out, they bring you right back into line by not buying."

Wiseman worked with Lester Flatt and Earl Scruggs during the late '40s and early '50s and went on his own with hit recordings such as "Love Letters in the Sand," "The Ballad of Davy Crockett," and numerous others.[2]

"Going back to what Tut said about the Model-A," he said. "The reason that bluegrass hasn't had more gross prior to this is that the bluegrass singers didn't progress. The new groups didn't bring new life and blood to the music. They just imitated the old-timers. But there are some good new groups around—the Blue-grass Alliance and the Country Gazette."

Someone commented that a lot of people still saw bluegrass as mixed in with all of country music. "Ha, country music is just a part of bluegrass," grinned Tay-lor. "Nashville still needs to discover bluegrass."

Wiseman, like the other musicians, expressed delight with his new and unex-pected generation of fans. "Frankly it's like buying yourself another ten years in the business. That may sound mercenary but that's my observation."

He said he had been impressed with the requests he'd been getting from the young festival crowd. "They were asking for some old ones—'Tragic Romance,'

---

2. Wiseman worked with Flatt and Scruggs in 1948 and with Monroe in 1949.

'Davy Crockett.' 'Davy Crockett' was a hit in '56 and here was a young guy requesting it—guy with a beard!"[3] He smiled and shook his head. "But you get a nice cross
section—some new converts, some purists, so you can play the things you like."

Wiseman acknowledged that he had performed or recorded some numbers that
would offend purists with their steel and electric backgrounding. "But the only difference was always the background. I sing the same way, just as simple."

"Look—there goes a 1925 Lloyd Loar mandolin," said Taylor. "That's $3,500."
He was pointing toward Frank Wakefield of the Greenbriar Boys, whose sound has
been called "primitive backwoods Bach." Clad in a white suit and with his hair a
dazzling shock of blonde, Wakefield looked like a lit cigarette.

Someone onstage was telling the crowd that his Bay-area group was so down-
home that their favorite cigarette was a pound of grits rolled up in a *Watchtower*
magazine.

Jerry Garcia, bluegrass' leading showpiece from the counterculture, sat on the
Chevy hood and explained that he does not foresee for bluegrass the kind of commercial success that might ruin it.

"This is no flash in the pan. Interest in bluegrass has paralleled that in the other forms of music. But it has never had the economic support, the promotion, the
industry assistance the others have had. If it had, then it probably would have hurt
the music.

"But I don't think bluegrass will ever 'thrill millions.' I think there will always
be people who like to listen to it a *lot.*"

As for electric strings, which cropped up here and there during the festival, he
said, "Electrified country music is a fabrication—it's really *suburban* music. Country music traditionally uses acoustic (non-electric) instruments. But these are just
labels. The point is they are *different* kinds of music. If you're playing electrified
instruments, for the most part, you could be playing any kind of music. The Nashville players are great in any idiom."

Doc Watson played the sun into the Pacific with the mellow campfire strains
of "Miss the Mississippi and You," his full-hearted voice resounding off the hills and
the unlikely scalloped backdrop of the sand-and-sea-colored Civic Center designed
by Frank Lloyd Wright. To Watson's sightless eyes, he might have been playing across
the hills of his native North Carolina.

As the stars rolled over the plinking echoes of the final song at the fairgrounds,
many of the spectators seemed numb.

But over in Room 135 at the nearby Holiday Inn, their public performances done
with, the musicians gathered again to jam happily into the small hours of the morning—just for themselves, their women clogging in the shag rugs.

Originally published in *The Tennessean* (Nashville), May 5, 1974, 35C. Copyright © by *The Tennessean*. Reprinted by permission.

3. "The Ballad of Davy Crockett" hit number 10 on the *Billboard* charts in May 1955.

In the later 1960s and throughout the 1970s, experimentation came to the fore-front in the work of bluegrass pickers. Mandolinists such as Frank Wakefield and John Duffey had for years been pushing the proverbial envelope on the instrument closely associated with Bill Monroe. Players still had to be able to crank out "Raw Hide" and the other familiar Monroe pieces—it was hard to deny that there was much to admire and learn from his extensive canon of mandolin music. Many, however, were also searching for wild new notes, exotic techniques, and unconventional rhythms on mandolin. This 1972 survey by mandolin authority Jack Tottle gives Monroe full credit for his leading role and considers some of the players who were then taking new directions. Some of the highest-profile bluegrass mandolinists—notably Ronnie McCoury, Ricky Skaggs, and Mike Compton—of the early twenty-first century reside principally in the Monroe fold. Players such as Chris Thile draw on jam-band, jazz, and pop influences in creating contemporary styles for the instrument.

41

"Bluegrass Mandolin ⅓rd Century Later"

JACK TOTTLE

In the early years of bluegrass the mandolin was frequently overshadowed by both fiddle and banjo. Bill Monroe is by no means the only one who took up the mandolin because it was the only instrument not already spoken for by his musician friends. Fiddle tunes and banjo tunes have always been in far greater supply than numbers written for the mandolin. And, a few years back, when the pop music industry began to take notice of bluegrass instrumental sounds, the mandolin seemed to get little or no attention.

Lately, in the never-ending rush to replace one fad with yet another fad, it looks like pop may be coming around to the mandolin. Rod Stewart has used it on several of his hits, including "Mandolin Wind," "Reason to Believe," and "Maggie May." So have the Rolling Stones, Elton John, Bob Dylan, the Nitty Gritty Dirt Band, The Doors, Oliver, Ry Cooder, Jesse Winchester, the Band and the Byrds. While this may or may not have further implications for bluegrass, it does serve to remind us that the mandolin has undergone considerable development over the years and continues to show additional promise for the future.

Fifteen years ago, if you were talking to a bluegrass enthusiast about mandolin playing you'd have found—as you'd find today—that Bill Monroe was occupying a place of healthy respect in the conversation. True, nearly all the bands which had achieved widespread popularity by the mid-1950s utilized the mandolin to some extent, and much of the playing was outstanding. Pee Wee Lambert's mandolin breaks on the Stanley Brothers' early records weren't fancy, but they were smooth and they were perfect for the songs they went with. Red Rector had done some fast and extremely agile picking with Reno and Smiley on tunes like "Choking the Strings" and "Double Banjo Blues" and could also be heard playing very pretty breaks on Charlie Monroe's "Down at the End of Memory Lane," "Clock of Time," etc. Bobby Osborne's mandolin on the Osborne Brothers' instrumentals like "Hand Me Down My Walking Cane," "Silver Rainbow" and "Wildwood Flower" was first rate and was very much his own. Benny Williams had a bit on Mac Wiseman's "Crazy Blues" that made you wish you could hear him cut loose on a few more tunes. Jesse McReynolds not only played lovely conventional mandolin but stood out as important innovator with his "roll" style of playing that was so perfectly suited to Jim and Jesse's "My Little Honeysuckle Rose," "Memory of You," "I Like the Old Time Way" and many more. Jethro Burns of Homer and Jethro didn't record bluegrass music, but after hearing him play you could tell he knew things about his instrument that most mandolin players don't approach in a lifetime. (The album *Down Yonder* by the Country Fiddlers and Wade Ray, recorded much later on RCA Camden features Jethro's amazing picking.)

Nevertheless, in the midst of all this strong stuff it was Bill Monroe who stood out most. Bill's rhythm playing provided a solid and distinctive base on which his music rested. Many people agreed with Carlton Haney that "Bill plays a different time than any other mandolin player" and felt that this was the most important single aspect of his band's driving sound.

Monroe's lead mandolin playing was, however, every bit as strong and distinctive, and perhaps a lot more obvious to the average listener. He could play smoothly and powerfully on slow songs like "In the Pines" or "Get Down on Your Knees and Pray." He combined a strong syncopation with "blues notes" (minor thirds and sevenths) in medium tempo numbers like "New Mule Skinner Blues" and "The First Whippoorwill." And when he got wound up into playing fast and furious as in "White House Blues," "Prisoner's Song," "Roanoke," etc., it didn't seem likely that anyone else would come along and do them better.

In writing and recording instrumental tunes which primarily feature the mandolin, Bill was also way ahead of the competition. He played bouncy, bluesy pieces like "Blue Grass Stomp" and "Blue Grass Special." He returned the mandolin for a compelling and different sound on "Get Up John" and "Blue Grass Ramble." And with "Raw Hide," "Blue Grass Breakdown" and "Pike County Breakdown" he gave aspiring young mandolin players something to sink their teeth into for years to come.

Skillful and inventive as many of the other mandolin pickers were, by the time Monroe had released all the above-mentioned mandolin tunes plus a few more, no one else had recorded a memorable mandolin number. And, while there were quite a few young guys working to learn Monroe's playing note-for-note off the records, it was rare to hear anyone emulating the styles of the good mandolin players who recorded with other bands.

All in all, if you were just listening to records at the time, you might have been figuring that with the exception of Monroe's band, the mandolin was going to remain a kind of fill-in instrument to be used chiefly for variety from the usual banjo and fiddle breaks. However, if you happened to be living in the Washington, D.C./Baltimore area, you might have been aware that below the surface, the caldron was bubbling considerably. From the middle to late fifties a number of new talents were boiling up into public view.

There was Earl Taylor with his forceful, Monroe-influenced style. There was Bennie Cain playing a gentler, slightly old-time-sounding mandolin. Jerry Stuart recorded just one tune ("Rocky Run" on the Folkways *Mountain Music Bluegrass Style*) but showed a promising sensitivity and original turn of mind. Smiley Hobbs, after a stint with Reno and Smiley, did some excellent mandolin work with Bill Harrell. Donna Stoneman was a major attraction not only because she was considerably better looking than most of the other mandolin players around, but also for her showy picking.

One of the most interesting musicians was Buzz Buzby. While there may have been players who knew more mandolin, Buzz was a heavy contender for the fastest right hand in the business. When he was feeling right he would squeeze out more notes per lick than you'd expect in three or four times that space. Buzz's band, called the Bayou Boys, featured at various times such widely known musicians as Scott Stoneman, Bill Emerson, Charlie Waller, Don Stover and Pete (Roberts) Kuykendall. Buzz and the Bayou Boys released a series of singles, many of them highly inspired, on Starday and other labels.

Around the same time an energetic young mandolin player named John Duffey helped start a new band which would open up new musical territory to bluegrass. Leaving aside his contributions in singing, arranging, and songwriting, John's powerful, showy and imaginative mandolin playing alone would have made him a prime asset to the Country Gentlemen.

His approach to the mandolin sometimes appeared to be aimed at seeing how many different and unexpected sounds could be coaxed, squeezed or beaten out of his instrument. In addition to his own impressive high-energy variations on Monroe-style mandolin playing, John did such unheard of things as playing breaks on three or four strings simultaneously instead of the usual one or two. He twisted the strings, he played jazz chords, played breaks alternating between first and fourth strings and sometimes he'd use fingerpicks instead of a flat pick. John used the mandolin as a principle instrument on such unusual (for bluegrass) instrumental numbers as "Sunrise," "Dixie Lookaway" ("Dixie"), "Backwoods Blues" ("Bye Bye Blues"), "Exodus," "Windy and Warm" and many others.

Some traditional-minded fans used to complain that what John played wasn't really bluegrass. "You may like it or you may not, but it's *mine*," he sometimes said of his unorthodox approach to the mandolin. (Occasionally he'd add: "What's *your* contribution?") As time passed the complaints dwindled and appreciation of John's contributions grew to the point that his influence now shows clearly on records by younger bands in such diverse locations as Boston, North Carolina, Wisconsin, California and Japan to name just a few.

1961 saw yet another important mandolin player making his first appearance in Washington.

(Phone rings.)

Frank Wakefield: "Hello, this is you speaking."

Puzzled voice on the other end (after a pause): "Who is this?"

Frank: "This is you speaking."

Voice: "I must have the wrong number." (Hangs up.)

(A minute passes. Phone rings again.)

Frank (answering it): "The number you have reached is the one you have just dialed."

The above could have occurred in Washington in 1961 instead of in January 1972, as it did at the apartment of a friend in Boston, Massachusetts. Today, at thirty-seven, Frank seems as whimsical and loose as he did when he first arrived with Red Allen in Washington and promptly earned deep respect for his ability on the mandolin.

During the years with Red and later with the Greenbriar Boys, Frank won himself a loyal following of enthusiasts who swore by his own individual version of Monroe-style bluegrass picking. His Folkways album with Red Allen and his work on Vanguard with the Greenbriar Boys are perhaps his most widely heard recordings to date, although he has recorded on several other labels as well, including Starday, Rebel and SilverBelle. Lately he has recorded with pop singer Oliver and has completed his own album for Rounder Records.

In recent years Frank began playing some tunes unlike anything he—or anyone else—had previously recorded. The tunes had rather strange names such as: "Jesus Loves His Mandolin Player No. 16," etc. He is currently working on "Jesus Loves His Mandolin Player No. 30." Frank describes why he named his tunes as he did: "When I was sixteen, I had my hands prayed over in church, and that was the reason I was able to get as good as I could on the mandolin. One day I was to play at the Performing Arts Center in Saratoga (New York) and suddenly when I was supposed to go on, I couldn't play at all. I finally realized that I had been taking all the credit for my playing without giving any to the Lord, where it belonged. After I realized it, I told the people in the audience the story, and I was able to play again."

The following is a brief discussion of Frank's playing prepared for the notes for his upcoming Rounder album:

Records by Bill Monroe, Jim and Jesse McReynolds, and the Blue Sky Boys are Frank's earliest recollection of the kind of playing which aroused his interest in the mandolin. Like many another aspiring young picker, he worked especially hard at copying Monroe's style, which stood out from others in its aggressive rhythmical drive as a backup instrument and in the "blues notes" and distinctive syncopations which figured prominently in lead playing. Unlike most of his contemporaries, Frank succeeded to an astounding degree. So complete became his grasp of Monroe's approach to the instrument that many people felt that when Bill's time came to retire, Frank would be the only musician capable of continuing the Monroe style in its true form.

Monroe's view was a little different, however. Frank recalls a jam session with Bill a few years ago during which Bill seemed to be intent on seeing how hard he could push Frank's abilities. Apparently satisfied, Monroe finally conceded. "Well, you're about as good as I am at my style. Now let's see you get a style of your own."

In actual fact, Frank has never limited himself to simple imitation. His "New Camptown Races," first recorded in 1952 (in the unlikely key—for the mandolin—of B flat), showed plenty of original thought. So did his later recordings.

Particularly striking was the way Frank began utilizing the "blues notes," using them as part of a minor scale against major chords played by the accompanying instruments. Nevertheless, for many years his playing did consist essentially of Monroe's style augmented by his own ideas.

Rounder Record's new album presents for the first time on record Frank's answer to Monroe's challenge. On his bluegrass numbers, it is true, Frank generally takes a somewhat Monroe-influenced approach. (Compare the beginning of Frank's "Sleepy Eyed John" with the original "Get Up John" by Monroe or Frank's break on "Nobody's Darling but Mine" with Monroe's on "The Prisoner's Song.") His instrumentals in the "Jesus Loves His Mandolin Player" series, however, introduce some wholly different concepts via what Frank calls his "classical style."

Frank asserts that he did not consciously imitate classical compositions. "If I ever picked up classical music on the radio I'd switch right away to nearest country station." Nevertheless, his new style does depart from previous bluegrass mandolin playing in directions which strongly suggest classical forms.

In bluegrass mandolin, when two strings are hit simultaneously the notes sounded normally consist of the melody plus a simple harmony, usually a third or a fifth above the melody. Frank, however, plays passages in which the two parts move independently—that is, one part might move upward as the other moves downward so that the effect is that of melody and countermelody. In some cases three parts instead of two are played.

Frank has also developed some interesting righthand techniques which produce a very full sound. While playing one part on the low strings with a tremolo he reaches over to the high strings between tremolo strokes and plays individual single notes without breaking the rhythm. At other times he plays a tremolo on the high strings and, again between strokes, hits individual bass strings. On "Jesus Loves His Mandolin Player No. 2" he achieves additional complexity by the use of a fingerpick on the third finger of the right hand. In this way Frank is able to play separate parts which are not on adjacent strings at precisely the same time.

These technical innovations combined with Frank's mastery of bluegrass mandolin playing and with his keen musical sense produce a unique style so full that it requires no accompaniment by additional instruments. In creating this new approach to his instrument, Frank has opened the door for a broader range of musical development of the mandolin. And perhaps somewhere there is a young picker who will successfully set out to master Frank's style, and end up having Frank tell him, as Monroe told Frank: "Now let's see you get a style of your own."

During the period when the Washington/Baltimore players were first making their presence felt, the older, established bands did not seem to share any common view about the mandolin's common role. Some, like Flatt and Scruggs and like Reno and Smiley, seemed less and less interested in it. The Stanley Brothers featured Bill Napier's skillful playing for a while and then seemed to lean toward the lead guitar in its stead. Bobby Osborne's mandolin seemed to be given a major role infrequently, but every so often (as on his instrumental "Surefire") it was right out in front again.

On the other hand, there was Jesse McReynolds. From his superb work discussed earlier, Jesse went on to explore still more deeply the possibilities inherent both in his fast, clean, conventional picking and in his own original "roll" style. Dazzling and complicated instrumentals like "Farewell Blues," "Border Ride," "Dill Pickle Rag," "El Comanchero," "Sugar Foot Rag," and "Tennessee Blues" were the result. (Not all are available on record, unfortunately.) So are a host of exciting breaks on songs like "Standing on the Mountain," "Salty Dog Blues," and "(I'm Going Back to) Alabam."

The 1960s saw a new crop of young pickers emerge, some of whom stayed with it and some of whom left for other instruments or different professions. Some of the best were Roland White (now with Lester Flatt), Ronnie Reno, Frank Wakefield protege David Grisman, Sam Bush (of the New Grass Revival), Jimmy Gaudreau (now with the II Generation), and Frank Greathouse (of the New Deal String Band). None have, perhaps, yet had the profound impact on bluegrass of certain of their elders. Among them, however, are some exceptionally talented musicians who have shown the ability to learn from what has gone before, as well as to add original and exciting concepts of their own.

The above is clearly far from a complete discussion of bluegrass mandolin playing. Much more space would be needed to trace all the subtleties of Bill Monroe's musical development, let alone deal fully with the styles of other highly regarded players like Paul Williams, Everett Lilly, Hershel Sizemore, Joe Val, Doyle Lawson and others. However, a survey of the various tunes and songs referred to throughout the article does point up the fact that bluegrass mandolin is far from a static skill. It is a vital and variable component of a music which survives and flourishes through a ceaseless blending of the old with the new.

Originally published in *Bluegrass Unlimited* 6 (March 1972): 5–9. Reprinted by permission of the author and *Bluegrass Unlimited*.

As Jack Tottle did in the preceding article on evolving mandolin styles, banjoist Steve Arkin surveyed tradition and innovation in this 1972 *Pickin'* piece. As Bill Monroe represented the totemic reference point for mandolin, so his former bandmate Earl Scruggs was the starting point for anyone studying bluegrass banjo. Arkin touches on some of the enduring controversies that continue to enliven bluegrass discussions—electronic and otherwise. Did Scruggs just enlarge on what South Carolina's Snuffy Jenkins was already doing with three-finger banjo-picking? Shouldn't Don Reno get more credit for his contributions to the three-finger style? And who came up with the "melodic" style—Bill Keith or Bobby Thompson? The answers are complex and to some degree subjective, but Arkin sheds considerable light on them, particularly on the Keith/Thompson issue.

In another parallel to the way mandolin styles have evolved, Scruggs's style has not only endured but also prevailed. These days, it is the sometimes overly ornate, "melodic" style that tends to sound dated, while Scruggs and admirers such as Jim Mills and Rob McCoury sound as forceful and hypnotic as Earl himself did in 1945. Finally, in the music of banjo innovator Bela Fleck, adept at both Scruggs and melodic techniques, stylistic roots lose importance, submerged as they should be in the flow of music.

42

"Banjo Playing: Reno, Thompson, Scruggs, Keith Style and Beyond"

STEVE ARKIN

Steve Arkin is a former Blue Grass Boy (1964) and is now a marketing executive for Oxford University Press.

From the mid-forties to the mid-sixties, the history of the bluegrass banjo was the history of "Scruggs style" and the history of its early practitioners: Earl Scruggs, Don Stover, Sonny Osborne, Ralph Stanley, Allen Shelton, and others. During this period, the role played by the banjo in the context of a band was an unusual one. It was a lead instrument, to be sure, but unlike the mandolin and the fiddle, it was not actually a melody instrument. Rather, when played in Scruggs style, the banjo was capable of only rough (or smooth) approximations of the melody on most tunes, and camouflaged this inadequacy with a marvelous barrage of arpeggios, rolls, licks, riffs, cliches, and gimmicks. It was a wonderful and exciting, but limited, instrument.

All this is not meant to imply that no one had—up to that point—discovered how to play melodic passages on a banjo. To the contrary, the earliest practitioners of the five-string banjo, back in the minstrel show days, played marches, jigs, reels, and so on in a style which closely resembled classical guitar technique. This approach reached its culmination in the music of the great classical banjo players at the turn of the century—most notably Fred Van Epps, and Paul Cadwell (who can still be heard occasionally). But this type of banjo playing was little known among bluegrass musicians, and the techniques of classical banjo playing rarely lent themselves to the driving rhythms of bluegrass music.

The most notable early attempt to introduce melody into bluegrass banjo came in the fifties from Don Reno, who inserted into his playing single-note runs achieved by alternating the thumb and index finger on single strings. While this style was adaptable to the fast pace of the music, the repeated use of single strings made for a staccato sound which contrasted poorly with the richness of Scruggs style. Nevertheless, single-string work became, for a while, the hip thing for a forward-looking banjo player to do, and the fad attained considerable proportions in the late fifties and early sixties—particularly in New York and environs. Still, the single-string style was adopted by very few professionals and was to remain an idiosyncrasy of Reno and his close followers—much admired, but never really accepted into the music. Throughout this period Scruggs style continued to reign supreme and unchallenged.

Today, the situation is different. Through a gradual process, a new approach has infiltrated the banjo scene; it is variously called "melodic," "chromatic," or "[Bill] Keith style." [*Note:* Until referred to otherwise in the article only the term *melodic* is used to described the new style. The term *chromatic* has a different meaning musically. "Keith style" is a layman's term.] The fundamental principle of this approach is to play straight melodies, unadorned by arpeggios, pedal points, and the other extraneous, if appealing, baggage of Scruggs style. The drive that is sacrificed in melodic playing is compensated for by a new agility in this style—a capacity to follow the fiddle, note for note, with all its turns, scales, triplets, and trills.

As with Scruggs style, melodic banjo playing depends on the fifth string for its very existence. But, whereas the role of the fifth string in the former is to act as a drone (or pedal point), this string has a very different function in the melodic style. It acts as an alternate first string (and is fretted), thus allowing the musician to execute scales without having to use the same finger (and usually string) twice in a row. This, in turn, permits the speed so essential to bluegrass.

When you think about it, there is nothing really ingenious or surprising about using a lead instrument like the five-string banjo to play melody. What is far more curious is the fact that the banjo passed through two decades of bluegrass history, during which none of its leading exponents had a fully satisfactory style for even the simplest melodic passage. It is a tribute to Earl Scruggs and his complex and subtle style that the banjo was able to assume such a preeminent position in the bluegrass arsenal without being able to fulfill the first requisite of a lead instrument—the ability to execute scales.

All this has changed. A walk through a festival parking lot will quickly inundate the hapless listener with more scales than a thousand-pound tuna. Major scales, minor scales, chromatic scales, modal scales—ad infinitum/ad nauseum. The age of melodic banjo playing is surely upon us, and it has brought with it a whole new generation of stars who play in this style: Bill Keith, Bobby Thompson, Jack Hicks, Carl Jackson, Larry McNeely, Tony Trischka, Pat Cloud, Courtney Johnson, Alan Munde, etc.

In discussing these new stars, as in discussing their predecessors, one pointless dispute persists in conversations among bluegrass musicians and fans: who should be credited with the development of a particular style? Surely we have all heard that Snuffy Jenkins did it all before Earl Scruggs. Even some of Scruggs' defenders will credit him only with the dissemination of the style, not its creation. It seems to me that anyone listening to these two musicians would realize that Earl's playing is a quantum jump ahead of Snuffy's—much as the latter represents an advance over that early three-finger pioneer Charlie Poole.

Likewise, there has been much speculation as to whether Don Reno preceded Earl Scruggs in the development of the three-finger bluegrass banjo style, and whether it wasn't just an accident that the style wasn't called "Reno style." Again, this strikes me as an inane argument. Obviously both of these fine musicians were influenced by Snuffy Jenkins, but it is also obvious to anyone who has heard records of the early Reno that he didn't play like Scruggs then any more than now. Earl's right hand is smoother, more articulate, and more syncopated; his style is tighter and more coherent than Don's. Of course, Don Reno compensates for this with a dazzling, unique, and inventive style of his own. But that's the point—it is his own, not the progenitor of Scruggs.

This leads us to look at what I believe to be yet another example of this type of inane argument: whether Bill Keith or Bobby Thompson was the originator of the melodic style. Each claims to have developed this style independently. Thompson dates his innovation to the late 1950s. Keith learned "Devil's Dream" in 1961. From my own vantage point, I'm inclined to believe the genesis was independent. In fact, I was responsible for introducing the two to each other.

I first met Bill Keith in the summer of 1962. At that time, the thing which most impressed me about his playing was the incredible fidelity with which he could duplicate Scruggs' playing—right down to that indescribable tone that has eluded everyone I've ever heard.

Another important aspect was one of the tunes in Keith's repertoire: "Noah's Breakdown." It was not until after I learned Keith's arrangement that I appreciated its true significance. This tune (recorded by Noah Crase in the fifties) had a bridge utilizing the position which should be considered the key to the new style: the alternation between open strings and fretting at the fifth and seventh frets. Runs using this same position were redistributed throughout Keith's playing and had already been dubbed "Keith runs" by his fans.

A third impressive component of his playing back then was the prevalence of Don Stover/Allen Shelton–style syncopation—a rarity in the North, except in that the Shelton "bounce" was advocated by Roger Sprung (by precept and not example).

At the time, the above elements of Keith's playing made a greater impression on me than two newly learned tunes, which were his earliest totally melodic pieces—"Devil's Dream" and "Sailor's Hornpipe." Up to that point neither tune was an established standard in the bluegrass repertoire, though both were very nice fiddle tunes nevertheless. Keith's inspiration to work out these tunes had been suggested by the similarity of the fret positions to "Noah's Breakdown." The term *Keith style* was first applied to his rendition of these tunes.

However, progressive bluegrass circles in the early sixties were still monopolized by Renophiles who regarded the melodic style as a shortcut for people who lacked the chops for single-string work. An important victory in the fight for respectability of the new style was won by Eric Weissberg and Marshall Brickman. Their album *New Dimensions in Banjo and Bluegrass* (Elektra) was a veritable orgy of melodic tunes which is still much listened to today. At that time, it was the first exposure of many to the new style.

Over the next two years, Keith's playing improved considerably as his experience spanned long hitches with Jim Rooney, Red Allen, Frank Wakefield, and—most especially—Bill Monroe. Keith's stint with Monroe put the final imprimatur on the new style, although not without input from the Great Man. For one thing, Monroe persistently suggested that Keith avoid entire breaks in the melodic style and frowned on whimsical non-sequiturs, such as Keith's introduction of a quotation from "Nola" into "Footprints in the Snow." (Keith got his revenge by recording "Footprints," "Nola" and all, on the recent Warner Brothers' *Muleskinner* album.) By the end of his tenure with Monroe, Keith was the "complete" banjo player—tasteful, flashy, flawless, complex, versatile, and very original.

As with other bluegrass banjo players worth their salt, Keith collected mountains of banjo "trivia"—unusual tunes that require lots of technique and that were difficult to integrate into the bluegrass repertoire. Keith's collection ranged from Bach sonatas to "Mr. Sandman" to an abbreviated (two part) version of "Nola." It was this repertoire which was really the laboratory for new techniques and which ultimately seems to have seduced Keith away from bluegrass altogether and toward the pedal steel—a laboratory instrument if ever there was one.

Shortly after Keith left the Blue Grass Boys, he suggested to me that I might profit by the same experience. I was in college at the time, and the prospect of such an exotic summer job was irresistible. Consequently, as soon as my 1964 vacation began, I was on a bus for Nashville and an audition. Bill Monroe was pleased to acquire another, albeit more limited, exponent of the melodic style. I had my summer job.

It was in the course of my travels with Bill that I first met Bobby Thompson. We were backstage in a high school somewhere in the wilds of Georgia and this very martial-looking guy with a brush cut came in looking for Bill. After Bill and the stranger exchanged warm greetings, Bill turned to me and asked me to play "something fancy." I think I played "Turkey in the Straw," "Salt Creek," and my own rip-off rendition of "Nola."

At Bill's suggestion, I then surrendered my instrument to the visitor, whom I took to be a "huglie" (pronounced hyooglee—Bill's word for people who come backstage to demonstrate a groundless familiarity with bluegrass stars and to finger their instruments, etc.—i.e., a bluegrass groupie). He wasn't. He was Bobby Thompson, newly returned from the service and "out of practice." But not really. He was fantastic: effortless guitar-style, single-string work, dazzling Chet Atkins' show-pieces like "Swanee River" and the "Humoresque" simultaneously and (wonder of wonders) melodic banjo playing! I vividly recall a nice rendition of "The Arkansas Traveler" in open D and "Sugarfoot Rag." All very like—and yet unlike—Keith. And had he heard of Keith? "Yes." Heard him? "No." How then did Thompson, living in the relatively isolated town of Converse, S.C., acquire this "new" style. By his own account, he'd been playing like that for years! Jeepers!

I made sure that I got Bobby's address. When I returned to New York at the end of the summer Keith immediately called me to find out how things had gone with Bill. In the course of the conversation, I mentioned that I had met Bobby Thompson, the best banjo player I had ever heard (although I'm not sure I meant that with utter conviction). There was a long, thoughtful silence at the other end of the line—followed by, "Well let's go down and see him." And within an hour I, who earlier that day had emerged from a grueling twenty-three-hour bus ride from Nashville, found myself in Keith's car—once again heading south.

We arrived in Converse to find Bobby relaxing on his front porch. He had no advance warning of our arrival, but he greeted us hospitably all the same. He didn't go out of his way to express any emotion upon being introduced to Keith (about whom I am convinced he had heard more than he let on). We were invited inside, and after some idle chatter there commenced a classic Alphonse and Gaston routine: "You play first, Bobby." "Why don't you kick it off, Bill?" After far too much of this, Bobby picked up his banjo and Bill switched on the tape recorder. But for this important debut, Bobby selected nothing more spectacular than a super-straight Scruggs-style rendition of "Shuckin' the Corn." Keith glowered at me and I could detect him silently questioning whether a two-month diet of grits hadn't eroded my connoisseurship.

After "Shuckin' the Corn" the ball was on Bill's side of the net, and he ran through much of his repertoire of fiddle tunes—finishing up with an abbreviated version of "Nola" which I had learned from him. With that, Bobby announced that he had liked the tune when I had played it for him two months earlier and had, therefore, gone out and bought the sheet music to learn it. He then proceeded to play the entire four parts, and all very, very fancy. Bill's jaw and mine dropped and remained in that position as Bobby winged through all of the flashy stuff he had played for me, plus a few surprises like Duke Ellington's "Caravan." As before, my dominant emotion was serendipity: that such a fine musician could have remained so obscure—just a footnote on some old Carl Story and Jim and Jesse records.

Keith's reaction was more constructive. He retired to Boston with the precious tape of that encounter, to emerge, some months later, with virtually all of it assimilated into his repertoire. At that point, it would be fair to say that Bobby was an influence on Bill. And yet, the tunes Bill learned from him were fully incorporated into Keith's richer, if less flashy, style.

Even with much of Bobby's repertoire under his belt, Keith's playing remained uniquely his own. Bobby Thompson plays with the effortless ease of the studio musician: infinite versatility, first in one style, then the other—melodic, Scruggs, single-string. Bill Keith's playing is more integrated, more architectural, more homogenized. His melodic passages merge imperceptibly with his rhythmically and harmonically complex Scruggs style. Single-string is a last resort for him. His playing throughout is dominated by a sophisticated chord structure—a legacy from his early years as a tenor banjo player in Brockton, Mass.

It is ironic that, although Keith was for years the better known exponent of the style, most of the melodic players he influenced utilize the melodic technique in a manner that more closely resembles Thompson's playing. I think the main reason for this is that Keith's style is just too complex and difficult for most newcomers to want to sink their teeth into. It requires a grasp of Scruggs-style basics and chord theory that are a chore to learn for a new picker wanting to get right down to the latest hot licks.

And yet, perhaps it is just as misleading to talk of melodic-style banjo playing as it would be to speak of melodic-style trumpet playing. Now that the capacity for melodic banjo playing has been established, any number of individual styles are possible—each having perhaps as little to do with the other as Miles Davis has to do with Harry James. The experimentation has now gone even further, however, with some banjo players exploring the "chromatic" style briefly mentioned at the beginning of the article. The melodic style uses only the notes of the familiar major and minor (diatonic) scale. True chromatic playing utilizes all twelve notes of the chromatic scale and is characterized by nonharmonic tones and dissonant notes. It offers complete freedom to the banjo player. Pat Cloud, Tony Trischka and Pete Schwimmer are three good examples of such musicians in the vanguard of this experimentation.

The floodgates were opened, and suddenly no note was too weird, no chord too far out, no passage too difficult. Chords which had previously been at home only in jazz—major sevenths, thirteenths, augminisheds, dementeds—now found themselves coexisting congruously with centuries-old fiddle tunes. The myth that the banjo is a limited instrument rapidly faded and, as it faded, one fine banjo player after another slipped outside the world of bluegrass and into the larger community of just plain musicians.

While I find it delightful that such a vast range of possibilities is now before us, I think that all lovers of bluegrass music are saddened to see so many of the most outstanding musicians defect to other musical idioms. The best hope of keeping them at home where they belong is for the dyed-in-the-wool traditionalists to allow the experimenters to coexist peacefully with the high lonesome sound we all know and love. If bluegrass music can become as rich and diverse as its potential, we might even see the day when Bill Keith is seduced back from his apostasy on the pedal steel.

Originally published in *Pickin'* 1 (Oct. 1974): 12–17. Reprinted by permission of Roger Siminoff.

3

Another Roots Revival

1980–2000

Well-placed articles in influential publications can suddenly broaden the horizon for new performers in any field. Dick Kimmel—himself a musician, songwriter, and recording artist as well as a journalist—recalled in an e-mail to me in 2002 how this *Bluegrass Unlimited* article came about: "Hot Rize approached me about doing an article on them for *Bluegrass Unlimited* during one of *BU*'s Indian Springs Bluegrass Festivals. At this point, I remember it was the 1970s and it may have been the first time Hot Rize appeared at this fine festival. Hot Rize drove over to my house in West Virginia for the interviews and photo session. The cover shot with the sunflowers was in my garden. Many years after the article had appeared, I sat in on an IBMA session that Pete Wernick was hosting. He mentioned the first big break for Hot Rize was appearing on the cover of *Bluegrass Unlimited*. I sat there very proud and realized how we all touch people's lives in different ways. Pete was very influential on my playing with his attitudes about keeping music rhythmic and leaving out some of those notes that seem to get in the way."

Hot Rize, which had formed in 1978, went on to become one of the genre's most influential and popular bands, breaking up in 1990.[1]

43

"Hot Rize: Pete Wernick's Secret Ingredient"

DICK KIMMEL

Mention "Hot Rize" to a bluegrass addict and you're liable to get a variety of responses. Within range of Nashville's WSM radio, "Hot Rize" not only brings to mind the secret ingredient responsible for biscuits made from Martha White Self-Rising Flour, but also Lester Flatt's early morning bluegrass radio program and theme song that many folks enjoyed with their morning coffee. Within the past year Hot Rize has also meant a hot young bluegrass band. Pete Wernick on banjo, Tim O'Brien on mandolin and fiddle, Charles Sawtelle on guitar and Nick Forster on electric bass have made themselves known as Hot Rize to audiences in at least a dozen states in the short time they've been together. The fact that Hot Rize became somewhat of an overnight success was not a surprise to those who have followed these individual musicians in the past.

1. Member Charles Sawtelle died in 1999 of leukemia. Gary B. Reid, "Hot Rize," in *The Encyclopedia of Country Music: The Ultimate Guide to the Music,* comp. by the staff of the Country Music Hall of Fame and Museum, ed. Paul Kingsbury (New York: Oxford University Press, 1998), 248.

When Pete Wernick moved to Colorado early in 1976, he had made no definite plans to play music. The years he spent in upstate New York had been good to him, a product of his sense of professional direction and plain hard work, but the hard winters and rainy summers had gotten to be too much, so he moved west. While the north means low pay and little recognition for most traditional musicians, Wernick recorded three well-recognized LPs with Country Cooking, wrote *Bluegrass Songbook* and *Bluegrass Banjo* (which has sold over a hundred thousand copies to date) for Oak Publications, produced a series of Music Minus One instruction records, wrote many bluegrass songs and tunes of which some have almost been declared bluegrass standards ("Armadillo Breakdown," "It's in My Mind to Ramble") and started his solo album for Flying Fish Records.

Shortly after arriving in the West, Wernick started playing bluegrass with Warren Kennison and Charles Sawtelle. Sawtelle was an experienced bluegrass guitarist who had played with The XX-string Bluegrass Band (*Bluegrass Unlimited,* March 1971) and The Monroe Doctrine (*Bluegrass Unlimited,* September 1973). Wernick, Sawtelle, and Kennison became known as The Rambling Drifters. According to Wernick, "Anyplace I go I want to be in a bluegrass band, even if I have some other professional objective which may not even be music. I'm a banjo player and you can't stay in shape as a banjo player if you don't play regularly. I just like it, anyway. So I got this band together with Charles (Sawtelle) and Warren Kennison within a couple of weeks after arriving in Denver." The band was an informal one, exemplified by the fact that they were not only known as The Rambling Drifters, but also as The Drifting Ramblers, The Lonesome Drifting Rambling Cowboys and The Rebuilt Ramblers.

Like Wernick, Charles Sawtelle was a bluegrass musician in his thirties. Sawtelle's father was in the oil exploration business so the family moved from his birthplace in Texas throughout the western United States and Canada. He had learned some steel guitar by the late '50's and by the early '60's was starting flat-top guitar. "I really couldn't play. I just started out watching people that played. My brother had left a guitar at home and I didn't even know how to tune it. I looked at a record album cover to see where the pegs were. I figured if I looked at a record jacket of Josh White or somebody that had a guitar, I'd be able to take the knobs on the guitar and position them exactly where they were on the record it would be in tune. Of course it didn't work." Sawtelle's persistence paid off and eventually he began to learn bluegrass guitar with the help of Colorado musicians. Throughout the '60's and '70's he performed with a number of groups and eventually settled down as the manager of the instrument shop for the Denver Folklore Center. At that time he was also playing on a part-time basis as well as collecting old Martin guitars, elderly Cadillacs and working with his own Sawtelle-Wilson Sound Company which has provided sound for concerts by the likes of John Prine, John Hartford and Joan Baez as well as some of the larger festivals in the area (Colorado Bluegrass Festival and Winfield, Kansas). One of Sawtelle's part-time involvements was The Rambling Drifters. As he puts it:

Sawtelle—"We had ten fiddle players and twenty bass players."

Wernick—"At different times."

Sawtelle—"There were just three of us, but we always played as a four- or five-piece band. Tim (O'Brien) was our usual fiddle player, but he was also playing with the Ophelia Swing Band."

For a musician in his mid-twenties, Tim O'Brien has carved out quite a niche for himself. He's known as not only a fine bluegrass performer, but also a top-notch old-time as well as swing musician. He's been featured on ten LP's including a solo LP *Guess Who's in Town—Tim O'Brien* (Biscuit City 1317), which includes his fiddling, mandolin, lead guitar and fine vocal work on an assortment of old-time, swing and bluegrass arrangements. O'Brien was born in Wheeling, West Virginia, to a musical family. "My father played the banjo-mandolin and my mother played the piano. And of course, we all sang, especially my sister Mollie and I." He gained an early exposure to bluegrass and other forms of music through the folks at the WWVA Jamboree (especially Roger Bland, a banjoist who has since played with Lester Flatt) and by playing guitar in a variety of performing bands. O'Brien was part of West Virginia Grass, a band which played regularly in and around his home state. After a short stint at Colby College in Maine, where O'Brien learned mandolin and played in another band, The Northern Valley Boys, he took to the road as a solo act in western ski areas and in the "Old Town" section in Chicago.

O'Brien—"The fall of 1974 found me in Boulder, Colorado, working at a music store and playing fiddle in a band called Towne and Country Review. I was drafted into the newly formed Ophelia Swing Band where I played mostly guitar at first, but later mandolin and fiddle. We played swing music of the '30's, sort of like Hot Club of France, but with vocals and more arrangements. The rhythm section of Dan (Sadowsky), Duane (Webster), and Chaz (Leary) was great and it really built up my chops."

With The Ophelia Swing Band, O'Brien recorded a very popular LP, *Swing Tunes of the 30's and 40's* (Biscuit City 1313), a unique recording of swing by this mostly acoustic string band. During O'Brien's last year with Ophelia he would frequently sit in with Wernick and Sawtelle in The Rambling Drifters. It was during this period that O'Brien, Wernick, and Sawtelle did some recording together for O'Brien's solo LP (Biscuit City 1317) and Wernick's LP *Dr. Banjo Steps Out* (Flying Fish 046).

The *Dr. Banjo* LP had a number of elements that eventually led to the association of O'Brien, Wernick and Sawtelle in the context of a band. Wernick had been fooling around with phase-shifted banjo and what he calls "Niwot" music. (Niwot is a town near where Wernick lives in Colorado.) Wernick's use of the phase shifter has been both an inspiration to bluegrass buffs and source of contention among them. He has been using it for a number of years.

Wernick—"I first got a phase shifter in 1974. When I heard an electric guitar through a phase shifter, I just figured I'd like to hear a banjo through it. I went to 48th St. in New York, into the different music stores, using a pick-up on my banjo, which I normally don't use. I tried a lot of our modern gadgets which give us our rock 'n' roll sounds of today. I picked out an MXR Phase 90 and also a thing called a Mutron III, which I later got rid of."

He also used the phase shifter when he was with Country Cooking.

Wernick—"In the last version with the Fiction Brothers, I used it on stage on a few numbers every set. When it came time to record our album (*Country Cooking with the Fiction Brothers*—Flying Fish 019), I used it on one number so it was recorded as of 1975. It was only with the release of my album (*Dr. Banjo Steps Out*) that I really got into presenting it."

The phase shifter produces a strange effect, to say the least, and an explanation of how it is produced should be in order.

Wernick—"It is an electronic imitation of a Leslie organ speaker. A Leslie cabinet has two speakers that actually rotate in opposite directions and they get out of phase with each other, causing cancellations of different frequencies. It was eventually figured out that it could be done by electrically altering a signal with tone-filters and transistors and put into a little box which sold for less than $100."

The sound is definitely a banjo, but Pete is able to work with the tones the gadget produces.

"It sustains the banjo a little bit. At festivals the mike gets plugged into the box and a wire just like the regular mike wire goes to the mixing board. The connectors are completely adaptable and it is low-impedance just like most sound systems. It can be hooked up in a short time and then it's just up to me whether I step on the button; if I do, I get the phase-shifted sound. It has a way of expanding the tonal properties so it's a much broader sound. It accentuates the overtones."

The bluegrass audiences have reacted to it in a variety of ways.

Wernick—"I had an incredible range of reactions. Like when Joe Meadows, who fiddles with Jim and Jesse, heard it he came up to the stage and wanted to know where he could get one. Alan Munde bought one the day after he tried mine out and he is now starting to use his at shows. I know for a fact that I like it, but I'm not into trying to present professionally music that a lot of people are turned off by. Generally the reactions have been very positive."

On the *Dr. Banjo Steps Out* LP the phase-shifted banjo was an integral part of Wernick's Niwot music, which he describes as "basically bluegrass without guitar." Wernick had put together the Niwot sound when jamming with Andy Statman without guitar backup. Both Statman and O'Brien played the Niwot mandolin-style on the *Dr. Banjo* LP. Wernick relates, "The first thing that attracted me to Tim O'Brien's music is that he played this fantastic rhythm mandolin-style, which is so easy to play banjo over. It just gives you so much beat that it picks you up and just floats you along and you don't have to worry about laying down a steady rhythm. He'd heard Andy (Statman) play and knew what to do. Most bluegrass mandolin players do not play that kind of rhythm."

That mandolin rhythm coupled with Wernick's banjo style is the basis of the distinctive sound of Hot Rize. The group officially formed early in 1978 as a result of the *Dr. Banjo* LP. The first group included Mike Scap on guitar, Pete Wernick on banjo, Charles Sawtelle on bass and Tim O'Brien on fiddle and mandolin, Niwot-style. According to O'Brien, "The Niwot mandolin sound has to do with the chop, which is not really a chop at all. Chop means that it is stopped, the notes stop—you take your fingers off the frets or damp them. In Niwot you let the notes ring as much as you can and instead of playing only off-beats you play eighth notes (chords) emphasizing the off-beats. Also instead of standard bluegrass chords, I'll play more open chords, and whatever adds to it; sevenths, cross-rhythms and things like that."

Nick Forster had had a loose association with the members of the band for many years. Forster had grown up in upstate New York with a background that included the musical interests of his father (jazz and swing), fooling with guitar and banjo at an early age, the square dances and fiddlers that are so much a part of life in the mountains of New York and Vermont and an introduction to bluegrass by a group from Poughkeepsie, New York, The Arm Brothers. The mid-seventies found Forster working as an instrument repairman at the Denver Folklore Center, which included such responsibilities as working the sound system for the Rambling Drifters and occasionally performing with them on dobro, mandolin or as their square dance caller. When Hot Rize needed a replacement for guitarist Mike Scap in May 1978, Sawtelle moved to guitar and Forster joined the group on bass.

Wernick—"I am partial to the sound of electric bass if it is really played well and sensitively. It is capable of adding more punch. I chose it for my album, because I liked the way it sounded."

Forster—"I try to make the bass sound as acoustic as possible. I also think one reason that I like it is that it is real easy to travel with."

Sawtelle—"The thing that's significant about our bass sound is that the amp onstage is used only as a monitor. The bass amp is turned down, just about as loud as an acoustic bass. It is wired directly to the mixing board and amplified and EQ'ed by the soundman."

Forster—"I really have a lot of control on how it sounds. It gives the soundman control over the volume and I have control over the tone on the amp. I can hear what the tone is like from the PA monitor on stage."

To satisfy the instrument nuts, Forster uses a Fender Precision Bass and various components as an amplifier. O'Brien uses a "Nugget" teardrop-shaped mandolin made by Mike Kemnitzer of Nederland. "It's a German factory job made in the twenties or thirties." Sawtelle prefers his 1937 D-28 Martin guitar, but occasionally uses a 1930 OM-28 for recording or a 1943 D-18 as a second stage guitar. About his guitar Sawtelle says, "I'd never own a herringbone at today's prices. I wouldn't even consider paying over $1,200 for one. Well, I might if I wanted one so bad, because if you're a bluegrass guitar player, it's the tool you've got to have. The new herringbones are better for the money, but the old ones sound better because they're aged. What would be good to say about my guitar is I'd like to sell it and see if I can get enough money to buy a new one."

No one is really sure about Pete Wernick's banjo. According to Wernick, "My banjo is an original five-string flathead Gibson RB-1 from around 1930. Although it is not officially a Mastertone, it certainly has the kind of ring I like in a Master-tone. I got it from Porter Church in 1966 when he was with Red Allen. It's been my only banjo all this time." Typically, RB-1 banjos did not come with the heavy tone-ring, but his banjo was either a special factory job or had been customized by the time Wernick acquired it from Church.

The group's interest in phase shifters, the Niwot sound, hefty PA systems, swing and other forms of music may tend to eclipse the similar interests that brought these four musicians together. This common ground is a respect for traditional bluegrass. After spending even a short time with the band members, their repertoire comes as no surprise.

Wernick—"We do a lot of straight bluegrass material. This is a pretty impor-tant aspect of the band. Other than our original material, almost everything we do was written before 1955. We hardly do any material that's like newgrass and yet we try not to do stuff that would be considered standards or shopworn material."

Wernick's preference for traditional bluegrass is a product of his early associa-tions in the New York City bluegrass scene. Wernick was attracted to banjo through early Flatt and Scruggs recordings he heard during the "folk boom of the late 1950's." During his college years at Columbia, study breaks involved picking a bow-tie Mas-tertone and serving as a disc jockey for his weekly show Bluegrass Special on WKCR radio. The show, which ran from 1964 to 1970, enabled Wernick to meet and inter-view many of the stars of bluegrass. "Also Washington Square during warm weather was just like a festival parking lot jam." While in New York he met and played mu-sic with many musicians such as Winnie Winston and Steve Arkin. "David Grisman and Jody Stecher were very influential in cultivating my interest in the old groups. At this point I consider myself lucky to have heard early Monroe, Flatt and Scruggs, the Stanley Brothers, etc. at that stage because I got into bluegrass earlier on in my learning, whereas now people will listen to an awful lot of, well, Alan Munde, who is great but it's not the roots. It takes folks a long time to develop a concern for the roots. I think it's important to get as deep an understanding as you can of the basis of bluegrass as well as the later development of the music."

The years Wernick spent in New York City introduced him to the banjo and the essence of bluegrass music. His musicianship developed while he was living in Ith-aca, New York, during the early 1970's. "I've been developing in the last seven years or so under the influence of Tony Trischka. He's just a fantastic player who impro-vises all the time and does things at a hard technical level. He has very few techni-cal limitations and makes you want to learn to play what he's doing." With Trisch-ka, Wernick recorded two Country Cooking albums, *Fourteen Bluegrass Instrumentals* (Rounder 0006) which is one of the most revered twin banjo LP's, and *Barrel of Fun* (Rounder 0033). Trischka also appeared on two cuts of Wernick's *Dr. Banjo* LP. By completing a Ph.D. in Sociology while in Ithaca, Wernick truly became Dr. Banjo.

It's frequently fruitless to try to intellectualize the various facets of traditional bluegrass that work themselves into a modern band composed of musicians from outside the bluegrass belt. Wernick demonstrated his insights into this dichotomy of the northern bluegrass musician in his article "Confessions of a Bluegrass Musician from New York" (*Bluegrass Unlimited*, May 1977). It seems that one of the hardest things for musicians newly exposed to bluegrass to grasp is the idea of keeping the music simple so as to release the soul. This approach, which is so much the essence of the music of bluegrass greats like Ralph Stanley, is definitely a part of Hot Rize.

Wernick—"If you come down a little bit off of the best that you are capable of and just get into grooving on the tone of the instrument, the tone of all the band blending together playing right into the same rhythm, you can just enjoy it more. And when you enjoy it more, it just communicates better within the band and outside the band. Music doesn't sound necessarily better, the higher the technical level. Music sounds good the more the musicians are getting into what they are doing."

O'Brien—"In this band we all can play some pretty bizarre stuff, but we all really try to not step too close to the edge ever."

As with any band, Hot Rize is a product of a group of musicians. Besides being a group of real comedians, their abilities in a number of different areas combine to make a unique band. Charles Sawtelle is a seasoned lead and rhythm guitarist who also supplies the band with sound system and recording experience. Bass player Nick Forster can repair instruments and call square dances, a definite asset at a rowdy wedding party. Either the swing-oriented mandolin and fiddle breaks or the strong lead voice of Tim O'Brien would be a sparkplug for any bluegrass band. Add to this the experience and solid banjo playing of Dr. Banjo, Pete Wernick, and you have Hot Rize.

What can we expect of Hot Rize in the future? According to Wernick, "I think our style is still forming, but I would guess the main developments in our music will be writing and finding good material that fits us. And of course, we'll be regularly checking our mailbox for invitations from people like Helen Reddy, The White House, etc." O'Brien adds, "Of course, I'd like to have my own Cadillac, a Lloyd Loar and a fiddle-shaped swimming pool, but I don't want to compromise the music. I take pride in the fact that we are putting out the real stuff and that people may know what is and what isn't bluegrass after hearing us."

For the immediate future anyway, the band will be featured on two LP's, the Kenny Kosek–Matt Glaser twin fiddle record and the upcoming recording by Hot Rize on Flying Fish. This month Hot Rize will be on their second eastern tour, entertaining audiences in such locations as Chicago, Delaware, Virginia, New York and Pennsylvania.

Originally published in *Bluegrass Unlimited* 13 (March 1979): 13–18. Reprinted by permission of the author and *Bluegrass Unlimited*.

R ecord reviews have been an essential part of bluegrass journalism since the earliest days of *Bluegrass Unlimited* and *Muleskinner News*. A dependable cast of reviewers, particularly at *BU,* offer up healthy servings of opinion. But that's not the only function these mostly brief pieces serve. The reviews also provide news of what favorite artists are up to this time out, notice that a new and noteworthy act is on the scene, or give an update on a band that readers may know only through reputation. Here long-time *BU* contributor Jon Hartley Fox heaps praise on the star-studded *Bluegrass Album* band and also places them in useful perspective. Fox points out the more carefree parts they play in this act, as opposed to their "serious" roles as band leaders or star sidemen. As Fox also notes, the *Bluegrass Album* band was part of a generalized, "back to basics" movement that emerged as some of the new-fangled excesses of the 1970s began to wear thin.

44

"Record Reviews: *The Bluegrass Album,* Vol. 2"

JON HARTLEY FOX

The Bluegrass Album, Volume Two
J. D. Crowe, Tony Rice, Doyle Lawson, Bobby Hicks, Todd Phillips
Rounder 0164

"Your Love Is Like a Flower" / "We May Meet Again Someday" / "Take Me in the Lifeboat" / "Sittin' Alone in the Moonlight" / "Back to the Cross" / "Just When I Needed You" / "One Tear" / "Ocean of Diamonds" / "Is It Too Late Now" / "So Happy I'll Be" / "Don't This Road Look Rough and Rocky" / "I'll Never Shed Another Tear"

J. D. Crowe–banjo and baritone vocals; Tony Rice–guitar and lead vocals; Doyle Lawson–mandolin and tenor vocals; Bobby Hicks–fiddle and bass vocals; Todd Phillips–bass.

I have a secret vice to confess. It's one that I suspect I share with other bluegrass fans: a little game called "Armchair Record Producer." In it one schemes and plans and matches personnel like some power-mad impresario. The object, of course, is to create the perfect bluegrass record and the perfect bluegrass band. A bluegrass All-Star team, if you will. On many occasions my starting five were the ones on this record. Imagine my surprise and delight when last year Rounder released *The Blue-grass Album* (Rounder 0140) with Crowe, Rice, Lawson, Hicks and Phillips togeth-

er, and playing traditional bluegrass, to boot. And now, here is *Volume Two*. Hard to imagine, but it's even better than its predecessor. I hope this becomes a regular occurrence.

The selection of material is once again excellent, drawing mostly from the pioneers of the "Golden Age" of bluegrass. Each of the twelve songs is a gem, but I think many fans will particularly enjoy the gospel quartets from the repertoire of Flatt and Scruggs ("Take Me in the Lifeboat" and "So Happy I'll Be"). Tony Rice just keeps getting better as a lead singer and joins with Doyle Lawson for several powerful duets, especially Flatt and Scruggs' "Back to the Cross." With J. D. Crowe added, one of the best baritone singers in the business, you strike trio paydirt.

Crowe, Rice and company are individually known as red-hot pickers capable of scorching the strings with hot licks. But hot licks are not the point on *Volume Two*, though there are plenty of blistering breaks to be heard. This is a vocal record and, above all, a true band effort. The picking, eminently solid throughout, is there to set up and complement the singing. It does so extremely well.

Crowe, Rice, Lawson, Hicks and Phillips are, of course, not a "real" working band, and that, ironically, is part of their strength. Because each of these five men has his own career and his own muse to follow, a project like this one brings them together for just one reason: a chance to play the music they love with a truly exceptional group of their peers. And without many of the day-to-day hassles and frustrations that have torn so many good bands apart.

Hats off to Rounder, producer Tony Rice, and J. D. Crowe, Doyle Lawson, Bobby Hicks and Todd Phillips for making possible this delightful busman's holiday. Let's hope there are many more such projects in the works, like perhaps a Keith Whitley–Ricky Skaggs pairing. *The Bluegrass Album, Volume Two* is a beautiful, essential album and highly recommended.

Recommended for airplay: Take your pick. You can't lose.

Originally published in *Bluegrass Unlimited* 17 (Oct. 1982): 4. Reprinted by permission of the author and *Bluegrass Unlimited*.

Musician/journalist Tim Stafford did a comprehensive job with these liner notes from Sugar Hill's 1999 CD reissue of Doyle Lawson's early albums with Quicksilver. Using fresh interviews and copious detail, Stafford sets out the history of the band, its origins in the musical scene of the day, and its strong influence on the next generation of bluegrass musicians. As Stafford points out, Quicksilver from the very beginning set a high standard of professionalism, polish, and musical impact. Stafford and other savants were attempting precise distinctions among terms such as *progressive* and *contemporary,* which saw wide use in bluegrass as key new bands formed and the style entered a new era. The account brings out interesting sidelights as well. Bassist Lou Reid, for example, about to join one of the most acclaimed bands in bluegrass history, had to be called away from employment at a factory in Greer, South Carolina, to play with it.

45

"Doyle Lawson and Quicksilver: *The Original Band*"

TIM STAFFORD

The Decision

Doyle Lawson decided in 1979 that he was going to start his own band. He had been playing with the Country Gentlemen for seven and a half years, eventually doing much of the arranging and record producing for that seminal group of the early and mid-1970s.

Doyle had nearly left that band some years before, opting to join the Navy with bandmate Bill Emerson. Deciding at the last minute to rejoin the Gentlemen, he was extremely sensitive to keeping bridges to the past intact when he finally left for good. That included not booking any shows for the new band until he played his last engagement with the Gents (on March 30, 1979), shying away from any material he had done with the earlier band, not recording on the same label and of course keeping the actual sound of the band distant from the Country Gentlemen.

"That was and still is kind of an institution in music, and I'd been there for almost eight years. I had been given the opportunity to do a lot of things with the Country Gentlemen. I learned a lot about how to entertain people. I had the freedom to pick and choose the material, produce the albums, arrange the material . . . I just wanted to make sure when I left that band that I could leave with the feeling that I had done everything in the right and respectful way for them. . . . But it was one of those things I had to try. I was nervous about it, although I was confident I could make it float."

As his mother recalls, "He said he wasn't getting any younger and he always had a desire to go out on his own. He said if he was ever going to do anything on his own, he'd better be doing it." At first, the band was going to be named Doyle Lawson and Foxfire, but after Doyle found a group named "Foxfire" in Oregon, he was faced with choosing another name. Ironically, his mother would come up with the solution: "So they were trying to decide on a name. I said, 'What about Quicksilver?' I said, 'There's no stopping Quicksilver. It goes.'"

The Group

But who to get? The way Doyle recalls, "I thought about Jimmy Haley. A year or so before that I produced one side of an album that they (the group, Southbound) were doing for Rebel Records. I remembered that he was a really good guitar player. Just a super rhythm player. That's what I was looking for—more than a lead player, I was looking for a rhythm player. Asked him about a banjo player, he mentioned Terry. Said Terry was playing some with him. Asked him if he knew anybody that played bass. Jimmy mentioned Lou Reid, or Louis Pyrtle. Louis was not playing any at all. He was working in a factory some place.

Anyway, the result was they all three drove up. We talked about it. Picked a little bit. Nothing magical happened. Just sounded like we were looking, trying to get something together. On the second day, they came up, we rehearsed. About an hour into rehearsal it clicked. I mean, I really believe we all felt it about the same time. It was like it just happened. It became a sound, right then. We found a groove."

Terry Baucom had played with perhaps the most important "progressive" bluegrass group of the 1970s, Boone Creek. Originally a fiddle player with that band, Terry switched to banjo when Marc Pruett, the original banjo player, decided he couldn't play music full time. Baucom's driving, powerful style seemed rooted most heavily in J. D. Crowe's Scruggs-based approach. It became a hallmark of the Quicksilver sound, one that's been quoted in one or more ways by every banjo player in the band since. According to Terry, "'Drive,' to me, is simply timing. Once you start playing in time, then you will begin playing on top of the beat of the music, not rushing but just on top of it. I would call that drive." Terry's bass singing was another important facet of his contribution to the band; according to Doyle, it was one of the earliest things that he noticed about Terry: "I wanted a real strong quartet."

Louis Reid Pyrtle was born on Bill Monroe's birthday, raised on the British rock invasion as well as Flatt and Scruggs, and possessed a beautiful natural tone to his voice, along with an impressive range that allowed him to sing many parts. He sang all the parts and played several instruments in a band with his school buddies, Jeff Hooker, Myron Nunn and a young North Carolina guitar-picker named Jimmy Haley. By 1973, Reid (on banjo) and Haley were playing, along with Jimmy Smith and Hersie McMillan, in a group named Southbound at the Apothecary Lounge in Atlanta. By the time Doyle called Jimmy Haley, Lou had burned out on music and was working at the Homelite/Textron Corporation in Greer, S.C., and Terry Baucom was filling in. Doyle called Lou, and that was it; suddenly, with only a few calls, Doyle had the nucleus of the band ready.

The band dedicated itself for six weeks to an intensive rehearsal schedule that included unusual strategies. Doyle said, "I thought, boy these guys are either gonna be really appreciative of what we've done or they're gonna hate me forever. But we did all kinds of things." This included starting a song together in one area of the house and then moving out of earshot, coming back and seeing how close everyone was, both on a cappella quartets and songs with instruments. "One guy would go maybe outside, one would go to a bedroom, one to a kitchen, wherever—just out of earshot. And then when we all came back together, we wanted to still be together. And if we weren't, we started over again" (much in the same way Earl Scruggs and his brother played banjos together around the homestead some forty years earlier).

The first weekend out was a three-show swing in May beginning in Knoxville, Tenn., at Buddy's Bar-b-Que on a Thursday; The Down Home in Johnson City, Tenn., on Friday; and Pickens, S.C., on Saturday. As a member of the audience at the Down Home, I remember the excitement running through the crowd, the wild response to nearly everything the group did.

Sometimes the shows weren't such huge successes, Lou recalls. "I also remember playing in front of three people in Grundy, Va. That was a funny night. We got so tickled at each other that we had to stop in the middle of the first song and apologize to the crowd of three. It's a night I'll never forget. I think we had one vocal mic, Terry and Doyle had to share an instrument mic, Jimmy had to run his guitar with a Barcus Berry pick-up through my bass amp. One could only imagine was it sounded like."

Other times, especially in reaction to the gospel numbers, it was obvious the four had stumbled on something quite magical. Again, Lou summed it up: "We all were overwhelmed by the response from the audiences. I can't believe how much they loved our gospel quartets. I still don't understand it. But I let them be the judge. The expression on Doyle Lawson's face after doing 'Jesus Gave Me Water' or 'On the Sea of Life' would have summed up how much fun we were having."

Here was a group of four men, flying around the country in a '79 Ford van— which Doyle would eventually put four engines in—usually passing the time singing (Barry Poss was struck by how the band "was always making music; I mean they would sing spontaneously in the bus, backstage, everywhere") and listening to live tapes as well as occasional material sent in by writers and classic bluegrass by Flatt and Scruggs, Bill Monroe and the Stanley Brothers. According to Terry Baucom, "We were so much into it that's all we thought about." By the second year, they were playing between 125 and 175 dates per year.

The Recordings

The need for a record to sell at personal appearances—always a staple of professional bluegrass musicians' income—led Doyle to think of Barry Poss and his new Sugar Hill label: "I did a solo instrumental project, *Tennessee Dream,* when Barry worked for County. It was Barry's idea to do it. And he had just gotten this Sugar Hill thing off the ground. I think the Whites were there, and Boone Creek had done one album for him. But he was in the early stage. At Rebel, it was like I would have been almost a competitor to Charlie and Bill, and I didn't want to do anything like that. So I thought about Barry and called him. He said, 'Yeah, sure, we'll try it.' He asked me to send him a tape, and I sent him a rough one from some of the rehearsals, and he called back and said, 'Oh, yeah, man, whenever you're ready, we'll go.'"

The group assembled in Bias Studios near Washington in August 1979 to record. Lou Reid looks back fondly: "I remember how much fun it was recording the first album." The entire album was cut in three to four days, mixed and ready to be mastered. Essentially, it was done live, with very little overdubbing; this was necessary because of the amount of bleed-over from one mic to another in such a set-up. Today this approach is used less often in favor of multi-tracking parts and getting more precise sounds—what's often lost, though, is the soul, the raw, live feeling that is impossible to duplicate. When asked to describe the first records, Lou Reid replied simply, "The albums were cut pretty much live, and came off being a little bit rough when I listened to them. But I think the soul in them will stand the test of time."

There was a mixture of traditional favorites, gospel pieces, vocal showcases and pop tunes which would also become a signature of early Quicksilver records. Doyle, of course, wanted the heritage of gospel singing he had grown up with to be a big part of the group, as well as the traditional bluegrass he had heard first on the radio as a child in East Tennessee. Lou and Jimmy were heavily influenced by the popular music of the sixties and seventies; thus tunes like "Don't Cross the River" and later "Yellow River" became part of the recorded repertoire. Terry, Lou and Jimmy were great fans of the stylings of several of J. D. Crowe's bands, including the Kentucky Mountain Boys of Doyle's tenure and the later New South. Fiddler Bobby Hicks, who sat in with the band a number of times in the early years and even toyed for a time with the idea of becoming a full-time member, added his soulful sounds to the record as a guest.

According to Doyle, "The first one is special to me because it was the first one, and it certainly was a good measuring stick to go by. I felt like it was a good project in spite of the fact that we were hurried along into the studio because we needed something to sell. But we didn't sacrifice the music for it. On the first project I thought there was a little something for everybody. I try to think that way generally. There's no way to be sure. You just go by your heart and hope that you're right."

The follow-up to the band's second record, the all-gospel *Rock My Soul,* which has since become recognized as a classic in the field of bluegrass gospel, was going to be important to maintaining the momentum the group had established. It would be a bluegrass record on the model of the first, but as Doyle pointed out, with more original material, better and stronger material: "To me, the material [on *Quicksilver Rides Again*] is second to none, really. I've had so many people talk about the material. I've heard Travis Tritt say one of his favorite songs is 'Georgia Girl.'"

The band began recording this album at Bull Run Studios in Ashland, Tennessee,[1] but Doyle quickly decided to scrap this session and start over again at Bias in early 1982. At the time, they had no idea for a title until doing a photo session with Jim McGuire. Doyle remembers "I was looking at his truck. I got in that old pickup truck of his and was sitting there looking at it. He said, 'Hold it! Don't move!' So he goes out and comes back with a light, sets it up and says, 'Hold it, hold it!' Looking through the camera then he said, 'All you guys get in the truck!' And that's how the cover came about." From the cover came the idea for the title, *Quicksilver Rides Again.*

The Impact

"I have had some younger players that were between the ages of eight and twelve around the time that we recorded this (who are now in their late twenties) tell me

---

1. Actually, between Nashville and Ashland City, Tennessee.

that we were their Flatt and Scruggs. We had no idea that we had this kind of impact on the younger generation. And, by no means, do I compare Quicksilver to Flatt and Scruggs. I would never go there. I think we probably established a sound that a lot of new bands would later pattern themselves after."—Lou Reid

There can be no doubt that these records became a sort of canon for the young players who grew up learning bluegrass in the 1980s. Banjoist and educator John Lawless of Acutab Publications notes that these records "defined the 'sound' for the next generation of bluegrassers just as *0044* (J. D. Crowe and the New South's eponymous 1975 record *Rounder 0044*) had done for the generation before and the early Gentlemen records for the generation before that."

To David Pendley, a mandolinist and singer with the group Last Run, DL&Q's influence is even easier to spot: "Go to a fiddler's convention or an amateur band contest sometime. As you listen to each band practice, you can almost bet your last dollar that they'll break into a DL&Q song before you walk away. That tells me that their music appeals to the biggest critics: musicians."

Pat Collins of Kansas City, Missouri, an amateur bluegrass musician with his brothers and others in an award-winning band named The Drifters, put it this way: "Historians will say . . . that these were groundbreaking in their contemporary, yet traditional feel. Great use of unknown songwriters and his arrangements of older songs sent contemporary bluegrass to a new level. It had a great deal to do with impressing younger bands to copy the sound. Personally, when these albums came out the material was strong enough that everyone in the Midwest tried to learn the material . . . our band included. I think on the 'family tree' of bluegrass, Lawson will have a branch of his very own. Mainly due to all the influx of newer songs and players into the genre."

It's impossible and probably unfair to gauge just yet what historians will say about these recordings. Neil Rosenberg, whose definitive book *Bluegrass: A History* (University of Illinois Press, 1985) traced the genre from its folk beginnings through the festival phenomenon of the late 1960s and beyond, sees the early Quicksilver records as "setting a standard that many musicians aspired to. And they moved the gospel quartet as a part of bluegrass much more into the spotlight than it had ever been before."

Yet putting these records in the "progressive" camp is something Rosenberg has a hard time with: "In terms of the Country Gentlemen and the Seldom Scene, bands that everyone seems to agree were 'progressive,' Doyle Lawson and Quicksilver were, to my way of seeing it, somewhat more conservative. There was more emphasis on hard-driving straight-ahead delivery, as contrasted with the tendency of those other groups to try softer, more folk-rockish arrangements. On the other hand, they broke a major taboo in using an electric bass from the start as part of their sound. Before that, among the 'name' groups, only the Osbornes, who were working to cross over as a country group in those years, had electric bass. And again, the emphasis on great gospel singing with a strong bass singer reflected the influence of southern gospel as well as Doyle's personal convictions. I think they had what all great

bluegrass bands have—a mixture of old and new influences from the past of bluegrass music and from outside forms, mixed in a unique way. I think they changed
the course of bluegrass in the Southeast in the '80s. I think of younger bands that
followed and seemed to me to have some of the same sound like Virginia Squires
and Summer Wages and early Lonesome River Band. I guess I'd prefer 'contemporary' to 'progressive.'"

"Progressive" bluegrass was a charged term by the late 1970s, indicating perhaps
something more along the lines of New Grass Revival or IInd Generation rather than
Boone Creek or Quicksilver. Certainly the term had its foundation in the stylistic
devices of the Country Gentlemen in the early 1960s and the groups who were to
follow them: Cliff Waldron's groups; the Bluegrass Alliance; the Seldom Scene; and
Red, White and Blue (Grass).

According to those like Frank Godbey, a musician and student of the music who
reviewed the first record for *Bluegrass Unlimited* magazine in April 1980, "They will
probably be considered 'evolutionary' as opposed to 'revolutionary.' Doyle's vision
was not the same as, say, Sam Bush's—e.g. Doyle might adapt a rock 'n' roll song
to play in a bluegrass style, whereas Sam would play rock 'n' roll on the mandolin.
I think I'd use the word 'contemporary' instead."

Barry Poss looks at these recordings as progressive "in the sense that they were
making new music, but it was always grounded in tradition, so the newness felt
natural and connected."

Liner notes for *Doyle Lawson and Quicksilver: The Original Band,* SH2210 (1999). Reprinted
by permission of the author and Sugar Hill Records.

These liner notes by musician/journalist Bill Vernon have as a reference point
the breakup of the Johnson Mountain Boys, a fondly remembered "neotradi-
tionalist" band that rose to prominence in the early 1980s. The article serves as a
history of the band and the role it played in reviving hard-core bluegrass. By 1979,
when the band formed in the Washington, D.C., area, newgrass or progressive bluegrass had explored the far corners of the musical universe for more than a decade.
For some tastes, all that experimentation had played itself out; it was time to get back
to the basics of bluegrass.

Emblematic of that instinct was JMB fiddler Eddie Stubbs's devotion to the hard-
hitting musicianship of stalwarts Paul Warren and Chubby Anthony, forsaking, as
Vernon points out, "the illustrious smooth single-string stylists." In the years since
the band's breakup, Stubbs, now an announcer for WSM-AM, has become perhaps
Nashville's single most effective voice for old-time country and bluegrass music. In
the spring of 2002, the station announced a new focus on bluegrass, a startling development even for the Opry's home station. Vernon died in 1996 at age fifty-nine.

46

"The Johnson Mountain Boys: *At the Old Schoolhouse*"

BILL VERNON

One bluegrass music authority called it the most dramatic event since the breakup of Flatt and Scruggs. The news made its way during the fall of 1987 around the bluegrass circuit even faster than a rumor, and this time the "rumor" was undeniable fact. The Johnson Mountain Boys, young and at the height of their popularity after a rise that had been little short of meteoric, had decided to disband. By that year's Thanksgiving weekend Myrtle Beach, South Carolina, bluegrass festival, some of the music's important veteran personalities were already offering onstage spoken tributes to The Johnson Mountain Boys and their contributions to the music. Thus, the bluegrass community reluctantly began finding ways to come to terms with the fact that the group's last shows would be held the following February 20, where it had first developed a strong and loyal following, the old schoolhouse now serving as the Lucketts, Virginia, Community Center.

Lucketts is a town small enough that it doesn't always appear on road maps of Virginia. It is so close to one of Virginia's northernmost borders that a driver passing through town with his mind on something else might find himself in Point of Rocks, Maryland, before he knew it. On any other day, the Lucketts Community Center, situated across a lawn a bit back from the town's main road, would have been quietly going about its business of antiquating without visibly dilapidating. But, on that raw, grayish February Saturday, it was suddenly a human anthill. The line of Johnson Mountain Boys enthusiasts for whom attending the band's last public appearance was no less than a mandate had begun forming several hours before the afternoon show; ultimately it encircled the entire building before extending all the way out to the main road. By the time every last possible determined loyalist had been shoehorned into the small auditorium and The Johnson Mountain Boys were preparing to take the small but serviceable stage, not only the old building itself, but the emotions of all its occupants, band members perhaps most of all, were at very nearly critical mass.

People who mass-merchandise music are fond of viewing its potential audiences not as living human beings but as "demographic targets." By contrast, bluegrass fans tend to be strongly individualistic. Older rural bluegrass fans may tend to appreciate the music because it has always been part of the fabric of their daily lives. Younger urban bluegrass fans, on the other hand, may come to the music because it offers something that is otherwise not in their lives. One of the important ways in which The Johnson Mountain Boys were truly a phenomenon is the extraordinary following they developed among individuals from all segments of the bluegrass audience, as a glance around that auditorium during either show that day would bear out.

Through the years, most of the composite personnel of The Johnson Mountain Boys came from the Maryland suburbs of the greater Washington, D.C., area. The area is well known as a hub of bluegrass popularity, but most of the bluegrass music played around Washington tends to be of the contemporary variety, a fact which undoubtedly served to cast the tradition-oriented music of The Johnson Mountain Boys almost immediately in sharp relief. But at first, the band was often considered "southern" by northern audiences, and, especially in its earliest days, occasionally suspiciously "northern" by southern audiences. This initial dichotomy of perception notwithstanding, The Johnson Mountain Boys were definitely in the right place at the right time. As the band began to emerge on the national scene in the late 1970s, it had been a long time since any new traditional performers (except Dave Evans, with whom the band was often cross-referenced in those days) had come along to join the music's original masters, so the rise of The Johnson Mountain Boys was especially welcome in that respect as well. (The longer the tide stays out, the better reception it gets when it comes in.)

The Johnson Mountain Boys could not have accomplished all that they did, especially in such a relatively short time, without bringing to their music a uniquely catalytic amalgam of dynamism, creativity, and a thorough appreciation of its roots. The band could not be described, in this age of musical labels, as retro-traditional; one could not dub into their recordings 78 rpm-style surface noise and hope to hear Johnson City, Tennessee, 1947. They could more accurately be described as, in the fullest, finest sense of the phrase, neo-traditional. Whereas many present-day music groups are willing to graft onto their sound anything that makes them sound contemporaneous, The Johnson Mountain Boys created and always nurtured their distinctively healthy musical identity by allowing their strongly rooted music to grow from within. ("Contemporary" is often nothing more than the intersection of time and place on a graph; roots can be forever.)

"We all grew up listening to hillbilly radio." The statement comes from Johnson Mountain Boys high lead/tenor singer, guitarist and songwriter Dudley Connell; in it is the genesis and definition of the sound and style of The Johnson Mountain Boys. "Hillbilly" is the term that, through the years, has been as much maligned as it has been misunderstood. Even some of hillbilly music's original champions have in later years been heard to use the term pejoratively, and very few of even the best bluegrass bands performing today still have any hillbilly "intangibles" left in their sound. Yet, more specifically than it is "country" music and before it wakes up one bright morning to discover that suddenly it is "folk" music, original bluegrass music is hillbilly music, with values and virtues and heart and soul all its own. By the time The Johnson Mountain Boys began gathering steam in the late 1970's, hillbilly music had had as many of its life-support systems severed as the country music industry could reach, but there were still many who, having heard it, would always love it. And among these were some, like The Johnson Mountain Boys, who could not only cherish and preserve it but perform it and make it flourish anew.

The Johnson Mountain Boys began as a duet. (For an intensive look at their early years, see Walter V. Saunders' excellent liner notes to their first Rounder LP; for an overview of much of their career, see the November, 1987 *Bluegrass Unlimited*.) Dudley remembers listening with his original partner in the mid-1970s to the nightly WAMU radio programs of long-time Washington air personality and devoted traditionalist Gary Henderson. Carter Stanley became Dudley's hero. "When I hear him sing, that's what really made me want to sing bluegrass music." Richard Underwood brought a strong, Stanley-tinged (though unintentionally so) banjo style to the group. Mandolinist David McLaughlin is also thoroughly versed in the Stanley style, so it's not surprising that, on occasion, the music of The Johnson Mountain Boys would pressure-cook in the great Stanley tradition.

The members of the group never fit any of the pre-cast molds, however, either musically or personally. In demeanor, they were neither terse originalists nor smoothly upscale modernists. As Dudley put it, "You couldn't find a more diverse group of people." But everything fit seamlessly together because "we all really listened to the same kind of music, and had been influenced by the same people. It was really a charged atmosphere when we got together, because everybody was learning new things for the first time, hearing old, old records that were new to us—it was really an exciting time."

By the time their first Rounder LP appeared in April of 1981, The Johnson Mountain Boys may still have been a new name to many bluegrass fans, but they were already an experienced professional band. For a band of unestablished reputation, playing for any kind of money meant playing in clubs, which The Johnson Mountain Boys did for several years. But, "those weren't clubs, they were honky-tonks," asserts fiddler Eddie Stubbs. Eddie remembers them as being "not particularly violent," which probably meant that there were occasional mornings after which there were no eyeballs for the janitor to sweep up, even if on countless nights before the assembled gentry had submitted real or imagined differences of opinion to their own style of binding arbitrations. As Dudley put it, people came there primarily to "drink and release." In this atmosphere, the band was free to experiment and improvise, and because they often played in the same "club" several nights in a row they would keep as many as sixteen different full sets of material worked up at any given time. As their friend and early mentor Bill Harrell told them, "one thing I'll always respect you for—you built your show and learned to play in the clubs, and not at festival patrons' expense." Dudley, in turn, recalls that Bill "helped us a lot; he looked at the music as a serious profession, and instilled that in us as very young guys." Even in later years, when many of their most devoted fans might be able to see them just a handful of times on the festival circuit each summer, The Johnson Mountain Boys always kept more of their recorded material up to request-ready performance standard than perhaps any other prominent bluegrass band.

The rise of The Johnson Mountain Boys may have been rapid, but it was by no means automatic. Many a band has developed a frenzied following at the roadhouse where it gets its mail only to be greeted by unilateral stupefaction almost anywhere else. As the band graduated from local to national status, the Washington-based Johnson Mountain Boys often found themselves playing deep into the rural-southern areas where bluegrass music was originally nurtured. This placed them in the anomalous position of bringing the "home folks" their own music. To a large extent, the original audience for bluegrass had seen its access to its own music diminish, even as it appeared to be being taken over by "outsiders." But it was extremely important to The Johnson Mountain Boys to take their music into those areas and be accepted by that audience, and, after some initial skepticism, that's exactly what happened. (Eddie Stubbs, though, still sees a sad and tragic irony in the fact that, in at least some of the areas where bluegrass originally was most popular, the local people seem to have no present-day awareness of their rich musical heritage.)

One milestone for The Johnson Mountain Boys, Dudley remembers, was the 1981 Lavonia, Georgia, festival. "We went down there," he recalls, "and people really accepted the band." They were always dedicated and industrious, and from then on The Johnson Mountain Boys became one of the most in-demand, hardest-working bands in bluegrass. It was not unusual to scan the group's list of upcoming personal appearances and find them working three or four nights a week (sometimes as many as five nights in a row), for several months on end. Often, the distance from one night's show to the next was several hundred miles. They might be playing in Michigan one day and upstate New York the next. To arrive at their last shows at Lucketts, they drove all night from Columbus, Ohio. But no matter how far they had to travel from one show to the next, the show they put on was always great. They were there not only to perform their great music, but in the fullest sense of the word to entertain. (By contrast, an observer of some of today's groups, each member at parade rest at his separate microphone, might conclude that he had happened upon not performers but sentries in the desert.)

The Johnson Mountain Boys may have been made up of diverse personalities, but their musical affinities made them completely musically compatible. During and after the life of the band, talking with the band members about their music has always brought out how much they like and respect one another. A composite quote might well read, "we are all still friends, and we still love to play music together," a fact which several planned "reunion" concerts will undoubtedly bear out. Dudley Connell and Eddie Stubbs seem to have brought in the lion's share of the material the group would record. Many of the songs were strong originals written by Dudley, each one a creative, forthright expression of the traditions the entire band reveres. Dudley and Eddie quickly single out David McLaughlin as the one who can "be selective among ideas" and who can put harmonies together "just like that." Eddie disclaims any ability to assemble harmonies, yet every time he plays one of his patented "double-stops," he makes it manifest that he is hearing harmony where another fiddler might be hearing only one melody or backup line. Eddie's fiddle heroes are not the illustrious, smooth, single-string stylists, but the perhaps less-appreciated, solid, straight-ahead "hillbilly" fiddlers like the late Paul Warren and Chubby Anthony and Tater Tate and Mack Magaha. All these greats have approached their work with unfailing directness and intensity, and their influence strongly permeates Eddie's own unique style to this day. David pays Eddie the ultimate compliment: nowadays, he says, you can't always tell who the fiddler is on any given record, "unless it's Eddie Stubbs."

In Nashville music, for instance, the spotlight is on the lead singer, while his band lurks somewhere in the background, looking like wallpaper with sideburns. In bluegrass music, however, every band member makes a difference. Every musician who joined The Johnson Mountain Boys through the years made a specific difference in the texture and overall composition of their music. When the need arose in 1986, senior group members Eddie, Dudley and David were all delighted that they were able to acquire the services of musicians of the caliber of Tom Adams and Marshall Wilborn. Yet, almost every encomium for the new arrivals begins with the assertion that they "don't mean to take anything away from" their predecessors. According to Dudley, "Richard Underwood set a style and a precedent." David, who replaced Richard as lead singer under Dudley's tenor in the duets, is the first to add that when Richard left, "we lost a great voice." Dudley agrees wholeheartedly, but remembers that the first time he and David sang together, "it was right there."

Because Richard had been such an integral part of the band, replacing him put The Johnson Mountain Boys at an important crossroads. The band had first heard Tom Adams in March 1985 at a festival in Dunnellon, Florida, near the end of his two-year tenure as a member of Jimmy Martin's Sunny Mountain Boys. They were impressed with his power and drive, what Dudley calls Tom's "eatin' Coke bottles" style of playing. When he auditioned for the band, Eddie remembers, it became evident "after about three songs" that Tom was the ideal man for the job. Earl Scruggs had been Tom's hero from the start—"his playing is still what excites me to this day." (Since The Johnson Mountain Boys disbanded before Tom could get too much biographical attention in album liner notes, a bit of chronology is in order here. Tom played in his family bluegrass band in Gettysburg, Pennsylvania, from 1969 until his father passed away in 1979. He and his brother Dale played together for a while, and in 1981 Tom, Chris Warner and Warren Blair formed a band together. Tom worked with Jimmy Martin from 1983 until 1985, and then joined The Johnson Mountain Boys in October of 1986.)

Just as replacing Richard's lead voice with David's had changed the group's whole approach to their singing, Tom's arrival engendered changes as well. As Dudley states, "the fact that Tom played with such fire not only 'sold' the band, but actually stimulated it. I think it also kindled a lot of (new) respect for the band among our musical peers, because it showed that we could indeed have somebody play, not in the same style, but still in a style that would fit our music, and move it along to another plane. I feel Tom is one of the most creative and innovative banjo players in bluegrass music."

Tom remembers borrowing an arch-top banjo and, in preparation for joining The Johnson Mountain Boys, learning all the banjo parts off their records. When he joined the band, he was surprised to discover that what was needed was not precisely what he had learned from the records, because in the interim their "timing" had changed significantly. This was directly due to the contributions of bassist

Marshall Wilborn. Marshall had worked with the fine Pennsylvania bluegrass group Whetstone Run, and, like Tom, had done his time as a member of Jimmy Martin's Sunny Mountain Boys. He joined The Johnson Mountain Boys in June 1986, in his words, "thrilled at the chance to work with them." Rapport and mutual admiration were immediate—the band fully appreciated his solid bass playing, his just-right baritone singing, and his songwriting ability as well. Marshall points out that "every group plays with a different 'timing,' a different 'feel'; The Johnson Mountain Boys' approach to timing really made bass playing a joy for me. They seemed to have a way of playing the appropriate thing at just the right time!"

An important facet of The Johnson Mountain Boys' success was their long association with Rounder Records, beginning in 1980. The band appreciated the freedom the people at Rounder gave them. Eddie remembered, they "never told us once we couldn't record a song—communication lines were always open." Rounder's Ken Irwin would sometimes suggest that the group not record a certain song, and Dudley remembers that his reasons were always to the point. There was one song in particular that Ken strongly advised them not to record; they recorded it anyway. In retrospect, Dudley was highly amused. "Ken was right—it didn't do a thing for us!" Rounder's enlightened approach allowed the band to grow in its own way, and that growth was invariably reflected in their records.

From their first Rounder album, The Johnson Mountain Boys never allowed anything to compromise their own distinctive approach. The band had a predilection for undeservedly obscure old bluegrass and old-time songs, and these were always an important part of their repertoire. In Dudley Connell, they had an outstanding songwriter who could write original bluegrass songs that went right to the soul of bluegrass tradition. Several band members wrote strong instrumentals, including two from their 1984 release *Live at the Birchmere.* Both "Sugarloaf Mountain Special" and "Georgia Stomp" were nominated for Grammy Awards as "Best Country Instrumental," and several country songs of the 1950's and '60's found a new home with The Johnson Mountain Boys. Any song that's authentically country—as opposed to bankrupt rock 'n' roll that's trying to reorganize as country— is potential bluegrass material. All it needs is the utilization of bluegrass instrumentation and the intensification that bluegrass always brings to any kind of country song. The Johnson Mountain Boys knew this, and they made it work for them perfectly.

Many bluegrass bands become prisoners of their own few "greatest hits." The Johnson Mountain Boys were more fortunate; their sound, their approach, their repertoire were all uniquely theirs, and at least half the songs in all their albums became audience-request numbers. (So determined was the group to establish its own identity that it never recorded songs received on "demo" tapes from outside professional writers who might also be supplying other groups with material, even though, as Dudley recalled, "we got some good ones, too.")

In 1987 The Johnson Mountain Boys had what all concerned agree was their breakthrough song, "Let the Whole World Talk." There was no conscious commercial calculation involved, but once the group had recorded the song, with its inspired twin fiddling by Eddie Stubbs and David McLaughlin and Dudley Connell's soaring vocal, they knew they had hit on something new and different. "Let the Whole World Talk" brought new acclaim to the group from people who had never paid any particular attention to them in the past, and even from some who had regarded The Johnson Mountain Boys' traditional groove as a rut. People who had not previously especially liked bluegrass music took a second listen on the strength of the song, and radio stations that played little or no bluegrass added "Let the Whole World Talk" to their playlists.

Many new doors thus opened to The Johnson Mountain Boys—but not, unfortunately, those of the Nashville country music television programs that would have brought them even greater exposure and acclaim. They had in their corner important supporters such as The Country Music Hall of Fame's Bob Pinson, but somehow they never connected, even though other bands of equal or less stature would frequently appear on these programs. More important in the long run, however, was the fact that the commercial success of "Let the Whole World Talk" in no way changed the rest of what the band was doing. The song itself created instant greater accessibility, with no hidden costs—no musical compromise, not even any accommodation of anything that would in any way dilute the worth of their sound—and, because they were recording for a major *bluegrass* label, no mercenary pressures to make any concessions that might result in even broader appeal.

But now, after eight and a half years on the road as a nationally acclaimed band, after playing in thirty-six states and ten (six in Africa, England, Ontario, Nova Scotia and British Columbia) foreign countries, appearing as guests on The Grand Ole Opry, and even performing at The White House, The Johnson Mountain Boys had found it necessary to disband. It was an emotional decision, and one not easily made. "We did everything we could possibly do," Dudley said, "to leave the music with dignity—we tried to give the music back something of what we'd (gotten out) of it." So personal and so strong were the feelings of their fans that many reacted as though they personally, and not the band professionally, were in terminal straits. In retrospect, this is where an ironic quirk of human nature came into play. Had the group merely issued the standard, pro forma, the-truth-but-not-the-whole-truth press release, everyone would probably just have shrugged, swallowed hard, and accepted the news, however reluctantly. But when the band, in good faith, tried to clarify their reasoning, some of their followers seem to subliminally feel that they'd been given sufficient data that they should have been in on the decision-making process itself. After all, as Dudley said, the members of the band just needed "to do something else for a living for a while."

"The end" for The Johnson Mountain Boys was no somber shambling off into the musical sunset. Rather there occurred a rebirth—a kind of musical Indian summer. The group played as many shows as ever, continuing till the last moment to polish their music and work up new material. (The arrangement of "Sweetest Gift" heard in this album was worked up scarcely a week beforehand.) Rounder's Ken

Irwin noted that Dudley's singing seemed, if anything, to become more intense and more improvisational. Dudley returns the ball to Ken's court, noting that people as enthusiastic about their music as Ken and Rounder artist Hazel Dickens sitting on the front row at any show always serve as an automatic catalyst. Dudley states that seeing people they knew they might not see again for some time and probably never as often again made "each show a very emotional event. We tended to approach each show as if it was our last—it wasn't just the way we sang, it was our approach to our shows they were just wide open. The people wanted it; I didn't bring it out—they did!"

Those two shows on that last day at Lucketts were less "shows" than communions. Emotion flowed freely, even onstage. Frequently, during his spoken remarks, Dudley found the need to defer to Eddie to get him through to the next tune. "I didn't think I was going to make the second show," Dudley would say afterwards. All eyes and hearts were on the five members of The Johnson Mountain Boys—Dudley Connell, Eddie Stubbs, David McLaughlin, Tom Adams and Marshall Wilborn—who were onstage in front of them, but many in the room thought, too, of two other fine musicians, Richard Underwood and bassist Larry Robbins, who from 1979 till 1986 did so much to make The Johnson Mountain Boys one of the nation's premier bluegrass bands. That day, the group could have sung the tax code and received a standing ovation. Even if they had not been at their very best, the audience might well have come away thinking they had. But that day, the finely honed music of The Johnson Mountain Boys had the glint of a perfect diamond. Dudley's singing had never been more emotive and commanding; his duets with David created, as always, a close, strong blend that only a pair of blood brothers could hope to equal, and David's mandolin work was a model of lean, concise authority. Tom's banjo crackled with authority, Eddie's fiddle never sounded better, and Marshall played his bass as if he had been a Johnson Mountain Boy from the beginning. Eddie wrapped his rich bass-baritone voice around a solo performance and anchored (with Marshall singing baritone) a series of flawless gospel quartets. The tunes performed that day were an artful blend of familiar favorites and songs those fortunate enough to be in attendance that day might not have previously heard the group play. The music was, in a word, triumphant, and the shows not so much a series of high points as one long, memorable occasion. No less a bluegrass personage than Sonny Osborne had summed it up for bluegrass fans everywhere, onstage at the Myrtle Beach festival that prior Thanksgiving weekend. "The Johnson Mountain Boys," said Sonny, "have been a class group since they started . . . they look the way they're supposed to, they act the way they're supposed to, and the main thing is, they've entertained the way they're supposed to—and I hate very much to see them go." But, with the playing of "Wake Up Susan," go they did. In a weird sort of post-climactic twist some members of the group rose early the next morning to fly to the Far East on a long-scheduled tour that would not end for more than a month, improbably enough in Indonesia. But for the bluegrass community as a whole, an important chapter in bluegrass music came to a close on February 20, 1988, in Lucketts, Virginia. A dozen or so years is a very short time in which to become one of the all-time great blue-grass bands, but that's exactly what The Johnson Mountain Boys accomplished. At a time when the force of tradition was ebbing in bluegrass music, The Johnson Mountain Boys took that tradition, ameliorated it, revitalized it, and made it their own. They brought to their music unique creativity, dynamism and dedication. They went out at the top of their form, and at the top of their profession. We can all be gratified they were here.[1]

Liner notes for LP 0200/0261 (1989). Reprinted by permission of Rounder Records.

As Alan Steiner points out in this 1979 *Bluegrass Unlimited* piece, multi-talented Peter Rowan has roamed far and wide in his long musical career. During a period between 1964 and 1967, when some of his fellow New Englanders were delv-ing into bluegrass versions of Beatles songs and the like, Rowan had reached the mountain's top—playing and singing with Bill Monroe himself. Like some of the other non-southern musicians who did Blue Grass Boys stints during this period, Rowan brought influences from outside bluegrass along with an aggressively exper-imental nature that sometimes put him at odds with Monroe. In the years since this article ran Rowan has ventured into all sorts of music, but he has returned to blue-grass again and again, teaming with the Nashville Bluegrass Band for tours and re-cordings and releasing a Monroe tribute, *Bluegrass Boy*, in 1996.

47

"Peter Rowan: Wandering Boy Returns to His Roots"

ALAN STEINER

Bluegrass fans often bemoan the loss of a first-class performer to other styles of music. Lately, however, those fans have had the opportunity to celebrate the return to bluegrass of at least one musician. Peter Rowan, once lead singer and guitar player for Bill Monroe, passed through a couple of rock bands, came back to bluegrass and then wandered away again. Now, with super-successful performances at recent blue-grass festivals, a tour of Japan with a full bluegrass band and an all-acoustic LP re-corded on the Flying Fish label, Peter Rowan is back.

In his multi-faceted career that has already spanned a decade and a half, Peter has thrilled audiences across this country and abroad. From Nashville's Grand Ole Opry and West Virginia bluegrass festivals to New York's Carnegie Hall and from

---

1. The Johnson Mountain Boys held several successful reunions, leading to the group's refor-mation and further CD releases.

the Armadillo World Headquarters in Austin, Texas, to San Francisco's premier showcase—Winterland—Peter has constantly cut loose with his original "stuff," and in the process has emerged as a major talent whose power and distinction have captivated audiences far and wide.

Rowan began his musical odyssey in eastern Massachusetts. As a child, he was drawn to his uncle's guitar "like a magnet." Country music on Boston's Hayloft Jamboree was within earshot via the radio, and he strummed along on a tennis racket that he substituted for a guitar.

At the age of twelve, Rowan first heard Elvis Presley, and he recalls that at that point, "the tennis racket was gettin' a lot of use. . . . Something really reached me in Elvis' music." With some junior high school friends, Rowan formed a rockabilly band that played "mostly Buddy Holly stuff."

Interests in the blues and ballads led Rowan to bluegrass. When he was sixteen, he heard Eric von Schmidt playing the blues in Harvard Square and "couldn't believe it." Seeing the black country blues as the roots of the rock and roll he was playing, Rowan traded in his electric guitar for a Martin. The blues really appealed to him, but he "couldn't just play blues. I didn't have the experience in life . . . to really understand what those songs were about."

Around the same time, Rowan heard Joan Baez singing Child ballads in Harvard Square. The folk sound also appealed to him. Rowan saw white folk music forms as offering him a way to explore his roots as a white person, his British heritage. He played folk and old-time music, but still felt that the blues were *the* American expression and that they simply did not come through enough in the forms Pete was involved in.

In his early college years Rowan pursued two interests. He read literature of the American experience (Hemingway, Dos Passos and Kerouac) and after seeing the Country Gentlemen and hearing the Stanley Brothers, he dug deeply into the recorded history of bluegrass. There, in the early bluegrass music of Bill Monroe, he found the feeling for which he had been searching. "Back in the beginning," Rowan says, "it had the blues." The traditional ballads that were a part of the bluegrass repertoire also attracted Rowan. He began to play bluegrass and dropped out of college. Through an association with innovative banjoist Bill Keith, an ex-member of the Monroe band, Rowan was given an opportunity to play guitar for Monroe when the master toured up north without his regular band. Monroe was impressed enough to tell the young picker, "Boy, you ought to come to Nashville, I can help you."

Soon Rowan was driving to Nashville with Keith. There he became guitar player and lead vocalist for the Blue Grass Boys. The rest of the band consisted of fiddler Richard Greene, banjoist Lamar Grier and Monroe's son James on bass. Rowan quickly found out that the band did not rehearse. "If you'd go in to rehearse, Bill would just start playing some obscure fiddle tune or 'Moonlight Waltz' or the schottisches . . . just to kind of teach you what he wanted you to know. I learned all of his old duets . . . everything he'd ever sung with anyone else. At one time or another we did 'em all live on the Opry."

The recording side of the band left Rowan a little dissatisfied. Whereas onstage he sang lead in duets under Monroe's soaring tenor, James Monroe did the leads on the records, and Rowan was left with the baritone parts and only an occasional lead. Furthermore, the band did not record the music that they had been performing: "On that album *Bluegrass Time* . . . it's all stuff the producer said to record. Bill was just going along with the producer. He wasn't sticking behind the vision of the band. I can see why after having been in the business longer."

While most musicians who played with Monroe "would just go in there and just do what he told them to do," Rowan tried to do a little bit more. His attempts apparently resulted in personality clashes. "Bill's very happy having a band of people that he can tell exactly what to do. Within that structure, Bill comes forth amazing. . . . Now I could *really* play with Bill. I feel like Bill Monroe and I, right now, should make a lot of albums and get really on it, because there's some uniqueness there. . . . Now when I play with Bill, I swear, it's rhythm and blues, rhythm and bluegrass is what I call it."

Rowan still is excited by the music and the movement produced in a Bill Monroe performance. This past summer "he came on . . . and from the first moment that guy was just boogieing. He was moving and playing runs like he used to when he was younger, but runs much more into rhythm and blues than they are into country sound. That's the way I feel about bluegrass because if Bill Monroe was an electric guitar player, can you imagine, it would be the most blues-funk country you ever heard. Because that's the way he plays, it's just . . . hard-driving."

After two and a half years with the Blue Grass Boys, Rowan left the band to enter the world of rock.[1] He had been writing some "strange" songs in Nashville and got together with mandolinist David Grisman to play them. The pair made a demo that led to the release of the album *Earth Opera*. The new band was to have been acoustic, but the group found itself opening for the Doors, a psychedelic rock band. Rowan "caught the spirit" of the sixties, the rebellious, mind-expanding spirit of rock. Earth Opera's sound changed from what Rowan labels "the first real newgrass" to a synthesis of styles, a musical theater that included "free saxophone passages, wild stuff going on . . . kind of country . . . kind of psychedelic . . . kind of medieval." Rowan wrote songs for the group's two records, the first of which showed some of the effect of the Beatles' *Sergeant Pepper's* album on American rock.

Following the demise of Earth Opera, Rowan joined a California band, Seatrain, which already included fiddler Richard Greene. Seatrain used written arrangements and would play songs note for note onstage; this was a practice that Rowan had not experienced in bluegrass. Seatrain employed a heavy, insistent rock rhythm, yet occasionally the bluegrass would come through on record, as in the versions of "Sally Goodin" and "Orange Blossom Special" on the group's second album. While Rowan was getting into playing electric guitar and "keeping that rhythm tight," another energy, "that warm acoustic sound, was going in my mind, 'come on . . . let me

---

1. According to Tom Ewing's chronology, Rowan played with Monroe from March 1965 until March 1, 1967 (personal communication with Tom Ewing, 2003).

out.'" Rowan left Seatrain when he found that the band's constant touring was taking too heavy a toll on his songwriting.

Rowan returned to California and again teamed with Richard Greene. Together with Bill Keith, David Grisman and guitarist Clarence White, they formed Muleskinner, a bluegrass band. The group produced one now out-of-print album (though soon to be re-released) that included some country and rock as well as straight bluegrass. At the same time Rowan and Grisman started another bluegrass band, Old and In the Way, with Vassar Clements on fiddle and Grateful Dead member Jerry Garcia on banjo. The group released a live album which included "Panama Red," "Midnight Moonlight" and "Land of the Navajo," three Rowan songs which also appear on his new album on Flying Fish. Although the group lasted only around a year, Rowan feels that he gained many of his current fans from the followers of Old and In the Way. After the group broke up, Rowan joined his brothers' rock band and stayed with it for about three years until the individual musical interests of the siblings diverged.

Since leaving his brothers' band in 1977, Rowan has not played in a group with drums. He has toured Japan with Richard Greene and the nucleus of the old Breakfast Special bluegrass band, played clubs with Greene and New Jersey–based fiddler Tex Logan and appeared at bluegrass festivals with a band known as Peter Rowan and the Green Grass Gringos. Rowan sees bluegrass not as "a folkie tradition," but "as a modern music as viable as rock and roll or anything else. I always did, except being young you have these other things in your viewpoint." He believes that young musicians should approach bluegrass as music and not just as tradition. "If you try and just play it as bluegrass, it's kind of stilted. If you can play an instrument medium-well and pick with other people, that's the joy of bluegrass as the people's music it is today . . . like it's, wow, pass the instrument around. It's opened way, way up in the last ten years. I find it easy to relate to a bluegrass audience; they seem to understand what I'm trying to do."

What Rowan is trying to do is to convey "expressions of the heart and of the mystical inner soul of America . . . in its historical sense." He now finds that "super-competitive loud brash rock and roll" is not "particularly applicable to the way people need to have things expressed from their heart. To me rock and roll and super-commercial music is all a gigantic advertising blitz-hype. People will accept it as saying how they feel only because there's nothing else, they never get to hear anything else."

Rowan, along with veteran bluegrass fiddler Tex Logan and the amazing banjo-picking of Lamar Grier, combined with Barry Mitterhoff on the mandolin and Roger Mason on bass, have played this past season to standing ovations. They have constantly whipped the crowds into a frenzy at what many consider the high point of the summer festivals. "The atmosphere of a festival is great for music," he says of the outdoor scene. "It's more healthy for you and it just makes you feel good."

"Oh, that gave me chills," promoter Rod Kennedy of the Kerrville, Texas, festivals said later, in what has to be the single best description of a Rowan performance.

"That single moment when they did 'Land of the Navajo' was the best of all, and that whole first set just touched every emotion I ever thought I had. It was incredible."

Rowan hopes to express the tenderness of life in a musical form usually known for its flashy instrumentation at breakneck speed. He has explored his musical roots and searched for America. As an artist, Rowan is back and ready to complete his task and offer a new vision in bluegrass.

Originally published in *Bluegrass Unlimited* 13 (Feb. 1979): 12–13. Reprinted by permission of the author and *Bluegrass Unlimited*.

The most obscure acts and weirdly eccentric records can create the biggest excitement among record collectors and bluegrass scholars. Calling on all his own real-life stock of lore, Charles Wolfe got into the spirit of collecting with his fanciful, in-joke-driven survey of a group of acts that would have made bluegrass a richer place—had they actually existed.

48

"The Early Days of Bluegrass, Vol. 117 (Fiction)"

CHARLES WOLFE

Liner notes: With this final volume, Wonder Wecords brings to a close its series documenting the early days of bluegrass. In this album, we document what might be called "peripheral" influences on the development of bluegrass: rare small-label issues, significant old-time string band sides, and material by artists who are not as well known as they deserve to be. Notes on the individual tunes and performers follow.

Sleen Toddle and His Small Mouth Bass. "Sawmill Stomp" (Champion 16989)

For all its poor acoustical quality, this rare side is a fine example of the passion and raw power many bands put into their numbers. The lyrics derive from the old cliché about a man tied down in front of an advancing buzz saw while his rescuers race against time. The kazoo player sounds remarkably like a buzz saw, so much so that some scholars think the side was recorded on location in a sawmill. One must admit that the screams at the end are most convincing.

Ada Haddis and Smokey Brown. "What Will I Do if My Jesus Don't Come?" (Fentress 28)

Ada Haddis and Smokey Brown, a fiddle and guitar team, were for many years a star attraction on the Murrel Tent Show Circuit. The team is remarkable in the respect that at least one of its members was a bear, though stories conflict as to which member it was. One musician who worked with them, ninety-five-year-old Clive Fumml, has said, "The bear was Brown," but this may have simply meant, "the bear was brown." (See R. Rinzlurp, "The Bear Facts of Haddis-Brown," *Journal of Ethnomusicology*, XVII, June 1969, pp. 118–190.) Unless the bear could yodel (and few bears could in the 1920's), he presumably sings bass on this selection. Whoever is who, their message is driven home with a graphic immediacy on this romping old gospel tune.

The Big Mouth Sacred Singers. "No Potholes in Heaven" (Backhoe 5440–B)

This was apparently a family group headed by a self-styled preacher named Tyler Tyree, who was the founder of a sect called the Church of the Speckled Bird, which venerated wrens. They were fond of singing out of round-note songbooks in shape-note style, giving their music a striking diatonic effect. Their special significance to bluegrass stems from the fact that they moved to Rosine, Kentucky, in 1929; a few short weeks later young Bill Monroe left Rosine. So did several other people.

Medwick's Incredible Sheep. "Pretty Little Thing of Mine" (Bubbletone 209)

This is the only known copy of this unusual Bubbletone issue. The sheep seem horribly out of tune with each other, and only the unique guitar style of Shep Medwick (he reportedly licked the strings with his tongue) saves this from being just another sheep record. Medwick, a Mississippi shepherd, reported in an interview that he fed the sheep nothing but bluegrass.

Mother Furalee McLellan Fossbank. "Terrible and Tremblin'" (Ork 2356)

Mother Fossbank, from Taney County, Missouri, apparently sings an old hymn, though the imagery gets a little confusing in the last three stanzas. For instance, does "he" in stanza 3 refer to god (stanza 1), or the great white bullfrog (stanza 2)? The cracks you hear on this 1929 recording are not defects in the original master; some scholars feel that Mother Fossbank had the hiccups during this session; in other recordings she giggles a lot.

Carson's Lodge Band. "Down on Gaitor Creek" (Gennett mx. 167945)

This 1931 recording shows what happens when three strong-willed old-time fiddlers get together for a good old breakdown. There's a lot of excitement here, but there might have been even more had the three chosen to play in a common key. This is an unissued Gennett test pressing probably unissued because the tune breaks up toward the end, and several oaths are heard amidst scuffling sounds.

Lepingwell Freeze and His Briscoe Bird Pushers. "Bird Pushers Breakdown" (Police 10–4–A, recorded in 1933)

Here is the legendary Texas fiddler who supposedly invented the long bow style back on 1926, when he had to use his bow to fend off buzzards who kept trying to attack him during a fiddling contest at Briscoe, Texas. (Hence the name "Bird Pushers" for his band.) Lepingwell's career has been documented in *The Devil's Box*. The rare label "Lep" recorded on, Police, was a regional label started by a Tyler County sheriff; it was not successful. According to Freeze, people would go into a record store, ask the salesman if he had a police record, and the salesman would invariably reply, "No sir, I'm clean and honest." The records did poorly, and are collector's items today.

The Bluegrass Nuns. "Yellow Road to Camptown" (Merton 102–A, recorded ca. 1949)

The Bluegrass Nuns were three or four sisters from an obscure Carmelite order in south central Kentucky who entertained in various orphans homes from 1948 to about 1952. Little is known about them except that they used an unusual three-stringed banjo, and they often sang part of their songs in Latin. They are one of the first real sister acts in bluegrass. In 1975 bluegrass scholar Boggs Hickey disguised himself as a nun and went around the area trying to learn more about this band, but he was arrested in Corbin.

Blind Oscar Thornton. "She Poisoned Me Boys" (Vocalion 5890)

This is Blind Thornton's last recorded number, thought by some scholars to be autobiographical.

Cyrus Leech's Creole Jazz Band. "Yack Yack Burboun" (Thumper 256–B-a)

This is a rare alternate take of a regional jazz band. It is included here because at the end of the take you can hear a series of coughs. This is none other than Hector Stovepipe, who had wandered into the studio looking for a bathroom; it is the only known recording of his famous cough.

Doc Stanley. "Corn Cob Blues"
(Harry Ace 345–A, recorded 1947)

This is Doc Stanley's famous complaint about how rough dried corn cobs are; some scholars think Doc was trying to comb his hair with them, and there is speculation that this custom might have once been quite common in West Virginia. Others see this song as related to Woody Guthrie's "Hard, Ain't It Hard."

The Rudd Family with Kaw Hendricks.
"Courtship and Crowbait"(Bluebird 3498–A)

This is the Rudd Family's only record about crows, and offers interesting insights into how the hill people of Kentucky felt about crows in 1934. Kaw Hendricks was noted throughout the South for his crow imitations; he was shot by a confused farmer in 1941.

Originally published in *Bluegrass Unlimited* 13 (Dec. 1978): 20–21. Reprinted by permission of the author and *Bluegrass Unlimited*.

E arl Scruggs and Bill Monroe did it. Louis Armstrong and Charlie Parker did it. And so did Jerry Douglas. Only a few times in American musical history has a player significantly revised the accepted notion of the way a specific instrument works in music. There were undeniably great players of the Dobro, or resonator guitar, before Jerry Douglas came along. And during his long apprenticeship in bluegrass, Douglas learned from Josh Graves and myriad others. But the mix of impossible virtuosity and lyrical soul that Douglas brought to his instrument set an entirely new standard for what Graves used to call the "hound dog" guitar. In this 1998 article, Raleigh *News and Observer* contributor Jack Bernhardt set out Douglas's challenge: How does even a star picker establish his own identity in a musical landscape dominated by vocal artists?

49

"An Instrumentalist with a Name"

JACK BERNHARDT

It's noon on Thursday and Jerry Douglas is hanging out—hiding out, actually—in his Louisville, Ky., hotel room, trying to steal a few precious moments of solitude.

Douglas has been attending the International Bluegrass Music Association's annual trade show since Monday, attending board meetings, conducting seminars and playing showcases, socializing and talking business with veterans and young hopefuls looking for ways to get the six-time Grammy winner involved in their careers. Now, he's trying to get some rest before the night's awards show, when he'll learn if he's been voted Dobro Player of the Year for a record seventh time.

With more than a thousand album credits as player and producer, Douglas is one of the architects of contemporary bluegrass and country music. But as an artist he's always been a pioneer, choosing to push the boundaries of his instrument into unexplored territory.

While the Dobro, or resophonic guitar, is his primary instrument, Douglas considers himself to be a musician who just happens to play the Dobro.

"I've made a lot of choices, a lot of decisions, and looking back on them I think they were all the right ones," says Douglas, who performs at Durham's Carolina Theater on the 7th as part of a tour to support his current album, *Restless on the Farm* (Sugar Hill). (Douglas' band will include Tim O'Brien, Russ Barenberg and Maura O'Connell; bluegrass legends Josh Graves and Kenny Baker are also on the bill.)

Looking back on his various associations, he says: "It's taken me some pretty crazy places. Last year I played on a record for [jazz guitarist] Bill Frisell, and it won *Down Beat's* jazz album of the year. So just being an instrumentalist, it doesn't really matter what kind of music you play. If you have the ability to adapt to different situations, you can go a few places."

Douglas, forty-two, was born and raised in Warren, Ohio. His father was a steel-worker who also played in a bluegrass band. By age five, Jerry was playing mandolin. When he was eleven, he switched to Dobro after attending a concert where he saw Josh Graves, the legendary picker who had popularized the instrument in the 1950s as a member of Flatt and Scruggs and the Foggy Mountain Boys.

While still in high school, Douglas began his professional career, traveling to summer festivals with the Country Gentlemen. By the age of nineteen, he was playing with J. D. Crowe and the New South in a band that also included Ricky Skaggs and Tony Rice. In '76, he and Skaggs left Crowe and formed the influential band Boone Creek, and three years later he joined Buck White and the Down Home Folks.

Douglas also worked in Nashville's recording studios as a session player, contributing to projects by Skaggs, Emmylou Harris, Johnny Cash, Ray Charles and others. His own albums include *Under the Wire* (MCA) and *Yonder,* with Peter Rowan (Sugar Hill). And he's recorded as a member of the supergroup Strength in Numbers, which also features mandolinist Sam Bush, fiddler Mark O'Connor, banjoist Bela Fleck and bassist Edgar Meyer.

Douglas' musical wanderlust has taken him in new directions and has given him the opportunity to advance his instrument beyond its traditional role. It's also led to friendships with other trendsetters who have established themselves as a community of artists who support and push each other in creative directions.

"I think living in Nashville and doing lots of sessions trained me to adapt to different situations," Douglas says. "I met a lot of interesting people and that led me to different kinds of music. Hanging out with Bela Fleck and Sam Bush, Edgar Meyer, Mark O'Connor—we all went in different directions, and we all pulled each other this way and that."

These are the artists who, through their innovative work as session musicians in Nashville recording studios and their own adventuresome solo careers, have redefined country music in the last couple of decades.

"It's sort of like, 'What could we have done in our lives that would have made us any happier, that we could have gotten more joy from?' We're just really lucky, and if we talk about it too much, we may jinx it.

"And part of it is the instrument I play. It's sort of a real vocal instrument—it has a vocal quality. People think of it as a country instrument, but it's a slide guitar, really, so it's pretty boundless. And that's helped me go a lot of places."

The IBMA trade show is a place where the past, present and future of bluegrass music meet. As an artist and producer who has contributed to changing the definition of bluegrass, Douglas is acutely aware of trends.

So, what does he think will happen to the music of Bill Monroe as it moves into the new millennium?

"I see music as a whole as becoming more entwined," he says. "And from that will come new music. From watching the festivals like Telluride and MerleFest—those big gathering places of musicians and fans—they're all bringing their different ideas and they all survive in one little space for a weekend. They all entertain each other, and they all appreciate each other.

"I think it's going to come down to a time when radio is not so powerful—formatted radio. I think that's going to change, and I think that's going to be for the better, where everybody's more open. I think that's one thing that's going to change in the new millennium.

"And if you walk the halls of IBMA you see whole bands of kids. It's pretty cool to walk up on a jam session and it's all ten-year-old kids. It's changing all the time. It's just about giving kids a chance and not letting our record labels get stale."

As for his future, Douglas plans to continue pushing the boundaries of his music while helping others define the quality of theirs. Since May, he's toured as a member of Alison Krauss' band, Union Station. When his *Restless on the Farm* tour ends at the end of November, he will don his producer's hat and guide albums by the Del McCoury Band, Krauss and Jesse Winchester.

Douglas enjoys staying busy, but he worries that his fans may lose track of his primary identity as an artist. That, he says, is a primary reason for this tour.

"I would like to be known as someone like Ry Cooder or David Lindley—an instrumentalist with a name. That's what I'm after, for people to know who I am and what I do, and maybe give it more of a direction. This tour is a main thrust for me—to get out and be at the front of it, to play that band. That's what this tour's all about."

And about the IBMA awards? Douglas missed out on his seventh straight Dobro Player of the Year honor. It went to Blue Highway's Rob Ickes, a young picker who was inspired by the example set by Douglas for more than two decades.

Originally published in the *News and Observer* (Raleigh, N.C.), Oct. 30, 1998, 16. Reprinted by permission of the author.

North Carolinian Jack Bernhardt has for more than a decade chronicled country, bluegrass, and old-time music for the *News and Observer,* Raleigh's morning daily. His expertise and affection for the music come through in this brief example of what people in the newspaper trade would call an "advance." A worthwhile act is coming to town, the reporter either knows about them or studies up, perhaps does a short interview, and spreads the news. In about fifteen column inches, Bernhardt places the Nashville Bluegrass Band in the great sweep of bluegrass history, offers some background on the band and some of their famous collaborators, and relates a few thoughtful quotes from front man Alan O'Bryant. Readers who already knew about the band—or who were intrigued by his account—could turn out for the band's show at a local nightclub. As of this writing, Roland White is concentrating on a solo career and has been replaced by another sterling mandolinist and original NBB member, Mike Compton. Ace bassist and session player Dennis Crouch had replaced Gene Libbea by 2003.

50

"Country Preview: From Roots to Wings— The Nashville Bluegrass Band's Deference to Tradition Allows Its Music to Soar"

JACK BERNHARDT

Since the late Bill Monroe assembled his classic quintet in 1945, bluegrass music has changed with the times.

The '50s brought diversification as the popularity of bluegrass spread throughout the country. In the '70s, bands such as New Grass Revival combined tradition with rock 'n' roll. And the '80s and '90s have brought elaboration, as artists such as the Nashville Bluegrass Band have taken Monroe's brilliant vision to a new level of perfection. On the 10th, they'll bring their award-winning music to Carrboro for a show at the Cat's Cradle.

Formed in 1984, NBB has remained one of the most consistently excellent bands on the circuit. They've won two Grammy Awards, been named the International Bluegrass Music Association's top vocal group from 1990 to '93, and entertainer of the year in '92 and '93. With a keen ear for great songs, a vocal style that leans heavily on the blues and instrumental talents at the top of their field, NBB is a band that pleases in all dimensions.

Collectively, the band members possess a wealth of experience, having played with some of the most definitive artists in bluegrass. Before joining NBB, guitarist and vocalist Pat Enright, a dynamic tenor with a passion for the blues, played with California's Phantoms of the Opry and the progressive Dreadful Snakes.

Fiddler Stuart Duncan has been an A-list session player, lending his tasteful fiddle to recordings by John Prine, Nanci Griffith, Dolly Parton, Ricky Skaggs and others. Mandolin player Roland White has spent time with Bill Monroe and with Lester Flatt, and co-founded the legendary Kentucky Colonels with his brother, the late Clarence White.

Gene Libbea's credits include playing bass with Byron Berline and Vince Gill. And banjoist/vocalist Alan O'Bryant, a native of Reidsville, has played with Monroe and Doc Watson.

One quality that sets NBB apart from other bluegrass acts is impeccable choice of material. To fit its personality, the band finds songs from some of the best writers in and beyond Nashville. For example, the band's current CD, *American Beauty,* includes selections from Gillian Welch ("Red Clay Halo"), Flatt and Scruggs ("The Johnson Boys") and Triangle-area songwriter Carl Jones ("Homeless Waltz" and "Just Like a Fiddle").

The Nashville Bluegrass Band also has earned a well-deserved reputation for their arrangements of gospel music. They draw from both Anglo- and African-American traditions, often working the songs into finely crafted a cappella renditions of such gospel standards as "Up above My Head / Blind Bartemus," and "Roll Jordan, Roll."

By combining elements from the past with a contemporary interpretation of the music that Bill Monroe devised, NBB remains rooted in tradition while advancing the music beyond its earlier limits.

"Bluegrass is considered by many these days to be a 'roots' music, a big component of country music," said O'Bryant. "The interesting thing about these traditions of gospel music is that that are really a root of bluegrass.

"We're not trying to re-create music of the '40s or '50s. But I believe the only way to create a new and original music is to go back to the elements it was created from."

Originally published in the *News and Observer* (Raleigh, N.C.), April 2, 1999, 16. Reprinted by permission of the author.

When I was hired as a music reporter by the *Nashville Tennessean* in 1985, I jumped at the chance to interview and write about Bill Monroe, Jim and Jesse, the Osbornes, and a host of bluegrass acts on the Opry and elsewhere. As is the case with most daily music journalists, I was covering bluegrass along with mainstream country, pop, jazz, blues, and whatever else came along. Because Owensboro was just up the road, I got approval from the newspaper to cover the Fan Fest and trade show put on there in 1987 by the International Bluegrass Music Association. The organization and event have grown along with the music, but the atmosphere that year was of a down-home get-together coupled with an increasing professionalism. The IBMA event also provided an important early performance by the teenaged Alison Krauss. I can't take too much credit for predicting a bright future for Krauss in this piece; virtually everyone in bluegrass was saying the same thing.

51

"IBMA's World of Bluegrass"

THOMAS GOLDSMITH

Even the setting was perfect—the Banks of the Ohio in the Bluegrass State.

During the last week of September, the International Bluegrass Music Association put on a celebration in Owensboro, Kentucky, that had something for just about everyone who loves bluegrass—or who makes a living from it.

IBMA's World of Bluegrass trade show, which got its start in 1986 under a tent in Peter B. English Park in Owensboro, moved to the Executive Inn Rivermont for its first full-scale edition. More than two hundred businesses were represented at the trade show, which was coupled with a series of Fan Fest concerts at the nearby riverfront park.

"It went wonderfully—I don't know any other way to say it," was the assessment of Nashville agent-manager Keith Case, a member of IBMA's board and one of the main craftsmen who produced the event.

"For a first-year event I think the representation was incredible."

Taken as a whole, the trade show/concert series represented both the music-obsessed tradition and the business-oriented leanings of bluegrass. About 150 musicians registered both to attend trade show events and perform free at the Fan Fest, which benefited the IBMA trust fund for bluegrass professionals' emergencies. As at any convocation with more than thirty bands and lots of other musicians present, there was formal and informal music around the clock and time to greet old acquaintances and meet new ones.

If a new professionalism was in the air at the World of Bluegrass, the event was driven by the high-quality, exciting music heard at the outdoor festival including the Father of Bluegrass, Bill Monroe and the Blue Grass Boys, and at showcases in the Rivermont's classy Show Room Lounge. In the same venue where the hotel presents acts such as Willie Nelson and Dolly Parton, the finest in traditional and innovative bluegrass acts held forth.

Former Blue Grass Boy Peter Rowan, whose music features a variety of different styles on a traditional foundation, proclaimed his allegiance to bluegrass during an ecstatically received showcase with the Nashville Bluegrass Band.

"As you can see, we're not going to let it die and I know you're not," Rowan told the audience of musicians and professionals. "So let's keep it going together, what do you say?"

More than thirty acts performed at the hotel showcases. They were mostly top-grade, up-and-coming bands who benefited from exposure before the promoters and label heads present.

"The established acts that did showcase—like Hot Rize, the Country Gentlemen and Doyle (Lawson)—did it purely to show support and be part of the event," Case said.

Friday night's showcase was noted by many of those present as especially full of musical fire. Chicago's Special Consensus got things rolling with a triple-yodel version of the Sons of the Pioneers' "Way Out There." The Short Crick Flatpickers ranged from straight bluegrass to hard country.

A real highlight of the week's music was the appearance of sixteen-year-old fiddler-vocalist Alison Krauss with the Union Station band from Champaign, Illinois. Krauss' co-lead vocalist Dave Denman missed the show because of a family tragedy, but his place was ably filled on short notice by Hot Rize's multi-talented Tim O'Brien. Krauss' performance was simply astonishing—she's a very good, aggressive bluegrass fiddler and a strong, moving vocalist. The sky seems to be the limit for her.

The Nashville Bluegrass Band continued their rise to recognition as a top-line festival and recording attraction with their sizzling performance at Friday night's showcase. Their combination of classy picking, bluesy bluegrass singing, black gospel harmony and unaffected showmanship won them top marks with the promoters and others present.

In his gesture of IBMA solidarity, Charlie Waller showcased the latest edition of the Country Gentlemen. They obliged with some new tunes as well as perennials such as "Matterhorn" and "The Rebel Soldier."

The evening concluded with Rowan's performance. He came out first with Dobro king Jerry Douglas for a taste of the Crucial Country band gigs the two have played in Nashville with acoustic stars Roy Huskey and Mark O'Connor. Then the Nashville Bluegrass Band returned.

With Douglas still onstage, the all-star assemblage rocked through a satisfyingly long set of Rowan tunes and straight bluegrass that cracked with energy and excitement. The Rowan-NBB combination has been in the studio recording for an album project for a label yet to be selected, so fans should have a chance to hear this music sometime in 1988.

If all the great music heard at IBMA '87 is to reach wider audiences, the bluegrass industry will have to seek new means of adding to the music's faithful core audience. There was recognition of that in the real-world, professional atmosphere surrounding the trade show's many opportunities to exchange information. Perhaps IBMA executive director Art Menius wasn't exaggerating so wildly after all when he predicted the event would be "the most significant business event in the history of the bluegrass music industry."

"All the attendees were just blown away by the amount of energy and activity," Case, who represents artists such as Rowan and John Hartford, said after returning to Nashville.

On a meat-and-potatoes level, the trade show consisted of a series of professional seminars and an exhibit floor representing talent, publications, radio stations, sound reinforcement and other areas. Seminar topics included record labels and albums, contract negotiations and riders, band marketing, radio and records, festival planning, insurance for promoters, bluegrass associations and bluegrass radio.

"At the two meetings that really related directly to promoting, I had the most successful promoters in bluegrass coming out saying, 'My God I can't believe what I've learned,'" Case said.

A sampling of the several dozen exhibit-floor booths would include those of Martin Guitar, Gibson Guitar, South Plains College, Lee Olsen and Associates, Southard Audio, *Bluegrass Unlimited,* the *Grassometer,* Chestnut Mandolins and record companies including Sugar Hill, Rounder, Rebel, Flying Fish, and Turquoise.

The exhibit area, in the Executive Inn's basement, was a favorite hangout for pickers or industry people in between seminars or showcases. Norman Blake took a break from picking fiddle tunes on the newest products from Martin to record station IDs for a bluegrass radio station. Gibson's Nashville plant sent what looked like a pickup load of its new acoustic models. Picker-educators Alan Munde and Joe Carr touted the opportunities offered at South Plains College in Levelland, Texas, where both are faculty members.

"Levelland is the truth in advertising capital of America," Carr said about the table-flat country around the West Texas school.

Friday's magic several hours of music were preceded by a banquet and awards ceremony in which five pioneering souls were honored for "lifelong, significant and selfless contributions to bluegrass music." Washington-area radio announcer Don Owens was remembered posthumously for his unstinting efforts to promote bluegrass records over the air and his favored practice of "back-announcing," naming sidemen on a record after it was over.

County Gentlemen kingpin Waller was honored for his more than thirty years of picking and singing and his championing of legions of sidemen, about whom it was remarked that "some have gone on to great success and others have just gone."

"I'm not much for saying words unless they're in a song, but I appreciate it," Waller told the IBMA crowd.

Snuffy Jenkins got an IBMA certificate in absentia for his early three-finger banjo style and his decades of entertaining. Promoter Bill Jones got the organization's nod for taking bluegrass into uncharted territories. And musician-scholar-manager

Ralph Rinzler, whose award was accepted by singer-songwriter Hazel Dickens, was recognized for furthering Bill Monroe's career and myriad other services to bluegrass.

Terry Woodward, an IBMA board member and head of a local tourism commission, announced the association's move to permanent headquarters in Owensboro and the establishment of a committee to seek state funds for a bluegrass museum there.

Originally published in *Bluegrass Unlimited* 22 (Nov. 1987): 73–74. Reprinted by permission of the author and *Bluegrass Unlimited*.

Alison Krauss, born in 1971 in Decatur, Illinois, emerged in the second half of the 1980s as a defining bluegrass artist for a new generation. First making her mark at age twelve as a champion fiddler, she developed into an increasingly accomplished singer, recording artist, record producer, and leader of the band Union Station. In 1993 she was inducted into the Grand Ole Opry. In interviews, recordings, and performance, Krauss has made plain her affection for hard-core bluegrass acts such as J. D. Crowe and Mac Wiseman.

Her wide-ranging tastes, however, are also typical of a period in which MTV and niche radio brought all sorts of music within easy reach of American teenagers. Vintage jazz, heavy metal, urban dance music, and singer-songwriter sentimentality are all part of Krauss's musical vocabulary. Her high level of accomplishment and versatility have lent broad appeal to her acoustic-based sound. And her apparent willingness to voice almost any thought have made her an interviewer's delight, as revealed in this piece from the pop-world standard *Rolling Stone.*

52

"Country Artist of the Year: Alison Krauss"

JIM MACNIE

The route taken by bluegrass over the years has been straight and narrow, just like the path Alison Krauss followed at the Country Music Association Awards last October while strolling to the podium to pick up one, two, three—why stop now?— four different honors. But the twenty-four-year-old leader of Union Station earned her prizes by adding a pop-rock twist to her versions of traditional standards. Her last album, *Now That I've Found You: A Collection,* is made up of songs culled from Krauss' previous records for the Rounder label as well as bluegrass-style covers of tunes by Bad Company and the Beatles. The album has gone platinum, and it has made a whole new audience familiar with bluegrass, putting Krauss and her band in the mainstream spotlight.

You and your brother Viktor—a member of Lyle Lovett's band—have made home recordings of heavy-metal tunes for kicks in the past. Have you done any new ones lately?

"Well, Viktor got me an amplifier for my birthday, and Gary Paczosa, our engineer, got me a Danelectro guitar, so my brother and I sit around and play AC/DC songs in the living room with the amps turned up as loud as they will go. We walk outside with the guitars and play 'Highway to Hell.' It's pretty fun, except Vik's good and I suck."

Are there now audience members who show up at shows because of your hit "When You Say Nothing at All" and are turned on by the more orthodox bluegrass stuff?

"I notice that there are more people, but I don't really notice that anyone is waiting for something—which is great, because we feared that. We feel that the other stuff we do is just as important as the newer songs."

Are the songs from your current studio sessions closer to the modern sound of "Now That I've Found You"?

"I think so, but they're more far-out songs. I feel like we've grown into what we're going to sound like."

You and your band have changed some perceptions about what bluegrass can be and what country is.

"I think whatever we have slipped by somebody is great. [Laughs.] If they call it country, that's cool."

Have you warmed up to making videos?

"If I had a stomach like Shania Twain, I might be a little more confident."

You've said that in the past you felt like a child singing adult songs, and it's only been recently that you could accurately convey the emotions in songs like "Baby, Now That I've Found You."

"Well, I still don't feel that I'm quite there yet. I listened to Merle Haggard last night. Talk about a mash."

A mash?

"Yeah, he mashed me down. Unbelievable. I tell you, I can't believe anybody is like that. When I was listening to that, I just about crapped myself. It's incredible."

Because your voice is so clean, people can't believe you smoke cigarettes.

"I used to do it because everybody would get so mad. Me and my friend used to say, 'Man, it's so gross when women smoke—let's smoke.' So we'd smoke and play the fiddle outside. We'd get the tape recorder out and say (puts on a thick Southern accent), 'Here's a song about my old boyfriend. This is one called "He Smelled Bad."' We'd just be nasty. There's a tape somewhere—I need to find it. I hear that stuff about which band members smoke cigarettes is on the Internet. I don't do it much, and I sure don't recommend smoking to anyone."

Which bluegrass records would you nudge a beginner toward?

"J. D. Crowe and the New South, on Rounder, the first one. Ralph Stanley's Clinch Mountain Gospel, on Rebel. Oh, boy, I don't know what else."

You're producing your friends the Cox Family. Are you getting happier with arranging and producing?

"Well, I like what we come up with. There was an article—I forget which magazine—that said my arrangements sound like hymns. I think the writer was slamming us, but I don't take it as a slam."

Do you remember the fiddle contests you used to play in?

"Yeah, I had a really good time. If I hadn't entered contests, I probably wouldn't have wanted to play. That's what kept me going. It's a place to try to perfect what you do. I learned a lot by listening to the records and learning what the fiddle players did. You use that every day."

Your singing has been stressed over the fiddling of late.

"Well, I don't think I'm progressing so much fiddlewise. It's slack sometimes. I've played on recording sessions where I've had to stretch out; it made me think, 'Oh, I don't suck as bad as I thought—that's nice.' But the band has so many other things to do that we don't sit around and pick a lot any more. And that will make you come to a halt pretty quick."

I heard the guys in the band still make fun of your voice.

"Want to hear 'em? Hey guys, it's *Rolling Stone,* and they want to know if you make fun of my voice."

A chorus of Alvin and the Chipmunks voices erupts.

What's with the scandal-sheet reports of you being entwined with Lyle Lovett?

"I think it's funny. I mean, where did that come from? My friends and I started in with the stupid stuff like 'We make out one time, and look what they turn it into.' So it was funny. But what was even funnier was they said I was helping him get over his broken heart. Like, yeah, sure, he forgot all about Julia Roberts when he and I were hanging out. Right."

Has there been a day yet when you've felt like chucking your newfound popularity in the trash can?

"Well, you don't notice it that much when you're in the middle of it. Nothing has really changed with us—we're on the road so much, we don't notice a difference. But I feel that I should probably shower before I go out of the house now. A shower would be a good idea."

As Alison Krauss and a few other bluegrass-rooted musicians emerged as popular favorites outside the music's traditional mainstream, their music more frequently became subject to high-minded criticism in publications such as the *New York Times.* Showing familiarity with Krauss's career as well as a broad range of other styles, *NYT* reviewer Ben Ratliff placed her band's Town Hall performance in a broad context of American music. Where else would Krauss have been called a "Godzilla of pop"? This and other "outside" looks at bluegrass surely helped its rise to unprecedented levels of popularity near the turn of the millennium.

53

"Focusing on the Music, Not on Those Playing It"

BEN RATLIFF

The bluegrass singer and fiddler Alison Krauss, and her band, Union Station, have sold millions of records and still aren't cool. None of the band members project much of an onstage persona other than affability; they're not the sort of glib technical wizards who appeal to string-instrument gear-heads, and they don't show discomfort with the conventions of bluegrass by playing it like giddy scholars or specter-haunted old-timers.

Instead, as they demonstrated at Town Hall on Tuesday night, they turn their attention to one another and achieve something as close to perfection as can be found in popular music: a fully integrated sound in which the musicians, fully at ease, melt their projections together so that it's hard to tell who's playing what. A perfectly calibrated ensemble mix rises from their hands and mouths. Ms. Krauss, who has been touring for twelve years and still isn't thirty, has gradually turned to pop ballads; she leans toward songs from the 1960's or '70's that aren't in the forefront of anyone's consciousness, and rearranges them to the strengths of the band. The Town Hall set included old songs by Todd Rundgren and Michael McDonald, and in her restorations they have become perfect mainstream pop songs, the kind that aren't limited by an artist's race or genre. It's easy to imagine those songs and other material from her latest album, *Forget about It* (Rounder), sung by Whitney Houston. (Or by Garth Brooks: his and Ms. Krauss's new album include versions of the song "Maybe," written by Gordon Kennedy and Phil Madeira.)

Her alarmingly pretty spring-water soprano, controlled and insinuating, makes her a Godzilla of pop. But her concerts defy the logic of pop performance because she's unfailingly modest onstage. She talks softly and sings softly—at least at the beginning of songs—and whenever she shifted from talking to singing a song it felt like a surprisingly seamless segue.

The core quartet of Union Station—Ms. Krauss, the guitarist Dan Tyminski, the banjoist Ron Block, and the bassist Barry Bales—has added the dobro player Jerry Douglas for its current tour, and for the more pop material, the drummer Larry Atamanuik. On Tuesday night, Mr. Atamanuik kept his playing to a minimum, with often nothing but a shaker in his right hand and a brush for the snare drum in his left hand; Mr. Douglas stayed deep within his own style, making the instrument sound like a sighing human voice when he plays melodies. His individuality is a blessing and a curse; his is the sound of the American radio format, so patented that it's difficult for him to blend in anymore.

But the core band musicians limited their solos and sang with careful microphone technique, backing away slightly when their voices rose. They interspersed pop songs with traditional bluegrass—the murder ballad "Wild Bill Jones," Don Rich's instrumental "Pike Country Breakdown"—and each musician slid into his improvisation gracefully, gathering steam and then letting go.[1]

Originally published in *The New York Times*, Nov. 19, 1999, B30. Copyright © by *The New York Times*. Reprinted by permission.

As bluegrass marched into the mainstream in the later 1990s, coverage of the genre increasingly appeared in daily newspapers. Robert Oermann, a high-profile music journalist and mainstay of the *Nashville Tennessean*'s entertainment coverage during the 1980s and 1990s, had left the staff and was contributing as a free-lancer when he wrote this article. (Full disclosure: Oermann and I were partners in the *Tennessean*'s popular music coverage from 1985 until 1992).

Oermann's perspective on female performers was especially acute; he and wife Mary Bufwack are the authors of *Finding Her Voice: The Saga of Women in Country Music*. In Dale Ann Bradley, Oermann profiled a performer whose evocative voice and interesting song choice would have made her a mainstream country standout in a more rational music industry. In fewer than five hundred words, the writer put Bradley in historical and contemporary perspective, offered a brief bio, and gave readers an idea of the sound of her music.

54

"It's All in the Emotion: Dale Ann Bradley Is 'Real Deal' Bluegrass"

ROBERT K. OERMANN

Dale Ann Bradley has graduated from the all-female string band The New Coon Creek Girls at Kentucky's Renfro Valley Barn Dance to solo success.

The singer plays Friday at the durable country music barn dance show. Her debut album, *East Kentucky Morning*, was produced by a veteran of another: Sonny Osborne of the Grand Ole Opry.

1. "Pike County Breakdown" was composed by Bill Monroe and recorded by Monroe, Flatt and Scruggs, and many others.

"Sonny knows how to capture the moment" Bradley says with admiration for the legendary Osborne Brothers banjo player. "I'm awfully happy to be associated with him."

Osborne, in turn, calls her "the real deal . . . one of the best singers this style of music has ever produced."

East Kentucky Morning was named one of the ten best albums of 1997 by one of *Billboard* magazine's editors and ascended to No. 6 on the Gavin Americana chart. It joins a growing group of albums by women that are reinvigorating the bluegrass field. Alison Krauss, Laurie Lewis, Claire Lynch and others have invaded a style that was almost exclusively male twenty years ago.

"I think bluegrass music is so emotion-filled, more than any other music," Bradley says. "And as it has become more popular, it has captured women's attention. That's what reaches out and touches women: emotion."

Dale Ann Bradley has a classic background for the style. Born in 1964 near the Cumberland Gap, she is a child of the Kentucky coal fields.

"Daddy was a coal miner and a hardshell Baptist minister. We weren't allowed to have any musical instruments in the church. I had to be really persistent until he came around and got me a guitar when I was fourteen. I can't remember not wanting to sing."

By age five she was onstage; by her teens she was winning local talent contests. Bradley put music aside when she married in 1985 and had a son. The young family moved to Jacksonville, Fla., but the marriage faltered. Bradley went back home to the mountains.

In 1989 she auditioned for the cast of the Renfro Valley Barn Dance, a show that has been staged south of Lexington since the late 1930's.

In 1992 she joined its all-female bluegrass group, The New Coon Creek Girls, and began recording. With Bradley as lead singer, the band has recorded three albums in Nashville. Last year, the all-female moniker was dropped. Now billed as Dale Ann Bradley and Coon Creek, they're performing more than a hundred shows a year.

East Kentucky Morning includes six songs written by Bradley and Coon Creek founder Vicki Simmons, as well as contributions from such Music Row notables as Dave Olney, Larry Cordle, Billy Smith, Irene Kelly and Dallas Frazier. There's also a bluegrass treatment of U2's rock hit "I Still Haven't Found What I'm Looking For."

Originally published in *The Tennessean* (Nashville), Jan. 23, 1998, F4. Reprinted by permission of the author.

Robert Oermann and Mary Bufwack filled a major void in country music journalism with their intensively researched, broadly conceived 1993 volume *Finding Her Voice.* Using their extensive backgrounds in both music and sociology, the pair—they are married—drew all sorts of fascinating connections between women's historical condition and the music they have made. Oermann is perhaps Nashville's highest-profile music journalist, his scholar's love of history and lore augmented by a keen sense of popular taste.

In addition to her work in journalism. Bufwack is director of Nashville's United Neighborhood Health Services. As of this writing, *Finding Her Voice* is set for updating and reissue. As the authors note in this excerpt, women in bluegrass hoed a tough row for the first several decades of the music—and still encounter noteworthy obstacles.

55

"'Little Darlin's Not My Name': Women in Bluegrass"

ROBERT OERMANN AND MARY BUFWACK

In 1989 Tanya Tucker scored a major hit by reviving the 1928 Jimmie Rodgers classic "Daddy and Home," one of several old-time music revivals that occurred in mainstream country music as a result of the outlaw, folk revival, and country-rock movements. Like Tanya, many country music women who came of age during the late 1970s were interested in stripping country of its showy, choreographed excesses and reconnecting it with its roots. So in addition to giving The Nashville Sound a country-rock kick, female performers of the day dug into its history and heritage. Linda Ronstadt had a Top 10 hit in 1978 with the Appalachian chestnut "I Never Will Marry." Dolly Parton did "Mule Skinner Blues" (1970), and Crystal Gayle recorded "Miss the Mississippi" (1979), both Jimmie Rodgers numbers.

The role model was Emmylou Harris, whose repertoire included The Carter Family's "Hello Stranger," The Louvin Brothers' "If I Could Only Win Your Love," and entire albums devoted to old-time gospel and bluegrass. Emmy's explorations of antique country sounds were an outgrowth of a widespread old-time music revival movement spurred by the folk revival.

A striking number of old-time revival bands of the 1970s showcased female singers and musicians. Even more revolutionary was women's full-scale invasion of the closely related bluegrass world. Created in the mid-1940s by adding hot-picking, hard-edged singing and overdrive tempo to the string band tradition, bluegrass music remained an almost completely male domain during its first twenty-five years. Its emphasis on instrumental flash, aggressive vocals, and conservative social structure made it the most male-defined of all country's styles. But as in so many other aspects of American life, that began to change in the seventies. Suddenly, as if from nowhere, there were women fiddlers, singers, banjo-pickers, guitarists, and bandleaders at bluegrass festivals, on bluegrass albums, and in bluegrass clubs.

Bluegrass men responded to the invasion by shouting derisively at female pickers, making sexual overtures backstage, or snickering behind their backs. "She picks pretty good, for a girl" was a typical backhanded compliment. As women began participating in greater numbers, their presence became "a divisive topic of conversation among men," recalls folklorist Thomas A. Adler. "Many men resisted and continue to resist the very idea of women's participation in bluegrass. Some flatly assert that women can't pick bluegrass, can't sing bluegrass, and don't belong in bluegrass."

"It's a fact that bluegrass music has traditionally been a man's world," noted a *Bluegrass Unlimited* reviewer in 1979. "At one time, if women were found in bluegrass bands at all . . . it was in minor roles such as bass player, and they hardly ever sang."

Bluegrass music's earliest women were relatives of its male stars—Bill Monroe's daughter Melissa and girlfriend Bessie Lee Mauldin; Lester Flatt's wife, Gladys; Howdy Forrester's wife, Sally Ann. This heritage continued into the fifties and sixties with such talented wives as Carl Tipton's Sophie and Hubert Davis's Rubye working in their husbands' shadows. Family groups and male-female duet teams— often working in the bluegrass-gospel idiom—were the most common entry points for women. John and Margie Cook, Rex and Eleanor Parker, Bill and Mary Reid, and Benny and Vallie Cain became active in the late 1940s and persevered as teams into the 1970s. But although cast in a bluegrass setting, most of these women were closer to the parlor-song style of The Carter Family than to the hair-raising "high lonesome sound" of Bill Monroe.

A surge in popularity for bluegrass music occurred as a direct result of the folk festivals of the sixties. Country veteran Barbara Allen performed at what is regarded as the first bluegrass festival, in Luray, Virginia, in 1965.[1] Mother Maybelle Carter was another early participant, both at festivals and on a Flatt and Scruggs LP of 1961 called *Songs of the Famous Carter Family.* Roni Stoneman was among those recorded on the 1957 Folkways LP *American Banjo Scruggs Style,* which historian Neil V. Rosenberg cites as the first bluegrass album. Her sister Donna contributed mandolin to the 1962 LP *Rose Maddox Sings Bluegrass.* "Bluegrass has been almost exclusively man's music," said Ken Nelson in its liner notes. "Now, just as if to prove that it's a man's world only till a woman decides she wants some of it for herself, along comes the wonderful Rose Maddox with a bluegrass album." Cousin Emmy also became part of bluegrass history when The Osborne Brothers transformed her "Ruby" into a bluegrass standard in 1970.

Perhaps not surprisingly, several of the female bluegrass pioneers came from collegiate, folk revival backgrounds rather than from more repressive rural roots. Joan Baez performed and recorded with The Greenbriar Boys in the 1960s, collaborated often with Earl Scruggs, and promoted the music of the bluegrass world throughout her career. New York-born, Hollywood-raised Dian James recorded a bluegrass LP backed by the Greenbriars in 1963.

---

1. A one-day show in Luray on July 4, 1961, featured bluegrass, but the first bluegrass festival is generally considered the September 3–5, 1965, event in Fincastle, Virginia.

But for over-the-top performance passion in women's early days in bluegrass, you have to look to gospel. Mountain wailers such as Wilma Lee Cooper and Molly O'Day were the overwhelming influences, and their fervor was carried on by the seminal bluegrass-gospel act The Lewis Family. With its trio of lead-singing sisters, this gifted Georgia clan has epitomized bluegrass showmanship on the festival circuit for thirty years. In the wake of the spectacular Lewis Family came Alabama's two Sullivan Family acts, the first featuring the fervent, husky belting of Margie Sullivan, and the second starring the hard-driving style of her cousin Tammy Sullivan. Of Ohio's gospel-singing Marshall Family, *Bluegrass Unlimited* opined, "If you don't like the Marshalls' music you've got stone ears and a lead heart." The Marshalls began performing in 1967; guitarist/songwriter/vocalist Judy Marshall was the leader. Born in 1951, she was deeply influenced by the religious sincerity and musical skills of Kentucky gospel great Dottie Rambo.

Bluegrass families, usually singing gospel, were launchpads for women in the field. But as bluegrass instrumentalists, lead singers, and bandleaders, women were rare. Among the earliest to shine as pickers were the Stoneman women, who began performing in their father's Bluegrass Champs band around 1956.[2] Patsy, the oldest Stoneman daughter, led her own group in the Washington, D.C., area shortly afterward. Pennsylvania's Gloria Belle (Flickinger) was probably the first female lead singer in bluegrass. She was active as early as 1957. Gloria led her own Green Mountain Travelers, recorded solo LPs, and served a long stint as a singer and bass player with Jimmy Martin. "She's been taking Jimmy's on-stage insults since 1968," observed writer Bob Artis in 1974. "She breaks into a rousing song while Jimmy makes faces at her, holds his nose in a gesture of blunt criticism, and encourages the audience to boo, which it is too polite to do. Gloria Belle, like most women bluegrass singers, leans toward that belt-'em-out Molly O'Day style."

Lillimae was another Molly O'Day/Wilma Lee Cooper disciple. Born near Roundhead, Ohio, in 1940, Lillimae Haney was named after Lily May Ledford of the famed all-girl 1930s' string band The Coon Creek Girls. Her father played guitar in the Maybelle Carter style, and by the time Lillimae was eight, she and her sister Wilma Jean were performing gospel as The Haney Sisters, with him as their accompanist. Wilma Jean got married and quit the act, but Lillimae and her father pressed on with mandolinist Charles Whitaker, whom she married. The Whitakers formed their own group, first recording in 1959. As Lillimae and The Dixie Gospel-Aires, they recorded again in 1967 and 1968, and throughout the 1970s the group performed steadily. Scholars Ivan and Deanna Tribe got to know Lillimae in 1976 and came away with this impression: "She feels it is tough being a woman in bluegrass and would welcome more ready acceptance of women in the field."

North Carolina–bred Betty Fisher would echo that sentiment. Betty became the third major female bluegrass bandleader of the early seventies. "I'm not after es-

---

2. Fiddler Scott Stoneman started the Bluegrass Champs, although Pop Stoneman later appeared with the group.

tablishing records like being the only women performer on a certain show or being one of the few women in bluegrass music to front a band," Betty told writer Don Rhodes. "But I do feel a part of history. I feel like I'm helping to start a movement of women in bluegrass music." Although never a spectacular singer, Betty took a back seat to no man as a guitarist, songwriter, and bandleader. "I feel a responsibility. I feel people are looking at me, and I have to set high standards for myself. . . . There were not many women in country music a few years ago, but now there are a lot. I believe bluegrass music is going to be the same way. And if women love the music and want to perform it, I'm going to help them all I can.

"The audiences generally have over 50 percent women," said Betty, "and I think they like to see another woman on the stage. I have as many women fans as men. We talk about soap operas and swap recipes. The reason I think there are not many women in bluegrass . . . is because the men [in bluegrass] tend to be more old-line in their thinking about the role of women. . . . Men in bluegrass music feel differently about women, partly because so many of them come from the sticks and were raised in a traditional way and on old-fashioned beliefs. A woman in the old days used to walk in back of her man. Now the woman is walking with him, but she is still not walking ahead of him."

By the 1970s bluegrass music had drifted outside the country mainstream to occupy its own cultural niche. Bluegrass created its own publications, popularity charts, record labels, and touring circuits. Its fans are not nearly so numerous as those of mainstream country music, but they are fanatical devotees. Artists measure success in the size of outdoor festivals rather than in record sales; yet hundreds also record profitably by selling their wares at live shows. Specialty labels rather than international conglomerates tend to market the style. Bluegrass developed a strong us-against-them attitude toward the rest of the music world, with rigid musical definitions, an almost vicious internal gossip network, and a highly self-critical nature. Change was threatening, and innovation was difficult.

By 1975 this climate was changing. Several writers noted that the number of females performing bluegrass seemed to be increasing. In addition to Betty Fisher, the women who were recording included North Carolinian Arlene Kesterson; Georgia's "Queen of Bluegrass" Mary Padgett; Washington, D.C.,'s Liz Meyer; New Hampshire's Judy Carrier; and Kentuckians Audrey Barger and Emma Smith.

The finest of them was Oklahoma's Delia Bell. "If Hank Williams and Kitty Wells had married and had a daughter, she would have sounded like Delia Bell," raved Emmylou Harris after her first experience with the mournful, lonesome sound of Delia's voice. Emmy brought Delia to national prominence in 1983, but the bluegrass diva's saga starts long before that.

Delia Nowell Bell is a product of the Depression, a sharecropper's daughter and an ironworker's wife who began singing in a fundamentalist church in her hometown of Hugo, Oklahoma, when she was in her teens. After marrying Bobby Bell, she met his boyhood friend, mandolinist Bill Grant. Bill and Delia formed a singing team in 1959 and began appearing on Hugo's KIHN Little Dixie Hayride radio show. By the late 1960s they'd gathered their Kiamichi Mountain Boys band and were recording. Delia became the talk of the bluegrass festival circuit during the 1970s. She, Bill, and the band made more than a dozen albums locally and toured England and Ireland eleven times.

"I used to be so shy," Delia recalls. "When I met Bill, I couldn't hardly get up in front of people and open my mouth. He just kept pushing me out there. If it hadn't been for him, I never would have done it publicly like I have. . . . Our parents like to hear us sing, and friends and family. But I never thought about singing anywhere else. I just like to sing. I knew I could sing, but that's as far as I thought."

Delia Bell's first solo LP, *Bluer Than Midnight,* appeared in 1978. It included "Roses in the Snow," the song that became the centerpiece and title tune of Emmylou Harris's bluegrass album two years later. Emmy was so smitten with Delia's singing that she produced, arranged, and sang harmony on 1983's *Delia Bell,* released nationally by the big-time Warner Bros. label. That collection revived The Davis Sisters' classic "I Forgot More (Than You'll Ever Know)," Kitty Well's timeless "Back Street Affair," and The Carter Family chestnuts "Wildwood Flower" and "Will You Miss Me." Using country star John Anderson as her duet foil, Delia made the charts with the LP's George Jones oldie "Flame in My Heart."

Critics began praising her as "the female Ricky Skaggs"; Music Row agencies vied to book her; Warners urged her to pursue mainstream country stardom. "All of this scared me to death," Delia recalls. "I didn't know what was happening. . . . I'd be so depressed. It scared me to death if the record went up the charts, and it scared me if it didn't!" The big-label LP elevated her stature enormously in the bluegrass world, but the company dropped its confused and reluctant female bluegrass star. Delia and Bill began appearing as an old-timey mandolin/guitar duo in the mid-1980s, sometimes with Delia's beautician sister Mona on bass. But on Rounder Records albums, they continued to perform with bluegrass backing.

"Women haven't had the opportunity men do," says the breakthrough bluegrass woman. "Men can just pick up and stay out a week, go to a festival, while women stay at home, take care of the kids, keep house, and all of that. They don't have the opportunity to get out and learn. . . . When I started, there weren't any women in bluegrass, at least around where we lived."

More and more women were. Ginger Hammond Boatwright was another pioneer, with her Red, White and Blue (Grass) group. "I'm probably one of the longest-running and original women in bluegrass," says the guitarist/songwriter/singer. Raised in Pickens County, Alabama, Ginger learned bluegrass from her father and put together Red, White and Blue (Grass) in Birmingham when she was a college student in 1966.

Red, White and Blue (Grass) was probably the most eclectic bluegrass act of the time and was often criticized by purists for its fancy production touches, off-the-wall antics, and pop influences. But Ginger's band won a Grammy nomination with its 1972 LP, made the country charts in 1973, and won Most Promising Vocal Group from *Billboard* in 1974. Still, "the acceptance of their album will depend largely on

how one feels about the role of the female voice in bluegrass," cautioned a reviewer in 1975.

Ginger moved to Nashville in 1974 and opened her Old Time Pickin' Parlor
nightclub. She disbanded Red, White and Blue (Grass) in 1979. "I stayed off the road
for two and a half years, and nearly went nuts." She began fronting The Doug Dillard Band in 1981 and recorded *Fertile Ground* as her first solo CD with backing by
Dillard and other star pickers in 1991. "If the money were there, there'd be more
women in bluegrass," Ginger believes. "In country music, women can have a bus
or fly; and the work is just on weekends or in the summer. In bluegrass you have to
stay out on the road a good long while. It's really hard to leave your family and go
on the road. But I made a decision in 1967 that I would do whatever it took."

Little by little, band by band, women infiltrated the male bluegrass domain.
South Carolina native Martha Hearon Adcock plays guitar and sings lead in Talk
of the Town, the band led by her banjo/guitar virtuoso husband, Eddie Adcock.
Active on the bluegrass scene since the late 1970s, Martha has a pure, folk-country
contralto that she generally applies to songs with old-timey sentiments on the
group's albums.

Sweet-voiced Cincinnatian Katie Laur used Alabama-bred charm in fronting
her popular 1970s band. A highlight of each show was a witty medley of fifties teen
golden oldies performed by the Katie Laur Band in bluegrass style with doo-wop
vocals. The group also did a takeoff on "The Flintstones" TV theme titled "Bedrock
Breakdown." And Katie gave the feminist movement a wink by titling a 1979 LP
Msbehavin'.

Excerpted from *Finding Her Voice: The Saga of Women in Country Music* (New York: Crown
Publishers, 1993), 454–61; reproduced by permission of the authors.

S cholar Thomas Adler entered the fray over the role of women in bluegrass with
this paper, originally titled "Women in Bluegrass," delivered to an annual meeting of the American Folklore Society in Baltimore. Reprinted and retitled in the magazine *Women in Bluegrass* in 1999, the article looks perceptively at bluegrass and pre-
bluegrass traditions and forces that have affected the role of women in the music,
particularly as instrumental soloists. The editor's notes appeared in the original
version and are from *Women in Bluegrass* editor Murphy Henry.

In almost a side note that probably merits its own article, Adler suggests that
part of the reason bluegrass festivals became so popular is that they offer a "model
of a formulaic musical and social architecture that enables strangers to come together in the image of a family and, in the name of tradition, to make complex, beautiful, improvisational music." There's also an interesting theory on another enduring question: Why do bluegrass bands usually look so serious onstage?

56

"Is There a Link between Bluegrass Music and Sexuality?"

THOMAS A. ADLER

Twenty-one years ago, in his *Journal of American Folklore* article "Introduction to Bluegrass," Mayne Smith helped us all by formulating a clear and informed socio-musical definition of this music. Bluegrass, said Smith, though not in these exact words, is music performed by groups of four to seven male musicians, who are culturally aligned with life in the rural, upland South, who play certain non-electrified stringed instruments—you all know which ones—in a tightly organized and highly-constrained set of tradition-based styles, and who sing together in as many as four parts, creating and re-creating a repertoire that includes many textually-traditional songs. Explicit in Smith's discussion was the assumption that bluegrass music-making is a purely male enterprise, and he wrote that most bluegrass aficionados are young men under forty who own instruments and attempt to play the music. But "twenty-one years, boys, is a mighty long time," and there have been significant developments in every aspect of the demographics of bluegrass.

To give the topic of women in bluegrass music the proper background, we really should begin by considering the historic sexual division of artistic roles in the various root traditions that precipitated bluegrass. Anglo-American folksong, viewed in broad generic terms, has certainly always been supported as much by female tradition-bearers as by male ones. Remember, some of the largest song repertoires ever collected have been those of women ballad singers like Mrs. Brown of Falkland; Texas Gladden of Virginia; or Almeda Riddle of Arkansas. And unaccompanied ballad performance has frequently been assumed by trained folklore collectors to be dominated by women singers. For example, when Henry Belden collected folksong texts in Missouri in the 1940s, he pointed out that both sexes shared participation in the ballad tradition there, but his actual words were: "Men and boys sing . . . [ballads] equally with women and girls," with the implication that that was not typically the case elsewhere in the country. So, anecdotally, at least, we should begin by noting that women have long been tradition-bearers in the venerable parade of folksong and balladry that led towards bluegrass.

But bluegrass is more easily definable instrumentally than vocally, and women's participation in instrumental Anglo-American music presents a very different picture. Among the ranks of fiddlers and pipers who brought traditional instrumental skills and repertoires from the British Isles to America, women apparently always formed a very tiny minority, though, as usual, reliable quantified data are lacking. We should note that throughout most of European and American history, the cost and the value of musical instruments has been relatively high. Men, as the heads of households, have often been the nominal owners of all property, and the unequal division of instruments themselves would obviously contribute to generic male "ownership" of folk instrumental traditions. Women seem always to have "participated in tradition," in folklorist Kay Cothran's general sense, but perhaps not so much in the past by playing the instruments themselves as by responding appropriately to male-dominated instrumental music with socially-complementary singing and dancing.

Tangentially, I'd note a similar domination of instrumental music by males in the African-American tradition. Not one of the early illustrations and references to banjos and large drums cited by Dena Epstein suggests that women were ever seen performing on them in the seventeenth and eighteenth centuries. In the nineteenth century, minstrelsy remained almost exclusively male until after 1870, when a number of all-female minstrel troupes came suddenly into being, but these shows were a parody of the minstrel parody itself, and chiefly existed, according to Robert Toll, to sell "a revealing glimpse at scantily clad women." At any rate, the banjo and other instruments of minstrelsy were presented in that popular forum for nearly a half century in association with men only. By the 1880s, many women outside the rural Southeast had indeed taken up the banjo, but typically to play it in the popular "parlor instrument tradition," the transmission of which was grounded in written instruction books, printed sheet music, and a rhetoric of elitist white European assimilation and improvement of the humble African-American instrument.

Many Southern mountain women born in the last quarter of the nineteenth century apparently played the five-string banjo, but almost without exception they confined the exercise of their art to the family circle. Very few early women instrumentalists crossed the boundary from amateur to professional status, or even semiprofessional status, as entertainers. Even purely local string bands assembled on a temporary basis to play for home and community dances seem always to have been dominated by men. This pattern surely represents both the male assertion of a perceived primary male right to engage in men-only socializing and perception, on the part of both sexes, that playing music in a band, even for friends and neighbors to dance to, is a kind of work outside the home and therefore construed as men's business, whether it's enjoyable or not. In support of this last point, we should recall how many early bluegrass bands have been described as workmanlike and "pokerfaced." It seems right to reinforce the point that bluegrass, like a lot of other men-only enterprises, has always been an uncommonly serious-looking form of "playing."

If we turn to the broad history of commercial country music prior to the crystallization of bluegrass in Bill Monroe's 1945 band, a modest number of semiprofessional and professional women stars will come immediately to mind. And these were not always women who dreamed of being stars, but rather women who extended the tradition of their music-making beyond the family circle where they had developed it. Many of them were certainly talented instrumentalists: Eva Davis and Samantha Bumgarner were pioneering recording artists in the fiddle-and-banjo duet tradition; Maybelle and Sara Carter's autoharp and guitars carried the melody of many Carter Family performances and spawned fifty years of imitators of their own; the Coon Creek Girls, invented first in the imaginative minds of John Lair and Lily May Ledford, played and recorded some rousing mountain string band music; Cousin Emmy and Rachel Veach, the latter of whom played with Roy Acuff, were spirited banjo players who also specialized in comedy acts. Then there were many male-and-female duet groups whose artistic presentations-of-self always played on the homology between vocal harmony and romantic harmony. These groups generally featured women who were competent and comfortable, if not virtuosic, in instrumental performance: think of Lulu Belle and Red Foley, or Lulu Belle and Scotty, or Wilma Lee and Stoney Cooper, or James Roberts and Martha Carson, or Lynn Davis and Molly O'Day.

I believe none of these women stars of early country music would be identified as bluegrass musicians by the other members of this panel, even though almost all the women whom I've named profoundly influenced the development of bluegrass song repertoires and many of them were excellent instrumental performers. Like their male counterparts in commercial hillbilly and old-time country music, early women performers featured instruments and styles and tunes and songs that overlap with those of the bluegrass canon, but in general their performing careers antedated the invention of bluegrass music. More to the point, none of them ever played in a bluegrass band created in the instrumentally-participatory image of Monroe's Blue Grass Boys, in which each member has an obligation to pursue and demonstrate both the instrumental virtuosity and mutual instrumental support.

But there were a few women who got involved with bluegrass music in the early days, when the "sound" was emerging and just starting to become the "style." In fact, at least five different women might lay reasonable claims to having been the first female bluegrass musician.

Taking their cases chronologically, we begin with Wilene Forrester, wife of Tennessee fiddler Howard "Howdy" Forrester. Howdy was Bill Monroe's third fiddler, having succeeded Art Wooten and Tommy Magness.[1] Forrester played two times with Monroe, but his first stint lasted until he joined the Navy in 1943 and was replaced by Chubby Wise. About that time, Monroe hired Wilene "Sally Ann" Forrester to play accordion, probably to insure Howdy's return and also in partial response to Roy Acuff's hiring of Jimmy Riddle to play accordion in his band; but in compiling his monumental bluegrass history, Neil Rosenberg found a 1943 *Billboard* article in which Monroe says he really hired Sally Ann as a tribute to the memory of his own mother's accordion playing. No matter why she was hired, Sally Ann was the first women to perform regularly as a nominal "Blue Grass Boy," and her musical imprint is stamped indelibly on the first Columbia recordings of such songs as "Rocky Road Blues," "Nobody Loves Me," "Come Back to Me in My Dreams," and "Footprints in the Snow". (Editor's note: My own research into Sally Ann's life

---

1. Forrester was actually Monroe's fourth fiddler; Carl Story was third (personal communication with Tom Ewing, 2002).

points out that she was not hired to insure Howdy's return but rather because she was an accomplished musician in her own right who pulled her own weight in the show.)

The second woman "Blue Grass Boy" was Bessie Lee Mauldin from North Carolina. Bessie Lee has been almost completely overlooked by writers of fan magazine biographies and is acknowledged only sketchily in the stack of scholarly literature produced by today's distinguished panelists and others. This neglect is somewhat surprising since she played hundreds of live shows and took part in thirty-one recording sessions with the Blue Grass Boys between 1955 and 1964. Rosenberg has published a few early 1960s' photos of Monroe's band in which Bessie Lee can be seen. And Bessie Lee Mauldin's name is certainly preserved in the memories of many of today's practicing bluegrass musicians, even if it's only spoken in the midst of late-night sessions of Bill Monroe reminiscences, where it certifies the speaker's depth of knowledge of Monrovian bluegrass. In such contexts, too, Bessie Lee is sometimes alluded to by male bluegrass musicians with winks, leers, and the implication that her ties to Monroe were more sexual than musical. Apparently she considered herself to be Monroe's common-law wife, but he did not; there have been tales of a real or threatened lawsuit over this issue in the past few years. Regardless of the actual truth behind Mauldin's extra-musical relationship with Monroe, I raise the point now because I intend to return later in this paper to the critical concept of a link between bluegrass musicianship and sexuality. At any rate, since she played string bass only, and, at least to my knowledge, never sang with the Blue Grass Boys onstage, Bessie Lee remained in the musical background throughout her career, and is almost never referred to as an inspiring role model for today's generation of women bluegrass musicians. (Editor's note: New information indicates that Bessie Lee did, indeed, sing with the Blue Grass Boys onstage. Two of the songs she sang were the solo "Answer to the Wild Side of Life" and high harmony on "Walking in Jerusalem Just Like John.")

Sally Ann Forrester and Bessie Lee were the only "Blue Grass Girls," that is, the only women musicians employed by Bill Monroe. But among the daughters of pioneer recording star Ernest V. Stoneman, three played important parts in the early days of the bluegrass style. I am, of course, referring to Patsy Stoneman, who plays guitar and autoharp, Donna Stoneman, who plays mandolin, and Veronica ("Roni") Stoneman, who plays banjo and is famous for her music and comedy performances on *Hee Haw*. All three women played in various Stoneman family groups of the post–World War II years, and Patsy, the oldest, also worked in the early 1950s as a single musician and singer with notable bluegrass musicians like Bill Emerson and Wayne Yates. Around 1956, the Stoneman family band coalesced as the Bluegrass Champs, and Donna and Roni began to really come into their own as instrumentalists. Donna had begun to play mandolin seriously during the years of the Second World War, and in 1956 Roni, already married to a good Virginia Scruggs-style banjoist named Eugene Cox, was herself a good enough Scruggs-style player to take second place in an open banjo contest. In 1957, Roni recorded "Lonesome Road Blues" on the important Folkways record *American Banjo Tunes and Songs in Scruggs Style,* and on and off through the rest of the late 1950s and the early 1960s, the Stonemans performed in various family-based configurations, maintaining the visibility of both Donna and Roni as lead instrument–playing women bluegrass musicians.

In the latter half of the '50s and the early 1960s, a few other women began to shift from western, folk, old-time, gospel, or other country music genres into bluegrass, but most of them continued in the proven female roles of vocalists and/or rhythm instrument players. Such women as Ola Belle Reed, Rose Maddox, and Gloria Belle all come into mind here; all helped pave the way for those that followed in bluegrass, but none made or enhanced their reputations because of instrumental prowess. Miggie, Polly and Janis Lewis of Georgia's bluegrass-gospel Lewis Family began their careers during this period, too, but as vocalists only; they are the prototypes, in bluegrass, of a performance role that allows women, and women only, to participate in bluegrass without being instrumentally competent. Though Polly did play bass for a time in the '50s, and the Lewis Family's women members are sometimes seen keeping time with a tambourine, the band's lead instrumental roles have been filled by the men: Pop, Wallace, Talmadge, Little Roy, Travis, and Lewis Phillips. The women's roles in the Lewis Family followed the general trend in country music, where there has been a slow steady separation of vocalist and instrumentalists roles, both for men and for women. Fifty years ago on the Opry, a much higher percentage of the performers accompanied themselves instrumentally as they sang and had reputations as instrumental virtuosos. Where bluegrass played by men preserves the old ratio of at least one instrument per performer, women could and did begin to participate in family-based bluegrass bands in a way that owed more to popular music than country music, without becoming instrumentalists at all. For such women, the art of bluegrass was recentered on vocals, and instrumental virtuosity remained a male prerogative.

It was similar in the bluegrass–gospel singing Sullivan family. Margie Sullivan was featured from the beginning as a vocalist and only secondarily as a rhythm guitarist. The serious instrumental work of playing Sullivan Family bluegrass was left to Enoch, Emmett, Arthur, and Aubrey Sullivan, and later on to talented Sullivan Family sidemen like Joe Stuart, Marty Stuart, and Carl Jackson.

During the 1960s, two important developments changed forever the way women related to bluegrass. First was the Folksong Revival, which stimulated the exposure of bluegrass far beyond its original regional and cultural provenance. The second was the beginning of weekend bluegrass festivals in 1965, which created a new context for unmediated presentations of bluegrass in general, and for family-based secular bluegrass performance in particular.

The Folksong Revival and various pop cultural events of the 1960s, like the *Beverly Hillbillies* television show and later on the soundtrack to *Bonnie and Clyde,* brought the sound of bluegrass—specifically the influential sounds of Flatt and Scruggs and the Foggy Mountain Boys—to huge new audiences outside the rural Southeast. The story of the first bluegrass college concerts and the incredibly influential urban Folk Festivals at New York, Philadelphia, Newport, Chicago, and in other northern cities and towns has already been told in part. I only wish to remind you here that among the millions who heard bluegrass through national mass media at that time were a great many women who were moved by what they heard, and who quietly began to take up bluegrass instruments in earnest.

Part of the attraction of bluegrass to new listeners certainly lies in the sound of the music itself, but I would argue that a significant part of the attractiveness of bluegrass for those raised outside the cultural region of its origins is the way it provides ready rhetorical access to an exotic and interesting culture, or at least its image. Bluegrass has thrived because it offers all its willing exponents not only a musical art form to learn, but also a kind of voluntary and controllable participation in tradition. To post-sixties generations, north and south, urban and rural, male and female, bluegrass offered the useful burden of its associations, its history, and above all its model of a formulaic musical and social architecture that enables strangers to come together in the image of a family and, in the name of tradition, to make complex, beautiful, improvisational music. This is a model that fulfills needs for modern urban women as well as modern urban men, and the mass media's inevitable separation of traditional bluegrass music from traditional bluegrass culture made it easier for women to move into any bluegrass roles they chose, including those of lead instrumentalists.

Because the concept of family is so critical to this whole discussion, the bluegrass festival movement should be understood as a novel amalgamation of bluegrass performance with the safe context of family togetherness. The participation of actual families who set up temporary home sites and became the constituent units of bluegrass festival audiences marks the beginning of the festival era as a clear watershed moment in the history of women's participation in bluegrass. Neil Rosenberg flatly states in his history that "women . . . were practically unknown as bluegrass musicians prior to the beginning of the festival movement." And the handful of exceptions I've reviewed so far certainly prove the rule about the importance of family, for before diffusion of bluegrass and the rise of festivals—and to some extent, even now—a woman's only safe route into bluegrass was via direct kinship with male musicians. From the 1920s on, any unmarried woman who tried to be a professional hillbilly musician outside the safety of the family circle, and any bandleader that tried to employ her, had to endure or circumvent the presumptions of promiscuity and loose living commonly held of all popular musicians. This was a problem for pre-bluegrass women performers like Rachel Veach, and this reinforces the point I was trying to make about Bessie Lee Mauldin's role as a Blue Grass Girl. Where men could form hillbilly and bluegrass bands in which the sidemen were described as "boys," "ramblers," "cut-ups," and "playboys," women had to grow up in a real singing family, like the Stoneman and Lewis sisters, or had to have some other direct kinship relationship to a male musicians (like Sally Ann being Howdy's wife). The performance rhetoric of family membership in hillbilly bands, which had always provided a reason for unrelated or distantly-related band members to adopt the fictitious role of "brothers," was therefore crucial for women, too. And it's fascinating to note that once the festival movement provided the opportunity, married women in families moved into bluegrass principally as players of the supporting instrument roles, much as they play a critical supporting role in the family's emotional life.

After these two watershed events of the 1960s, the absolute number of women bluegrass musicians began to rise dramatically, and women's participation in bluegrass, like other tangible evidences of the Women's Liberation movement, became a divisive topic of conversation among men. Many men have resisted and continue to resist the very idea of women's participation in bluegrass. Some flatly assert that women can't pick bluegrass, can't sing bluegrass, and don't belong in bluegrass. Probably many more, including me, have tried to take a more tolerant stance, but we still probably greeted our first sights of competent women bluegrass musicians with the startled realization, and maybe even the infuriating vocalization of the thought: "She picks pretty good, for a girl." And we kept on picking in groups that were mostly male anyway, whether or not we consciously wanted to exclude women from bluegrass, because—as with any vernacular music—there are lots more so-so learners than accomplished virtuosos. Bluegrass defines a performance arena in which instrumental virtuosity was valued right from the start, especially on the lead instruments that women were so late to take up. So even though women began to be seen playing bluegrass in the 1960s, it was a long time before there began to be enough really good women bluegrass musicians—women who were not only competent, but excellent—to begin to break down the male observation that women couldn't pick.

While I want to concentrate here on the different implications and connotations of instrumental performance for the two sexes, I have to take at least a moment to address the crucial question of singing. There is no doubt that a real difference in average vocal range distinguishes women from men, and this difference is enough all by itself to cause problems. As the woman banjoist and banjo teacher Murphy Henry put it, "women cannot sing 'traditional' songs in the 'traditional' 'right' keys. This confuses most men. And when you get away from 'traditional keys' and move to a higher range, who can tenor a woman? Only another woman. Who can then sing baritone? It's too high for conventional men baritone singers, yet usually too low for another woman. . . . So usually women are confined to singing tenor to a man or occasionally giving a solo lead or sometimes high baritone. How could you have a woman's gospel quartet? Who would sing bass? If you can't sing lead in a conventional key, you can't have any control at a jam session of average musicians. You can't say, 'Let's sing "Uncle Pen,"' and then sing it—you have to say, 'Does anyone know "Uncle Pen"? I can tenor'—quite a handicap."

Compounding the problem of vocal range, the narrative orientation of many traditional bluegrass songs is purely and unalterably male. Some women respond by writing new songs, or by bringing songs into bluegrass from country or popular music that represent a woman's viewpoint ("Blue Kentucky Girl" may be the most popular of all these), but a significant response is also the simple avoidance of songs that are unequivocally male, like "Dirty Dishes" or "Home Run Man."

Another set of challenges to women pickers relates to the social dynamics of instrumental bluegrass. The bluegrass performance arena has always been one in which musical assertiveness is the norm and outright musical competition or dueling is a principle mode of "play." Assertiveness in bluegrass means stepping up authoritatively to take your break, and it means playing the lead instruments forcefully, hard. The aesthetic vocabulary of banjoists and mandolinists is filled with terms like "cut," "chop," "punch," "drive," "spark," "bark," "spang," "wang," "power," and "pop," all of which suggest the bundling of enormous and tightly controlled energy in the timbre of each properly-played note. When women pickers first came along in significant numbers, they often seemed to pick in a soft, relaxed or even languid manner deemed inappropriate by many male bluegrass critics. One has to learn to channel musical energy through an instrument, and that takes time. Today, those women who have first perceived and then achieved an appropriate assertiveness in their own bluegrass are likely to be the most vocal critics of beginning women players, especially those who "use being a woman as an excuse for 'dinky' playing."

Additionally, the musical dueling that takes place between all-male bluegrass bands has been likened to all-male team sports competitions. Most of us here probably already know about Bill Monroe's Blue Grass Boys baseball teams and his own positive views of both music-making and sports as arenas for tough competition. When women first entered the male bluegrass world, they sometimes felt they were being treated as competitors, and they were, but they were not always expecting that. To the eyes of non-pickers, the cooperative aspects of band membership probably are more apparent than the competitive ones.

Another dimension of meaning follows from this pattern of male bluegrass assertiveness and competition, namely the use of one's musical ability as a kind of romantic or courtship display. Many of the young male bluegrass musicians I've interviewed through the years have commented frankly that their membership in bands and their ability to pick bluegrass were assets when it came to picking up girls. Some women—including a significant number of the women I interviewed and corresponded with last summer in preparing this paper—freely acknowledged that they found male bluegrass musicianship romantically attractive and effective in a courtship sense. I heard and read comments like "yes, boys use bluegrass to get girls; in fact, that's what drawed me to Timmy." A more complex description of one California woman musician's motivation to learn began: "My mother wanted me to be a symphony musician. When my best girlfriend started banjo lessons, I decided I had to myself. I loved the sound of the banjo. Then I developed a mad crush on my banjo teacher, so I was inspired [to learn] by rebellion, competitiveness, emotionalism, and lust."

Many male pickers have, no doubt, been inspired by the same factors. The connection between the competitive performance of bluegrass and the romantic presentation of one's self to the opposite sex involves what psychologists would surely call a kind of sublimation; and the understanding that this function underlies male bluegrass performance goes a long way towards explaining the reluctance of women themselves to invade the bluegrass arena in ways that essentially challenge the masculinity of male pickers.

In this connection, too, I may as well refer once again to the "gender" of instruments themselves. Robert Cantwell may have startled some readers with his assertion that the banjo is "the only stringed instrument in American tradition which has not been feminized," but he was only reiterating an observation made often before about the generalized symbolic phallic use of bluegrass instruments. Whatever connotations of maleness and femaleness may be read into the instruments of bluegrass themselves, the traditional ways of playing and competing in bluegrass bear the full historic burden of male association and thus present inescapable mental obstacles for women, especially women with no direct ties of kinship or impending kinship to one or more men who already play in a band.

One fascinating response to the many dilemmas bluegrass presents for women has been the formation of "liberated," mixed-membership bands, like the group called the "Good Ol' Persons," or even "all-girl" professional bluegrass bands. I believe bassist Gloria Belle was part of an all-female bluegrass band in the mid-1960s, and Betty Fisher, who began fronting her own band in 1972, had talked to Bill Monroe a couple years before about an all-girl bluegrass band. "He told me it was a good idea," she said, but "he thought I would have a hard time finding girls in one area who played well enough." Since the early 1970s, a few bluegrass bands have been formed entirely of unmarried women pickers (e.g., the Buffalo Gals, the New Coon Creek Girls, Side-saddle, the Wildwood Pickers, Cherokee Rose, Sweet Dixie, Mountain Lace, and Feminine Grass), most of which write and perform bluegrass songs with a female, if not always feminist, point of view. Even so, such bands create as many cognitive problems as they solve for bluegrass audiences. For example, the women in an all-girl band may still be stereotyped as promiscuous. Neil Rosenberg recounted to me the interesting story of a woman performer at the Mariposa Folk Festival whose singing partner, the year a five-member, all-female bluegrass band was there, called them "Five Easy Pieces" because of their behind-the-scenes flirting with male festival performers. If jealousy enters into such assessments, it only underscores my assertion of a thoroughgoing link between the presentation of one's gender-identity and the presentation of one's self as a bluegrass musician.

Participation by women in bluegrass music is the focus of some genuine tensions between tradition and innovation, but such participation is a fact and it will undoubtedly continue to increase and to reshape the sound of the music itself. While individuals, both male and female, will always make their own accommodations to women's presences in bluegrass, their varied responses affirm that the sexual identity of performers is rhetorically critical for all traditional bluegrass musicians.

Originally published in *Women in Bluegrass*, no. 19 (Spring 1999): 1–6. Reprinted by permission of the author.

B anjo-picker, journalist, and unflagging feminist Murphy Henry institutional-
ized a long-simmering movement when she started her *Women in Bluegrass*
magazine in September 1994. In a music that so reveres its founding fathers, there
has been historical resistance among men to the idea that women could actually hit
the hard, high, and lonesome notes that first arose from Monroe, the Stanleys, and
the rest. But musician after musician has shown that of course women can play
bluegrass, excel at it, and bring new levels of meaning and excitement to the music.

One piece of this, alluded to by Henry in her speech, has to do with the reluctance of many male musicians to change the key of certain songs to fit female vocal
ranges. That had something to do with the way certain instrumental parts sounded and were played in a particular key. It also reflected a generalized refusal to change
the way things had "always" been done. As Henry notes, many obstacles remain for
women musicians, despite the success of Alison Krauss, Laurie Lewis, Rhonda Vincent, and many others.

57

"'Women in Bluegrass': Keynote Address
at the IBMA Trade Show"

MURPHY HENRY

Thanks, Lynn [Morris]. I appreciate those kind words. It's an honor for me to be
addressing the membership of the IBMA today. I've never really considered myself
to be a public speaker, in spite of the fact that I do feel very comfortable onstage. I
tell you right now, I'd be a lot more comfortable if I were up here with my Stelling
banjo slung across my shoulder and a set list on the floor in front of me. Or I'd be
even more comfortable if I were back in Winchester in our studio at the house where
we make our Murphy Method videos. Where my husband Red can edit out any
mistakes I might make or take out what he likes to call "excess verbiage." [Chuck-
les.] I hope there won't be much excess verbiage today. Or I'd feel the most comfortable in the world if I were sitting down and giving a banjo lesson to one of my
students because all my students think that every word that comes out of my mouth
is the gospel truth [chuckles] which, of course, is the primary reason I teach.

But I'm sure that you're not going to take every word that I have to say as the
gospel truth today, and one reason for that is that I've picked a little bit of a controversial subject to talk about. And one of the reasons I know it's controversial is when
I was mentioning this talk to my friends in Winchester, they were all saying things
like, "Well, Murphy, if you've got to talk about this, do it nicely. Don't tick anybody
off."

You know, the other day, Andy Owens called me on the telephone. And he said to me, "Murphy, whatcha doing?" And I answered truthfully, I said, "Well, Andy, I'm listening to a Rose Maddox CD." And Andy says, "Murphy, don't you think you're carrying this women in bluegrass thing just a little bit too far?" [Light laughter.] He says, "Don't you ever listen to any men?" And I said, "Sure, Andy, I listen to men all the time. But don't tell anybody because I don't want to ruin my reputation." [Light laughter.]

Well, what Andy didn't realize is that the first twenty years of my bluegrass career I spent listening to nothing but men playing bluegrass music. It was all-male bands and the Lewis Family. That's who I was listening to. So I feel like I've got a lot of catching up to do. Now, some of you might remember at the Awards Show last year, Laurie Lewis got onstage to present a Certificate of Merit to Vern and Ray. And Laurie said she'd learned a lot about playing bluegrass music from Vern. And Vern had told her that if she wanted to play bluegrass music and do it right, that she had to learn to spill her guts on the stage and then walk in them. [Light titters.] Perhaps that's a little graphic for lunch. Sorry. [Laughter.]

Well, I kind of feel like that's what I'm going to be doing today because I'm going to be talking about a subject that is near and dear to my heart, and it's a subject that I think is really important for the bluegrass community, for IBMA, and for all of us if we want to grow and prosper as an industry and as we move into the twenty-first century. So my topic today is "Women in Bluegrass." I guess you're not surprised. [Light applause.]

Right here at the beginning I would like to say that I think IBMA has done some good things for women in bluegrass. And I would like especially to thank Dan Hays and Kitsy Kuykendall for that. It was through their encouragement and support that last year at the Fan Fest women in bluegrass had a forty-minute set on the program. We put eight bands onstage—eight all-female bands—each band playing one number, and then we all congregated at the end for a great big jam session led by the magnificent Katie Laur. We sang "Banjo Picking Girl." And the thing that I was most impressed with was after we got finished picking, a lot of people were coming up to me and saying, "I was so impressed by the level of the musicianship of all the women onstage." And that's a wonderful thing. I'm very proud of that.

Two years ago, when we were at Owensboro, at the Fan Fest on the river, we had the world's largest all-female jam. We put seventy-three women onstage to pick three numbers. Of course, we did have to do it in the supper break, but that was okay. I was proud that we were up there. And I can tell you right now, that I have never felt so much estrogen in one spot. [Laughter.] And the thing that was interesting about that is, after we got finished with that jam onstage, some of the guys were saying things—they were kind of saying this tongue in cheek—but nevertheless they were saying, "Okay, we've had the world's largest all-female jam. When do we get to have the male jam?" And what they were forgetting was that for the first twenty-five years of the history of bluegrass music, almost every time there was a finale onstage or a jam session at the end of a festival, it was almost always all men. At least that's the

way it was down in the Southeast where I was raised in bluegrass. I understand from
the work I do with my women in bluegrass database that things are a little bit different out in California. [A few chuckles.]

But if you think that that's just history, that it's past and that things have changed
significantly for women in bluegrass, then we only have to look at our own IBMA
Awards Show to find out that things have not changed as much as we would like.
Now I know a lot of you get caught up in the Awards Show. And so do I. It's a won-
derful production. We're excited to see our friends and fellow musicians on the stage.
But this is what I've noticed.

Last year we had a finale onstage. It was great. We had Earl Scruggs onstage picking the banjo, we had Uncle Josh on the dobro, George Shuffler on the bass fiddle,
Kenny Baker on the fiddle. We had one woman on the stage for that grand finale.
Rhonda Vincent—playing the rhythm guitar. The year before that was the year that
we had a tribute to Bill Monroe and were remembering Chubby Wise. When we had
the last number onstage, everybody was gathered together to pick "Raw Hide." No
women onstage. About halfway through the song, Laurie Lewis came bounding out
from the side with her fiddle, but she stood in the back, and she didn't take a break
on the fiddle.

The year before that, Jimmy Martin was inducted into the Hall of Honor, and
for the closing number, present and former members of Jimmy's band joined Jimmy onstage to pick. One woman—Gloria Belle. Thank goodness for Gloria Belle.
Where would we be without Gloria Belle? She stood in the back of the band and
played her heart out on the mandolin, but she didn't get to sing, and she didn't get
anywhere near a microphone. Gloria, thank you just for being there. [Applause.] It
was an inspiration to me.

I feel like the IBMA is not sending a good signal to the women pickers who are
members of IBMA. We're not sending a good signal to potential women players,
and we're not sending a good signal to the world at large, who, if they only saw our
IBMA Awards Show, could come away with the perception that we're still an all-
male industry. And we know that is far from being the truth. Sometimes the IBMA
is guilty of simply not thinking. In 1993, the focus of our Trade Show was on youth
in bluegrass. And it's a wonderful focus. Youth in bluegrass is very important. But,
again, as part of our Awards Show, we put a band onstage that was the Bluegrass
Youth All-Stars. And I was sitting in the audience when the curtain went up on this
band. And the announcer said, "Ladies and gentlemen, the future of bluegrass
music!" And I watched the curtain go up on five young men standing onstage playing instruments. This was a put-together band. And it didn't have to be that way.
And it shouldn't have been that way. Because I'm here to tell you that the future of
bluegrass music is not five men standing onstage playing their instruments. The
future of bluegrass music simply must include women onstage playing their instruments and singing! [Loud applause and a whistle.]

It was this episode at the Awards Show that led me to start my database of wom-
en in bluegrass. Because I wanted to have a list of names, if this ever came up again,

so we could get in touch with women, young and old. And it's from the database that I did start my *Women in Bluegrass* newsletter. We're starting our fifth year in December. I wanted somebody to be in a position to address issues that were facing women in bluegrass and to talk about us and some of our stories. And I've kind of adopted the motto for the newsletter "We're little, but we're loud." [Small chuckles.]

Today, as you know from being here at the Trade Show, we have more women in bluegrass than ever before. But old attitudes about women and old attitudes about women in bluegrass are still around. And I want to give you an example.

Like a lot of you, when the old bluegrass is reissued on CDs, I like to buy the boxed sets. So when Columbia Records came out with a boxed set called *The Essential Bill Monroe,* I bought a copy of that. And this was two CDs of Bill Monroe's music from 1945 to 1949. And I opened the booklet that came along with the boxed CDs, and I was reading about Bill Monroe. It's a very fine-looking booklet and very well done. I got to the part where the author was talking about Bill Monroe and the mandolin. And he was telling a story that most of us know pretty well—how Bill Monroe came to play the mandolin. You know that Bill Monroe was the youngest of his family, so when Birch took the fiddle, and Charlie took the guitar, Bill Monroe was left with the mandolin. Well, there's nothing gender-related about that story. But this author chooses to inject gender into this little story. He points out that if we look at family band photos from that era, that the mandolin is usually being played by a kid or a girl. [A few light chuckles.] And the way the guy has written this up, it's like, nothing could be worse—the mandolin is a girl's instrument—isn't that awful? [More light chuckles.] And in the next paragraph he goes on to talk about how Bill Monroe spoke proudly of the times when he played the guitar. And he did. He spoke about playing the guitar behind Uncle Pen, when he would play dances. And he spoke about playing the guitar behind Arnold Shultz. And this author says, and these are the author's words, not Bill Monroe's, the author says that Bill Monroe liked to play the guitar because it was a man's instrument. And then he speaks about how Bill Monroe had some of his early Opry photos taken with the guitar. And how Bill Monroe played the guitar on the original bluegrass cut of "Mule Skinner Blues." And then the author says, "Did Bill Monroe harbor some fear that the mandolin, a kid's instrument, even a girl's, was not fit for the image he would project as an adult band leader?"

Oh, my goodness. What could be worse than playing a girl's instrument? The author concludes by saying that Bill Monroe would create a "ferocious and hell-bent man's music on an instrument disparaged as a kid's or even a woman's." A "ferocious and hell-bent man's music." [Small chuckles.]

Well, I'm here today to tell you that Bill Monroe did not create a ferocious and hell-bent man's music. It might have been ferocious at times. And it might have been hell-bent at times. But it was not then, and it is not now, a man's music. Bill Monroe created a music for anybody that wants to play it—any gender, men and women. [Moderately loud applause.]

And history shows us that Bill Monroe himself was both inclusive and supportive of women who played bluegrass, and I'd like to give you a few examples of that.

In this very boxed set that I've been talking about, the Columbia reissues, the first eight cuts that Bill Monroe made for Columbia Records featured a woman playing the accordion. Sally Ann Forrester. [Applause.] Sally Ann sang tenor on two numbers, and she took an accordion break on "Blue Grass Special." She was with Bill Monroe and the Blue Grass Boys for at least three years, which is quite a bit longer than many of the Blue Grass Boys stayed with Monroe. [Laughter.] She was a professional musician in her own right, and she added to Bill Monroe's show. I always find it interesting and curious that when we mention Sally Ann Forrester and the accordion, everybody chuckles a little bit. And I'm not sure if they're chuckling because we don't consider the accordion to be a bluegrass instrument anymore, or because, in the past, we didn't consider women to be bluegrass players.

Many of you are familiar with Bessie Lee Mauldin, who played the bass and recorded with Bill Monroe for a number of years. [Light applause.] But you're probably not familiar with a woman named Juanita Sheehan. She and her husband Shorty were part of the house band at the Brown County Jamboree up in Bean Blossom, Indiana. And sometimes when Bill Monroe would come through, he wouldn't have a full band with him to play a show. So Juanita would back him up on the guitar. And Neil Rosenberg says that Juanita was a wonderful guitar player. Bill Monroe didn't have a problem playing in a band that had a woman on the guitar.

Many of you also know that when Bill Monroe went out on the road sometimes he wouldn't carry a full band with him. He went to Washington State in the '60s without enough musicians to fill out his contract, so he used Vivian Williams on the fiddle for two shows. [Applause.] The thing that Bill Monroe said about Vivian Williams was this. He said, "I have never heard a lady fiddler that could beat Vivian, and a lot of men fiddlers can't beat her."

Bill Monroe was the one that encouraged Rose Maddox to record her landmark bluegrass album—the first bluegrass album ever recorded by a woman. Bill Monroe played mandolin on the album himself, he sang on the album, and Rose Maddox recorded a number of Bill Monroe's songs.[1] If you've ever had any question in your mind, any doubts about whether women can sing bluegrass, get this album and listen to Rose Maddox. Now, as a little aside about Rose Maddox's personality, when she came in from California to do this album, she brought her steel player with her. And when she got in the studio, the folks said, "You can't use a steel on bluegrass music." Rose Maddox had two words for these people. [Tentative laughter.] No, not those! [Loud burst of laughter.] Never thought of that. [More laughter.] Her words were, "Watch me!" [More laughter.] It's a great album.

Just one more example. The first professional bluegrass band that I played with was a group called Betty Fisher and the Dixie Bluegrass Band. I played bass in that group. Bill Monroe was the one that encouraged Betty to start this bluegrass band. He gave her tips on how to recruit young musicians to play in the band, and he hired

---

1. Bill Monroe played mandolin but did not sing on Maddox's album *Rose Maddox Sings Bluegrass* (Capitol T1799).

her to play his festival at Bean Blossom. Bill Monroe didn't have a problem with women being bluegrass band leaders.

Today I am proud to say that we've got more women leading bluegrass bands than ever before. We've got Alison Krauss, Lynn Morris, Laurie Lewis, Claire Lynch, Kate MacKenzie, Dale Ann Bradley, and we've got Rhonda Vincent. It's a great list of women. And slowly [hesitant applause], thank you, you can applaud those women [applause]. And slowly but surely we're seeing some women move up through the ranks as side musicians in all-male bands. And, of course, Kristin Scott is a prime example of this. [Applause.] Kristin's been playing with the Larry Stephenson Band now for three years. And I think we have to give Larry a lot of credit because some of you may not know that when Larry hired Kristin, he got quite a number of telephone calls from friends and acquaintances that said, "Larry, what are you thinking? It'll never work. You can't have a woman playing the banjo in an all-male band." Well, every time Kristin and Larry get onstage, they prove that you can have a woman as a side musician in a band. And Kristin plays great banjo.

We have women in bluegrass now that are great songwriters, following in the footsteps of the legendary and great Hazel Dickens. [Applause.] And we can't forget the women who work behind the scenes in bluegrass. We have women who are event producers like Mary Tyler Doub and Jean Cornett. We've got women who are newsletter editors all over the country—Elizabeth Burkett, with *inTune* magazine from California. We've got women who are magazine editors—Julie Koehler, the associate editor of *Bluegrass Now,* and Sharon Watts, my boss down at *Bluegrass Unlimited.* We've got women who are association presidents, and we've got women who are booking agents. How can I stand up here and talk about women in bluegrass without mentioning Louise Scruggs, one of the first women to be a booking agent and a manager and one of the best? [Applause.] She delighted in putting Flatt and Scruggs into places that had never even considered having bluegrass music before. And if you like the Carnegie Hall album, you have Louise Scruggs to thank for that, because that was her idea.

But in spite of all the progress that we've made down through the years, we still end up with a situation like we ended up with this year with the IBMA Awards ballots. We have two women on the final ballot—Missy Raines, nominated for Bass Player of the Year, and Dale Ann Bradley and Coon Creek, nominated for Emerging Artist. Of course, this is in addition to the five women who were nominated for Female Vocalist. And we can't forget, of course, that Vicki Simmons plays the bass in Coon Creek. Also the Freight Hoppers were nominated for Emerging Artist, and they have Cary Fridley playing guitar. So a total of four women being recognized by the IBMA for their contributions. And we have nobody to blame but ourselves because we're the ones that are doing the nominating from the ground floor up, and we're the ones that are doing the voting.

And this is a problem. I don't know what the answer to the problem is. But I do think the problem stems from the fact that we don't have as many women in bluegrass as we do men.

So if we don't have as many women in the organization, in the music, we don't have as many women making records, and if they're not making the records, they're not going to get on the air. And if they're not going to get on the air, they're not going to get on the charts. And if they're not going to get on the charts, then we're probably not going to vote for them because we're just not going to remember them when it comes time to make those nominations.

We need more women making records. We need more women making solo projects. So many of the men are coming out with great solo projects. Where are the women making solo projects? Of course, the example that comes to mind, the exception to that rule, as she is the exception to many if not most rules, is Suzanne Thomas, who has just come out with a solo project. [Applause.]

We need more women making instrumental CDs. Missy Raines just came out with a great CD that features her bass playing. [Applause.] We need more women making group projects—women that don't normally play together. This year we'll see a release from Hazel Dickens, along with Ginny Hawker and Carol Elizabeth Jones. They made a wonderful group project. And we need more women playing as side musicians on all the projects.

Part of the problem is that the women who do make records don't get the airplay that they need. I can't tell you the number of times I've turned off my car radio because I was listening to a bluegrass program that plays all-men bands all the time. And if I am doing this—somebody that loves bluegrass music—what are other women in the radio audience doing? Are they switching to talk radio? What are the other people in the audience doing? One of the complaints that we hear about bluegrass music is that it all sounds alike to people that are not used to listening to it. Well, if you'd interject some women's voices, some women's bands, into the radio airplay mix, then all bluegrass would not sound alike. And I hope we can grow our audience that way, by reaching out to people that we have not reached before.

In closing, I'd like to mention just two things. Musicians, I'd like to offer a challenge to you to stretch yourselves musically. I was in a jam session with Bill Evans this summer at Augusta Heritage Center, and Bill and I were both playing banjo, and Bill said he thought that everyone in bluegrass should learn to play the old standards in the keys that they were originally written in. And I think that's a good idea. It's good training. But then Bill went further and said, "And then I think all musicians should turn right around and learn to play these same songs in keys where women can sing them." [Applause.]

And banjo players, right, that means you have to learn how to play "Roll in My Sweet Baby's Arms" in D. [Laughter.] Fiddle players, what about "Footprints in the Snow" in G? And how about you folks who want to crosspick the guitar? How about "Will You Miss Me When I'm Gone" in the key of E? [More quiet laughter.]

And, ladies, when you're out jamming tonight I want you to think about that. And if you get the urge to sing "Uncle Pen" in the key of C, and somebody says, "But you can't do 'Uncle Pen' in the key of C," I want you to remember what Rose Maddox said . . . [laughter, starting small, and then getting louder as the audience remembered my earlier faux pas] . . . not that! Not that! I want you to remember what Rose Maddox said and just turn around and say, "Watch me!"

And, DJs, if I could just make one small suggestion. When May comes around and you do your annual program, the salute to mothers that a lot of you like to do, would it be possible to include some songs in your program that were not about dead mothers? [Loud laughter and applause.] I realize that in bluegrass music as it is today that may be a challenge. So I'd like to offer two songs for suggestions. Number one you are very familiar with. Our Song of the Year that Hazel Dickens wrote, the one called "Mama's Hand." Such a fine song. [Applause.] But the second song you might not be as familiar with. It's a song that Kathy Kallick wrote. It's called "Don't Leave Your Little Girl All Alone." And I'd like to quote just a little bit of that.

It starts out, in true bluegrass fashion, with a little girl begging her mother not to die. It says, "Don't leave your little girl all alone / Don't leave your little girl without a home / Mama, don't go / Her cry was soft and low / Don't leave your little girl all alone." Now, if this had been a traditional bluegrass song, of course, in the second verse the mother would be dead, and in the third verse, she'd be rejoicing with the angels up in heaven. [Laughter.]

But, Kathy's a mother herself. And she has two little girls. So she took this, and she wrote it a different way. She put a different ending on it. She says, "When the mother heard her daughter's little plea / Her fever disappeared so magically / Baby girl, don't cry / I'm not about to die / Come and kiss your mama / Let me dry your eyes."

The mother says, "Baby girl, don't cry / I'm not about to die." In bluegrass music? I didn't think that was allowed. [Laughter.] Thank you very much. [Applause.]

Originally published in *Women in Bluegrass*, no. 18 (Fall 1998): 2–5. Reprinted by permission of the author.

As any other tightly knit community, bluegrass has its political disputes. Following Murphy Henry's amusing yet pointed IBMA address about the role of women in bluegrass, banjoist and IBMA stalwart Pete Wernick felt moved to respond. Henry made some good points, Wernick said in the pages of *Women in Bluegrass*, but left out others that would have left a different impression. In a letter to me about the use of this article, Wernick listed the names of young bluegrass performers whom the IBMA had spotlighted in 1993: mandolinist Chris Thile, guitarist and banjo player Cody Kilby, banjo player Josh Williams, fiddler Michael Cleveland, and bassist Brady Stogdill. Thile, of course, has gone on to stardom in Nickel Creek, while Cleveland has starred in several high-profile bluegrass acts and made his own recordings. The performance helped spark a "youth in bluegrass" movement during the next several years, Wernick said.

58

"Keynote: 'Bones to Pick'"

PETE WERNICK

Thank you, Murphy, for the invitation to offer information and comments on issues you raised in your keynote speech at IBMA. First, my congratulations and thanks for raising the feminist view. Your delivery was great, and you made a lot of good points.

I do have some bones to pick, but I'll start with common ground: the need to be fair and clear with one another. The Golden Rule points us toward honesty and, on gender issues, to the view: Women and men should be encouraged to be all they can be, and no one should be denied fair rights based on gender.

Your history traced scenes at the IBMA Awards Show. It seems you feel the IBMA is not giving women a fair shake. But the picture you gave was exaggerated by your choosing to omit some important facts which I'd like to offer now.

Item one: the Bluegrass Youth All-Stars, the group I assembled for the 1993 Awards Show. The concept of this group was virtuosity, to powerfully raise a banner still not yet raised just five years ago: "young people in bluegrass." Twelve-year-old virtuosos are hard to come by, and of those I was able to locate, only one was a girl. As I told you back in '93, she was invited but was unavailable.

I asked you, after your speech, what was I to do, include a non-virtuoso girl mainly for her gender, out of her league? You said no, you just would have chosen not to present the group.

Thank goodness, it never occurred to me to sacrifice this great opportunity at the altar of gender representation. In my twelve years in IBMA, I've never seen a performance catalyze people the way this one did. Its long-range effects surely have been, and will be, positive for bluegrassers of all ages and genders. I regret that, for some, this event is memorable as just another slight to females.

But, for the record, regarding IBMA's role in presenting the band, they were not billed or introduced as "the future of bluegrass" as you stated. I daresay anyone using the phrase after hearing them (as did an announcer on the show) was surely making reference to the age, not the gender, of the musicians.

Item two: The bands in the finale of the 1996 Awards Show were all-male. As stated clearly in the show, the concept was to include all past IBMA Entertainer of the Year winners in a tribute to the classic 1946 Blue Grass Boys recordings. And there again, as you know, a female-led band qualified but declined the invitation.

In the two cases above, had the schedules/priorities of two particular females been different, your portrait of gender-insensitive IBMA would have lost a big part of its zing. It would have been nice to hear: "In all fairness, two women were asked," and, in fact, your leaving it out seems rather unfair. In particular as good as I feel about the powerful message sent by the youth band, I feel stung by the public attempt to tarnish the memory of it.

Item three: Our awards voting is based strictly on merit, not on gender (it's all in the awards criteria). Though indeed most nominees and winners have been male, do you know of instances of deserving females being ignored, based on gender? I hope in these discussions people don't suppose that who wins awards is based on IBMA policies. We intend for IBMA members to vote for whoever they think did best, period.

Item four: I appreciate the forum where I can proudly state that IBMA has always strived for balance in our leadership. The Awards Show itself has been produced for years by a team of one woman and one man. Our staff is ⅔ female. We have had a female Board chair and three female vice presidents. Women are well represented among awards presenters and honorees of our special awards (voted by committees). Each year we call on women to be part of the Board nomination process, and try for gender balance (as well as other types of balance) among the nominees. I feel that in an historically very-high-percentage-male industry, we are doing what we can.

Do we agree that in making selections of all sorts, talent and accomplishments should be the bottom line? Despite raised sensitivity to sexism, gender representation is regrettably skewed at times. In the bluegrass world, as in most of the world, progress is steady but painfully slow.

How to help it? I feel the ball is mainly in the court of the female talent itself. If they do what it takes to rise in the industry, they will be rewarded. But they need to step forward and take themselves seriously (like Rose, Louise, Lynn, Alison, Laurie, Alison, you, et al.). Still the gap persists. For example, at my banjo camps, typically two or three of twenty who register are female. I note a similar ratio among bands submitting their work to Prime Cuts of Bluegrass. These pathways up are not restricted by gender. The opportunities are there. As we say, "Pick it up!"

What can the rest of us do? Be encouraging, both publicly and privately, as I don't need to tell you, of all people! I've been doing this for awhile, too. I regularly teach pickers to play in typical "women's keys," something I do a lot myself when my wife, Joan ("Nondi"), and I perform. In 1988 at IBMA I spoke and issued a written statement advocating hiring more female talent at festivals.

I was glad you applauded actions and statements made by Bill Monroe and by Larry Stephenson that have advanced women in bluegrass. It's both pleasant and effective to acknowledge those who do the right thing.

Summing up, my theme is "choose your battles well." There are important ones to keep fighting. I hope you will not waste effort and good will putting your allies on the defensive by attacking them for circumstances they can't control.

Meanwhile, with much thanks to you and many others, thank goodness it's getting better.

Originally published in *Women in Bluegrass*, no. 18 (Fall 1998): 8–9. Reprinted by permission of the author.

Sandy Rothman, who posted this insider's portrait of Bill Monroe on the Internet after Monroe's death, says he first encountered bluegrass music in northern California at the time of the "folk revival" during the late 1950s and early 1960s, came to Nashville, and played guitar and banjo with Bill Monroe and his Blue Grass Boys in 1964. In addition, Rothman has worked with a number of other groups, including Earl Taylor and his Stoney Mountain Boys and the Jerry Garcia Acoustic Band. For what it's worth, my experiences with Monroe's leg-pulling side lead me to believe he was doing just that in the wonderful episode of the Christmas bathrobe cited in this piece.

59

"First Christmas without Bill"

SANDY ROTHMAN

Backstage at the Grand Ole Opry, or wherever he happened to be at Christmastime, Bill Monroe personified "Father Christmas" to me. I first met him in the springtime, but through his records and shows, especially a live tape recording of a 1955 Christmas show in California that made the collectors' rounds, I associated Bill with the holiday long before meeting him. Bill never sang any lyrics he couldn't believe in completely, so when he would later sing "I always have loved Christmas, it's my fave-rite time of year," it confirmed my feelings about his relationship with the season.

Well into the early 1960s it was traditional for Bill and the band to plan their West Coast tour for the wintertime. In those pre-festival times it wasn't unheardof for club bookings on the folk circuit to run into days and even weeks, and for a number of years at Christmastime, Bill's entire entourage would camp out at the Ash Grove, the well-known Los Angeles folk club, for a two-week engagement there. On one occasion, Christmas of 1963, the extended booking even saw a major personnel change: Bill Keith left the band and was replaced on banjo by Bobby Diamond, flown in from the East Coast.

That Ash Grove Christmas was memorable for me and several bluegrass friends because it was our first chance to spend any personal time with Bill. I didn't know how accessible he'd be at the club, but I wasn't going to let anything, not the four-hundred-mile driving trip from the Bay Area or a car that might not make it, deter me from going to see him. If we expected a brief audience with the Master, what we got was as warm a welcome as if we'd been to see him at the Opry. Part of the reason for that must have been the relationship between him and Ash Grove owner Ed Pearl, the most significant bluegrass advocate in California during the Sixties.

Pearl's private office at the club had become a kind of receiving area for Bill and the Boys. One night I knocked on the door and went in with Butch Waller, who had brought along his newly-acquired Gibson mandolin, a woody-sounding 1923 F-5 just a few serial numbers away from Bill's. I don't recall whether this was between shows, before, or after—but Bill got his mandolin out and sat with Butch for what seemed like hours, painstakingly showing him how to play "Raw Hide."

The image of a calm and patient Bill Monroe, never one to "get in a hurry" no matter the circumstances, passing along his mandolin brilliance to an eager young student is one I cherish always—a true expression of the generous spirit that is at the heart of Christmas.

As always with Bill, there was seriousness and there was fun. One Eighties' winter I visited his dressing room at the Opry and listened as the band rehearsed "That's Christmas Time to Me," his seasonal offering from 1977, a line of which was quoted near the beginning of this story. At one point Bill brought the proceedings to a halt after the banjo player played some fancy Earl Scruggs–like backup licks instead of the simple, bell-like harmonic "chimes" that Bill Holden had picked on the recording. He told the young musician, "You've got to get that Christmas banjo tone." This broke everyone up, although the room was silent. We didn't know whether "Christmas banjo tone" meant those expected harmonics or just some kind of sparkling tone that pleased Bill's ear on a holiday number. Whatever it was, Bill wasn't hearing it, and he wanted it . . . and it was, after all, Christmas. Things had to be especially right.

I feel fortunate and grateful to have shared a few holiday times with Bill over four decades, but my two most treasured close experiences with "Father Christmas" came during some of his last Christmases on earth in Nashville in the early Nineties.

The first of these was Christmas of 1992. Bill's guitarist and lead singer, Tom Ewing, was taking some time off for the holidays and asked me if I'd like to fly out and fill in for him on the Opry. Tom even left his guitar and hat in an Opry locker for me to use in this dream come true. On Christmas Eve we played the Friday Night Opry. On Saturday it was cold for Nashville. I'd been invited out to Bill's farm for early Christmas dinner with family and friends, the first Christmas I'd shared with the Bluegrass Father in years and the first one ever at his own home. This was especially important to me because, as a kid raised in a Jewish home without Christmas, I'd felt closer to the holiday in part through Bill's evocative 1951 recording of "Christmas Time's a-Comin'" and, later, from him personally.

Inside Bill's two-hundred-year-old log house there was a lot of warmth and conviviality, smoke curling up the old stone chimney to the crisp air outside. Bill was standing there quietly tending the fire in the rustic living room, wearing his comfortable blue jeans and flannel shirt. He would go out to the porch for logs occasionally while dogs, kitties, and kids scampered around him like something from the verses of an unwritten song. Later, after supper, he sat in his easy chair, circled by son James and grandson "Jimbo" and all the gathered friends and family, and it was time to watch him open his presents (and for him to give some: I got a wallet and key ring set that served several years from that day on).

While all this joy was happening, we barely noticed that it had become very, very quiet outside. A few more presents—an unforgettable look of delight filling the flame-illuminated hollows of that sculpted Monroe face as he unwrapped a lifelike model of a cute little puppy dog—and suddenly we realized it was snowing, and not just a little. We stepped out on the porch to watch in wonder and hear the sound-lessness of the best white Christmas ever . . . then quickly back inside to Bill's care-fully-tended fire.

It was still early afternoon, but with his years of road experience, it took Bill no time at all to make the decision that we needed to get dressed and ready and get to town and the Opry while we still could. He was worried that we'd be late for the Christmas show. The snow was falling so fast and furious that staying the night at the Opryland Hotel wasn't ruled out, so we packed up the long white limousine, which had become nearly invisible under the snowy blanket, and headed for the front gate. Bill was right. It turned out that we didn't have to stay in Nashville over-night, but the roads out from the farm were treacherous.

Our bluegrass caravan snaked along the country lanes, carrying Mr. Monroe and his family and friends to town. He was in the front passenger seat, hat on as usual. At one point, after he seemed comfortable with the way his driver was handling the car, Bill's snow-white hat started to turn towards me, and I leaned forward from the back seat. I thought he was going to say something about the weather or the roads or tonight's show. Instead, momentarily softening his vigilance about driving safe-ly and getting to the Opry on time, he pointed to a corner house we were just pass-ing and told me wistfully, "That's where Bradley Kincaid used to live." Kincaid had died three years earlier. I knew how important this influential songster and fellow Kentuckian was to Bill, and I could imagine him stopping by to visit in years past.

We were at the Opry hours early. Hardly anyone was around backstage. We un-packed the mandolin and guitar and played and sang, had coffee, talked, and were quiet for long periods of time like you always were with Bill. One by one the rest of the Blue Grass Boys arrived; Bill greeted each of them with a spirited "Merry Christ-mas!" as if they were dignitaries instead of the hired musicians he saw almost every day. We didn't decide what songs we were going to do for each stage segment—an instrumental, the gospel quartet, a Monroe chestnut or two—until shortly before going on. That was his method.

A year later I had a chance to fill in with Bill again, on a different instrument. His banjo player, Dana Cupp, was going home for Christmas and offered me the holiday weekend at the Opry. I was surprised when Bill came to get me at the air-port and will never forget how he grabbed my banjo case from me and carried it to the car! Before the weekend's broadcasts were to begin, on Thursday evening, he asked if I could drive the two of us to his church in the limo. (I'd only driven it once before, several years earlier, when he'd suddenly appointed me driver at his festival in Bean Blossom, Indiana.) When we got there the minister asked if we would sing a couple of songs from the pulpit. Bill and I looked at each other and we told him we didn't even have a guitar between us, just our mandolin and banjo in the car trunk. It never occurred to me that we would stand up in front of the congregation and play just with those two instruments, but that's what we did. It was sublime. Of all the times I was honored to play music with Bill Monroe, this occasion promised to be among the more perilous—but it was the best.

Without distraction from other instruments or voices, perhaps it was easy for Bill to hear well and be musically responsive. Perhaps the same was true for me. With just the two fine old Gibson instruments ringing together (his 1923 mandolin, my 1930s banjo), there seemed to be a blending of qualities you couldn't easily experience within the competing sounds of a full band. "Separate your notes, keep your timing right, and let your tones come out," Bill liked to say. He was a master musician who always set his mandolin notes like a fine craftsman setting gemstones into silver. Bill's instrumental and vocal articulation revealed his desire and ability to communicate the music with unwavering clarity.

As my stage fright receded in front of that small and earnest Tennessee congregation, I heard the two instruments talking to each other in a way I never had before and never would again. Bill's keen listening ability and refined musical responsiveness were at a powerful attunement. Every note I played he complemented on several levels at once, creating a seamless musical conversation: choice of notes, voicing and register, volume, tonal color. He relaxed and settled into the unusual duet format the way I remember him settling into the stage sound when we played an occasional show without microphones back in 1964. He just made it work. The next evening, Christmas Eve, we played the Opry and he surprised me by complimenting my banjo tone onstage. Walking next to me as the curtain went down after one of the many short segments you do at the Opry, his eyes twinkled in the dark as he asked in his best Good Uncle voice: "Did you enjoy that?" I said I sure did, and also told him what I felt from the playing we'd done at the church. He said yes, our two instruments had really sounded good together there.

And now for the anecdote that made me think about writing this story. I first heard Bill called "Father Christmas" this same night, backstage at the Opry. The person who called him that was Porter Wagoner, and it was echoed by Wilma Lee Cooper. Here's how it happened:

James Monroe came into the dressing room with a Christmas present for his daddy. Bill opened the large box to find a red-and-white-striped terry cloth bathrobe, reminiscent of a candy cane or Old Glory. Bill was delighted with it (Christmas candy and American patriotism at the same time) and immediately put it on over his dark suit, to everyone's surprise. He looked at himself in the mirror, smoothed out the robe and his special Christmas tie under it, and went striding out to the backstage hallway.

He would spot someone he knew, walk right up to them and stand really close (uncharacteristically close), ask how they liked his "coat," and then just grin. At one point he was doing this to Gwen McReynolds, Jesse's daughter, as she stood against the musicians' lockers in the hall. Gwen didn't quite know what to say. Tom Ewing (Bill's lead singer and guitarist at the time and Gwen's fiancé) was standing next to her and said, "That's a nice bathrobe, Bill!"

Bill got a strange expression on his face, drew himself up to his full height, looked Tom square in the eye, and said in seemingly utter seriousness, "You wouldn't take a bath in something like that!" Then he turned around and walked into the performers' lounge, straight into a bemused Chet Atkins, who was randomly filming with his video camera. At one point Bill even went onto the Opry stage while an act was performing, strode right out to the spotlight, and showed himself and his new overcoat to the audience. Impishly, he stayed dressed that way for the next Blue Grass Boys segment. He just seemed to love playing in it. That's when Porter called him "Father Christmas."

When he came back to his dressing room, thoroughly delighted and pleased with himself, Wilma Lee Cooper helped him take the "coat" off and hang it up, and then he (and everyone else) spent the rest of the night picking a thousand little red and white bits of thread from his dark blue suit. After we had rehearsed and played the rest of our segments, he put his "coat" back on again in the dressing room and went out to the hallway to show it off to some new people he'd noticed milling around there. Then we helped him pack up the robe, or coat, and all his other Christmas presents and take them out to the car.

We'll never know for sure if he did or didn't know what a bathrobe was. Knowing Bill, equal parts rough-hewn nineteenth-century pioneer and urbane leg-puller, it could have been just as likely either way.

He was eighty-two then. That was the last Christmas I got to spend with him. Three years later, Christmas 1996, was the first without him. There were "white candles burning," as he sang in "Christmas Time's a-Comin'," but they weren't as bright as they used to be. William Smith Monroe was Christmas, just as he was bluegrass, and neither Christmas nor bluegrass will ever be quite the same again.

––––––––

Internet posting, Nov. 1, 1998. Reprinted by permission of the author.

New Orleans author Tom Piazza caused a sensation in bluegrass with an essay on Jimmy Martin that first appeared in the magazine *Oxford American*. That was true even though fans and associates had long been aware of Martin's reputation for outlandish and sometimes dismaying behavior. No one, however, had ever put quite as all-revealing a lens to the great singer. Vanderbilt University Press and the Country Music Foundation Press released the essay in book form in 1999, along with an afterword, essay on Martin's music, and a timeline of the singer's career. That seemed to emphasize Piazza's desire to portray Martin's musical brilliance as well as his eccentricities. Piazza, a pianist, has published widely on American music styles, including jazz and blues. This excerpt from his landmark piece aptly portrays a familiar habitat for generations of bluegrass musicians and fans: the backslappingly convivial atmosphere that unfolds backstage at the Grand Ole Opry.

60

"From *True Adventures with the King of Bluegrass*"

TOM PIAZZA

I am at the Grand Ole Opry, backstage. It feels, indeed, like a big night at the high school, down to the putty-colored metal lockers that line the hall, the dressing rooms off the hall, with people crowding in and spilling out into the general stream—laughter, snatches of jokes and gossip overhead as you pass along—the halls even have the same dimensions of a high school hall, crowded with people, men and women, men with very dyed-looking hair and rhinestone-studded suits and guitars around their shoulders; at one point I recognize Charlie Louvin, of the Louvin Brothers. I follow Jimmy, who is alternately oblivious and glad-handing people as if he's running for senator. He attracts a fair amount of attention, even here, where flamboyance is part of the recipe.

Eventually we come to the dark, cave-like stage entrance, with heavy curtains going way up into the dark rigging above. The curtains at the front of the stage are closed, and I can hear the audience filing in out front. People in this area come and go with a more focused sense of purpose than out in the noisy halls; by the entrance to the area stand a guitarist and another young man and woman, harmonizing a bit. We walk into the bright, comfortable green room, just to the left of the stage entrance, and someone, a big man with stooped shoulders, comes over to Jimmy.

"Jimmy, how you doin' there?" he says, putting his arm around Martin and shaking his hand. "How's the old Hall of Fame member?"

"Well," Jimmy says, "I'm a Hall of Fame member, and the big booker ain't booked me shit."

Glancing at me a little embarrassedly, the other guy says, "Well, you never know; tomorrow's a brand-new day." We stand for a minute listening to the little group singing their song. "They're singing some bluegrass right over there," the man says. Martin grunts. This must be difficult for him being here, I think, like crashing a party. He seems to go in and out of his drunkenness; sometimes he's lucid, other times he has trouble putting a sentence together.

Now another man comes up and asks him, "Are you on the Opry tonight?"

Martin says, "No. They won't let me on it."

"Well, when are you going to get the hell on it?"

"Hey, Charlie," Martin says, grinning, "I can get out there and sing it and put it over!"

"I know it. I've seen you do it. Get out there and sing one."

Martin seems pleased by the encounter. He gets the two men seated; he's going to tell them a joke. Two women are walking around a shopping mall, carrying heavy baskets full of all the stuff they bought. They get tired at one point and they sit down. After they've been sitting fifteen, twenty minutes, one of them says, "I tell you, I got to get up here; my rear end done plum went to sleep on me." The other one says, "I thought it did; I thought I heard it snore three or four times."

Great laughter at the joke. "Now you beat that, goddamn it," Martin says, triumphantly. We walk away, toward the stage area.

This is going okay, I think. He's seen some old friends, his ego's getting stroked, people seem to like having him around. Who knows? I think. Maybe they will invite him to join after all.

We approach the small group that had been singing, and Jimmy stops. He says, "You're going to play on the Grand Ole Opry?"

"Yes, sir," the young man with the guitar says. He puts his hand out and says, "How are you doing, Mr. Martin?"

"What are you going to sing on it?" Jimmy asks.

"I'm playing with Ricky Skaggs," he says.

"Yeah?" Jimmy says.

"Yeah," the young man says. "Gonna play a little bluegrass tonight."

"A little bluegrass," Jimmy says.

"Yeah."

"Well," Jimmy begins, "he's about the *sorriest* fuckin' bluegrass you could ever hope to be on *with*, I'll tell you."

All three look at him, still smiling but a little stunned; the woman says, "Ohhhh," as if he must be trying to make a good-humored joke that he has just taken a little too far, and the young man with the guitar, smiling more broadly, says, "Well, bless your heart. . . ."

"Well," Martin says, even louder now, "I'm just telling you, he's about the sorriest bluegrass, and *tell him I said it.*"

"I'll do it," the young man says, smiling even more broadly, as Martin lumbers off.

I start off after Martin, who abruptly stops, turns around, and adds, "*Hey,* bring him over here and let *me* tell him that."

"He's back there," the young man yells after us.

Now we're making our way along through the dark backstage area, and I'm thinking maybe I should just lead Martin out of here before something really bad happens. He's heading for another well-lit area, where some instruments—fiddles, banjos—are tuning up, sawing away, warming up. "Didn't I tell him?" Jimmy says to me, proudly. "Let's see if we can see anybody back here."

Now we enter a brightly lit, garage-like area, with musicians milling around, and a number of older men who look like a certain type you still see behind the scenes at prizefights—slit-eyed, white-shoed, pencil moustaches, sitting in chairs, watching everything. "Hello, Jimmy," someone says; a middle-aged man walking toward us, with a banjo, wearing a plaid sports shirt. "Good to see you, man," the man says, with genuine warmth. They shake hands. They make some small talk, mostly Jimmy talking about his hunting plans. The banjoist seems to know all about the hunting and the dogs. Then Jimmy tells him the joke about the two women. The banjoist laughs and laughs. "I don't want you to *steal* this on me, now." Jimmy says. Everything seems to be cool again.

Then Jimmy says, "Let's me, you, and Brewster do a tune." The banjoist calls the guitarist and singer Paul Brewster over. Across the room I see a big guy walk by, with a kind of combination crewcut and bouffant hairstyle, carrying a mandolin; it's Ricky Skaggs.

From my left side I suddenly hear Martin's voice, loud, hollering, "Is that the BIGGEST ASSHOLE in Nashville?"

Immediately the banjoist launches into a loud, unaccompanied solo, Earl Scruggs–style, an old Bill Monroe–Lester Flatt tune from the late 1940s called "Will You Be Loving Another Man?" and it is beautiful, ringing, pure and uncut, and, his attention distracted like a bull's by a red cape, Martin begins singing the refrain, the banjoist and the guitarist joining in with the harmony; then Martin sings the first verse over just the banjo, his voice piercing and brilliant, then the refrain again, with the harmony, and the banjo comes in for a solo, so spangling and stinging and precise, the melody appearing out of a shower of rhythmic sequins and winking lights and now Martin comes in for another chorus, with the banjo underneath him telegraphing a constant commentary, goading and dancing around Martin's melody, and it's as if they have all levitated about six inches off the floor, pure exhilaration, and by far the best music I have heard during my time in Nashville.

When it's over there is that lag of a few seconds that it always takes for reality to be sucked back into the vacuum where great music has been, and as reality returns, along with it strides Ricky Skaggs.

"Hey, Jimmy," he says, pleasantly, walking over to our little group, strumming his mandolin, perhaps a little bit nervously. "How you doin'?"

"Okay," Martin says, making it sound, somehow, like a challenge. "How *you* doin'?"

"Okay." Strum, strum.

"Think you can still sing tenor to me?" Oh, no I think.

Skaggs laughs, strums a little more. "I don't know. If you don't get it too high for me."

"Ricky, it's left up to you." Martin says. "It's not left up to me. If you want to make a ass out of yourself and don't want to sing tenor with me, don't do it. *He* can sing tenor with me," indicating Paul Brewster, who had been taking the high part in the song they had just sung.

"He sure can," Skaggs says, strumming, already regretting that he has come over. "He sings a good tenor to me."

"But you can't sing tenor to me," Martin persists. "You did with Ralph Stanley, didn't you?"

"I was sixteen then," Skaggs answers.

"He lost his balls, huh?" Martin says, to the few of us gathered around. "He lost his balls; he can't sing tenor with Jimmy no more."

Strum, strum.

"I can sing lead with any sumbitch who's ever sung," Martin says.

"You sure can," Skaggs says.

"Huh?"

"You sure can," Skaggs says, no longer looking at Martin.

Not to be placated, Martin goes on, "You let me down."

"I couldn't sing it that high, Jimmy."

"You didn't *hurt* me," Martin says, "about making money. I made it."

"That's right, you sure did," Skaggs says. Then, wearing a Mona Lisa smile and nodding politely, he says, "Good to see you guys," and steps away.

Excerpted from *True Adventures with the King of Bluegrass* (Nashville: Vanderbilt University Press in cooperation with the Country Music Foundation Press, 1999), 53–62. Reprinted by permission of the author.

Good journalism often takes readers into places and situations where they would very much like to be. And an effective profile puts you in the room with the subject. In this instance, *New York Times* staff writer Neil Strauss took his readers into John Hartford's kitchen and other rooms of his Cumberland River home, making plain an ailing Hartford who was nonetheless as involved as ever in music. "I probably only have two years left," Hartford told Strauss. Tragically, Hartford didn't last that long; cancer brought his life to an end on June 4, 2001.

61

"Fiddling and Picking His Way to Perfection"

NEIL STRAUSS

Nashville, Oct. 5. Sitting in the kitchen of John Hartford's house feels a lot like being on a riverboat. Through the irregular wooden room's small white-fringed windows, all that can be seen is a whitewashed rail and a picturesque stretch of the Cumberland River. Gathered in that room one afternoon late last week were three young pickers, with Mr. Hartford—surrounded by a metronome, a microphone and a tape recorder—perched at the head of the long kitchen table.

Picking up his fiddle, Mr. Hartford pressed the record button on the tape deck and began a bluegrass tune he recently learned from French-Canadian musicians.

The other players joined in or struggled to keep up. Between songs he stopped the tape deck and told stories about growing up in Missouri, rested his head on his hands and rubbed his bleary eyes and stringy gray hair, and lounged on the couch with his legs raised on cushions. Scattered around the table were copies of Mr. Hartford's new CD (estimated to be his thirty-sixth album), *Good Old Boys* (Rounder), and his recent collaboration with David Grisman and Mike Seeger, *Retrograss* (Acoustic Disc).

Best known as a banjo player and songwriter, Mr. Hartford wrote one of the most recorded and broadcast songs in country music, "Gentle on My Mind," which has been performed by over two hundred artists, most famously Glen Campbell.

He played on the seminal Byrds album, *Sweetheart of the Rodeo* (1968). Soon after, he spent a few years in Los Angeles writing and performing for *The Smothers Brothers Comedy Hour* and *The Glen Campbell Goodtime Hour* (on which he worked with everyone from Stevie Wonder to Johnny Cash to a young Steve Martin). He has also been a disk jockey (the job that brought him to Tennessee in 1965) and provided voice-overs for film and television (including Ken Burns's *Civil War* series).

He has been a historian (he is writing a biography of the blind fiddler Ed Haley) and a riverboat pilot, his obsession after music.

But Mr. Hartford does not have the stamina he once had. He said he did not plan to tour much to support his new albums.

"I probably only have two years left," he said in his genial, aw-shucks voice. "Promoting a record is a lot less important to me than having a heck of a time with what I've got left."

Although he is only sixty-one, Mr. Hartford says he often feels as if he is falling apart. "Cancer has just about emptied my phone book, and I've got it, too," he said.

Mr. Hartford also has anemia, and in the last few months he had a sinus operation and developed knee problems that require him to elevate his leg throughout the day.

But the older he becomes, the more obsessive he is about getting better at his instrument. When he took a break to rest his knee, the younger pickers—Chris Sharp on guitar, Matt Combs on fiddle and Avery Auger on banjo—gathered around him. "The reason I'm in the business is because I love to play, and I love to explore where to go," Mr. Hartford said. "What happens is you run up against a wall in your playing and you start searching along the wall and you find this door down here. And you open it up and there's this beautiful garden on the other side and you crawl through and all of a sudden every tune that you know becomes a whole new experience again."

Mr. Combs asked, "Where can I find that door?"

He was joking, but Mr. Hartford answered: "I've had so many instances where I've come against a wall and said, 'Well, that's the farthest I can go, and I just don't have the talent to go any further.' But I can hear that what I'm playing is wrong.

It doesn't match what I hear in my head. And I keep fussing and fooling and tinkering with it, and pretty soon I will discover what is basically a cheap trick that will keep me from doing that again. And that's what those little doors and gates are. And to be real honest with you, I have a terrible time with my records, all of them. Since we made *Good Old Boys* six or eight months ago, there are all kinds of little doors that I've found. In fact, I'd like to go back and re-record the whole thing."

He paused and smiled. "My ultimate goal is to rent my records rather than sell them," he said. "So when I get past a problem, I can call them back in and say, 'Listen, we've remodeled this piece of material.'"

There was a knock on the door, and another picker, a banjo player, entered the room. He reached a hand out in greeting, but Mr. Hartford did not want to shake hands. Clearly the banjo player had not met Mr. Hartford before; if he had, he would have known that Mr. Hartford has not shaken a hand for as long as anyone can remember. He is frightened that someone will bruise or break his bones. Among Mr. Hartford's other eccentricities is his handwriting style: he gives autographs writing with both hands simultaneously in a beautiful baroque script.

After a little picking, the party adjourned into Mr. Hartford's back room, where the walls are lined with a bluegrass fan's dream: boxes and boxes of cassettes of unreleased sessions, picking parties and radio shows of Mr. Hartford and other bluegrass legends. He put in a tape of Lester Flatt and Earl Scruggs recordings from the 1950's, when the fiddler Benny Martin was in their band. Although Mr. Hartford spent his teen-age years in Missouri playing fiddle at square dances, weekend-long barn parties at which the men would sleep downstairs and the women upstairs, as soon as he heard Mr. Scruggs play banjo, he decided to switch instruments. Only recently has he returned to playing the fiddle.

"I would probably consider Earl Scruggs as much a father of rock-and-roll as anybody," Mr. Hartford said. "It's all very clear and obvious, especially if you've ever heard that record called *Million Dollar Quartet,* that Elvis was trying to fuse Delta blues with Bill Monroe when Lester and Earl were in the band."

"And I know it because I know Sam Phillips and Jack Clement," he concluded, citing names from Sun Records, where Presley made his first recordings.

When the pickers began to leave around 9 P.M., Mr. Hartford was sitting exactly where they first saw him hours earlier: at the head of his kitchen table flanked by microphone, metronome, tape deck and fiddle, still trying after almost fifty years of playing to get better.

"This," Mr. Hartford confided, gesturing to the display around him, "is the pain in the life of a guy who considers himself a mediocre musician."

Among the writers specializing in bluegrass of the early years, Jon Weisberger's perspective is exceptionally broad-based. As a contributing editor to the alt-country magazine *No Depression,* where his piece on Ricky Skaggs appeared, Weisberger has to make connections for readers whose primary orientation with country music comes from acts such as Steve Earle and Whiskeytown. His in-depth knowledge of bluegrass history has also, however, made him a welcome contributor in hard-core bluegrass circles, where he's won awards from the International Bluegrass Music Association.

His background? "I first encountered bluegrass as a part of the larger country music world I grew to love as a teenager in upstate New York in the late 1960s. But though I acquired a few Flatt and Scruggs, Stanley Brothers and Bill Monroe albums, it wasn't until I moved to Cincinnati some ten years later and heard Red Allen— first on records, then in person—that it became a preoccupation. That was in time to catch the waning days of the older bluegrass scene that had once flourished in the city's hillbilly bars as well as the festivals that predominate today, and the experience has shaped my view of the bluegrass world ever since."

62

"Going Back to Old Kentucky: Ricky Skaggs Rediscovers the Rules of Bluegrass"

JON WEISBERGER

Ricky Skaggs in *No Depression?* I can already see some readers scratching their heads—or, more likely, flinging their copies across the room. Skaggs, after all, has been a Nashvegas mainstream country fixture for years, and though his latest country album (*Life Is a Journey,* Atlantic) is doing well on Gavin's Americana chart, those familiar with the forty-three-year old singer only through his *Monday Night Concerts at the Ryman* series on TNN may wonder what he's doing in the pages of a magazine that mostly covers . . . well, you know.

The fact is, though, that these days Skaggs is a man with a mission, one that meshes nicely with this magazine's interests. Simply put, it's to bring what Steve Earle recently called "the original alternative country"—that is, bluegrass, and especially the hard-core bluegrass of the genre's early years—to new audiences. In pursuit of that goal, he's been preaching the gospel of bluegrass out on the road, and he's re-leased his first all-bluegrass album in fifteen or more years. Like any good missionary, he's found a way to simplify his message, in this case to a single, memorable phrase; the title of the album is *Bluegrass Rules*—as in "country rocks, but bluegrass rules"—and the music he's been making, both on the album and on his shows this past summer, is all the proof needed to drive home the point.

On a mild September Saturday evening I went down to Frankfort, Kentucky's Farnham Dudgeon Civic Auditorium to catch Skaggs's show-closing set at the Kentucky Folk Life Festival. To heighten the Skaggsian focus of the experience, I traveled with Dwight McCall, a friend and former bandmate of mine who presently occupies Skaggs's old tenor vocals/mandolin chair in J. D. Crowe's New South, one of two other acts on the bill. Dwight's a huge fan of Ricky's, the kind of guy who can knowledgeably discuss the variations between a dozen different bootlegged tapes of Skaggs singing "Molly and Tenbrooks" back in his New South days, and I was curious to see what he thought of Skaggs and his band, Kentucky Thunder.

Frankfort's Civic Center is mostly geared toward sporting events, and it made for a slightly peculiar bluegrass venue; thanks to a poor advertising strategy, it was only about half full by the time the show kicked off. If the crowd was small, it was nevertheless enthusiastic about a bill composed of native Kentucky frontmen and their bands, and Crowe (from Lexington) and the Osborne Brothers (from Hyden, though long-time Nashville residents), with Skaggs acting as a garrulous MC, were well received as they delivered sets of both old favorites and new material. Then it was time for Kentucky Thunder.

Though Skaggs began his journey back to bluegrass several years ago, it's only been recently—this past festival season, really—that he's been out and about putting on bluegrass shows, and for many in the audience—including myself and Dwight—it was the first opportunity to see the show first-hand, and I'm here to tell you, friends, it was a dandy. In keeping with the show's theme, a celebration of Bill Monroe, Skaggs and his band hit the stage hard with one of Monroe's best-known invocations of his native state, "I'm Going Back to Old Kentucky," and never let up. Pushing the band with his mandolin, much as Monroe used to do, he blazed through a set comprised almost exclusively of Monroe favorites, from the furious fiddle-led instrumental "Big Mon," through the biography of "Uncle Pen" to the dark gospel quartet, "Get Down on Your Knees and Pray," before winding up the scheduled set with the mandolin rave-up, "Get Up John."

It was an overpowering show, and Dwight wasn't the only musician who could be seen at the side of the stage alternately shaking his head and muttering in admiration both of Skaggs's flawless performance and the no less powerful work of the band—elder statesman and fiddler Bobby Hicks, guitar phenom Bryan Sutton, upright bass player Mark Fain, guitarist/tenor singer Paul Brewster, guitarist/baritone singer Darrin Vincent, and favored guest banjo player Jimmy Mills of North Carolina.

These are men who, though mostly young, have spent their lifetimes playing bluegrass—in Hicks' case, with Monroe himself throughout the immensely creative years of the 1950s—and their combined century and a half's worth of experience is tightly focussed on a sound that, while leavened with a few contemporary touches (notably Sutton's blistering lead guitar work), is so firmly traditionally-oriented that no one seemed to notice the virtually unheard-of three-guitar configuration; as Dwight said later, "it looks crazy, but when they're that good, who cares?"

"There's something coming with this music," Skaggs enthuses over the phone. "It's like it's been hidden for years." That may or may not be true, but if it is, part of the responsibility lies at the door of the label Skaggs was signed to for years, Columbia/Epic. At his Frankfort show, Skaggs launched into a brief but pithy description of the problem: "They wouldn't let me record any bluegrass. I even had to fight with 'em to get them to release 'Uncle Pen' [from his 1983 *Don't Cheat in Our Hometown* album] as a single—and it went to #1." When Skaggs moved to Atlantic in 1995, he says, new possibilities opened up; the label was willing to allow him outside projects, though it's apparently still uninterested in releasing bluegrass itself.

In the meantime, his mostly dormant interest in bluegrass had been reinvigorated. "Two or three years ago, Doc Watson invited me to Merlefest, and I asked if I could bring a bluegrass band; before I'd been going up there and playing with whomever. This time I took [then band member] Shawn Lane, Billy Joe Foster, and Keith Little. We had a blast." The experience was encouraging enough that Skaggs not only repeated it on a couple of occasions, but found himself spending more time playing bluegrass with Kentucky Thunder members on the bus and in hotel rooms. "After those first couple of bluegrass dates," he continues, "we did a tour of New Zealand, where we pretty much opened for ourselves as a bluegrass band. Afterwards, I would go to a preset place on the stage and do some solo country or play some fiddle while the stage was reset, and then we'd do a country show. After that, in some cities, we'd open as a country band, then talk about the roots of country, and finish up playing bluegrass. We were getting some confidence, we were having fun, and people were telling me that there was an expression of joy on my face that I hadn't had on shows in a long time."

"I started talking to my agent, saying 'go out and see if there are three or four festivals we can work.' We could afford to do them for less than the country show, because we had a smaller show and fewer equipment needs, etc. That netted us a few festivals—maybe ten to twenty bluegrass dates in all two years ago—and from there, things just grew to where we have sixty-five of them this year."

Though Skaggs had been wandering in the general direction of bluegrass for a while, the death of Bill Monroe last year kicked the process into a higher gear. "A lot of this I couldn't have done while Bill Monroe was alive," he says, "because I didn't want anyone to think I was trying to usurp his position." In Monroe's last months, however, following a stroke in the spring of 1996, Skaggs spent many hours with Monroe, and, he says, "I made a promise: I'm going to play bluegrass. I may do some country dates, but I'm going to do bluegrass from now on."

If Ricky Skaggs has been drawn away from country toward bluegrass, it's also true that he has, to a large extent, been pushed away from country by the increasing constriction and emptiness of the contemporary mainstream country scene. "Right now country is in such a place that I don't know if there's a place for me," he says—and quickly adds, "I'm not worried about it, though." Indeed, looking back over his career, he seems slightly bemused by his mainstream success. "Playing blue-grass, then going with Emmylou, and only then moving to Nashville, that back-ground set me apart from the whole *Urban Cowboy* thing. We were so surprised by what happened; we have a #1 with 'Crying My Heart Out over You?' Flatt and Scruggs!?"

While Skaggs avoids any hint of bitterness in his criticism of contemporary country music, his views aren't particularly complimentary, especially when he contrasts the mainstream radio scene with what's happening elsewhere. When I spoke to him, he had just appeared on the Country Music Association's awards show (to present, not perform), but he'd also been at the Gavin Americana radio retreat just a few days earlier, and the contrast between the latter and the world of the former—especially radio—was on his mind: "There was no judgmental criticism at the Gavin event, and that was a big difference. There's so much criticism in coun-try radio these days, people and labels trying to knock each other down; when you're up at the top, losing radio means losing dates. This is something I know; 'Loving Only Me' was my last #1 [in 1989], and without subsequent airplay we've seen a decline in dates, a decline in product sales and sometimes a decline in attendance."

"One thing I heard at Gavin," he continues, "was that with one radio group, the owner wrote a letter to country labels: 'we're drawing a line in the sand, you're not going to shove that stuff down our throats any more.' I almost turned a double back flip. There are twenty-five- or twenty-six-hundred full-time country music stations in this country, and only 10 percent report to *Billboard,* so in terms of what people are really listening to, it's sad to me. The chart is a facade, not the real thing; it's a fantasy."

Yet beyond these observations, and the impact their subject has had on his ca-reer, a talk with Skaggs reveals some deeper attitudinal explanations for the move; for one, though he's a skilled and soulful practitioner of country music, and though he understands that the two styles are intertwined—"it's kind of a chicken and egg thing, bluegrass and country; Bill and Charlie [Monroe], mandolin and guitar, that was pre-bluegrass country"—at bottom he finds bluegrass more demanding, and hence both more stimulating and rewarding.

"There's a difference this way," he tells me. "You can coast in country, be fairly decent and get by, because that music is based so much on the lead vocalist and rhythm section. To be a great bluegrass musician, you've got to excel. Like on the mandolin, there's Ronnie McCoury, Chris Thile, Sam Bush, Butch Baldassari, and David Grisman out there. If you're going to be a banjo player, it's the same way. The standards are raised in bluegrass; you're out there on a limb, either sawing yourself off or floating on the music." And bringing the point closer to home, he says of Kentucky Thunder, "To work in this group, you have to know your roots; the mu-sicians I really lean on have to have the file cards they can pull out from the '40s and '50s, they have to be able to pull out the licks."

Skaggs can demand of his band members that they be able to "pull out the licks . . . from the '40s and '50s" in large part because he's thoroughly mastered the ability himself. The career shift documented in *Bluegrass Rules* is, after all, not a move to new ground, but a return to home field. Born in Cordell, Kentucky, in 1954, "little Ricky" quickly showed himself as one of the most talented of the thousands of boys who lit out on the path of mastering bluegrass, performing on stage with Monroe and on TV with Flatt and Scruggs before he turned ten. A living-room tape from 1970 shows a fifteen-year-old Skaggs and equally youthful buddy Keith Whitley in full command of the instrumental and vocal styles of nearby Dickenson County, Virginia's Stanley Brothers, and sure enough, by the next year the two of them were working for surviving brother Ralph in his Clinch Mountain Boys because, as Ralph said, "they could sing the old Stanley Brothers songs better than I could."

Indeed, Skaggs' talent was so great and so quickly manifested that by the time he participated in the recording of the epochal *J. D. Crowe and The New South* (Rounder, 1975), he was almost matter-of-factly referred to by a reviewer as "of course [a] recognized master" of the mandolin and fiddle. Bootlegs and rare recordings of that band—frontman J. D. Crowe (himself a former child prodigy who began playing banjo with Jimmy Martin at fourteen), Skaggs, Tony Rice, a young Jerry Douglas and bassist Bobby Slone—are prized possessions among bluegrass enthusiasts, and Skaggs's contributions to the band account for much of their appeal.

Though he was barely twenty-one, he had forged personal styles on both the mandolin and the fiddle that seamlessly blended an intimate knowledge of predecessors like Bill Monroe and Bobby Osborne (to name only a couple of mandolinists) with a contemporary, jazz-influenced approach in ways that render his performances, even now, instantly recognizable; perhaps more importantly, he had already set a new standard for tenor singers, bringing together the curls and turns that characterize Ralph Stanley's style from the duets with brother Carter and an uncanny ability to match both tone and part with whatever lead singer he was working with, creating an effect that was at once powerful and supportive, always identifiable but never overwhelming.

These talents, displayed successively in the Clinch Mountain Boys, the Country Gentlemen, J. D. Crowe and The New South, and Boone Creek, as well as on numerous guest appearances, had made Skaggs a leading figure in bluegrass by the time he turned to country, first in a stint with Emmylou Harris's Hot Band and on his solo album, *Sweet Temptation*, and then in the full plunge of 1981's *Waiting for the Sun to Shine*. With his meteoric rise to the top of the country charts, his bluegrass appearances became a memory, kept alive by aging recordings and occasional—very occasional—appearances, as in the mid-1980s New South reunion included on Sugar Hill's Grammy-winning release, *Bluegrass: The World's Greatest Show;* ironically, when a 1980s' return to the traditional (one of the most powerful of several such cycles) took shape, it was driven, in large part, by the recordings and appearances of the Bluegrass Album Band, a project involving mostly musicians closely associated with Skaggs—Rice, Crowe, fiddler Bobby Hicks (then, as now, a member of Skaggs' band)—but Ricky himself was absent.

Now, with the release of *Bluegrass Rules* and a growing list of bluegrass gigs, Skaggs is poised to resume a prominent role in the world of bluegrass—and, perhaps more importantly, a prominent role in bringing the music that lies at its center into new arenas. Yet this is no simple picking up where he left off; where Skaggs had, toward the end of the 1970s, mined a progressive vein that was clearly different from, though indebted to, the sound of the earlier masters, he has now reached back to a more traditional sound, albeit one that has some distinctly modern characteristics, and a thoroughly traditional repertoire. He doesn't rule out a re-emergence of more modern sounds and material, but, he says, that's not what *Bluegrass Rules* is about: "This is my first new bluegrass album. I couldn't do twelve brand new songs, it just didn't feel right. We're going to pay honor and tribute to the originals. We'll probably incorporate more newer stuff as we go along; the floor is open for discussion. There'll be a lot of that old stuff, but I know that to keep moving on, I want to do new songs, if they have an edge to them. We can take what we've heard from the '40s and '50s and make it new and fresh."

Not coincidentally, that was exactly the dominant impression both Dwight and I had as we headed home from Frankfort. Ricky Skaggs and Kentucky Thunder have created a sound that comes as close as any to capturing the bluegrass dialectic— that yin and yang of the old and new, the recreative and the creative, the looking back and looking forward that must avoid both the sterility of simple imitation and the abandonment of the things that make bluegrass what it is. It is a remarkable achievement, especially for one who's so long been gone from the field.

Above all else, one thing Skaggs told me stands out as emblematic: "There's a power in that music," he said, "that hasn't been unleashed since the late '40s." Read that as a statement about bluegrass as a whole, and it's debatable; a lot of people might even argue that Skaggs himself has unleashed plenty of powerful bluegrass. Read it as a statement about a kind of bluegrass that welds the high mountain emotionalism of the Stanley Brothers' singing to the Blue Grass Boys' discipline and skill and Bill Monroe's steadfast vision, though, and it becomes almost a prediction—a prediction that Ricky Skaggs and Kentucky Thunder will be doing their best to make true. If anyone's up to the task, they are.

Originally published in *No Depression*, no. 12 (Nov.–Dec. 1997): 56–63. Reprinted by permission of the author.

Spartanburg, South Carolina, journalist Baker Maultsby hooked up with bluegrass veteran Del McCoury in 1999 for a frank interview on topics including McCoury's sometimes controversial partnership with Steve Earle. Earle, the talented, outspoken emblem of Nashville's darker side, took bluegrass to some places it had never been with his acoustic CD *The Mountain* and his tours with McCoury's band.

However, onstage language that was accepted by Earle's alt-country fans was offensive to McCoury, who opted out of further road work with Earle. Maultsby, himself a talented songwriter, also drew interesting comment from McCoury about being defined by tradition without being hamstrung by it.

63

"Progress Rooted in Tradition: Del McCoury Talks about Work with Bill Monroe, Steve Earle"

BAKER MAULTSBY

Bluegrass' old-time sounds and rigid constraints would have us believe that it's some ancient music form. Actually, it's barely older than Mick Jagger.[1] And literally hundreds of musicians who played with the genre's originator, Bill Monroe, are still in their natural prime. Among the best of Monroe's Blue Grass Boys alumni is Del McCoury.

McCoury had been turned on to Monroe's music as a kid around the time that rock and roll was, as he says, "making it tough on everybody in country and bluegrass. In my age group—that's when it hit, when I was in high school. I should have been a rock and roller.[2] But I had heard Bill Monroe and Earl Scruggs just before this rock and roll thing. I was already hooked on something else."

It was 1962 when McCoury was introduced to Monroe through Jack Cooke, a musical friend and ex-Blue Grass Boy, in Baltimore. Though McCoury was then a banjo player, Monroe needed a guitarist and singer. Aside from being the top bluegrass band on the road, Monroe's band was (and continued to be for many years) a springboard for the successful careers of quite a few bluegrass musicians, including Lester Flatt and Earl Scruggs. McCoury took the job and moved to Nashville.

McCoury is respectful of Monroe's legacy, and he still sounds genuinely appreciative of the education playing in Monroe's band afforded him. "I learned a lot from Bill," he says. "And I've learned that a lot of jazz, country, blues musicians wish they had gotten to be Blue Grass Boys. I was lucky to have gotten to play with him."

"He created the music," McCoury continues. "I just tried to sing with him and play with him. I thought if I could do that, I couldn't go wrong. When I was with him, he never told me how to sing. He just expected me to get onstage and work hard. Well, that was the easiest thing I'd ever done in my life."

The Del McCoury Band is a most interesting study in modern bluegrass in that McCoury has found ways to keep his music forward-thinking, while adhering to the basic foundations of what Monroe taught him over thirty-five years ago.

---

1. Jagger was born on July 26, 1943, so some might argue that the "classic" bluegrass sound is actually younger than the Rolling Stone.

2. Born February 1, 1939, McCoury was in his mid-teens when Elvis Presley's first hits signaled the new rock 'n' roll era.

On one hand, McCoury's purist tendencies can be heard in his band and specifically in the playing of his two sons, Ronnie, on mandolin, and Rob, on banjo, who have joined him in his group. He explains, "When they were young, they had all kind of different records, and I didn't know what kind of music it was, really. And they *listened* to all that. But they still knew who Earl Scruggs and Bill Monroe were. And they had a lot of respect for those two guys. I said, 'Look, if you're going to play these two instruments, these are the two guys to listen to. Don't listen to none of these young punks, you know. Because Bill Monroe invented the bluegrass mandolin. Earl Scruggs invented the bluegrass banjo. So, don't listen to anybody but those two guys.'"

And though McCoury admits his sons' playing has been influenced by younger players—he mentions Sonny Osborne and David Grisman—Ronnie and Rob's award-winning instrumental work is still largely based on the sound of the men who inspired their father.

While modern sound equipment has made live sound mixing a matter of technical expertise, McCoury's recent innovation is almost reactionary: he and his band perform with only *one* onstage microphone. "When I started playing in the '50s, bands played with one microphone. Then, in the mid-'60s, they started using microphones for everything. It got so complicated—the mains, the monitors. I thought, 'This is ridiculous.' So, two years ago, we started using just one mic. It takes a lot of effort for a soundman to mess up one mic. This way, we can mix ourselves onstage."

If all this makes McCoury sound like a staunch traditionalist, in other ways, he is taking bluegrass places it has never been. It's not that the Del McCoury Band is looking to venture out with the likes of Bela Fleck into the popular realm of jazz-influenced bluegrass improvisation. But, whereas many older groups rarely stray from the traditional canon of bluegrass tunes, the McCourys have recorded songs by the likes of Tom Petty, Steve Earle, and Robert Cray.

McCoury explains: "There are a lot of good songs. There are plenty of songs I like that are in some other musical genre. A good song is a good song. And I think you can do almost any song as a bluegrass song."

And McCoury's appreciation of good songwriting spawned a recent collaboration with Steve Earle—first as Earle's backup band on his album *The Mountain*, then on a tour of live shows. While the artistic collision of new and old suited McCoury fine, matters of non-musical taste were a concern.

Earle, who has made a reputation for his rocking country songs and hard-living, was eager to learn to play and sing with one mic onstage. He even wore a suit. For McCoury's part, he enjoyed Earle's songs and appreciated getting to reach a non-bluegrass audiences by playing with Earle. But some of Earle's less savory onstage habits spilled over into shows with the McCourys, and this obviously bothered Del.

"Well, you know, I really didn't know Steve Earle as far as playing a show with him until we did our first tour," McCoury explains. "And I did learn that he was a little bit too wild. And, that's actually why I quit touring when I did."

Especially troubling to McCoury was the notion of Earle's rough language at bluegrass festivals. "He wanted to do ten more dates on the East Coast, ten more on the West Coast, and he wanted to do some bluegrass festivals," McCoury says.

"And I kind of didn't want him in the bluegrass community because I always like to have a clean show, you know, and I think your music is what's carrying you—the songs you've written. And there's no place on stage, I don't think, for vulgarity, for anything like that. After touring, I thought, 'No, I don't want this. I don't want this in the bluegrass community.' So, I just nipped it in the bud."

Given McCoury's link to the founder of bluegrass as well as his own contributions to the genre, it is easy to understand his being protective of the bluegrass community and its festival scene. But that won't keep McCoury from opening himself up to new musical ideas and experiences. He recently agreed to perform on a track for the *Groove Grass 101* project featuring funk master Bootsy Collins. "A producer I knew called me in to sing on a track he was working on for it. I thought, 'Who is Bootsy Collins?' I didn't know who he was."

The recording was a far cry from the stripped-down approach taken by the McCoury Band. "It was *really* way out. There were a lot of sound effects," he says, laughing. "I'm just lucky I didn't have to tour with him."

Originally published in *Creative Loafing* (Greenville, S.C.), July 10, 1999, n.p. Reprinted by permission of *Creating Loafing.*

R are is the journalist who has not cherished the secret desire to write a novel. Veteran music critic David Gates, who wrote this perceptive *New Yorker* profile of Ralph Stanley, has actually done it. His novels *Jernigan* and *Preston Falls* have won praise from the likes of the *New York Times,* which noted Gates's "pitch-perfect ear for contemporary speech" and "keen, journalistic eye." Gates employed both after spending time with Stanley, who was riding high on the popularity of *O Brother, Where Art Thou?* Some of the background in this piece will be familiar to Stanley Brothers fans, but Gates's skillful account of how Ralph functions in and out of traditional settings made it stand out. Its location in the aristocratically hip pages of *The New Yorker* was one more illustration of the ever-broadening reach of bluegrass.

64

"Annals of Bluegrass: Constant Sorrow—The Long Road of Ralph Stanley"

DAVID GATES

Looked at from the world's point of view, it was a triumphant day for Ralph Stanley. Looked at from his own, it was a long wait to sing three songs. He hadn't slept well—"I must've turned over a hundred times"—partly because his two-year-old grandson was in the hospital back home, in Virginia, with pneumonia, and partly because no normal person could sleep in New York. His description of the hotel where he and his wife, Jimmi, were staying made it sound like an S.R.O. in Hell's Kitchen. (In fact, it was the aggressively fashionable Hudson, on West Fifty-eighth Street.) And Carnegie Hall's Dressing Room D, where he'd been hanging out behind a closed door since one-thirty in the afternoon for an evening performance, had just about everything a man didn't need: an upright piano, plates of fruit and cold cuts, and air-conditioning that wouldn't go off.

Stanley had come here during a hot spell in June as the culminating attraction of a sold-out concert featuring music on the best-selling soundtrack album from the film *O Brother, Where Art Thou?,* for which he had joined such roots-music loyalists as the late John Hartford, Emmylou Harris, Gillian Welch and David Rawlings, the Cox Family, and three sweet-and-sour-voiced little girls from Tennessee called the Peasall Sisters. Since May of last year, when these people were last onstage together, at Nashville's Ryman Auditorium, they had had occasion to reflect on the truisms about mortality and mutability in the songs they sing. Just a few days before the Carnegie Hall concert, Hartford had died of cancer. Several months earlier, the fiddler Willard Cox had broken his back in a car wreck; tonight he was playing in a wheelchair.

As the concert began, Stanley changed into his stage clothes, remarking—not without a certain sly satisfaction—that they made him look like "an undertaker": black suit with a blacker stripe; black shirt; busy tie in muted red; and a tiepin with a tiny clockface. His physical presence is not commanding. He's a short, owlish-looking man with wire-rimmed glasses and tightly curled, meticulously styled gray hair; when he's not playing the banjo, he often does his hell-harrowing singing with his hands in his pockets. And since he had come here only to sing and not perform with his own band, he had left his custom-made Stanleytone five-string and his trademark white Stetson at home. He stood in the wings with Jimmi, listening to the others, until it was time for him to go on and close the show. A few performers respectfully approached him, but he glad-handed no one. At last, he squared his shoulders and strode onto the stage to a standing ovation.

Backed by a few of the evening's other performers, he sang three of his strongest, most death-haunted songs. (Probably half of the two thousand or so numbers that he has recorded involve lonesome graves, cold dark shrouds, murders, dying parents—also dying children, siblings, sweethearts, and Saviors—and the prospective glories of Heaven.) His first song, "Oh Death," was an unaccompanied solo on the ancient theme of bargaining with the Reaper to "spare me over till another year." Next came "Man of Constant Sorrow." With its insistent, chugging rhythm, as much blues as bluegrass, and its weird, angular melody, it has been his signature number for more than fifty years. He closed the program with "Angel Band," a song that he first recorded in 1955 with his late brother, Carter. "My latest sun is sinking fast," it begins. "My race is nearly run." The performance was Ralph Stanley at his present-day best: his well-aged tenor voice strong and hard, its edge unblunted, as he navigated the turns and ornaments that he learned as a boy, singing in a Primitive Baptist church. He had performed these songs thousands of times over half a century but, as usual, he changed a few nuances. In "Angel Band," when he got to "whose blood now cleanses from all sin / And gives me victory" his voice leaped up a clarion-call fifth on the word "me."

///

Ever since the death of Bill Monroe, the putative father of bluegrass, in 1996, Ralph Stanley has been the supreme icon of authenticity in American vernacular music. He is neither the last nor the oldest of the mountain-music patriarchs: Earl Scruggs, who is the prototypical bluegrass banjo player and served as an early model for Stanley, has just released his first album since 1984, *Earl Scruggs and Friends.* But Scruggs hasn't performed much in the past quarter century; Stanley, who is slightly younger, continues to do more than a hundred shows a year. Even when he was in his twenties, Stanley's voice—hard, piercing, with a touch of raspiness—made him sound like a scary old man. Today, he sounds even scarier, and he has begun appealing to an audience far beyond the usual bluegrass circuit of summer festivals, college-coffeehouses, and school and firehouse gigs throughout the rural South.

Stanley has striven for commercial success ever since 1946, when he and Carter started out as the Stanley Brothers. But since he's ultimately selling his own rugged unworldliness, he also needs to keep the culture of getting and spending at a distance. After his brother died, in 1966, he deliberately turned backward and inward. He cultivated his own conservative musical instincts—soon, for instance, he began featuring stark a cappella gospel quartets—and, over the years, he has kept as close as a touring musician can to the primal landscape of his childhood: Virginia's Clinch Mountain region. For years, he has listened to few recordings but his own—if he's in the mood for Nashville-type country, he chooses George Jones—and his duets with such admirers as Bob Dylan and Lucinda Williams suggest that these better-known musicians want to touch the source of an almost mystical purity. Unlike Monroe, who occasionally hired urban college types, Stanley won't take on a musician who's not from the Southern mountains. "With all due respect," he told me, "I don't think Northern city boys have got the natural . . . you know I like to have a man in my band that talks like me. I just like to keep it down simple."

Stanley often begins the ritual opening speech at his shows with "a big old howdy" and a promise to deliver "that old-time, mountain-style, what-they-call-bluegrass music." This bumpy formulation is an attempt to draw a fine distinction: the most revered performer in bluegrass isn't sure that the term fits him. The name originated with Monroe, a Kentuckian who boosterishly called his band the Blue Grass Boys. Ralph Stanley's music sounds, superficially, like Monroe's, but to a musician of Stanley's generation "bluegrass" still feels like a brand name. He generally refers to what he plays as "my kind of music," or, if you press him, "just that old-time mountain music."

In fact, mountain music was never that simple. By the time fiddlers, banjo players, and singers from the Southern Appalachians began to be recorded, in the nineteen-twenties, they had already synthesized influences as diverse as ballads and dance tunes from the British Isles; blue notes, the banjo, and rocking polyrhythms from Africa; ragtime tunes and Victorian parlor songs. Twentieth-century technology, which allowed the music to travel independently of the musicians, only encouraged such exchanges. Stanley, who was born in 1927, remembers when his parents got their first radio—a battery-powered model, as they had no electricity—and when he first heard the Grand Ole Opry broadcasts from Nashville. Well before the advent of bluegrass, mountain music had already become a media-disseminated entertainment.

The band that Monroe formed in 1945 inspired a revolution. For all of bluegrass's traditional roots, it is a recent—even modernist—form, only a few years younger than bebop. Unlike ensemble-oriented old-time mountain bands, Monroe's group allowed individual musicians to play jazz-like, semi-improvised solos, and ornate obbligatos behind the singing. To complement his own hopped-up, asymmetrical mandolin and his bluesy, androgynous tenor voice, Monroe picked a team of virtuosos—notably Scruggs, who had perfected an intricate system of three-finger picking that produced a dense, high-speed flow of notes, like a twanging tommy gun. From that day to this, almost every bluegrass band has been a variation of Monroe's: Scruggs-style banjo, fiddle, mandolin, rhythm guitar, and bass, with sometimes a lead guitar or a dobro, and a repertoire of retooled folk, gospel, and love-gone-wrong songs.

Bluegrass might be described as meta-mountain music—semi-referential and driven by an anxiety that the old ways of life, and the music that went with them, are vanishing. Monroe's "Uncle Pen" is the best-known example of a favorite bluegrass trope: an up-tempo fiddle showpiece about an old fiddler and the tunes he used to play. Song after song tells the same story of uprootedness and alienation; the genre's locus classicus is the Stanley Brothers' version of "Rank Strangers." "I wandered again to my home in the mountains / Where in youth's early dawn I was happy and free / I looked for my friends, but I never could find them / I found they were all rank strangers to me." "Rank Strangers" reflects the hard times that drove people away from the mountains of Virginia, West Virginia, Kentucky, and Tennessee after the Second World War. These new urban workers made up an appreciable part of the bluegrass audience; for them, Stanley's "Man of Constant Sorrow" ("I bid farewell to old Kentucky, the state where I was born and raised") was both a nostalgic reminder of home and a bitter anthem of loss. "I've saw it when we'd play the bars and things up in Ohio—Dayton and Columbus and Cincinnati and through there," George Shuffler, who was the Stanley Brothers' lead guitarist, told me. "That was where all the people migrated to get out of the coal mines. I've saw 'em raise the roof when Ralph would start into that thing."

Stanley has known that feeling of exile. In 1951, he and Carter briefly took jobs at the Ford plant in Detroit. "That was a pretty miserable ten weeks for me," he said, fifty years later. "I was a truck pan welder, spot welder. I was working night shift, about three until twelve or something. I got homesick. I thought they's something better to do than punch a clock. So I quit and went home."

Stanley still lives in a remote area of southwestern Virginia, between the towns of Coeburn and McClure, just a few miles from where he grew up. The country looks much the same as it did when he was a boy, except for some flattened hilltops that the coal companies once strip-mined, where cattle now graze. You're getting close when you hit a crossroads with a Kwik Stop, a Freewill Baptist church, and a sign that reads "Jesus Is the Answerer and Finisher of Our Faith."

Stanley's house is a large, elegant, one-story gray stone rambler on a gentle rise; a section of his thirty-five-acre property near the road is marked off with a gentleman farmer's white fences. Stanley's son and lead singer, Ralph II—his father and his bandmates call him Two—lives in a small white trailer next door with his wife, Kristi. When I pulled into the driveway one morning, I was greeted by Two's German shepherd, Harley. Stanley, dressed for company in slacks and a sports shirt, ignored Harley's tail-wagging. "I'm kinda mad at him," he said. "He goes after the horses. So I don't fool with him much." He showed off his palomino, Angel, who was about to foal, and his John Deere Gator, a six-wheel all-terrain vehicle that he'd wanted for several years, but which now sat unused in shed. "I bet it hasn't got more than fifteen miles on it," he said. (A few months later, he sold the thing.) Stanley clearly loved this place, but he also seemed at a distance from it—perhaps the consequence of spending most of his life on a tour bus, heading from one town to the next to sing about his home in the mountains.

In the kitchen, something smelled good: Stanley, who likes to cook, had some beans on the stove. He led me into the reddest living room I've ever seen: an acre of red carpet, a plush red sofa, red curtains pulled open to reveal a manicured lawn. The floor-to-ceiling picture window and the meticulous housekeeping made the room seem like a diorama; ceramic dogs here and there, a white ceramic pillar with a cupid holding a cornucopia of roses, a display case with china angels, china birds, and a china Jesus. The only thing that looked out of place was the banjo case on the floor. Jimmi Stanley came in to say hello, chatted about the weather and her allergies, and offered us coffee. Stanley has small hands, and it was hard not to stare at his fingers: they curl away from the thumb, which made me wonder how he still managed to play banjo as strongly as he does. As we talked he drummed his fingers on a glass-topped table.

In conversation, Stanley has his set pieces: The road-not-taken story about his once having to choose between spending five dollars on either a brood sow or his first banjo; the there-but-for-the-grace-of-God story of a drunk who shot and killed one of his lead singers, Roy Lee Centers, who sounded uncannily like Carter. "Roy went to a party, and of course they all got drunk," Stanley said. "Roy's little boy was with him. He was about eight or nine years old at that time, maybe ten. And the tale the little boy told, this fella drove Roy home and he changed routes a little bit. Roy said, 'Where you going?' The fella said, 'I'm gonna take you up this road here and kill you.' He took him up there, got him out, and said, 'I'm gonna silence that beautiful voice forever,' and shot him right in the mouth. Then he turned around and took the butt of the gun and beat him all to pieces."

Stanley walked me briskly through his childhood: the period when he worked in his father's sawmill; his early thoughts of being a veterinarian; his father's leaving the family when Ralph was thirteen. From that time on, he said, "we didn't see too much of him." Stanley began taking music seriously as a teenager singing brother-act harmonies with Carter, who played guitar; they sometimes performed for donations outside the Clinchfield Coal Company on paydays. He did a short stretch in the Army, just after the war ended. Then he and Carter formed a band with a mandolinist, Pee Wee Lambert, and a fiddler, Leslie Keith. Before long, they'd landed the midday spot on Farm and Fun Time on WCYB, in Bristol, on the Virginia-Tennessee border, fifty miles from home. Even then, the shy and taciturn Ralph let his older, taller, more outgoing brother do most of the talking and lead singing. "Carter would've just as soon called the President as he would've called me," Stanley said. "He was a good mixer, a lot more forward than I am. Easier to get acquainted with."

At first, Stanley played banjo in the archaic clawhammer style that his mother had taught him: a clip-clopping sound produced by a downstroke of the index fingernail, followed by the thumb playing accents on the fifth string. He had also mastered the smoother two-finger style, in which the index finger picks upward. But, in the forties, a few banjo players—mainly in North Carolina—were refining a more complex three-finger style, attacking the strings in repeating sequences called "rolls"; on fast tunes, an overpowering technician like Earl Scruggs could unleash as many as fifteen notes per second. "I believe the first person I heard do that was a man by the name of Hoke Jenkins," Stanley said. "He was playing it on the radio somewhere. And I thought I needed to be doing it that way. There was just more of a drive to it. Then I heard Earl Scruggs with Bill Monroe on the Grand Ole Opry. I could tell they was using three fingers. But I never could copy anybody. When I found out there was a sort of a roll, I wanted to just play it the way I felt it, and I didn't want to hear them anymore. I guess I still don't have it right. Earl Scruggs probably knows a little bit more about music. I'd say he's more polished, you know." When I asked Steve Sparkman, a Stanley disciple who now plays the more difficult banjo parts with the Clinch Mountain Boys, to characterize the difference between the two masters, he said, "Ralph took the drive and put more drive in. You might say overdrive. Just wham! Keep that forward roll jammin'."

Stanley's other contribution to the band's sound, his raw, yearning tenor voice, was even more distinctive. He sang lead mostly on the old-time songs—"Little Maggie," "Pretty Polly," and "Man of Constant Sorrow." On the others, he sang high harmony to Carter's lower, smoother-textured melody. Perhaps the most dramatic moment in all the Stanley Brothers' hundreds of recordings occurs in the chorus of "Rank Strangers." After Carter sings the verse, Ralph enters with the words "Everybody I met / Seemed to be a rank stranger" in a voice that stabs like an ice pick. He raised the tension in the Stanley Brothers' music to the nearly unbearable: singing above Carter's melody, he would hang on a dissonant note in anticipation of the chord that was about to arrive. Over time, these harmonies became wilder, more edgy and attention-getting—a separate drama that didn't cozy up to the melody but defied it before an ultimate reconciliation. "Every lead singer that sings with me will say I'm hard to sing with," Stanley said. "I hardly ever sing the same verse exactly the same way."

Initially, the Stanley Brothers so admired Monroe that they annoyed him by copying his sound. Their maniacally up-tempo 1948 recording of "Molly and Tenbrooks" was an almost note-for-note version of what Monroe was playing on his radio broadcasts, and when Columbia signed the Stanleys, later that year, Monroe left the label in protest. But the feud, such as it was, was short-lived. In 1951, Carter briefly became a Blue Grass Boy. And at one point both Stanleys did a few gigs with Monroe. "The last night I played with him, Bill said that he would like to have me join him and call it Bill Monroe and the Stanley Brothers," Stanley said. "But I just never did like to work for anybody." In later years, Stanley and Monroe sang together at festivals, where they indulged in the bluegrass world's mode of friendly rivalry: how high could they push the key before somebody's voice cracked? "After the shows," Stanley said, "we personalized. We'd talk about music, we'd talk about farming. Bill cut his hay with a horse-drawn mowing machine. He was an old-timer."

In contrast to Monroe, who was something of a martinet (he recruited band members to work on his farm when they weren't playing), the Stanley Brothers had a complementary partnership. Carter, who was the principal songwriter, had a gift for the country-style objective correlative—"For years they've been dead / The fields have turned brown"—while Ralph played the fiery instrumentals. Carter did the talking onstage, while the more retiring Ralph did most of the booking and the business. Musically, Carter was the progressive and Ralph the traditionalist. "Carter believed in searching a little bit, and I never did," Stanley said. Everyone who knew Carter was struck by his sharp intelligence, and George Shuffler likes to remember him laughing and throwing his head back so far that you could see his gold tooth. John Cohen, a member of the New Lost City Ramblers, saw a different man. "Carter was so deep into himself," Cohen recalled. "I think it was this huge drinking thing that he had. You couldn't get to where he was."

When Carter died of liver disease, at the age of forty-one, Shuffler was in the hospital waiting room with Ralph. "When the nurse came in and told us," Shuffler recalled, "Ralph was just as limp as a string." Monroe flew to Bristol and was driven up the icy mountain roads to sing at Carter's funeral. (Thirty years later, when Monroe died, Stanley went to Nashville to "sing over Bill," as he put it.) Carter's death made Stanley think, briefly, about quitting music. "He had a hard time in his heart knowing what to do," Ricky Skaggs, who played mandolin for Stanley in the early seventies, told me. "But Ralph had a desire to keep the Stanley Brothers sound alive. And he didn't know any other trade. He didn't have anything else to do."

Stanley said, "I knew that I had one or the other of two ways to go: up or down. I wanted to go up."

///

Last spring, on a Thursday night in Berkeley, California, I caught up with Ralph Stanley and the Clinch Mountain Boys. They were in the middle of a two-week tour.

Freight & Salvage, a large coffeehouse on a side street near the university has been a regular stop of theirs since the seventies and both the Thursday and Friday shows were sold out. The band likes the West Coast: the audiences are knowledgeable and enthusiastic, and they tend to have more money than folks in the Deep South; on a tour like this, the band members who have solo CDs and tapes to sell can make fifteen hundred dollars above their usual wages. The audience was a typical folk-music crowd: faculty, grad students, a couple of Sikhs with beards and turbans, a biker in a Merle Haggard cap, an alert-looking young woman with a T-shirt that read "Got Banjo?" Median age: forty. Percentage wearing glasses: fifty. Randy Campbell, an agent who books the band on the West Coast, calls this sort of venue "the Church of Ralph Stanley."

The Clinch Mountain Boys are a seven-member repertory company. The fiddler, James Price, is so magisterially large that he looks as if he were holding a kid-size Suzuki violin. Price doubles as the comedian—Stanley, of course, is the straight man—and he does convincing onstage impressions of Johnny Cash and Willie Nelson (as well as a convincing offstage impression of Ralph Stanley). The lead guitarist, James Alan Shelton, has mastered George Shuffler's "cross-picking" technique, a wrist-twisting approximation of the three-finger banjo style; he's also the road manager. Steve Sparkman plays Stanley's old banjo pieces, such as "Hard Times" and "Clinch Mountain Backstep." The mandolinist, John Rigsby, can fill in singing either Carter-like lead or Ralph-like tenor—as the occasion demands.

Jack Cooke, who was once Bill Monroe's lead singer, has been Stanley's bass player for thirty-one years. He's a source of manic energy despite an arthritic hip and the open-heart surgery he had a couple of years ago. On the band's bus, he'll burst into a Little Richard song or deliver dire prophecies about the environment and the Bush Administration. (Like Stanley, he's a lifelong Democrat.)

Ralph Stanley II, who is twenty-two years old, has been the band's lead singer since he was sixteen. Two started riding the Stanley bus as a boy, and when he couldn't come along he'd play his favorite Stanley Brothers album and his favorite Ralph Stanley album each night on his bedside boom box. "I'd listen to every song on both them records," he told me. "They's twenty on one, twelve on the other. And then I'd go to sleep." With his beard and aviator sunglasses, Two looks like a video-ready young Nashville star. Longtime fans used to roll their eyes about him—his voice hadn't finished changing when he first took the job—but he's become a warm, moving singer, who combines the soul-fullness of his Uncle Carter with the more anguished mainstream country style of his hero Keith Whitley, who sang lead with Stanley in the seventies.

Onstage that Thursday night in Berkeley, the band locked into the usual sweetly aching harmonies and headlong rhythms: the heavy bass that brings the words "bull fiddle" to mind, the woody acoustic guitars, the bell-toned jack-hammering of the twin banjos, the keening and skittering fiddle. But Stanley sounded hoarse, and he looked as if he were having trouble keeping his eyes open. On "Man of Constant Sorrow" he strained to hit the top notes, and later apologized to the crowd:

"We left Virginia last Wednesday, and we've been playing for eight nights straight. I tell you, that works on you." He joked about his age and his problems remembering new songs: "'Doc, it seems like I can't remember anything anymore.' 'How long have you been that way?' 'What way?'" Then he took out his glasses and a piece of paper, and sang "Daddy's Wildwood Flower," a ghost story in which Mama dies and Daddy, with the help of "God's mighty power," summons her back by playing her favorite song on his guitar.

On Saturday morning, the bus, a standard-issue country-star Silver Eagle with "Dr. Ralph Stanley & His Clinch Mountain Boys" painted on its sides, took to the road again: a show in Palo Alto, an all-night run to Los Angeles, a last gig in Tempe, Arizona. On the way, the band members talked cuisine ("You ever eat that swordfish? I don't like that worth a shit"), football, music, and women. James Price read a motivational book by an ex-N.F.L. player; James Shelton read Seymour Hersh's "Dark Side of Camelot." But mostly the musicians dozed in their seats or looked out the windows. Stanley seldom said a word. "This must get rough on him," I said to Shelton. "It's all he knows," Shelton said.

In Tempe, the bus pulled up to a flat-roofed building in a dicey neighborhood, next to an adult bookstore. Price looked out the window and said, "Regular hole in the wall." Stanley shook his head and said, "It ain't even that." But Nita's Hideaway, as the place was called, turned out to be far better than it looked: an ironic simulacrum of the sort of bar that George Shuffler calls a "skull orchard," with black velvet paintings (J.F.K., a squatting cowboy with a lariat, bullfighters, galleons, a charioteer), a pool table, and comfortable easy chairs in a side room. It was the natural habitat of Stanley's newest admirers—the tattooed, the pierced, the dreadlocked, and the shaven-headed—who have discovered him either through "O Brother, Where Art Thou?" or through certifiably cool music stars (Yoakam, Welch, Dylan) who have certified him as even cooler. Yoakam has gone as far as to call him an "archangel."

Ricky Skaggs had suggested to me that Stanley now transcends bluegrass. "He's become like an old African," Skaggs said, "a world-music person." Stanley's best performances involve you so deeply that any sense of a particular genre gets lost, the way the book, the page, and finally the words disappear in a great work of literature. A few other American musicians have had this gift: Armstrong, Ellington, Bill Monroe, Merle Haggard, James Brown, Howlin' Wolf. Despite bluegrass's mystique of mountain purity and Afro-Druidic roots—what Monroe called its "ancient tones"—there's nothing inherently special about it. Good bluegrass—like good blues, good jazz, and good rock and roll—is sweet and sad, wild and sexy. Mediocre bluegrass, which you can hear at any festival from a dozen perfectly competent parking-lot bands, is among the most wearisome music on the planet; the more it tries to stretch its parameters—with arty lyrics or bebop licks—the more evident its limitations become. Ralph Stanley understood that the way to go was to simplify, intensify, and countrify. As Steve Sparkman explained it to me, "Take a little block about that big and put everything in it and keep it there. Ralph's been the king of that."

At Nita's, Stanley played the two best sets I heard him do. Sometimes fatigue or irritation revs him up more than a good night's rest, and maybe a long day of traveling to a hip hellhole did the trick. He delivered violently intense versions of "Pretty Polly" and "Little Maggie"; his two-banjo breaks with Sparkman had an unaccustomed aggressiveness; and his shamelessly over-the-top harmonies seemed to defy anybody who'd ever dared call him what he calls himself—"an old hillbilly." As he does now at every show he sang "Oh Death"—it has become his greatest hit—and the whole bar fell silent. When he got to "I come to take the soul," he executed a semi-yodelled upward turn on the last word that gave me chills. After two weeks on the road, Stanley's voice was shot, but he didn't apologize; he was overdriving it the way a rock-and-roll guitarist overdrives an amplifier into grainy distortion, and he seemed to be reveling in the rawness. The crowd at Nita's might not have been able to tell you—as the crowd at Freight & Salvage probably could—the name of everyone who had been a Clinch Mountain Boy in 1958, but they understood the truest secret of Ralph Stanley's appeal: a bedrock punkishness, a righteous lack of ease in this world, a refusal to comfort or be comforted.

///

From the beginning of his career, Stanley, like almost every country performer from Roy Acuff to George Jones, has sung mini-dramas of sin and redemption—"Are You Afraid to Die?," "My Sinful Past," "Cry from the Cross," "When I Wake Up to Sleep No More." Fifteen years ago, he wrote a song titled "I'll Answer the Call." Yet, until last summer, it was only words. "I went to this country church," Stanley told me, "and I heard this man preach, name's Ezra Junior Davis. After we left the church house, two ladies were going to be baptized. The Clinch River runs by there, and I thought that river was pretty—pretty shade trees. From then on, I could see that river. Well, one Saturday night I couldn't sleep much—worried, had that on my mind—and I got up about four-thirty and called Brother Junior and told him I wanted to be baptized there in the Clinch River that day."

Stanley took me to a graveyard near his old home, at the top of Smith Ridge. "There's Grandpa right here," he said, "and Grandma on the other side of that tree. My mother. And there's Carter"—he pointed to a mausoleum. Next to it was an identical mausoleum with two names and dates of birth carved on it—"Me and Jimmi's resting place someday." From below came a sound that might have been a woodpecker or an idling chain saw. I asked Stanley about a gravestone with a Harley-Davidson carved on it. A father and son, distant cousins on his mother's side, he guessed; they'd both died of drug overdoses. "You see that little bitty house over there, painted white on this end?" Stanley said. "That's the house my mother and I had. The old one burned that used to set there, where I was raised, and I built that little house for her." He pointed to another house. "Carter built that little yellow one. My first cousin lives there now." What about those houses, over to the left? "That's some of their son-in-laws, daughters, and so forth. It's all family down here."

The next day, a rainy Sunday morning, Stanley and I got into his Lincoln Town Car and drove over to Grundy. The Hale Creek Primitive Baptist Church, just outside town, was a new, plain white building, across the road from a rocky stream, a picnic pavilion, and a futuristic-looking power transfer station. Nearby stood the original log church, now in disrepair. Inside, rows of padded benches faced a table that had a display of artificial flowers and a box of tissues. Stanley's "brothers and sisters," as the members call themselves, were mostly around his age. He greeted them in the group's ritual embrace—a handshake, then a hug—and chatted about coon hunting, about which relative was in the hospital, about the grandkids.

The service began when one woman, then two, started singing amid the chit-chat. (Primitive Baptists allow no instruments in church, and sing only in unison.) Gradually, everyone joined in, but I could hardly hear Stanley: he's so used to leading other singers and obeying his own instincts that he finds it hard to follow the turns in the melodies. Several elders felt inspired to stand and preach. One prayed aloud for "the little children on drugs and alcohol"; another pointed to a window and said, with tears on his face, "All these raindrops, and I see them being taken away, one by one. And each one has a meaning."

Brother Junior, a well-barbered young man with wire-rimmed glasses, began to preach in an unprepossessing mumble, but soon he was singing a King James-like cadence in a scorching tenor that would have shone in any bluegrass band. Men and women wept; some rushed up to shake his hand and hug him. Stanley watched and listened.

After the service ended, the brothers and sisters remained standing to sing one more song: "Happy Birthday." Today, Brother Ralph turned seventy-four. He had momentarily forgotten all about it. But he smiled like a good sport at all the fuss over him—spared over, as the song says, till another year.

Originally published in *The New Yorker*, Aug. 20, 2001, 88–94. Reprinted by permission of the author.

INDEX

Pennell, John, 26
Perkins, Carl, 164
Phantoms of the Opry, 273
Phillips, Todd, 22, 246–47
Piazza, Tom, 29
"Pick Me Up on Your Way Down," 71
Pierce, Don, 14, 74
Pierce, Webb, 154
"Pike County Breakdown," 47, 218, 226, 281
Pine Tree Records, 196
Pinson, Bob, 260
Plank Road String Band, 163
Poole, Charlie, 3, 9, 62, 95, 138, 158, 161, 232
"Poor Ellen Smith," 63
"Poor Old Cora," 72
Poor Richard's Almanac, 213
Poss, Barry, 24, 158, 163, 250, 253
Potter, Dale, 122
Prairie Home Companion, 30
Presley, Elvis, 1, 48, 52, 67, 74, 89, 104, 122, 164, 165, 263, 318
"Pretty Bird," 146
"Pretty Polly," 332, 337
Price, James, 334, 335
Price, Joel, 119, 120
Prine, John, 273
"Prisoner's Song," 226
Pruett, Marc, 249
Puckett, Riley, 9, 62

Quicksilver (band). *See* Lawson, Doyle
Quicksilver Rides Again, 251

Raines, Missy, 303, 304
Ramblin' Blue Grass, 193
Rambling Drifters, the, 240–41, 243
Ramblin' Guitar, 196
"Rank Strangers," 330, 332
"Raw Hide," 29, 59, 118, 206, 225, 300, 309
Ray, Wade, 226
RCA Records, 17, 226
Rebel Records, 15, 158, 211, 228, 248, 250
"Rebel Soldier, The," 275
Record Depot, 158, 161
Rector, Red, 107, 123, 128, 160, 226
"Red River Valley," 60
"Red Rocking Chair," 64

Red, White and Blue (Grass), 253, 287–88
Reid, Lou, 248–53
Reinhardt, Django, 179
Reno, Don, 13, 17, 22, 54–58, 123, 124, 185, 205–6, 217; banjo style of, 56–57, 87, 103, 129, 130, 231, 232, 233; and Bill Monroe, 55–56, 87, 92, 119, 132, 140; guitar style of, 57–58
Reno, Ronnie, 54, 230
Reno and Smiley, and Tennessee Cutups, 7, 9, 12, 13, 54–56, 65, 87, 127–31, 154, 169, 185, 189, 194, 226, 230; breakup of, 56, 131, 187
Restless on the Farm, 270
Retrograss, 317
"Reuben," 205
Rice, Tony, 21, 22, 24, 25, 215, 246–47, 270, 323
Richardson, Larry, 107, 124, 160, 187
Rich-R-Tone Records, 11, 52, 212
Rigsby, John, 334
Rinzler, Ralph, 5, 6, 11, 14, 16, 97, 98–99, 137, 144, 155, 184, 187, 276–77
"Roanoke," 226
Robbins, Larry, 22, 261
Robbins, Marty, 67
"Rock Hearts," 60
Rock My Soul, 251
"Rocky Road Blues," 291
"Rocky Top," 19
Rodgers, Jimmie, 3, 44, 105, 133, 148, 187
"Roll Jordan, Roll," 273
Roll, Larry, 73
"Roll in My Sweet Baby's Arms," 141, 170, 304
Ronstadt, Linda, 283
Rooney, Jim, 16, 35, 97, 234
"Rose Connolly," 108
Rose Maddox Sings Bluegrass, 284
Rosenberg, Neil V., 30, 58, 252–53, 284, 291, 294, 297, 302
Roses in the Snow, 21, 51, 287
Rose, Wesley, 67, 69
Rounder Records, 15, 22, 24, 26, 228, 246, 247, 255, 256, 259, 276, 287, 317
Rowan, Peter, 16, 22, 218–20, 262–66, 270, 275
"Ruby," 67, 68, 284

THOMAS GOLDSMITH worked as a journalist and musician in Nashville for more than thirty years before taking the position of features editor at the *Raleigh News and Observer* in 2003. In addition to his newspaper journalism, including several posts at the *Tennessean* in Nashville, Goldsmith has written about music for a variety of trade and consumer publications as well as in collections published by various academic presses. In 2004 the International Bluegrass Music Association named him Print Media Personality of the Year. His songs have been recorded by artists who include the Nashville Bluegrass Band, Riders in the Sky, Uncle Walt's Band, and David Olney. He has also appeared as a sideman on recordings by Hazel Dickens, the Whitstein Brothers, Riders in the Sky, and others. He has produced recordings by Tracy Nelson, David Olney, Tom House, the Nashville Jug Band, and Elise Witt.

MUSIC IN AMERICAN LIFE

Charles Ives Remembered: An Oral History   *Vivian Perlis*
Henry Cowell, Bohemian   *Michael Hicks*
Rap Music and Street Consciousness   *Cheryl L. Keyes*
Louis Prima   *Garry Boulard*
Marian McPartland's Jazz World: All in Good Time   *Marian McPartland*
Robert Johnson: Lost and Found   *Barry Lee Pearson and Bill McCulloch*
Bound for America: Three British Composers   *Nicholas Temperley*
Lost Sounds: Blacks and the Birth of the Recording Industry, 1890–1919   *Tim Brooks*
Burn, Baby! BURN! The Autobiography of Magnificent Montague
   Magnificent Montague with Bob Baker
Way Up North in Dixie: A Black Family's Claim to the Confederate Anthem
   Howard L. Sacks and Judith Rose Sacks
The Bluegrass Reader   *Edited by Thomas Goldsmith*
Colin McPhee: Composer in Two Worlds   *Carol J. Oja*
Robert Johnson, Mythmaking, and Contemporary American Culture
   Patricia R. Schroeder
Composing a World: Lou Harrison, Musical Wayfarer   *Leta E. Miller and*
   Fredric Lieberman
Fritz Reiner, Maestro and Martinet   *Kenneth Morgan*
That Toddlin' Town: Chicago's White Dance Bands and Orchestras, 1900–1950
   Charles A. Sengstock Jr.
Dewey and Elvis: The Life and Times of a Rock 'n' Roll Deejay   *Louis Cantor*
Come Hither to Go Yonder: Playing Bluegrass with Bill Monroe   *Bob Black*
Chicago Blues: Portraits and Stories   *David Whiteis*
The Incredible Band of John Philip Sousa   *Paul E. Bierley*
"Maximum Clarity" and Other Writings on Music   *Ben Johnston, edited by Bob Gilmore*
Staging Tradition: John Lair and Sarah Gertrude Knot   *Michael Ann Williams*
Homegrown Music: Discovering Music   *Stephanie P. Ledgin*
Tales of a Theatrical Guru   *Danny Newman*

The University of Illinois Press
is a founding member of the
Association of American University Presses.

Composed in 10/12.5 Adobe Minion
with Caslon 224 display by Barbara Evans
at the University of Illinois Press

UNIVERSITY OF ILLINOIS PRESS
1325 South Oak Street   Champaign, IL 61820–6903
www.press.uillinois.edu